INTERNATIONAL TRADE

ECONOMIC ANALYSIS OF
GLOBALIZATION AND POLICY

John McLaren
University of Virginia

WILEY

VP & EXECUTIVE PUBLISHER	George Hoffman
EXECUTIVE EDITOR	Joel Hollenbeck
CONTENT EDITOR	Jennifer Manias
ASSISTANT EDITOR	Courtney Luzzi
EDITORIAL ASSISTANT	Erica Horowitz
ASSOCIATE DIRECTOR OF MARKETING	Amy Scholz
SENIOR MARKETING MANAGER	Jesse Cruz
PRODUCT DESIGNER	Greg Chaput
SENIOR MEDIA SPECIALIST	Elena Santa Maria
PRODUCTION MANAGER	Lucille Buonocore
SENIOR PRODUCTION EDITOR	Sujin Hong
PHOTO RESEARCHER	Ellinor Wagner
SENIOR DESIGNER	Maureen Eide
COVER PHOTO	L. Vest, Houston Pilots Association

This book was set in Times Regular by MPS Limited and printed and bound by Courier Companies. The cover was printed by Courier Companies.

This book is printed on acid free paper. ∞

Founded in 1807, John Wiley & Sons, Inc. has been a valued source of knowledge and understanding for more than 200 years, helping people around the world meet their needs and fulfill their aspirations. Our company is built on a foundation of principles that include responsibility to the communities we serve and where we live and work. In 2008, we launched a Corporate Citizenship Initiative, a global effort to address the environmental, social, economic, and ethical challenges we face in our business. Among the issues we are addressing are carbon impact, paper specifications and procurement, ethical conduct within our business and among our vendors, and community and charitable support. For more information, please visit our website: www.wiley.com/go/citizenship.

Evaluation copies are provided to qualified academics and professionals for review purposes only, for use in their courses during the next academic year. These copies are licensed and may not be sold or transferred to a third party. Upon completion of the review period, please return the evaluation copy to Wiley. Return instructions and a free of charge return mailing label are available at www.wiley.com/go/returnlabel. If you have chosen to adopt this textbook for use in your course, please accept this book as your complimentary desk copy. Outside of the United States, please contact your local sales representative.

ISBN-13: 978-0-470-40879-7

Printed in the United States of America

10 9 8 7 6 5 4 3 2 1

To Ella, Kennan, Alev, and, of course, to Mom.

ABOUT THE AUTHOR

John McLaren's research has ranged across the fields of international trade, development, industrial organization, and political economy, and has appeared in the *American Economic Review, Quarterly Journal of Economics*, the *Review of Economic Studies*, and a range of other outlets. He received his PhD at Princeton in 1992, has taught at the University of Virginia since 2000, and at one time or another has also taught at Princeton, Yale, Columbia, the University of Maryland, and—farthest afield—the University of World Economy and Diplomacy in Tashkent, Uzbekistan.

PREFACE

Approach

This is a textbook for undergraduate, MBA, and Master's of Public Administration courses in international economics. It is appropriate to either a one-semester course in international economics with two or three weeks of macroeconomics topics or a course specialized in international trade. This text covers all of the conventional theory that undergraduates are expected to learn in a course of that sort, but presented in a radically different way. A standard course in international trade will present a sequence of models—the Ricardian model, specific factors, Heckscher-Ohlin, and a few others—following up each theoretical model with an application to one or more policy questions or with a discussion of empirical evidence. This time-tested method works fairly well, particularly with highly motivated students, but it suffers from two important limitations that I have noticed after long experience.

- *The absorption of the theory* suffers from a lack of enthusiasm, because for most students it is difficult to sustain motivation through the many technical details required to understand the models well, before the *usefulness* of the model has been established in the mind of the student.

- *The application of the theory* suffers because the student tends to think of "theory" and "policy" as two different topics, which refer to each other but do not depend on each other in any crucial way. Often, the real-world applications are presented in text boxes, which signal to the students that they are not part of the core material and are unlikely to be on the exam. I have found that in practice, students tend to suffer through the theory, then perk up somewhat during discussion of policy controversies, but generally fail to make a strong connection between the two. When, at the end of my course, I have assigned a short written assignment in which students are required to analyze a real-world trade policy, I have found that even students who have understood the theoretical models reasonably well simply do not use them in analyzing real-world problems. Put differently, *using* economic theory is a different skill from merely *understanding* economic theory, and our economics courses ought to aim to teach this skill.

In this text I have used what I call the *inversion technique*: I introduce a real-world policy problem at the *beginning* of each topic, and spend some time presenting the key facts and background, showing the students why the problem is important, achieving a certain level of emotional investment in the policy question. I then present one or more key arguments that are made in answering the question by advocates for one answer or another, and *then*, in the process of elucidating the particular argument I want to highlight, I present a theoretical model that is *necessary to understand that argument*. In this way, the theory model is not separate from an inquiry into the real world, but it is presented at the outset as a *tool* for understanding the world, and the students appreciate it as a possible solution to an important real-world question.

Since I began using this technique to present my course at the University of Virginia, I have found a sharp improvement in students' engagement with the material (and my own enjoyment of it). Each major theoretical idea can be motivated by a vivid problem from the real world. For example, I introduce the Ricardian model not as a theory of why nations trade in general, but as part of the answer to the question: "Should Nigeria pursue self-sufficiency in food?" The government of Nigeria has indeed had food self-sufficiency as an explicit goal for many years, and in fact for several years in the 1980s banned rice imports as a step to achieving it. Some arguments can be made in favor of this sort of policy in some cases, which I note, but economists overwhelmingly reject this as helpful policy, because it denies the country the benefits of specialization on the basis of comparative advantage. The Ricardian model makes that line of argument as clear as it can be, including the observation, surprising to many noneconomists, that a country may well boost its food consumption by abandoning food self-sufficiency, because of the higher incomes that result from the gains from trade. In this way, the Ricardian model unfortunately but literally becomes a matter of life and death, and vastly more interesting to students than if it was a mere abstract exercise.

Coverage

Although the manner of presentation is unusual, and the table of contents shows a series of real-world policy problems rather than theoretical topics, the textbook contains *the full set of theoretical models* contained in any standard international textbook, presented in *full analytical rigor*. As a result, one might well interpret this volume as a conventional trade theory textbook in disguise, although I hope its contribution will be greater than that. I have laid out in the accompanying two tables which model is covered in each chapter. The Theory Guide shows a brief list of the main theory ideas, with the chapter location of each one, and the Chapter List with Detailed Guide to Theory Contents shows the theory content in each chapter.

Technical Level

The technical level of the text is moderate. The text does not use calculus, but many models involve the simultaneous solution of two linear equations with two unknowns and a lot of fairly elaborate diagrams are analyzed with a lot of geometry. Key microeconomic tools are defined before being used, so one could use the course with only a Principles course as a prerequisite, although I think that students are likely to get the most out of it if they have already completed intermediate microeconomics. The analysis of the models is fairly detailed, but I have found that building each chapter around a motivating example enhances students' willingness to push through detailed equilibrium analysis. In that sense, the factual material that begins each chapter and the theoretical elaboration that makes up the bulk of the chapter should be seen as complements, not substitutes.

Additional Features

A few additional features of the text are worth mentioning.

(i)   *Empirical assignments.* Students can learn a great deal about globalization in practice by working out simple exercises with spreadsheets on actual data. I have found that students appreciate this feature both because of what they learn about globalization and because it sharpens some quantitative skills that are useful in every walk of life. For example, for Chapter 1, there is a simple spreadsheet of data from the World Bank on trade volumes, GDP, and populations by country and by year for a broad sample of countries. Problems at the end of that chapter ask students to identify both trends in openness over time and cross-country patterns, such as whether richer or larger countries tend to be more or less open than poorer or smaller ones. For the material on intra-industry trade for Chapter 3, a chapter problem asks students to pick a country and compute the fraction of U.S. trade with that country that is intra-industry in nature rather than inter-industry, and to speculate on the reasons it is high if it is high, and vice versa if it is low. This computation is easy to do with a spreadsheet with the formula given in the chapter.

(ii) *Theory exercises on spreadsheets.* For some problems, where a full mathematical analysis involves heavy algebra, a good bit of the mathematical insight can be obtained by manipulation of a spreadsheet. I have taken some inspiration on this from the work of Soumaya Tohamy and J. Wilson Mixon Jr. of Berry College on the pedagogical use of spreadsheets for trade theory. Student homework problems on optimal tariffs in Chapter 7 and the productivity effects of a Melitz-type model in Chapter 3 are set up in this way.

(iii) *The family tree of trade models.* Real-world trade is complicated; trade between the United States and Canada does not in any way resemble trade between the United States and Nigeria; the effect of a voluntary export restraint in a competitive industry such as the apparel sector is very different from the effect in an oligopolistic industry such as the auto sector. For this reason, we need a portfolio of very different models to analyze the world. Students can find the variety of models overwhelming, and so I have organized them in a diagram that I call "the family tree of trade models." This is a single image that summarizes all of the theory in the course at a glance, and as a result it can serve as a map to help us navigate the course material. It grows out of three branches, each representing one of the three main reasons for international trade (comparative advantage, increasing returns to scale, and imperfect competition), as developed in the insightful and, I believe, underappreciated textbook by Wilfred Ethier. I show the tree at the beginning of the course, pointing out its three main branches, and at the end of each topic in class I show it again to indicate which branch of the tree we have now learned. At the end of each chapter in the book, the portion of the tree that has been seen so far is reproduced under the heading "Where We Are." In that way, students always know how the different pieces of the course fit together. The full tree is reproduced on the inside back cover for convenience.

(iv) *Advanced theoretical topics.* The book incorporates a simplified account of the Melitz model; both the Feenstra-Hanson and the Grossman-Rossi-Hansberg models of offshoring; the Kala Krishna theory of voluntary export restraints (VER's) as facilitating practices; and simplified analytical equilibrium treatments of the ideas in theoretical work on the World Trade Organization by Bagwell and Staiger and on pollution by Copeland and Taylor. The last chapter incorporates a simple cash-in-advance model of international monetary equilibrium that builds on models of international trade developed earlier in the book. I do not believe that this collection of topics is treated in very many texts at this level.

Theory Guide: The Location of Key Pieces of Theory by Chapter

Ricardian model: Chapter 2
Specific-factors model: Chapter 5
Heckscher-Ohlin model: Chapter 6
Oligopoly models: Chapter 4
Increasing-returns-to-scale models— internal: Chapter 3
Increasing-returns-to-scale models—external: Chapter 9
Monopolistic competition: Chapter 3
Heterogeneous firms: Chapter 3
Tariffs and quotas with perfect competition: Chapter 7
Tariffs and quotas under oligopoly: Chapter 10
Infant-industry protection: Chapter 9
Trade creation and trade diversion: Chapter 15
Intertemporal trade and unbalanced trade: Chapter 16
Exchange-rate determination: Chapter 17

Chapter List with Detailed Guide to Theory Contents

I. Engines of Globalization

1. A Second Surge of Globalization.

Shows the key facts of rising globalization in historical context and introduces the three main reasons for trade, hence the idea behind each of the three main trade theories covered in the next three chapters.

2. Should Nigeria Strive for Food Self-sufficiency?

Introduces the Ricardian model and comparative advantage as a reason for trade.

3. Why Do Americans Get Their Impalas from Canada?

Introduces increasing returns to scale as a source of trade. Export-versus-FDI model of serving a foreign market. Monopolistic competition model of trade. Intuitive treatment of Melitz model.

4. Kodak and Fuji: Is World Trade Rigged in Favor of Large Corporations?	Introduces oligopolistic models of trade, showing how oligopoly in and of itself can be a reason for trade and how oligopolists themselves can be the losers, with consumers the beneficiaries. Baldwin-Krugman model of reciprocal dumping. Cournot and Bertrand models.

II. Politics and Policy in the World Economy

5. Why Did the North Want a Tariff, and Why Did the South Call It an Abomination?	Introduces specific-factors models.
6. Is Free Trade a Rip-off for American Workers?	Introduces the Heckscher-Ohlin model as well as empirical evidence on the trade-and-wages debate.
7. Why Doesn't Our Government Want Us to Import Sugar?	Introduces basic tariff and quota analysis in comparative-advantage models, partial and general equilibrium. Terms-of-trade versus interest-group motivations for trade policy. Extension to VERs.
8. Who Are the WTO, and What Do They Have Against Dolphins?	The prisoner's dilemma nature of protectionism and the rationale for multilateral cooperation. The problem of disguised protectionism and the intersection between trade and environmental policy.
9. Should Third World Governments Use Tariffs to Jump-start Growth?	Tariffs in an economy with external increasing returns; infant-industry protection.
10. Was Ronald Reagan Punked by Japanese Automakers?	Shows how VERs can have radically different effects in an oligopolistic model; examines evidence that Japanese firms benefited from VERs of the 1980s, and shows how this can arise in a Bertrand oligopoly. (Simplified version of Kala Krishna's theory of VERs as "facilitating practices.") Extension to strategic trade policy more generally: export subsidies and import tariffs under oligopoly.

III. Current Controversies

11. Should the iPod Be Made by American Workers?	Feenstra-Hanson and Grossman-Rossi-Hansberg models of offshoring; look at empirical evidence.
12. Should We Build a Border Fence?	Shows how the models of Chapters 5 and 6 can clarify the different arguments regarding immigration; look at empirical evidence.
13. Trade and the Environment: Is Globalization Green?	Reviews "pollution haven" argument that globalization harms the environment versus Antweiler-Copeland-Taylor Heckscher-Ohlin-based argument that globalization is good for the environment. Adds pollution and pollution regulation to the model of Chapter 6.

14. Sweatshops and Child Labor: Globalization and Human Rights	Adds Basu-Van-type child labor to the model of Chapter 5 to understand the approach and findings of Edmonds, Pavcnik, and Topolova; addresses other questions in globalization and human rights less formally.
15. Is NAFTA a Betrayal of the Poor or a Path to Prosperity?	Trade diversion, trade creation, and evidence on the effects of NAFTA on households in the United States and Mexico. Draws on models from Chapters 6, 7, and 11.
16. Is the Trade Deficit a Time Bomb?	Intertemporal trade and the reasons trade may be unbalanced. Critical look at current views on the U.S. trade deficit.
17. Trade and Exchange Rates: Is the Renminbi the Culprit?	Equilibrium model of exchange rates based on infinite-horizon cash-in-advance model. Critically evaluates claim that China achieves an unfair advantage through currency manipulation.

Additional Resources

Companion Web Site. A dedicated site for *International Trade* containing all of the following teaching and learning resources: www.wiley.com/college/mclaren

Instructor's Manual. Several valuable resources that enhance each chapter of the text, including a chapter summary, approaches to teaching the chapter, suggested related readings, and answers to all of the end-of-chapter questions.

Test Bank. Multiple choice and short-answer questions varying in level of difficulty for every chapter.

Lecture Slides. Slides of text art and lecture outlines for each chapter provided on the companion web site; can be viewed or downloaded to a computer.

Additional Questions and Problems. Similar to those found at the end of each chapter; additional questions and problems provided for further practice and/or assessment.

Student Practice Quizzes. Approximately 10 multiple-choice questions per chapter that help students evaluate individual progress.

Excel Spreadsheets. Throughout the book, the icon at left identifies selected problems that can be solved using Excel spreadsheets found on the book's companion web site.

Acknowledgments

Too many colleagues have provided help and guidance on particular portions of this book to be able to thank them all individually. A partial list includes Erhan Artuç, Peter Debaere, Bob Staiger, Mary Lovely, Arik Levinson, and Giovanni Peri. Former graduate teaching assistants who have shaped the book before going on to greater things include Felipe Benguria, Shushanik Hakobyan, and Gihoon Hong. I am grateful as well to the students whose feedback improved the text on many occasions. The reviewers who read draft chapters and provided detailed comments improved the book a great deal, and

I send them my sincere thanks. They are listed below among others who wish to remain anonymous. The Wiley team has been a great help, and all have my gratitude; Jennifer Manias, Jeanine Furino of Furino Production, and Ellinor Wagner have worked particularly closely with me to bring the book together. Finally, I thank my family, who put up with a great deal indeed during the creation of this volume. Hearty thanks to all.

Reviewers

MANOJ ATOLIA, *Florida State University*

NICOLA BORRI, *Boston University*

JOSEF BRADA, *Arizona State University*

ADHIP CHAUDHURI, *Georgetown University*

JOSEPH DANIELS, *Marquette University*

SMILE DUBE, *California State University, Sacramento*

ERICK M. ELDER, *University of Arkansas*

ERIC FISHER, *California Polytechnic State University*

DAVID GHARAGOZLOU, *California State University, Sacramento*

AMY GLASS, *Texas A&M University*

KISHORE G. KULKARNI, *Metropolitan State College of Denver*

FREDDY LEE, *California State University, Los Angeles*

ANTHONY LIMA, *California State University, Eastbay*

CHRISTOPHER MAGEE, *Bucknell University*

KEITH MALONE, *University of North Alabama*

MICHAEL A. MCPHERSON, *University of North Texas*

USHA NAIR-REICHERT, *Georgia Tech University*

NINA PAVCNIK, *Dartmouth University*

SUNIL SAPRA, *California State University, Los Angeles*

CHARLIE TURNER, *Old Dominion University*

CHONG UK KIM, *Sonoma State University*

KEVIN ZHANG, *Illinois State University*

BRIEF CONTENTS

CONTENTS

A Second Wave of Globalization

A ship loaded with cargo in standardized containers. Containerization has revolutionized ocean shipping since the 1960s.

When the Phoenicians developed square-rigged sails to trade throughout the Mediterranean, that was globalization. When European explorers reached landmasses west of Europe but east of China, blazing the trail for transatlantic trade routes, that was globalization. When the first telegraphic communication messages flowed through a cable under the Atlantic, that was globalization. Globalization, defined as anything that facilitates expanded economic interaction across countries, has been going on for a very long time. It can entail anything that makes it easier to buy and sell goods and services across national borders; for a firm in one country to set up production facilities in another; for an investor to invest in securities originating in another country; and for a worker in one country to travel and seek employment in another.

This book is an introduction to the economic analysis of globalization. It presents many tools that are useful for investigating the questions about what globalization does and what policies regarding the world economy we should demand of our governments. This chapter provides an overview of the major globalization movements in history and analyzes the categories of, and key reasons for, globalization. The chapter also functions as an overview of the rest of the book.

1.1 The First Wave

Historians disagree on the degree of globalization in the distant past, but a strong case can be made that the first wave of rapid globalization that made a serious difference in ordinary peoples' lives occurred in the nineteenth century. Economic historians O'Rourke and Williamson (2002) have proposed that it occurred in the 1820s. This is a surprising conclusion because the two momentous developments that would have been expected to have the largest effect on international transactions costs did not occur until later in the century, namely, the rise of the steamship and the opening of the Suez Canal, which allowed ships to travel from the Mediterranean Sea to Asia and back without rounding the Cape of Good Hope at the southern tip of Africa. O'Rourke and Williamson suggest that something occurred quite early in the century to make the world economy substantially more integrated. Two key pieces of evidence stand out: direct evidence on transport costs and indirect evidence on product prices.

With regard to transport costs, Figure 1.1, based on data from Harley (1988), shows how freight rates changed over this period. The curve shows an index of the cost of shipping coal from the British city of Tyne to export destinations over the period 1741 to 1872, expressed in 1800 shillings per ton.[1] The horizontal blue line shows the freight cost as of the year 1800. Notice that for virtually every year before the 1820s, the cost is above the 1800 level, with the average far above; for virtually every year from the 1820s on, the cost is

---

[1] The freight rate index is a simple average of the four coal-shipping series presented in Harley (1988), Table 9. They are deflated by the consumer price index shown on p. 469 of Mitchell (1962) for 1741 to 1823, and on pp. 471–472 for 1800–1872, scaled to have the same price in 1800, with a simple average for the overlapping years.

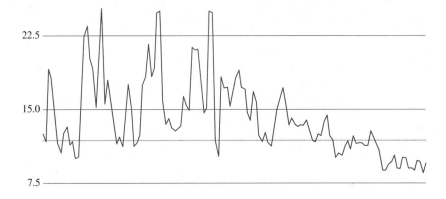

- Coal freight rates: 1800 shillings per ton
- 1800 rate

Source: Harley (1988, Table 9); Mitchell (1962, p.469, pp. 471-2).

FIGURE 1.1
British Shipping
Rates for Export of
Coal, 1741–1872.

below the 1800 level, with the average far below. The graph demonstrates that in the 1820s it became considerably easier to export coal.

With regard to product prices, a sample of the evidence is reproduced in Figure 1.2. This figure shows, for cloves, black pepper, and coffee—all commodities exported from Southeast Asia to Europe—the ratio of the price paid by the consumer in Amsterdam to the price received by the supplier in Southeast Asia between 1580 and 1939. For example, at one point in the 1660s, consumers in Amsterdam paid about 25 times for a pound of cloves what the same cloves could be purchased for in a market in Southeast Asia. These ratios fell dramatically after the 1820s, with the destination-price-to-origin-price ratio for cloves falling to about two quite quickly at that time. This evidence suggests that it became substantially easier to send commodities around the world in the first half of the nineteenth century—and so much so that not only would international trade statistics be affected, but ordinary peoples' lives (by, for example, making cloves newly affordable in Europe for people who had been priced out of the market).

Thus, both direct evidence on transport costs and indirect evidence on the convergence of product prices across countries suggest a wave of globalization in the nineteenth century, particularly around the 1820s, on a scale sufficient to affect ordinary peoples' lives.

1.2 The Second Wave

The first wave of globalization did not last, however, owing to a wave of protectionist policies in the early twentieth century. Barriers to international trade rose sharply in the first decades of that century before falling sharply

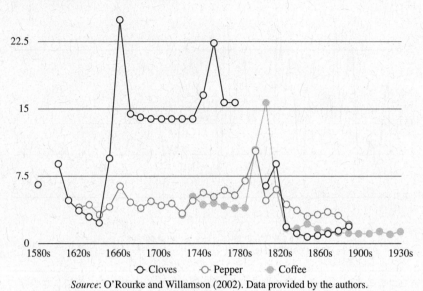

FIGURE 1.2
Spice and Coffee
Markups: Amsterdam
vs. Southeast Asia,
1580–1939.

Source: O'Rourke and Willamson (2002). Data provided by the authors.

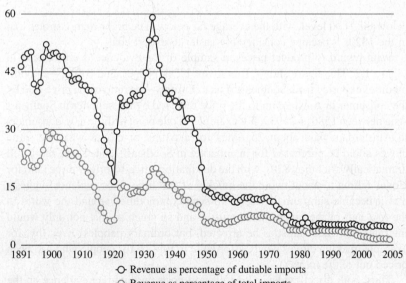

FIGURE 1.3
Average U.S. Tariffs,
1891–2005.

Source: U.S. International Trade Commission (USITC) (2006).

in the later decades. Figure 1.3 illustrates this by plotting the rise and fall of
U.S. tariffs over this period. A *tariff* is a tax on an imported good; the "average
tariff," as plotted in Figure 1.3, is the total revenue collected from tariffs on
imports into the United States in a given year divided by the total value of
goods imported. The dark blue time-plot in the figure shows revenues as a
percentage of dutiable imports, which means the product categories that are

subject to tariff, and the light blue time-plot shows revenues as a fraction of *all* imports, including those that are duty-free. Tariffs will be discussed at length much later, especially in Chapters 6, 7, and 10, but for now we need note only that high tariffs discourage trade.

As Figure 1.3 shows, U.S. tariffs surged in the early twentieth century but steadily declined after that. From their high point with the Smoot-Hawley Tariff of 1930 (see Chapter 8) to 1960, average U.S. tariffs fell by three quarters, and since then they have fallen another two-thirds. A similar picture would emerge from tariff data for other industrial countries. These tariff reductions were the result of international cooperation through the General Agreement on Tariffs and Trade (GATT) and the World Trade Organization (WTO). These together form a key feature of the world economic landscape and will be discussed in some detail in Chapter 8.

The striking reduction in tariffs and other government-imposed barriers to trade in the last half of the twentieth century is an example of *liberalization*. In general, liberalization denotes any reduction in barriers to international transactions that are created by government.

Aside from reductions in tariffs, a major force for globalization in the second half of the twentieth century was the technological advance in transport, which reduced international transport costs. Hummels (2007) surveys research on trends in transport cost worldwide. A major revolution in ocean shipping occurred as a result of *containerization*, a system of standardized shipping containers that can be used on rail cars, trucks, or ships, allowing a firm to pack a shipment, send it by truck to a rail line, by train to the harbor, by ship halfway around the world, then by rail and truck again to its destination, all without opening the container. Containerization originated in the United States in the 1960s and spread worldwide during the 1970s. It allows for substantial efficiencies, but it has not translated into sustained reductions in freight rates, partly because of increases in fuel prices (Hummels, 2007, pp. 140–145). The importance of fuel prices is something to keep in mind when pondering the future of globalization, as we will discuss later in Section 1.3. Freight rates *have* fallen in air transport, however, particularly with the introduction of jet engines; the average cost per ton-kilometer for air shipping fell by more than 90% from 1955 to 2004 (Hummels, 2007, p. 138). Overall, in the second half of the century reductions in tariffs appear to have been a more important force for globalization than reductions in transport cost. In 1958, average U.S. transport costs were half of average tariffs, while by the end of the century they were three times average tariffs (Hummels, 2007, p.136).[2] More recently, reductions in transactions costs brought about by the rise of the Internet appear to have been important for both goods and services trade (Freund and Weinhold, 2002, 2004).

This drop in trade tariffs and transport costs, combined with reduced impediments to movement of capital and people across borders, has resulted in a dramatic rise in the degree of integration of the world economy. We observe

---

[2] This basic message is underlined by Anderson and van Wincoop (2004), who analyze the size and nature of trade costs by studying trade patterns. One lesson is that trade costs remain substantial, even between countries with very few tariffs or other governmental trade impediments between them. In addition, physical proximity is still an important determinant of trade flows. These considerations suggest that transport costs remain very important in international trade, even where tariffs have essentially disappeared.

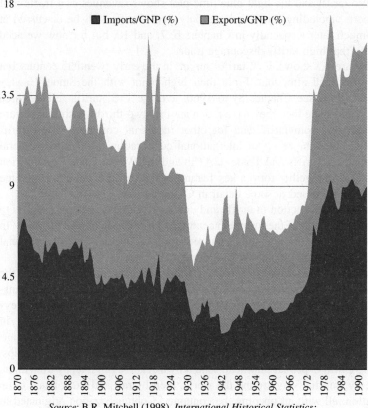

FIGURE 1.4
U.S. Trade Volume,
1870–1993 (as % of
GNP).

Source: B.R. Mitchell (1998), *International Historical Statistics: The Americas, 1750–1993*. New York, NY: Macmillan Reference.

U.S. Trade flows, 1793–1993 (% of GNP).

this integration in several ways. First, there has been a sharp rise in international trade. Consider Figure 1.4, which plots U.S. imports and exports as a percentage of U.S. gross national product (GNP) over a long time span. In this figure, the height of the light blue region at any date is the volume of U.S. exports as a percentage of GNP, and the height of the dark blue region is the volume of U.S. imports as a percentage of GNP. Their combined height is the sum of imports and exports as a percentage of GNP, which is often used as a measure of a country's "openness." For example, in 1958, U.S. exports were 3.9% of GNP; U.S. imports were 2.9% of GNP; and openness was 6.8% of GNP. Over this time span, the figure shows a clear U-shaped pattern. At the beginning of the twentieth century, total trade (imports plus exports) amounted to 10 to 12% of GNP in most years; with a few exceptions trade was unusually high. As a result of early-twentieth-century protectionism, trade fell markedly, reaching a low of around 5% in 1932. The recovery really did not occur until the 1970s, during and after which trade as a fraction of GNP surged to levels that had never been sustained for any long period in the past.

The second way in which we can see this late-twentieth-century surge in globalization is in movement of capital. On one hand, investors can purchase shares of foreign companies or other foreign securities without taking a large ownership stake in any one firm; in other words, they engage in foreign *portfolio investment*. On the other hand, if an investor or a firm purchases a

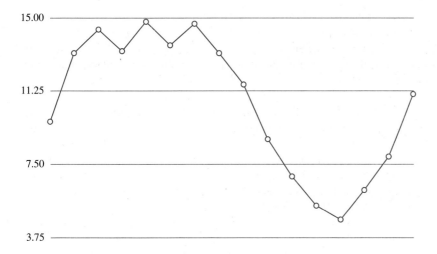

FIGURE 1.5
Foreign-born Fraction
of U.S. Population,
1850–1990.

Source: Gibson and Lennon (1999) and Malone et al., (2003).

controlling interest[3] in a foreign enterprise, or actually builds or expands a productive facility in another country, the investment is called *foreign direct investment*, or FDI. *Inward FDI*, in the case of the United States, occurs when foreigners buy U.S. productive enterprises or build or expand plants in the United States, and *outward FDI* occurs when Americans do the same in other countries. FDI has become a substantially larger piece of the world economy than it ever was in the past. To cite some illustrative data, Bordo, Irwin, and Eichengreen (1999) report that in 1914, the stock of accumulated U.S. FDI abroad stood at about 7% of U.S. GNP, in 1929/1930 the figure was still 7%, and in 1960 the figure had fallen slightly to 6%. By contrast, by 1996, it had jumped to 20%. Thus, outward FDI had exploded in the final decades of the twentieth century. Similarly, the stock of foreign capital in the United States stood at 3–4%, 1%, and 1% of U.S. GDP in 1914, 1929/1930, and 1960, respectively. By 1996, the stock of foreign capital had jumped to 16%. Clearly, both U.S. capital abroad and foreign capital in the United States have a much larger role in the U.S. economy than they ever had in the past.

The third way in which the surge in globalization manifested itself is in the integration of world labor markets. An employer can hire a foreign worker to perform a task, a practice known as *offshoring* (sometimes called outsourcing, but this is a more confusing term since it has other uses as well). Alternatively, a foreign worker can come to the country where the employer is, which implies either a guest-worker arrangement, if the move is temporary, or immigration, if it is permanent. All of these forms of labor-market integration increased in the late twentieth century. Figure 1.5 demonstrates these trends. The figure is

---

[3] The definition used for this varies quite a lot from one user to the next. The U.S. government's Bureau of Economic Analysis, for example, uses a 10% ownership threshold in its definition of foreign direct investment.

constructed using data from the U.S. Census and shows, over a century and a half, the share of foreign-born workers in the U.S. population (whether in the country legally or not). Since the United States was settled by immigrants, it is not surprising that the foreign-born share was fairly high in the nineteenth century, hovering close to 14% for much of the century. The numbers dropped off following the immigration restrictions of the early twentieth century, reaching a low of about 4% in 1970. However, in the last three decades of the century, the foreign-born share of the population surged again, reaching a high close to 12% by 2003.

To summarize our discussion so far, there have been two distinct waves of globalization, defined as changes in the economic environment that facilitate international transactions in goods, services, or factors of production. The first occurred in the nineteenth century and was a result of technological changes such as the rise of steam transport, the opening of the Suez Canal, and the transatlantic cable. This wave was interrupted in the early twentieth century by policy impediments to globalization, such as tariff walls and immigration restrictions. Finally, as governments loosened these impediments, a second wave of globalization followed in the last three decades of the twentieth century.

We can divide the increased integration into several categories. First, greater integration of world goods markets leads to increased trade volumes. Second, increased integration of labor markets shows up as increased offshoring, increased migrant labor, or increased immigration. Integration of financial markets manifests itself in increased foreign portfolio investment, and integration of capital markets more generally manifests itself in increased FDI. All of these forms of increased world economic integration have been in evidence, particularly since the 1970s.

1.3 Crisis, Peak Oil, Pirates—and De-Globalization?

In the first quarter of 2009, world trade fell by a startling 30% as the world economy entered a major downturn. This abrupt collapse of world trade left vast numbers of container ships idle as a kind of 'ghost fleet," larger than the combined navies of the United States and Britain, moored off the coast of Singapore, waiting empty for customers (Parry, 2009). Given the size of the recession, this drop is not out of line with the response of trade to macroeconomic fluctuations generally (Freund, 2009), but having looked at the historical trends, we can ask what the future long-run trends in globalization may be, and whether or not the decades-long trend toward international integration may be reversed. The following are a few factors that are likely to be important in determining the answers to these questions.

1. *Trade may become more volatile*. Freund (2009) has documented that, although world trade flows have always been correlated with macroeconomic fluctuations, trade is apparently becoming more sensitive to these fluctuations. This may be due to the increased globalization of production, with production networks for each product spread out increasingly over several countries—a topic discussed in detail in Chapter 11. If manufacturers offshore more of their production in boom times and reduce their

foreign workforce in downturns, they will thereby magnify the effect of aggregate demand shocks on trade flows. For example, a manufacturer of shirts might have trouble keeping up with demand in a boom and so might contract with a foreign supplier to produce some extra shirts to fill the gap; later, in a slump, the manufacturer will go back to meeting its demand with domestic production.

2. *Peak oil.* We have already discussed the impact of oil on ocean shipping rates (Hummels, 2007). If world oil production has already peaked, as some observers believe, those fuel costs will likely enter an implacable, rising upward trend that will have a negative effect on world trade.

3. *Piracy.* Political collapse in Somalia has given rise to a new problem of heavily armed gangs roaming the Eastern African coast and environs looking for ships to take over, stealing their contents, or holding their occupants for ransom. This problem has substantially raised shipping costs for sea lanes in that region (see Murphy, 2009, for an analysis). In general, criminals preying on ocean shipping are called *pirates*, and if piracy continues to worsen it can certainly dampen globalization.

4. *A new rise of protectionism?* We have already noted that the crisis of 1929 and the years after prompted a surge in protectionist policy. Some observers are concerned that recent economic troubles could have the same effect today. A group of economists sponsored by the Center for Economic Policy Research (CEPR) in Europe has set up a program to monitor this possibility, issuing regular reports called Global Trade Alerts to keep a careful watch for surging protectionism. These alerts can be found at the website www.voxeu.org.

5. *Global warming.* As concerns about the potential devastating effects of global warming rise, governments around the world are likely to impose increasingly more stringent restrictions or taxes on the use of fossil fuels. Since transport of goods around the world uses fossil fuels intensively (recall point 2 above), the resulting increases in fuel prices are likely to dampen world trade.

Time will tell if the second great wave of globalization will fade as the first one did.

1.4 The Forces at Work

We have discussed the many forms that globalization takes, as well as its ebb and flow over time. This all raises the question: What is the reason for all of this international economic activity? Once natural and policy impediments fall, is there any special reason for people to look outside of their own country for things to buy or people to sell to? Why trade? Why build a company through investments abroad? Why offshore jobs? Why emigrate? In other words, what is the driving force behind all of these big economic changes described above? And further, what are the effects of all of this globalization? Is it good or bad for humanity? Should governments be allowing it, slowing it, speeding it up, regulating it, taming it?

This book will examine these questions. The answers will differ for different industries, countries, and time periods, and in many cases there is dispute among experts about what the answers are. Although no one answer to any of these questions will apply to all cases, we can offer one simple principle that can help organize the inquiry: It is important to think about the answer to the first question before addressing any subsequent questions. In other words, once we have a tentative answer to the question "Why is there trade?," we have a theory of trade, and that theory of trade can then be applied to policy questions. But different answers to the question "Why is there trade?" imply different theories of trade, and thus, in general, different answers to the policy questions. We will see that there are several different theories of trade, all of which help explain real-world phenomena, so the theory chosen for a particular question regarding trade in a particular industry or country makes a big difference in deciding what policy to use. This same logic applies to the questions "Why is there FDI?," "Why is there offshoring?," and the others (and all of these questions are inextricably intertwined).[4]

To anticipate our discussion in future chapters, there are three broad answers to the question of why there is trade. First, countries differ, and any difference between two countries—in technology, climate, culture, factor supplies, and consumer preferences, for example—can lead to opportunities for mutual gain from trade. Theories based on this reasoning are called *comparative-advantage* theories. Second, many industries exhibit increasing returns to scale, meaning that an increase in output results in a less-than-proportional increase in costs. This can imply that it is most efficient and most profitable to concentrate production of a good in one location, serving all world markets from that location. Third, many industries are oligopolistic, meaning that they are dominated by a few large firms, each with some control over prices. Oligopoly can give rise to trade, as oligopolistic firms strive to grab oligopolistic profits from each other by invading each others' markets.

We can view all trade theories and all trade models as arising from one of these three reasons, and we can represent the types of trade models as three branches of the Family Tree of Trade Models, illustrated by the big diagram by that name in the Appendix. All of the models that are discussed in this book are located somewhere in that diagram, with the chapter number indicated. Each chapter adds a twig to the tree. (A diagram at the end of each chapter shows the new twig in its place, until the whole tree is done.)

We will examine comparative-advantage models, increasing-returns models, and oligopolistic models in detail. Each of the three types of model has a contribution to make in understanding the reasons for trade in the real world, and the way we think about policy in any given case depends on the relative importance of these three motivations in the case at hand. Along the way, we will discuss the parallel analysis of the other forms of globalization, FDI, offshoring, and immigration, which are just as important as trade, but not quite as well researched or understood. We will do all of this by examining a sequence of case studies and policy questions, in order to illustrate the usefulness of each model from the start.

---

[4] This approach to organizing the analysis of international economics follows Ethier (1994).

WHERE WE ARE

In this chapter, we have introduced the three main branches of the Family Tree of Trade Models.

Each chapter will add some twigs to one of these branches.

QUESTIONS AND PROBLEMS

1. Identify a technological change that has facilitated globalization, aside from those mentioned in the text. Identify a policy change that has contributed to globalization, aside from those mentioned in the text. Explain your answers.

    The following questions ask you to quantify some trends in globalization and are based on the Excel spreadsheet entitled "Trade.data.spread sheet.xls." The data are from the World Bank. Define the "openness" of a country as the sum of its imports and exports divided by its gross domestic product (GDP).

2. How has the average level of openness in the world economy changed over the years in question?

3. How many countries experienced an increase in openness between 1991 and 2001? How many experienced a decrease?

4. Looking at the last year of the data, compare the average openness of the 20 largest countries (measured in terms of population) and the 20 smallest countries. Which is more open?

5. Again looking at the last year of data, compare the average openness of the 20 richest countries (measured in terms of per capita GDP) and the 20 poorest countries. Which is more open?

6. Based on your results in questions (4) and (5), summarize what kind of countries tend to be more open, and what kind tend to be less open. Can you speculate as to why this is the case?

REFERENCES

Anderson, James E., and Eric van Wincoop (2004). "Trade Costs." *Journal of Economic Literature* 42 (September), pp. 691–751.

Bordo, Michael, Doug Irwin, and Barry Eichengreen (1999). "Is Globalization Today Really Different than Globalization a Hundred Years Ago?" *Brookings Trade Forum* 1999, Washington, DC: Brookings Institution.

Ethier, Wilfred (1994). *International Economics* (3rd edition). W.W. Norton & Co.

Freund, Caroline (2009). "Demystifying the Collapse in Trade." *VOX: Research-based Policy Analysis and Commentary from Leading Economists*, July 3 (available at voxeu.org).

Freund, Caroline, and Diana Weinhold (2002). "The Internet and International Trade in Services." *American Economic Review* 92:2 (May), pp. 236–240.

———— (2004). "The Effect of the Internet on International Trade." *Journal of International Economics* 62, pp. 171–189.

Gibson, Campbell J., and Emily Lennon (1999). "Historical Census Statistics on the Foreign-born Population of the United States: 1850–1990." Population Division Working Paper No. 29, Population Division, U.S. Bureau of the Census.

Harley, C. Knick (1988). "Ocean Freight Rates and Productivity, 1740–1913: The Primacy of Mechanical Invention Reaffirmed." *The Journal of Economic History* 48:4 (December), pp. 851–876.

Hummels, David (2007). "Transportation Costs and International Trade in the Second Era of Globalization." *Journal of Economic Perspectives* 21:3 (Summer), pp. 131–154.

Malone, Nolan, Kaari F. Baluja, Joseph M. Costanzo, and Cynthia J. Davis (2003). "The Foreign-Born Population: 2000." Census 2000 Brief C2KBR-34. Washington, DC: Bureau of the Census.

Mitchell, B.R. (with Phyllis Deane) (1962). *Abstract of British Historical Statistics*. Cambridge: Cambridge University Press.

Murphy, Martin (2009). "Somali Piracy: Not Just a Naval Problem." Washington, DC: Center for Strategic and Budgetary Assessments Backgrounder.

O'Rourke, Kevin, and Jeffrey Williamson (2002). "When Did Globalization Begin?" *European Review of Economic History* 6:1 (April), pp. 23–50.

Parry, Simon (2009). "Revealed: The Ghost Fleet of the Recession." *Daily Mail (UK)*, September 13.

USITC (2006). "Value of U.S. Imports for Consumption, Duties Collected, and Ratio of Duties to Values: 1891–2005." Statistical Services Division, Office of Investigations, Office of Operations, U.S. International Trade Commission (March).

Should Nigeria Strive for Self-Sufficiency in Food?

Billy Rizcallah

Girl in a Nigerian village.

2.1 A Presidential Agenda

Not many countries have been through more political and economic upheavals than Nigeria. Since its independence in 1960, it has dealt with an oil boom and bust, several coups and dictatorships, a devastating civil war, and religious and ethnic tensions. Under civilian government since 1999, it has attained some stability and has achieved some debt reduction and policy reform. A study published in *New Scientist* magazine in 2003 even listed Nigerians as the happiest people in the world.

Unfortunately, and despite enormous oil wealth, the country has never achieved sustained growth, and most of the population endures poor living standards.[1] What strategies the Nigerian government should pursue to raise incomes and living standards is a sprawling topic beyond our scope here, but we will examine one strategy that the government has tried in the past and may try again: use of trade policy to achieve self-sufficiency in food. Food self-sufficiency has often been a high priority for the government. For example, H.E. Olusegun Obasanjo, president of Nigeria from 1999 to 2007, while attending a 2004 conference on African food issues in Uganda, boasted of his government's "holistic agricultural and food self-sufficiency strategy," and explained how his government had "set targets, strategies, and time frames for the achievement of national self-sufficiency to be followed by export program and promotion."

President Obasanjo was proud of his efforts to move Nigeria toward food self-sufficiency as a growth strategy, an antipoverty strategy, and a food-security strategy. Nigerians generally import about 20% of the cereals they consume (Akande, 2005, p. 168), and the idea of producing all cereals consumption domestically has been promoted many times, both by various analysts who study the country and by the government itself. Indeed, during the years 1986–1995, the government *banned* rice imports in order to increase domestic rice production and bring about rice self-sufficiency (Akande, n.d.), along with other cereals and associated foods (Nwosu, 1992). As recently as 2006, the government considered adopting that tactic once again, before being persuaded against it on grounds that it would violate its international agreements (FAO, 2006).[2]

Are such policies wise? Are they likely to put a dent in Nigeria's poverty and malnutrition?

At times there are good reasons for a policy of food self-sufficiency. For example, if government were to be subject to blockade threats, food self-sufficiency could reduce its vulnerability to its foreign enemies. Even if a blockade never occurs, food self-sufficiency could improve the country's bargaining power by diminishing the power of credible threat from the other country. This geopolitical argument for food self-sufficiency policies has validity in a limited number of cases—medieval cities prone to siege, and perhaps the former Soviet Union in the 1970s, for example. This reasoning applies to beleaguered countries that may find themselves subject to international sanctions. It probably does not apply to Nigeria.

---

[1] According to the United Nations Development Program, life expectancy at birth is 43.3 years, and under-age-5 child mortality is 197 per 1,000 live births.

[2] Mpoyo (1992) and Akande (2005) provide commentary on Nigeria's agricultural policies, broadly supportive of the rice self-sufficiency agenda, and Holmén (2006) argues in support of food self-sufficiency policies more broadly as part of a comprehensive approach to development.

Setting aside geopolitical arguments, most economists reject food self-sufficiency policies because they argue, based on comparative advantage, that a self-sufficiency strategy blocks the country's gains from specialization. In this chapter, we will look at that argument in detail. Specifically, we will see that in a world in which trade is driven by comparative advantage, a country that avails itself of trade benefits by specialization, exporting what it is relatively best at producing and importing what it is relatively least good at producing, becomes richer as a result. Furthermore, even if engaging in trade causes a country to lose its food industry altogether, it still has higher utility and will even have a higher level of food consumption. Thus, a policy of food self-sufficiency can contribute to national undernourishment. This conclusion is exactly the opposite of what its proponents want.

We turn next to a simplified model of gains from trade based on comparative advantage to explain this reasoning, and then we will return to the question of whether or not Nigeria should pursue the goal of self-sufficiency in rice.

2.2 The Comparative Advantage Argument Formalized: Introducing the Ricardian Model

In setting up our model, we will adopt the classic formulation of comparative advantage by British economist David Ricardo, first published in 1817. We use a simplified numerical example to work through the model, but the main conclusions are far more general than this simple model.[3]

The self-sufficiency proponents generally argue that the problem is that countries like Nigeria have developed their agriculture to favor cash crops for export, such as cocoa, Nigeria's largest non-oil export, and palm oil, instead of food for domestic consumption. To capture the choice between export crops and domestic food crops in the simplest manner possible, suppose that there are only two commodities, rice and cocoa, and that each Nigerian farmer can produce 1 ton of rice or 3 tons of cocoa in a single growing season. Ignore all other trade partners, and suppose that Nigeria's only trading possibilities are with America. ("America" in this case refers to the region consisting of North and South America so that we can include cocoa-growing regions of South America, such as Brazil.) Again, to focus on agricultural issues, let us suppose that a farmer in America can produce either rice or cocoa, but the capabilities of American farmers are different; each is able to produce 2/3 ton of rice or 2/3 ton of cocoa in a single growing season. There are 130 million people in Nigeria, whom we will assume are all farmers,[4] and 390 million people in America. These assumptions allow us to work out the maximum amount of cocoa the economy can produce for any quantity of rice,

---

[3] For much more general treatments of the Ricardian model, see Bhagwati, Panagariya, and Srinivasan (1998), Chapters 2−4, and Dornbusch, Fisher, and Samuelson (1977).

[4] Since 70% of Nigerians work in agriculture, this is not too egregious an oversimplification. The major omission is, of course, oil, which is the country's largest export, but it does not employ many Nigerians. Again, the points being made here would generalize to a more complicated and realistic model incorporating those other features.

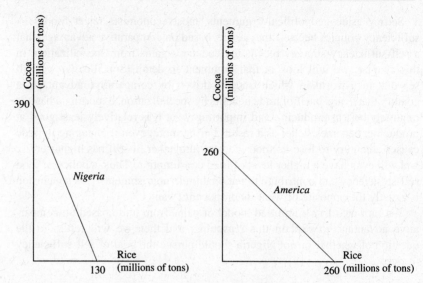

FIGURE 2.1
Production Possibility
Frontiers.

or the *production possibilities frontier*, for the two countries as shown in
Figure 2.1. The horizontal intercept for the Nigerian frontier, for example, is
the maximum amount of rice that could be produced by that economy, or 130
million people times 1 ton of rice production per person.

Note that for the Nigerian economy the opportunity cost of producing one
more ton of rice in Nigeria is 3 tons of cocoa. We determine the opportunity cost
by considering that 1 ton of rice requires one farmer for one growing season;
that farmer in that time frame could have produced 3 tons of cocoa instead. For
the American economy, the opportunity cost of one more ton of rice is 1 ton of
cocoa. We determine the opportunity cost by considering that 1 ton of rice
requires 3/2 farmer-growing seasons; those farmers in that time could
have produced 1 ton of cocoa instead. In each case, the opportunity cost of rice
production is the ratio of the marginal products of the two commodities, and in
each case it is the slope of the production possibilities frontier in Figure 2.1
(without the minus sign). Note that each country's opportunity cost of producing cocoa is the reciprocal of its opportunity cost for producing rice.

A country has an *absolute advantage* in a commodity if its workers are more
productive in producing that commodity than workers in the other country. A
country has a *comparative advantage* in a commodity if its opportunity cost in
producing that commodity is lower than that of the other country. Note that a
country can have an absolute advantage in every good; here in this example,
Nigeria does. However, it is impossible for one country to have a *comparative*
advantage (or a comparative disadvantage) in both commodities because if its
opportunity cost is lower in one good, its opportunity cost must be higher in the
other. In this example, since $1 < 3$, Nigeria has a comparative advantage in
cocoa, and America has a comparative advantage in rice.

To analyze equilibrium in this model, we will need to make some assumption
about consumer preferences. Let us assume that all consumers in both countries always spend one-half of their income on rice and one-half on cocoa.[5]

---

[5] In effect, we are assuming that all consumers have a Cobb-Douglas utility function with equal weights
on the two goods: $U(R, C) = R^{\frac{1}{2}}C^{\frac{1}{2}}$, where U denotes the utility function, R denotes consumption of
rice, and C denotes consumption of cocoa.

Assume that markets are competitive, meaning that all producers and all consumers take prices as given and that prices adjust to clear the markets. We will compare two situations: a ban on rice imports in Nigeria and free trade. The rice import ban is, of course, a crude way of enforcing self-sufficiency, but as we have seen it has been popular with the government in the Nigerian capital of Abuja. In this case, banning rice imports will be tantamount to cutting Nigeria off from trade altogether, since, as we will see, rice is the only commodity that Nigerians will want to import, and if no one can import anything, no one will want to export anything either. Economists use the term *autarky* to describe a situation in which trade is not possible or not permitted. In analyzing what trade actually does, it is often useful to imagine what would have happened in autarky and compare that to what happens with trade, and so we will use the term fairly often. For this discussion, we use the terms *rice import ban* and *autarky* interchangeably.

2.3 Autarky in the Ricardian Model

First, consider autarky in Nigeria. Under autarky, for markets to clear, the amount of each good produced in Nigeria must equal the amount of that good consumed in Nigeria. To see what the equilibrium will be, we need to figure out what each farmer will choose to produce. Suppose that the prices of rice and cocoa are given by P^R and P^C, respectively. Then a Nigerian household that produces rice will earn an income of P^R per growing season, and a household that produces cocoa will earn an income of $3P^C$ per growing season. As a result, the household will want to produce rice instead of cocoa if:

$$P^R > 3P^C, \ or$$

$$P^R/P^C > 3.$$

In that case, since all households in the country make the same decision, the country produces no cocoa at all and instead produces 130 million tons of rice each growing season. Similarly, if $P^R/P^C < 3$, all farmers will produce cocoa, so the economy will produce 390 million tons of cocoa each growing season and no rice. If $P^R/P^C = 3$, the economy could produce any mix of the two crops, since each farmer would be indifferent between the two. This is all we need to know about the supply behavior of the economy; this behavior is summarized in Figure 2.2 by Nigeria's *relative supply curve*, marked *RS*. The vertical axis in Figure 2.2 records the *relative price* of rice, P^R/P^C. The horizontal axis records the *relative supply* of rice, Q^R/Q^C, where Q^R denotes the total amount of rice produced nationwide and Q^C denotes the total amount of cocoa produced nationwide. If $P^R/P^C < 3$, no rice is produced and so the relative supply is equal to zero. If $P^R/P^C > 3$, no cocoa is produced and so the relative supply is infinite. At $P^R/P^C = 3$, any relative supply is possible, hence the flat part of the relative supply curve.

To find out what the autarky equilibrium is, we need to combine the national relative supply curve with the national *relative demand curve*. The relative demand for rice is defined as C^R/C^C, where C^R is nationwide consumption of rice and C^C is nationwide consumption of cocoa. Given our assumption about demand behavior, if a consumer has income I, then spending on rice will be

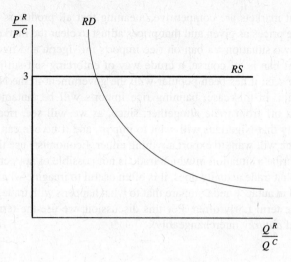

FIGURE 2.2
Autarky Equilibrium in Nigeria.

equal to $I/2$, for a quantity consumed equal to $I/(2P^R)$, and spending on cocoa will be $I/2$, for a quantity consumed equal to $I/(2P^C)$. Expressing these relationships in equation form, we get:

$$RD\left(\frac{P^R}{P^C}\right) \equiv \frac{C^R}{C^C} = \frac{P^C}{P^R}. \tag{2.1}$$

This is, then, the relative demand curve, plotted in Figure 2.2 as *RD*.

Since under autarky consumption of every good in Nigeria must equal the production of that good in Nigeria, it is also true that in any equilibrium the domestic relative supply must equal the domestic relative demand. Consequently, the equilibrium is given by the intersection of *RD* with *RS* in Figure 2.2. The equilibrium relative price is equal to 3, which makes sense since that is the opportunity cost of producing rice, and the relative price must take exactly that value if both goods are to be produced in equilibrium.

How well do Nigerian consumers do in this autarky equilibrium? Note that all households receive the same income whether they produce rice or cocoa, because prices have adjusted so that they are indifferent between producing rice and cocoa. A cocoa farmer will make 3 tons of output per growing season and sell them for P^C each, earning an income of $3P^C$. We can use this information to derive the farmer's *budget line*, which shows the set of all combinations of rice and cocoa that the farmer can consume (see Figure 2.3). Since, for example, the farmer could spend all income on cocoa, the cocoa-axis intercept of the budget line is equal to the farmer's income divided by the price of cocoa; this yields an intercept equal to 3. At the same time, the rice-axis intercept is equal to income divided by the price of rice, or $3P^C/P^R$, which is equal to 1, since $P^R/P^C = 3$. As with all budget lines, its slope is equal to -1 times the relative price, or -3.

The farmer maximizes utility by choosing the best consumption point on the budget line. Representing utility by *indifference curves*—curves that connect up consumption bundles that give the same consumer satisfaction or utility—the optimal consumption bundle will be at a point where the

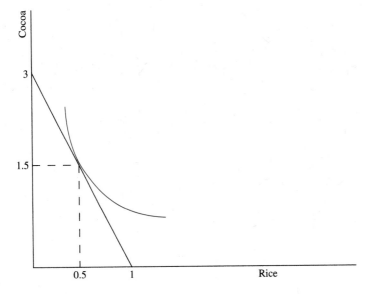

FIGURE 2.3
The Nigerian Farmer's
Autarkic Budget Line.

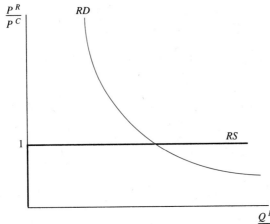

FIGURE 2.4
Autarky Equilibrium in America.

indifference curve is tangent to the budget line. Given our assumption about preferences (namely, that the farmer always spends one-half of her income on each good), this occurs at consumption of 0.5 ton of rice and 1.5 tons of cocoa, as indicated in the figure.

All of this works in parallel fashion for America, whose relative supply and demand curves are shown in Figure 2.4.

The autarky relative price of rice is equal to the opportunity cost 1, and the budget line for a typical American farmer has a cocoa-axis intercept and a rice-axis intercept equal to 2/3, as shown in Figure 2.5. Of course, the slope of the budget line is equal to -1 times the relative price, or −1. The American farmer consumes 1/3 ton both of rice and of cocoa; both this optimal point and the indifference curve it is on are shown.

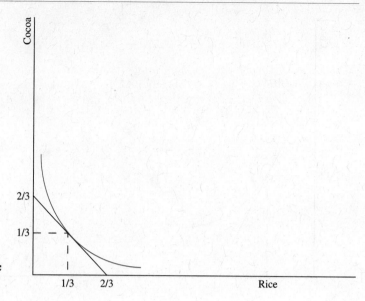

FIGURE 2.5
The American Farmer's Autarkic Budget Line.

2.4 Free Trade in the Ricardian Model

Now, we lift the import ban and let both countries trade freely. We will assume that there are no transport costs or other impediments to trade, so that the prices of both rice and cocoa are the same in America as they are in Nigeria. Thus, we henceforth will refer to the *world relative price*. To compute equilibrium, we need to put world relative supply RS^W together with world relative demand. The latter is easy to derive, since both countries have the same relative demand curves, as described in equation (2.1); this common relative demand curve is therefore also the relative demand curve for the world as a whole. To analyze the world relative supply curve requires three steps.

First, consider what happens to supply if P^R/P^C lies below 1, the opportunity cost of rice in America. In that case, farmers in both America and Nigeria will choose to produce cocoa, and, as a result, no rice will be produced anywhere in the world. Thus, for this price range, the world relative supply will equal zero, as shown in Figure 2.6. Second, if P^R/P^C lies above 3, farmers in both countries will produce only rice, so the world relative supply will be infinite. Finally, if P^R/P^C lies strictly in between these values, farmers in America will all produce rice, while farmers in Nigeria will all produce cocoa. Therefore, the world relative supply will equal America's maximum supply of rice (390 million farmers times 2/3 of a ton of rice per farmer per growing season, or 260 million tons) divided by Nigeria's maximum supply of cocoa (130 million farmers times 3 tons of cocoa per farmer per growing season, or 390 million tons). This yields a relative supply of rice equal to 2/3, shown in Figure 2.6 as a vertical line joining the portion with a relative price of 1 to the portion with a relative price of 3. Note that it is vertical because as long as the price is in that range, changes in the price do not affect output; each country simply continues producing the maximum possible amount of its particular commodity.

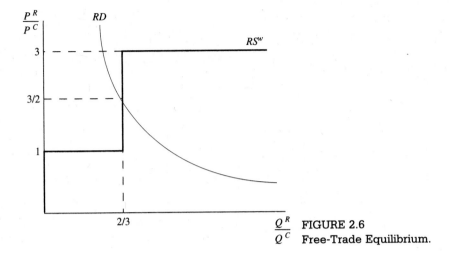

FIGURE 2.6
Free-Trade Equilibrium.

The complete curve in Figure 2.6 is the *world* relative supply curve, RS^W. Putting it together with the relative demand curve gives us the equilibrium. Algebraically, the price can be found as the solution to the equation:

$$RS^W\left(\frac{P^R}{P^C}\right) = RD\left(\frac{P^R}{P^C}\right). \qquad (2.2)$$

The solution will be the equilibrium world relative price of rice, which is called Nigeria's *terms of trade*.

More generally, a country's terms of trade is the price of its exported good divided by the price of its imported good. For a country with many imported goods and many exported goods, the terms of trade is computed by creating a price index for the country's exported goods and dividing it by price index for its imported goods. This is an important concept in international economics and will come up in many discussions in later chapters.

Let us make the assumption for the moment that (as shown in Figure 2.6) the intersection of the RS^W and RD curves occurs in the middle region where the RD is a vertical line. In this case, solving equation (2.2) is the same as solving:

$$\frac{2}{3} = \frac{P^C}{P^R},$$

allowing us to conclude that the relative price P^R/P^C equals 3/2. Since 3/2 is between 1 and 3, and thus indeed does lie on the vertical portion of the RS^W curve in Figure 2.6, we conclude that our assumption is correct and this is the equilibrium.[6]

---

[6] More generally, if this calculation produced a price in excess of 3, we would conclude that the intersection is in the upper flat portion of the RS^W curve (with, hence, an equilibrium relative price of 3), and if it had produced a price below 1, we would conclude that the intersection is in the lower flat portion of the RS^W curve (with an equilibrium relative price of 1).

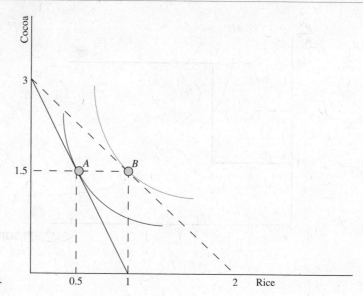

FIGURE 2.7
The Effects of Trade: Nigeria.

Notice that since America produces only rice but consumes both goods, while Nigeria produces only cocoa but consumes both goods, it follows that America exports rice and imports cocoa, while Nigeria exports cocoa and imports rice. In other words, *each country exports its comparative-advantage good and imports its comparative-disadvantage good*. This is a general principle in models of this sort, and it is clear from Figure 2.6 that it is inevitable: Nigeria has a comparative advantage in cocoa because its opportunity cost of producing cocoa is lower (so, geometrically, the flat portion of the RS^W curve that marks the boundary of American specialization occurs at a lower relative price than the flat portion corresponding to the boundary of Nigerian specialization). Note that even though America has an absolute disadvantage in rice, it produces all of the rice: Only comparative advantage, and not absolute advantage, matters for the pattern of trade.

Note that this equilibrium features *complete specialization*: Each country produces exactly one good. Complete specialization makes it simple to analyze the budget lines that result in equilibrium, as shown in Figure 2.7. In that graph, the autarky budget line is shown as a solid line, and the free-trade budget line is shown as a broken line. Under free trade, each Nigerian farmer produces only cocoa, producing 3 tons per growing season, for an income of $3P^C$ per season. Dividing this income by the price of cocoa gives the cocoa-axis intercept of the budget line, which is equal to 3 as before, but dividing by the price of rice to find the rice-axis intercept now gives $3P^C/P^R = 3(2/3) = 2$. This value is double the original intercept value of 1. Put differently, the new budget line shares the original point on the cocoa axis (because it is always feasible for a cocoa grower simply to consume his or her output), but now, because of the change in relative price, the budget line is flatter. Therefore, the budget line pivots outward, increasing the consumption opportunities for the farmer and raising his or her welfare. Note that as soon as we can see that the budget line with trade has pivoted out, so that the farmer can consume more of both goods than under autarky, we can

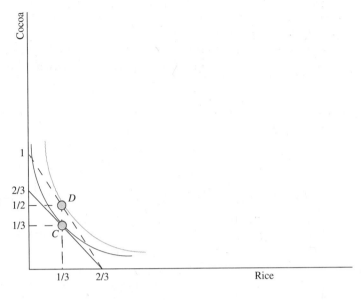

FIGURE 2.8
The Effects of Trade:
America.

conclude that he or she is better off with trade than with the import ban.[7] The autarky consumption bundle is marked as point *A* in Figure 2.7, while the free-trade consumption bundle, on a higher indifference curve, is marked as point *B*.

Analogously, we can derive the budget line of an American farmer, as shown in Figure 2.8. This time, since the farmer produces rice, the rice-axis intercept is unchanged, but the cocoa-axis intercept takes a value of 1 instead of 2/3, so the budget line has pivoted out. Note that for American farmers, the budget line is steeper than it was before, and once again we do not need any more information than the budget line to conclude that American farmers are better off.

Here is the essential point: In a model of this sort, a policy of food self-sufficiency makes the citizens of the country imposing it poorer, because it deprives them of the benefits of specialization along the lines of comparative advantage. When trade is allowed, the Nigerian farmers are able to maximize their real income, producing cocoa that is relatively more expensive than it was under the ban, and using the proceeds to purchase rice that is relatively cheaper than it was under the ban. In America, analogous welfare gains work in the opposite direction. Put differently, comparative advantage creates *gains from trade*, and both countries are better off as a result.

So now we know that lifting the ban makes all of the farmers richer. What of actual nutrition? Given that Nigeria has lost all of its rice production, do Nigerians actually consume less rice? We can find out by using the information that each farmer spends half of her income on rice; in both autarky and trade, that implies

---

[7] One serious issue we are glossing over is the existence of some coercive child labor in cocoa growing in West Africa. Obviously, the welfare analysis here does not apply in such cases. Fortunately, this practice appears to be the exception rather than the rule, comprising under 1% of cocoa workers (Aaronson, 2007), and it does not affect the point being made about the desirability of food self-sufficiency, but it is still a serious problem. The issue of globalization and child labor will be explored in Chapter 14.

rice expenditure of $(3/2)P^C$, and thus a quantity of rice consumed equal to $(3/2)P^C/P^R$. With the autarky relative rice price of 3, this implied consumption of 1/2 ton of rice per growing season, but with the free-trade relative rice price of 3/2, rice consumption goes up to 1 ton per growing season. Rice consumption in Nigeria increases both because of the income effect (real income is higher, as consumers are on a higher indifference curve) and because of the substitution effect (the relative price of rice has fallen). Thus, *by giving up the goal of food self-sufficiency, the government has allowed its citizens to become better fed.*

2.5 So What Actually Happened?

As we have seen, the Ricardian model predicts that nutrition should have worsened as a result of the rice import ban that was in force from 1986 to 1995. Was that the actual outcome?

Evaluating what happened to actual nutrition in Nigeria during this period is surprisingly difficult. In an early assessment, Nwosu (1992, p. 7) reports very rapid increases in food prices in the first two years after the ban was imposed, four to five times higher than the prevailing rate of inflation. Despite the increase in food prices, his data show net increases in the consumption of cereals per person, but reductions in other sources of nutrition, leading to overall decreases in average calories consumed per person (pp. 11–12).[8] World Health Organization (WHO) surveys suggest mild improvements in child nutrition during this period, but the data are subject to a range of interpretations.[9] Perhaps the most reliable measure of overall nutritional performance comes from the Food and Agriculture Organization (FAO) of the United Nations, which attempts to compile consistent measures of the numbers of undernourished people in all developing countries. For the years 1980–1996, the FAO figures show that the undernourished fraction of the Nigerian population fell from 40% to 8% (FAO, 1999, p. 30). Among all countries, this was the fourth-best improvement in nutritional performance in the world over this period (FAO, 1999, p. 10)—an impressive achievement.

Thus, the cereals import ban seems to have been associated with an improvement in nutrition. Does this refute the theory? No, because many other changes took place at the same time, in addition to the ban. The early 1980s were a time of economic crisis, and the cereals ban coincided with a time of macroeconomic recovery; the ban was part of a complex package of reforms

---

[8] At the same time, he acknowledges that the food consumption data available at that time were not reliable. In addition, we should note that per capita food consumption does not say anything about malnutrition unless the food consumption is evenly distributed across the population. If average food consumption rises but it becomes more unevenly distributed, the number of people with inadequate nutrition could rise.

[9] One useful measure of short-run nutritional outcomes is weight-for-height, which tends to fall in periods during which nutritional intake is below normal. Based on figures from the WHO Global Database on Child Growth and Malnutrition, posted on the WHO's website, the fraction of Nigerian children under 5 with weight-for-height more than two standard deviations below WHO's international population mean was 20.6% in 1983, 8.9% in 1990, 18.2% in 1993, 15.6% in 1999, 9.0% in 2001, and 9.3% in 2003. Thus, by this measure, child nutrition was better during the ban (1990 and 1993 figures) than before the ban, but better still after the ban. These figures are consistent with an interpretation that a steady improvement was in process and that the ban was irrelevant to it.

plus loans from international institutions known as the structural adjustment program (Nwosu, 1992); the government improved rural infrastructure and instituted programs to fight rural poverty and help small farmers (Akande, 2005); new high-yielding varieties of cassava (an important root crop) dramatically increased cassava output (FAO, 2001); and illiteracy fell dramatically during this period as well (FAO, 2001, Table 1). Any of these factors could have had a beneficial effect on nutrition independently of—or despite—the effect of the import ban. Unfortunately, the counterfactual indicated by the theory—what would have happened to Nigerian nutrition if the ban had not been imposed but everything else had been the same—is a matter on which we can only speculate.

This is a good example of the difficulties of making causal inference about the effects of policy in economics. An argument of the form, "The government banned rice imports and then nutrition improved—therefore, rice import bans improve nutrition," is called a *post-hoc* argument and is a poor way to do economics, exactly because while that one policy was changing so many other elements of the environment were also changing.

Billy Rizcallah

Nigerian children in a cocoa shop.

For the record, the FAO (2001) examined 13 success stories of nutritional improvement, including Nigeria, and concluded that improvements in literacy and in cassava productivity probably deserved much of the credit in the Nigerian success and that in several of the other countries studied, the availability of food imports was a contributor to their success. It is difficult to make a case that banning cereals imports helped matters for Nigerian consumers.[10]

---

[10] At the same time, it should be noted that a number *other* policies might be part of an overall food self-sufficiency strategy that is much easier to justify. Improving rural roads, increasing educational opportunities for farmers, and supporting research on high-yielding crop varieties, for example, all have strong economic rationales and have been extremely useful in many countries. What we are commenting on here is, first, the *policy goal* of food self-sufficiency, which is a very different goal from maximizing aggregate real income or minimizing poverty, and could serve merely as a distraction from those other development goals; and, second, the *specific policy* of restricting food imports as part of that strategy.

2.6 Additional Insights from Ricardo's Model

Three more useful points emerge from analysis of the model.

The role of absolute advantage. We have already noted that absolute advantage has no role at all in determining the pattern of trade; that is fixed by comparative advantage. However, absolute advantage is not irrelevant. Suppose that one country has an absolute advantage in both goods. Then its workers must receive a higher income in equilibrium than workers in the other country. (Whatever workers in the less productive country produce, a worker in the more productive country will have the option of producing the same thing, in which case that worker will receive a higher income because of her higher productivity. If she chooses to produce the other good instead, that must be because it earns her higher income still.)

Thus, roughly, comparative advantage determines the pattern of trade, while absolute advantage determines the international distribution of income. As an example, aggregate labor productivity in the United States is approximately eight times aggregate labor productivity in Mexico, but that does not mean that Mexican workers cannot compete with American workers. It merely means that their wages are approximately one-eighth of American wages. Viewed from the flip side, Mexican wages are one-eighth American wages, but that does not mean that American workers cannot compete with Mexican workers—because Mexican labor productivity is one-eighth American productivity.

The effect of size differences. Returning to the Nigeria/America example, suppose that we increase the size of the American labor force. As we do so, the maximum amount of rice that the American economy can produce increases, and so the relative supply of rice in the middle section of the RS^W curve in Figure 2.6 increases above 2/3, shifting the vertical segment of that curve to the right. This shift, of course, pushes the equilibrium relative price down. If we continue this process, eventually the price will be pushed to its minimum value of 1, at which point the RD curve will intersect the RS^W curve where the RS^W curve is flat. At this point, Nigeria is still producing only cocoa, but America is producing both goods. In other words, we now have an equilibrium with *incomplete specialization.* This outcome is quite natural, since if America is large enough compared to Nigeria, the small Nigerian economy will not be able to produce enough cocoa to meet American demand.

This is an important conclusion for the welfare effects of trade. Recalling Figure 2.8, if the equilibrium relative price under trade is equal to 1, since that is also the autarkic relative price in America, then the budget line for a farmer in America is the same as that farmer's autarkic budget line. In other words, in this case America does not gain from trade, but Nigeria still does. In fact, recalling Figure 2.7, Nigeria gains even more from a price of 1 than from a price of 3/2. In general, the cheaper are Nigeria's imports, the better off it is; for this reason we call a reduction in the relative price of rice *an improvement in Nigeria's terms of trade*, and by the same token we call it *a worsening in America's terms of trade*. Any increase in the size of America's labor force will improve Nigeria's terms of trade and worsen America's.

This is a general feature of Ricardian models: *Smaller countries capture most of the gains from trade*, and if the difference in country size is large enough, the small country will capture *all* of the gains from trade.

Possibilities for immigration. Finally, note that if some workers can move across borders to chase higher incomes, all of the movement of labor will be in the direction of the country with the higher labor productivity. Thus, although comparative advantage governs the direction of trade, in this model if immigration became possible, absolute advantage would govern the pattern of immigration (provided, of course, that a worker's productivity is a function of where that worker works, rather than his or her inherent skill).

In conclusion, comparative advantage does provide a powerful argument against food self-sufficiency as a development strategy. More generally, comparative advantage provides one powerful explanation for the fact of trade: Countries differ in their relative productive abilities, giving rise to different relative prices in the absence of trade and thus an incentive to ship commodities across borders. The Ricardian model treats these productivity differences as coming from exogenous and immutable differences in know-how or technology, but a similar story can emerge from many different sources. Comparative advantage can arise from differences in legal institutions, in labor-market frictions, in climate, in educational levels, in accumulated physical capital, or in endowments of land and other natural resources. In Chapter 6 we will see a model in which comparative advantage arises through differences in factor supplies across countries; this is called the Heckscher-Ohlin model.

Now that we are familiar with the idea of comparative advantage as a reason for trade, the next two chapters will explore two additional reasons for trade, which will help explain trade that is not compatible with comparative advantage.

MAIN IDEAS

1. One key reason for international trade is differences between countries, and a theory of trade based on these differences is called a comparative-advantage theory. The Ricardian model is a comparative-advantage theory that is based on differences in production technology across countries.

2. A country has a comparative advantage in a good if its opportunity cost of producing that good is smaller than its trade partners' opportunity cost, which is a statement about the different slopes of the two countries' production possibilities frontiers. Every country has a comparative advantage in something and a comparative disadvantage in something.

3. A country has an absolute advantage in a good if its workers are more productive in that good than its trade partners' workers are. A country could have an absolute advantage in all goods or in no goods.

4. In a Ricardian model, comparative advantage determines the pattern of trade, but absolute advantage determines the international distribution of income.

5. All countries gain from trade in a Ricardian world, or at least no country loses from trade. In fact, *every person* gains from trade in a Ricardian world, or at least no person loses from it. In this model, small countries capture most of the gains from trade, and if they are small enough they capture *all* of them.

6. In this model, small countries specialize completely in equilibrium. If a large country does not specialize completely, it does not gain from trade.

7. The logic of comparative advantage argues against a policy of using import restrictions to advance the goal of food self-sufficiency.

WHERE WE ARE

We have now added the first comparative advantage model to the family tree of trade models.

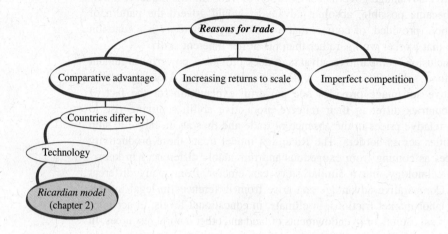

QUESTIONS AND PROBLEMS

1. In the model in the text, comparative advantage comes from a pure technological difference between the countries. Identify some other differences that might drive comparative advantage? Provide concrete examples from countries that are familiar to you.

2. In the model presented in the text, no one in Nigeria would have any reason to object to trade. Do you find this realistic? What assumptions does this depend on? Do you think these assumptions are crucial for the idea of the gains from trade, or for the question of how trade can affect nutrition?

    Consider the following model of trade between Iceland and Finland. Assume throughout that those two countries are the only two countries in the world, at least for purposes of trade. There are two goods: fish and wheat. Consumers always spend one fifth of their income on fish and the remainder on wheat. The only factor of production is labor. Each Icelandic worker can produce 1 unit of fish or 1 unit of wheat per unit of time, while each Finnish worker can produce 2 units of fish or 4 units of wheat per unit of time. There are 1 million workers in Iceland and 1.5 million in Finland.

3. Which country has an absolute advantage in fish? In wheat? Which country has a comparative advantage in fish? In wheat?

4. Find the autarky relative price of fish in both countries (i.e., the price of fish divided by the price of wheat), and draw the typical worker's budget line in both countries.

5. Derive the relative demand curve relating the relative demand for fish to the relative price of fish. Solve algebraically, and then draw the curve in a diagram with the relative price of fish on the vertical axis and the relative quantity of fish on the horizontal axis.

6. Derive the world relative supply curve and draw it on the diagram that you created in Problem 5.

7. Compute the equilibrium relative price of fish under free trade, and draw the budget lines for a typical worker in each country. Which country produces which good or goods? Is there complete specialization? Who gains from trade?

8. How does your answer in Problem 7 change if Finland has 3 million workers instead of 1.5 million? Answer verbally; no computation is needed.

REFERENCES

Aaronson, Susan Ariel (2007). "Globalization and Child Labor: The Cause Can Also Be a Cure." *YaleGlobal*, March 13, 2007.

Akande, 'Tunji (n.d.). "An Overview of the Nigerian Rice Economy." Working Paper, Agriculture and Rural Development Department, The Nigerian Institute of Social and Economic Research (NISER), Ibadan, Nigeria.

Akande, 'Tunji (n. d.) (2005). "The Role of the State in the Nigerian Green Revolution," in Djurfeldt, Goran, Hans Holmén, and Magnus Jirström (2005). *African Food Crisis : Lessons from the Asian Green Revolution*. Wallingham: CABI Publishing.

Bhagwati, Jagdish, Arvind Panagariya, and T. N. Srinivasan (1998). *Lectures in International Trade* (2nd edition). Cambridge, MA: MIT Press.

Dornbusch, R., S. Fischer, and P. Samuelson (1977). "Comparative Advantage, Trade, and Payments in a Ricardian Model with a Continuum of Goods." *American Economic Review* 67:5 (December), pp. 823–839.

FAO (1999). *The State of Food Insecurity in the World 1999*.

FAO (2001). "The Thirteen Countries Most Successful in reducing undernourishment, 1980–1997." FAO Council, One Hundred and Twentieth Session, Rome, June 18–23 2001.

FAO (2006). "Food Outlook: Global Market Analysis." No. 2, December.

Holmén, Hans (2006), "Myths about Agriculture, Obstacles to Solving the African Food Crisis," *The European Journal of Development Research* 18:3 (September), pp. 453–480 .

Mpoyo, Pierre-Victor (1992). "The Needs of African Agriculture," in Olusegun Obasanjo and Hans d'Orville (ed.), *The Challenges of Agricultural Production and Food Security in Africa*, Washington, DC: Crane Russak, pp. 93–97.

Nwosu, Aloysius C. (1992). *Structural Adjustment and Nigerian Agriculture: An Initial Assessment*. Washington, DC: United States Department of Agriculture Economic Research Service, Agriculture and Trade Analysis Division Staff Report No. AGES 9224.

Obasanjo, Olusegun, and Hans d'Orville (ed.) (1992), *The Challenges of Agricultural Production and Food Security in Africa*, Washington, DC: Crane Russak.

Obasanjo, H.E. Olusegun (2004). "Welcome and Opening Remarks," speech at conference "Assuring Food and Nutrition Security in Africa by 2020: Prioritizing Action, Strengthening Actors, and Facilitating Partnerships," April 1–3, 2004, Kampala, Uganda.

3

Why Do Americans Get Their Impalas from Canada?

SuperStock

1959 Chevrolet Impala Convertible.

3.1 Impalas on the Horizon

The Chevrolet Impala is an iconic American car. In the 1950s, it sported the extreme tail fins that were the quintessential signature of American automotive flamboyance. A 1959 Impala low-rider even has a speaking role in the Disney/Pixar movie *Cars*, which sentimentally personified famous vehicles. Now, the updated Impala is ubiquitous on American roads as a handsome and practical full-size sedan. As of February 2010, the Impala was the fourteenth best-selling car in the United States, selling at the rate of about 12,000 per month.

EVOX Images/AgeFotostock America, Inc.

2010 Chevrolet Impala.

It may come as a surprise, then, that this all-American vehicle is actually Canadian. Every modern Impala is built in the General Motors (GM) assembly plant in Oshawa, Ontario.

Why, precisely, should this be an imported product? The design and know-how originated in the United States, so it of course *could* be produced in the United States. Canada is certainly not a low-wage country; wages, education, infrastructure, and standards of living are very similar to what they are in the United States. It is hardly plausible to argue that Canadians simply have a comparative advantage in producing Impalas, while Americans have a comparative advantage in producing, say, the Cobalt (another Chevrolet sedan, built in Lordstown, Ohio), or the Buick Lucerne (another General Motors sedan built at the Detroit/Hamtramck Assembly Plant in Hamtramck, Michigan). Indeed, comparative-advantage theory appears perfectly useless in explaining the annual shipment of these 200,000-odd vehicles with a price tag of $21,000 per unit across the border. Clearly, the skills required to build any one of these imported vehicles are about identical to the skills required to build the others that are produced in the United States.

To understand the reasons the Impala is imported, we need to understand two features of the automotive industry: the 1965 Canada-U.S. Auto Pact and increasing returns to scale. Once the logic of the Impala case is clear, an important general point about increasing returns and international trade emerges, namely, that increasing returns is a major reason for international trade, completely separate from comparative advantage.

First, the Auto Pact. Before 1965, the auto sectors of both the United States and Canada were protected by significant tariff walls, which raised the cost of shipping vehicles or parts from either country to the other. As a result, the major U.S. automakers served most of their Canadian demand from assembly plants in Canada that duplicated much of the product line they were producing in the U.S. In 1965, the two governments, together with the major U.S. automakers, worked out an agreement under which, in essence, the two governments eliminated their tariffs against each others' automobile and auto parts exports. One proviso was imposed by the Canadian government in a side agreement with the automakers: a requirement that the automakers continue to increase their production of cars and car parts in Canada, following a specified formula. (See Hervey, 1978, for a concise account.)

Second, increasing returns to scale. An industry exhibits *increasing returns to scale* (IRS) if and only if an *x%* increase in all inputs increases the output by more than *x%*. Equivalently, an industry has IRS if an *x%* increase in output increases cost by less than *x%*, thus lowering average cost. IRS is important in automobile production because running a production line for a particular model of car requires a tremendous fixed cost. The machines required for that model of car must be set up in the right arrangement and calibrated for that model, and all workers on the line must be trained for the requirements of that model. These costs must be incurred even if only one unit is to be produced, and so they are indeed fixed costs. These fixed costs lead to increasing returns to scale over a range of output levels and give the automaker an incentive to try to concentrate all production of each model in one location.

An example can illustrate how this works. Suppose that GM has 11 models of car to produce. Sales of each model are expected to be 200,000 units in the U.S. market and 20,000 in Canada (since population and GDP are approximately one-tenth in Canada what they are in the United States). Suppose that maintaining an assembly line for a given model in a given location requires a fixed cost of F; that, in addition to the fixed cost, each car produced requires a units of labor in either country; and that labor is priced at the wage w in both countries. It is easy to confirm that this is an example of an increasing-returns-to-scale technology: Suppose that a given assembly line initially is producing Q units per year. Then, total cost for the assembly line is equal to $F + a \cdot w \cdot Q$. If we double the output, then the cost becomes $F + 2 \cdot a \cdot w \cdot Q$, which is less than $2(F + a \cdot w \cdot Q)$. This is the essence of increasing returns: Doubling the output less than doubles the cost.

Suppose that, initially, tariffs between the two countries are so high that it is prohibitively expensive to ship any vehicles from one country to the other. In that case, GM must produce 200,000 units of each model in the United States to meet U.S. demand, and 20,000 units of each model in Canada, to meet Canadian demand. Thus, GM must maintain 22 assembly plants, 11 on each side of the border, and its total costs are equal to $22F + w \cdot a \cdot 11 \cdot 220,000 = 22F + w \cdot a \cdot 2,420,000$.

Now suppose that the Auto Pact comes into effect, creating free trade between the United States and Canada in automobiles, and assume that there are no transport costs or other trade impediments between the two countries. Assume that GM is bound by the constraint that it must produce at least as many cars in Canada as it did before the Auto Pact, and assume, too, that, for political reasons, it is also required to produce at least as many cars in the United States as before the Pact. The company can now reallocate its production in the following way: It can keep 10 of the assembly lines in the United States, dropping one of them; close out 10 assembly lines in Canada, keeping only the model that is being shut down in the United States; and increase production at each plant in both countries to 220,000. This would keep output in Canada unchanged compared to output before the Auto Pact, since before the Pact there were 11 plants in Canada, producing 20,000 units each, for output of 220,000, while now there is one plant, producing one model, and it produces 220,000 units. In the United States, before the Pact, production was 200,000 at each of 11 plants, for a total of 2,200,000. After the Pact, it is 220,000 at each of 10 plants, for a total of 2,200,000. Thus, the total number of cars produced in each country is the same as it was before. Furthermore, the same total number of units of each model car is being produced as before the Pact. However, since GM is now maintaining only 11 assembly lines instead of 22, its total costs are $11F + w \cdot a \cdot 11 \cdot 220,000 = 11F + w \cdot a \cdot 2,420,000$. This is less than the costs it incurred before the Pact, by $11F$.

Clearly, GM has a powerful incentive to reallocate its production in this way, concentrating all production of each model in one location and distributing the finished cars to customers in both countries from that location. It allows the company to produce the same number of cars with only half the fixed costs, thus saving the company a lot of money. Notice as well that after it reallocates production in this way, the company will ship 200,000 units of one model from Canada to the United States and 20,000 each of 10 other models, or 200,000 units, from the United States to Canada. Thus, we have moved from an arrangement with no trade at all to an arrangement that generates a large amount of trade—200,000 vehicles in each direction per year. The point is that *increasing returns to scale creates a motivation for trade by encouraging the concentration of production of each good in a single location.*

This is more or less what actually happened in the case of the Canada-U.S. Auto Pact. Following the enactment of the Pact, the number of models produced in Canada dropped sharply, but the number of each model produced in Canada rose sharply, with a substantial portion of each plant's output going to export. This led to a dramatic explosion of trade between the two countries, both in completed vehicles and in parts. This is illustrated in Figure 3.1, which shows U.S.–Canada automotive trade from 1960 to 1974. The two upper curves show U.S. exports of cars and U.S. exports of trucks and buses to Canada, respectively. The two lower curves show the corresponding figures for U.S. imports from Canada (for convenience, U.S. imports from Canada are shown as negative values). Before 1965, trade in both directions and both categories was negligible, but after the Auto Pact came into effect in that year trade in both directions exhibited explosive growth, totaling 1.6 million vehicles in 1974. Over this period, U.S. car and truck exports to Canada increased tenfold in value, while Canadian car and truck exports to the United States increased *forty*fold (Hervey, 1978, p. 21). Figure 3.1 forcefully demonstrates the importance of increasing returns for trade: *All* of the rise in trade in that figure is due to IRS.

3.2 Increasing Returns More Generally

The example of the Impala shows that increasing returns can have an enormous effect on trade, generating trade in cases in which the concept of comparative advantage is irrelevant. The principle applies to many other industries beyond the auto industry and is crucial to understanding modern international trade. To explore the implications of IRS in trade more fully, we need to distinguish three types of IRS.

FIGURE 3.1
U.S.-Canada
Automotive Trade,
1960–74.

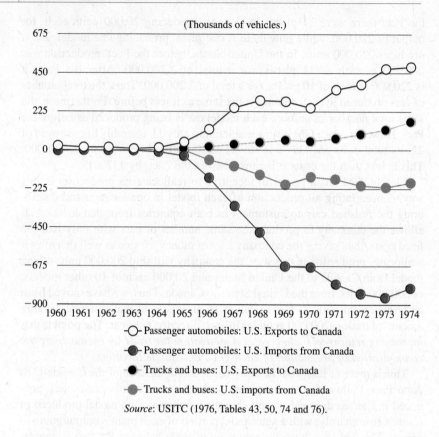

Source: USITC (1976, Tables 43, 50, 74 and 76).

First, if increasing *one firm's* inputs by *x*% increases *that firm's* output by more than *x*%, the firm exhibits *internal IRS*. As we have seen, one source of internal IRS is a simple fixed cost of setting up and maintaining a firm, plant, product line, or assembly line. Note that internal IRS shows up diagrammatically as a downward-sloping average cost curve.

Second, if increasing one firm's inputs by *x*% increases that firm's output by no more than *x*%, but increasing the inputs of *all* firms within the same industry within the same country by *x*% increases all of their outputs by more than *x*%, then the industry exhibits *external national IRS*.

Third, if increasing all of the inputs to firms within the industry *worldwide* by *x*% increases outputs by more than *x*%, the industry exhibits external, *international* IRS.

In this chapter, we focus on internal IRS; the external versions will come up later and will be central to the discussion of trade and economic development in Chapter 9. It should be noted that internal IRS is not in and of itself any kind of market failure, but since it is inconsistent with perfect competition, it implies imperfect competition, which itself is a form of market failure.

The example of the Impala makes the point that internal IRS can be a powerful reason for trade. In the next three sections we will expand on the point by looking at some additional international implications of IRS: the effect of IRS on corporate strategies for penetrating a foreign market (Section 3.3), the rise of monopolistic competition and intraindustry trade (Section 3.4), and the effect of trade on productivity (Section 3.5).

3.3 How to Tackle Europe: Trade versus FDI

Let us return to the topic of General Motors. Since the 1930s, one big piece of the company's strategy has been to maintain a major presence in Europe; on average the company supplies approximately 9% of the continent's cars. A major strategic question then is as follows: Would it be more profitable for GM to supply cars to Europe as exports, or would it be better to make cars in Europe for the local market? This decision is crucially affected by considerations of IRS.

The following thought experiment can show why. Suppose that you are the CEO of a corporation in country i trying to tap the market in some foreign country, j. You have two options: You can continue to produce in your home-market production facility and export to j, or you can set up a subsidiary in j to produce your product and sell to the j-market from that subsidiary. In order to decide which strategy to use, you must trade off the effects of increasing returns (which call for concentrating production in one location and exporting to meet the foreign market) against tariffs and transport costs (which argue in favor of setting up the subsidiary).

For concreteness, suppose that the foreign market has a demand for your product that can be summarized by the demand function $Q(P)$, a decreasing function of the price, P, that you charge in the foreign market.

On one hand, you can set up a subsidiary in j at a cost F, after which you can produce with a^j units of labor per unit produced. The labor in country j costs w^j per unit.

On the other hand, you can ship products to j by paying a transport cost of $k(d^{ij})$ per unit, where d^{ij} is the distance from i to j and $k(\cdot)$ is an increasing function. Country j also has an import tariff, which requires that you pay the government there an amount t for each unit that you ship to consumers in j. Production in i requires a^i units of labor per unit of output as well, which costs w^i per unit. Crucially, *there is no fixed cost to production in i for the j market*, because the home production facility has already been set up and is going to be maintained to satisfy country-i consumers, regardless of the decision on how to serve j.

Thus, to serve j's customers through a subsidiary requires a fixed cost of F and a marginal cost of $w^j \cdot a^j$. To serve j's customers through exports requires no fixed cost, but a marginal cost of $w^i \cdot a^i + k(d^{ij}) + t$.

Using the export strategy, you will need to choose the price, P^j, that you will charge customers in j, to maximize:

$$(P^j - [w^i a^i + k(d^{ij}) + t])Q(P^j),$$

producing a maximized profit that we can label $\Pi^{export}(w^i a^i, d^{ij}, t)$. Clearly, Π^{export} will decrease if $w^i a^i$, d^{ij} or t is increased. On the other hand, using the FDI strategy, you will need to choose P^j to maximize:

$$(P^j - w^j \cdot a^j)Q(P^j) - F,$$

producing a maximized profit that we can label $\Pi^{FDI}(w^j a^j, F)$. Clearly, Π^{FDI} is decreasing in $w^j a^j$ and F.

Your best option is to export when $\Pi^{export}(w^i a^i, d^{ij}, t) > \Pi^{FDI}(w^j a^j, F)$. Holding the other variables constant, you will find this to be true when:

1. The unit labor cost of production in country j, $w^j a^j$, is very high;

2. The distance between the two countries, d^{ij}, is low;

3. The tariff, t, charged by the government of country j is low; or

4. The fixed cost, F, to setting up and maintaining a subsidiary is high.

GM's Europe strategy is easily understood along these lines. Because of European tariffs and transoceanic transport costs, GM does not export many cars to Europe, but it does produce a large number in Europe for the local market, mostly through its Opel subsidiary, which it purchased in 1929. However, *within Europe*, its production is concentrated in a fairly small number of locations. For example, the Opel Vectra model is produced entirely at the assembly plant in Rüsselsheim, Germany. In 2006, GM produced 126,088 Vectras there and shipped them all over Europe. Essentially, between the United States and Europe, which have large transport costs and significant tariffs, trade costs are the dominant factor (see points 1 and 3 above), and the company has chosen local production for the European market instead of trade. However, within Europe, with smaller distances and with zero tariffs between European Union member countries, IRS is the dominant factor (point 4), and the company chose to export. As a result, GM does not export much to Europe from the United States, but it does export large numbers of vehicles from Germany to France, from Spain to Germany, and so on. Once again, trade can be driven by increasing returns.[1]

These predictions do describe corporate behavior fairly well more generally as well. For example, Brainard (1997), in a study of U.S. multinationals over a broad range of manufacturing industries, found that a U.S. firm is substantially more likely to serve a foreign market through trade rather than through a subsidiary if the foreign country has low tariffs (low t in our model), if transport costs are low (low d^{ij} in our model), or if the industry is characterized by large increasing returns to scale (large F in our model).[2]

3.4 On a Smaller Scale: Trade and Increasing Returns in Furniture

The presence of IRS in the automobile industry is hard to ignore because the indivisibilities of that industry result in gigantic plants of several thousand employees, each plant turning out many thousand vehicles per year. These indivisibilities are probably the main reason that in each country at most a handful of automakers exist. However, the same principles apply to industries with much smaller indivisibilities, in which fairly small enterprises can coexist by the hundreds. One example is furniture. The United States exported $1.919 billion worth of furniture to Canada in 2001, and Canada exported $3.974

---

[1] We could also add to this simple model the possibility that some firms are more efficient than others. Helpman, Melitz, and Yeaple (2004) show that in such a model, *ceteris paribus*, it is the more productive firms that choose FDI.

[2] That study did not examine the role of labor costs, $w^j a^j$. In general, the empirical literature has not found a strong connection between these FDI/trade decisions and labor costs, possibly because it is difficult to measure a^j in a way that is useful for a statistical study.

billion worth back to the United States.[3] This trade is not dominated by three or four giant firms, but rather by a large number of small and medium-sized enterprises, often firms with a distinctive style to offer. For example, Baronet is a medium-sized Canadian firm that produces its own designs, which are offered in showrooms throughout the United States. Here is its Java dining set, built out of simple rectangles with a slight and elegant curvature that the company says is a hint of Asian influence.

John Wiley & Sons

On the other side of the border, L. and J. G. Stickley is a firm producing high-quality wooden furniture in a factory in Manlius, New York. It built its reputation over more than a century, centered on traditional designs such as this Mission dining set, influenced by the Arts and Crafts movement in early twentieth-century design:

John Wiley & Sons

---

[3] These figures come from customs bureau data, as processed and documented in Feenstra, Romalis, and Schott (2002). "Furniture" is defined here as major Standard Industrial Classification (SIC) category 25, which includes fixtures.

These two dining sets would look identical in the data—wooden dining table plus matching chairs—and yet they are strikingly different in style and would appeal to different consumers. The point is that furniture is not a commodity, but a designer product. This implies that what each firm produces is different from what all other firms produce, even in such a narrowly defined category as a "dining table" or a "dining-room side chair." As a result, each firm needs to incur a fixed cost to create its own designs, as well as to set up and maintain production facilities, so there are two different reasons for internal IRS in the furniture business. Furthermore, each firm—even if it has no more than 1% of the market—has a certain amount of market power. If the Stickley Company were to raise the price of its Mission dining set by 10%, for example, it would know that it would lose some of its customers to competing firms, but not all of them, because no one else produces the same product.

A good model to approximate industries like this one is the *monopolistic competition* model, formulated by Harvard economist Edward Chamberlain in the 1930s. The key features of this model are as follows:

1. A large number of sellers compete, all with the same cost structure and none with a significant market share.

2. Each seller produces something distinctive, so that it is a monopolist in its unique product.

3. There is free entry, so that all producers make zero profits in equilibrium.

A diagrammatic exposition is presented in Figure 3.2. This is the decision problem for one firm—say, Baronet, deciding how to price its Java line. The firm's marginal and average cost curves are shown as *MC* and *AC*. The downward-sloping curve is the demand curve for Java dining-room sets *conditional on the number of other furniture firms in the industry*. If more firms were to enter with their own designs, at a given price Baronet would lose some customers to them, and so the demand curve would shift to the left. If some firms shut down, the demand curve would shift to the right.

The firm chooses its optimal price by setting marginal cost equal to marginal revenue, which is represented by the curve *MR*. This yields a price and quantity for the Java dining set equal to P^* and Q^*, respectively. Importantly,

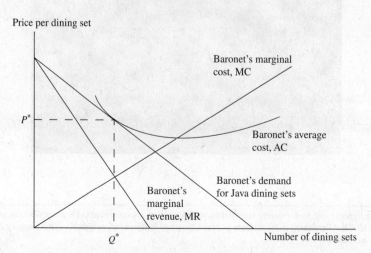

FIGURE 3.2
Monopolistic Competition.

at this point we have $P^* = AC$, so that profits are equal to zero. If this was not the case, so that, for example, we had $P^* > AC$ at Baronet's optimum, then that would mean that Baronet is receiving positive profits, which would imply that other firms could enter and also make a profit. The result would be entry, shifting Baronet's demand curve to the left, until profits are equal to zero. Similarly, if $P^* < AC$ at Baronet's optimum, Baronet and other firms would be incurring losses, which would lead to exit, shifting Baronet's demand curve to the right until zero profits are restored.

Put differently, the number of firms adjusts until the product-specific demand curve in Figure 3.2 is tangent to the average cost curve. If the demand curve is everywhere below the AC curve, there is no way the firm can choose a price and quantity combination that the market will bear that will also allow the firm to break even. If the demand curve cuts through the AC curve at any point, then the firm has the option of choosing a price-quantity combination that the market will bear and that will result in $P^* > AC$ and therefore strictly positive profits. The only way the zero-profit condition imposed by the free-entry condition can be satisfied is with a demand curve that is exactly tangent to the AC curve.

It should be noted that the equilibrium is necessarily in the downward-sloping portion of the AC curve (because the demand curve must be tangent to the AC curve). The lowest point on the AC curve is often called the point of *minimum efficient scale* because that is the quantity at which average cost is minimized. Therefore, a monopolistic-competition equilibrium always produces below minimum efficient scale. This can be interpreted loosely as the cost of providing product variety: If the number of firms was reduced by 10% and each firm produced 10% more output, total output would be unchanged and average costs would go down, but consumers would have less variety from which to choose.

Analyzing equilibrium fully in a model of this sort is rather beyond our scope, but we will offer an informal summary of what happens when such a model is opened to trade.[4] First, for simplicity, consider a model with two identical countries (with the possible exception that one country may be larger than the other). Suppose that one industry, the furniture industry, is monopolistically competitive and that initially trade in furniture is blocked. Now, allow free trade. The first thing to observe is that Baronet is likely to have to deal with some firms that have a style similar to its own, which it could previously ignore. Consumers who like that type of furniture now have more options that appeal to them than they did before, so now Baronet has to be more concerned that it will lose more of those consumers if it raises its price than it would have before. In other words, the demand for each firm's product will be more *elastic* than it was before trade was allowed. As a result, Baronet's demand curve will be flatter than it was before, as depicted in Figure 3.3(a). This implies that Baronet will price its dining sets closer to marginal cost (with the new price marked as P^{**}), selling a higher quantity than it did before (marked as Q^{**}).

Figure 3.3(a) does not show the new equilibrium, however. The reason is that these same changes are facing *every* firm in the industry on both sides of the borders, and with *each* firm similarly cutting its price and selling a larger quantity, Baronet's demand curve will shift inward, as indicated by the arrows.

---

[4] Interested readers can pursue a detailed analysis of trade in these models in Helpman and Krugman (1987).

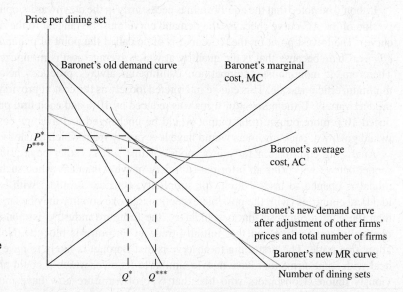

Price per dining set

Baronet's marginal cost, MC

P^*
P^{**}

Baronet's average cost, AC

Baronet's new demand curve

Baronet's old demand curve

Q^*Q^{**} Number of dining sets

FIGURE 3.3(a)
The Effect of Trade with Monopolistic Competition: Before other firms have adjusted prices, and before entry or exit.

Price per dining set

Baronet's old demand curve   Baronet's marginal cost, MC

P^*
P^{***}

Baronet's average cost, AC

Baronet's new demand curve after adjustment of other firms' prices and total number of firms

Baronet's new MR curve

Q^* Q^{***} Number of dining sets

FIGURE 3.3(b)
The Effect of Trade with Monopolistic Competition: Allowing for all firms' price adjustment, and entry and exit.

If this industry-wide price-cutting goes far enough, Baronet (and all other firms in the industry) will start to lose money, which will induce exit of firms,[5] shifting Baronet's demand curve back outward until Baronet can once again break even. Thus, in the trade equilibrium each country has fewer furniture makers, even though each consumer now has access to a greater variety of furniture (since each consumer can now choose from varieties produced in both countries). The new equilibrium is shown in Figure 3.3(b), which looks just like Figure 3.2, but with a flatter demand curve, higher quantity, and lower price per firm (marked, respectively, as Q^{***} and P^{***}).

---

[5] This is the outcome in the best-known formulations of these models, but it is conceivable that one can construct an example in which price-cutting is less vigorous and so entry results instead of exit. See Helpman (1981) for a very thorough mathematical analysis of the version described here. That analysis shows that the total number of firms goes down following trade, but each consumer has access to a larger number of varieties from which to choose because he or she has the option to choose a foreign variety.

The upshot is that each furniture producer sells some of its product to Canadian consumers; each Canadian producer sells some of its product to American consumers; some fraction of producers in both countries shut down; the price of each furniture line is closer to marginal cost, since the market is more competitive now and each product's demand curve is more elastic; and each consumer benefits from a greater variety of furniture designs from which to choose, as well as from lower prices due to the increase in competition. No one in either country loses from trade; even the owners of the furniture firms that closed down are not hurt because, due to the zero-profit condition, they were simply earning the opportunity return on their capital, which they will now earn in some other industry. Consumers benefit both from lower prices on furniture and from more variety.

This is a story with no comparative advantage (owing to the assumption that the countries are identical except for scale), and yet it is a story of trade. The reason is that each furniture producer has something unique to sell, so some Americans wish to buy from Baronet and some Canadians wish to buy from Stickley. This kind of trade is called *intraindustry trade*, meaning trade within an industry (dining sets headed in trucks south across the border at the same time other dining sets are headed in other trucks north across the border). This is in contrast to what we discussed in the previous chapter with Nigeria, for example, where cocoa was being exported in exchange for rice; such trade is called *interindustry trade*, or trade across industries.

To make the concept precise, suppose that exports by industry k in country i to country j, measured in dollars, are given by x_k^{ij}. Then total trade between the two countries is equal to $\Sigma_k x_k^{ij} + x_k^{ji}$, while for each industry *net* trade is equal to the absolute difference between shipments from i to j and shipments in the opposite direction, or $\left| x_k^{ij} - x_k^{ji} \right|$. As a result, interindustry trade as a fraction of total trade between i and j is given by:

$$ interindustry_{ij} = \frac{\Sigma_k \left| x_k^{ij} - x_k^{ji} \right|}{\Sigma_k x_k^{ij} + x_k^{ji}}. $$

We can then compute the fraction of trade between i and j due to intraindustry trade as:

$$ intraindustry_{ij} = 1 - interindustry_{ij}. $$

In general, trade with other industrial countries tends to be mostly intraindustry, while its trade with Third World countries tends to be much more interindustry. For example, by this measure manufacturing trade with Canada is 60% intraindustry, while trade with Nigeria is 2% intraindustry.[6]

3.5 Adding Heterogeneity: The Melitz Effect

Needless to say, the assumption in the monopolistic competition model above that all firms are equally productive is wildly unrealistic. What happens if we

---

[6] Based in 4-digit SIC-level trade data, again from Feenstra, Romalis, and Schott (2002).

allow for the obvious reality that some firms are better run and more pro-ductive than others?

A paper by Melitz (2003) presents a famous exploration of this question. Melitz modified the monopolistic competition model of trade by allowing firms to differ in their marginal cost, making it a *heterogeneous-firms model*, and he also complicated things a bit more by adding dynamics: Over time, some firms die off, and they are replaced by new entrants. A last, important assumption is that each firm must pay a fixed cost in order to export (it must learn about the foreign market, adapt its product to suit local regulations, develop a distribution network, and so on). But the key assumptions that each firm has internal increasing returns and produces a unique product are unchanged.

The main conclusion from this model is as follows. *First*, in any equilibrium, a more efficient firm, with its lower marginal cost, will produce and sell more output than a less efficient firm. Firms below a given productivity threshold drop out of the market altogether—with increasing returns, production on a very small scale is unprofitable because it does not generate enough variable profit to justify the fixed cost. *Second*, when trade is opened up, only the most efficient firms will pay the fixed cost required to export. (It is worthwhile to pay the fixed cost only for a firm that will export enough output to justify it, and only a low-marginal-cost firm will export that much output.) As a result, when trade is opened, all firms will be hit by import competition, but only the most productive firms will enjoy the offsetting benefit of export sales.

Therefore, with the coming of trade, all but the most productive firms face a drop in profits and reduce their output. Some at the bottom of the productivity range drop out of the market altogether, even though their productivity would have been enough to survive under autarky. At the same time, the most pro-ductive firms start to export and benefit from the exit of the less productive firms as well as the reductions in output by marginal firms that remain. The most productive firms thereby make higher profits and sell more output than they would have without trade.

The outcome is important: Trade causes the most productive firms to export and expand, while less productive firms serve the domestic market and shrink, and the least productive firms drop out entirely. This all implies that *globalization raises productivity*, partly because the least productive firms drop out, but also because among the surviving firms the market share of the more productive firms rises at the expense of the market share of the less productive. We can call the combination of these two changes and the resulting improvement in productivity the Melitz effect.

This outcome can be illustrated as in Figure 3.4. In the notation of the model, a firm that wants to produce q units of output must hire $f + q/\phi$ units of labor, where $f > 0$ is a fixed labor requirement, the same for all firms, and $\phi > 0$ is the marginal product of labor, which is constant for each firm but varies from firm to firm. Thus, ϕ is a measure of the firm's productivity. In addition to the fixed labor requirement f for production, a firm must pay a fixed cost plus transport costs in order to export. These fixed costs are the same for all firms. Only firms with a high enough value of ϕ will enter the market; only firms with a high enough value of ϕ will export; and the higher a firm's value of ϕ is, the more it will produce and the higher its profit will be. Figure 3.4 shows how much a firm will produce given its value of ϕ. Firm behavior under autarky is shown by the black line. In autarky, firms with a value of ϕ below

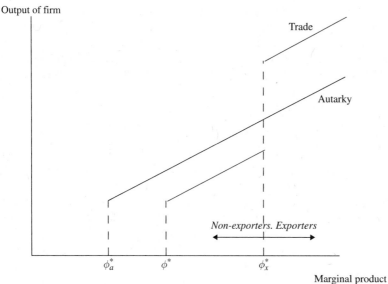

FIGURE 3.4
The Melitz Effect.

the cutoff value ϕ_a^* do not enter the market at all; those with a value above the cutoff value do enter, and the more productive they are, the more they produce, as indicated by the upward slope of the line. Firm behavior under free trade is shown by the blue line. Under free trade, firms with a value of ϕ below the cutoff value ϕ^* do not enter the market at all (and any such firm that has entered in the past will exit); those with a value above ϕ^* do enter, and the more productive they are, the more they produce. In addition, under trade, firms with a value of ϕ below the cutoff value ϕ_x^* do not export, and so their output is lower than it would have been in autarky, while firms with a value of ϕ *above* the cutoff value ϕ_x^* *do* export, and so their output is *higher* than it would have been under autarky. Note that $\phi_a^* < \phi^*$, since trade is tough on marginally profitable firms, who suffer from import competition and do not export, resulting in a higher cutoff productivity for entry in a trade equilibrium.

These changes in equilibrium resulting from trade together create the Melitz effect described above. Trade causes lower-productivity firms to drop out (as indicated by the fact that $\phi_a^* < \phi^*$), and among surviving firms, it causes the more productive to increase their market share at the expense of the less productive (as indicated by the fact that the blue line lies below the black one to the left of ϕ_x^* and above the black line to the right of ϕ_x^*). Both of these effects imply that the average firm productivity will rise as a result of trade.

These predictions come out of a particular theoretical model, but they actually have quite good empirical support. For example, Bernard and Jensen (1999, pp. 5−6) showed that in 1992 data, firms that engaged in exporting had on average 88% more employees and 13% higher total factor productivity than firms that did not export. This is consistent with the Melitz prediction that only more productive, and hence larger, firms will choose to export.

For another example, Trefler (2004) studied data on Canadian manufacturing before and after the 1988 Canada-Free-Trade Agreement

(CUFTA) was enacted. The agreement reduced and eventually eliminated each country's tariffs on the other country's manufactures. Since tariffs for different products were initially at different levels, moving them all toward zero created a larger change in tariff for some industries than for others. (For example, we have already seen that each country had zero tariffs on the other country's auto products due to the auto pact, so the CUFTA had no liberalizing effect on trade in the auto sector.) This does not exactly match the Melitz theoretical model because Canada and the United States did not move from autarky to free trade, but rather liberalized existing trade by reducing trade barriers. However, the theory still predicts the same sort of effects in this case: If the markets are monopolistically competitive with heterogeneous firms, mutual tariff reductions should intensify competition, increasing productivity.

Across industries, Trefler found a strong correlation between the size of the tariff drop and the change in labor productivity. He concluded that in the most affected industries, eliminating the tariffs had resulted in an annual improvement in labor productivity growth of 1.9% for the industries with the higher initial tariffs (Trefler, 2004, p. 880). This is an enormous number.[7] However, within each plant, the effect on labor productivity growth was only half as much. This suggests that much of the productivity improvement Trefler found was due to more efficient plants gaining market share at the expense of less efficient plants, or the exit of less efficient plants. The results are entirely consistent with the Melitz effect.

MAIN IDEAS

The observations on the importance of increasing returns to scale can be summarized as follows.

1. IRS generates a motivation for international trade, even when there is no comparative advantage, because it creates a reason to concentrate production of each good in one place and serve customers in all locations from that place, as GM does with the Impala (and most other models).

2. There are three kinds of IRS: internal, external national, and external international.

3. A corporation that is trying to decide how to serve a foreign market, either through exports or by production in the local market, must trade off trade impediments such as tariffs and transport costs against IRS. If IRS is the dominant factor, it will export, as GM does from its plants in Spain and Germany to the rest of Europe. If tariffs and transport costs are dominant, it will produce in the foreign market, as GM does by producing its cars for the European market in Europe rather than in the United States.

4. If internal IRS is present in an industry but fixed costs are low enough to allow for a large number of small producers; if entry is free and if each of these producers produces a unique good, then the model is called monopolistic competition.

5. Monopolistic competition implies intraindustry trade, and in addition benefits from trade that include lower price/marginal cost margins and greater product variety for consumers.

6. If firms in a monopolistically competitive market differ in their productivity, and if exporting requires a fixed cost, opening up international trade can have the additional benefit of improving productivity. This is so because trade benefits large, efficient firms that export, leading them to increase at the expense of small, less efficient firms that produce only for the domestic market, and because the least efficient firms drop out of the market. This can be called the Melitz effect and has quite good empirical support.

---

[7] What is meant here is an increase in 1.9 *percentage points*. For example, for an industry that would otherwise have had 1% annual productivity growth, it implies an increase to 2.9%.

WHERE WE ARE

We have added internal-increasing-returns to scale models to the family tree, which includes both single-firm models and monopolistic-competition models.

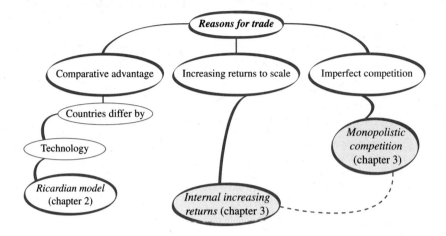

QUESTIONS AND PROBLEMS

1. Your firm wants to sell its product in each of several foreign countries, and you must decide whether to do so by exporting or by producing locally for that market through FDI. Suppose that in each country the demand for the product is the same, and is given by:

$$Q = 100 - P,$$

where P is the price your firm charges in that country in dollars and Q is the quantity sold there. In addition, the marginal cost of production in any country is the same and is equal to $20 per unit. Wherever you choose to produce, your firm is a monopolist. To produce in a foreign country, your firm must incur a fixed cost equal to $79. On the other hand, to produce in your home country and export to a country that is d miles away requires a transport cost of $d/5,000$ dollars per unit shipped.

For what range of values of d will your profit-maximizing decision be the export option? The FDI option?

2. Suppose that one of the countries discussed in question (1) imposed a tariff, or a tax on imports, which your firm must then add to the cost of exporting to that country. The tariff does not apply, however, to any units you produce in

that country to sell to its consumers directly. Suppose that you initially were exporting to that market, but the tariff is set high enough that you decide to switch to an FDI strategy. (This is often called tariff-jumping FDI.) What price will you now charge consumers in that country for your product? Is this tariff-induced change likely to be beneficial to that country? Should every importing country try this, or could it backfire?

3. In the model of reallocation of production under the Auto Pact in Section 3.1, we have assumed that GM takes the wage in each country as given. Suppose that the market wage, w, is unaffected by whatever happens in the auto industry and that workers can easily find a job in the other industries at that wage.

(a) If GM simply pays its workers their opportunity wage of w, then do GM's workers benefit from, lose from, or remain indifferent to the restructuring of production described in that model (reducing the number of models produced in each country but expanding output at each plant)?

(b) Now, suppose that GM workers are unionized, so that in addition to receiving their opportunity wage they bargain to receive a fraction of the economic rents the company generates. Assume for simplicity that the existence of the union does not affect the firm's output and pricing decisions.[8] Call the company's revenues minus the workers' opportunity cost the *bargaining surplus,* and assume that the workers always receive half of this bargaining surplus (divided up evenly among the workers) in addition to their opportunity wage. Will your answer to the question in (a) be different?

(c) Consider the political incentives of GM workers to support or oppose the Auto Pact and the rationalization of production that it allowed. Will those political incentives be more closely aligned with the political incentives of management if the workers are unionized or if they are not unionized? Explain.

4. The spreadsheet "bilateral trade data 2001.xls" records manufacturing trade between the United States and every other country, broken down into 374 industrial categories (all within manufacturing). The "export" column lists exports to the partner country, and the "imports" column lists imports from that country.

   Choose a country (other than Canada or Nigeria) and compute the fraction of manufacturing trade with that country that is intraindustry. Briefly analyze your finding. If you came up with a high number, comment on why it is so high; if it is low, comment on why it is so low. A couple of sentences should suffice. If you want to investigate the composition of trade to help in interpreting the data, you can look up the meaning of the industrial categories at http://www.osha.gov/pls/imis/sicsearch.html.

5. *The Melitz effect.* Open the spreadsheet "heterogeneous firms.xls." This provides data for a hypothetical monopolistically competitive market with heterogeneous firms. Each firm is numbered from 1 to 100 and has its marginal product

of labor ϕ marked. The common value of the fixed labor requirement, f, is marked at the top of the spreadsheet. For each firm, an assumed value for the firm's initial quantity produced is marked as well; assume that this has been derived by setting each firm's marginal cost equal to its marginal revenue. Note that firms with higher marginal products of labor are assumed to produce more output.

(a) Compute each firm's employment of labor under autarky.

(b) Use this information to compute the industry's labor productivity (total output per worker).

(c) Now, suppose that the industry is opened to trade, and in accordance with the Melitz effect, the least efficient 15% of the firms drop out. Furthermore, suppose that firm #54 and all of the firms more efficient than firm #54 export, while the remainder of the surviving firms produce only for the domestic market. Suppose that exporting firms increase their output by 10% compared to autarky, while nonexporters reduce their output by 10% compared to autarky. Now, redo your calculations in parts (a) and (b). Interpret your results. In particular, what happens to industry productivity and why?

(d) Graph the equivalent of Figure 3.4 to illustrate these results.

6. *More on the Melitz effect.* Using the calculations in the previous problem, you can do an exercise similar in spirit to Trefler (2004). Calculate labor productivity *for each firm* (once again, output per worker) before and after trade. (Ignore the firms that drop out of the market when trade opens.) Compute the growth rate of labor productivity for each firm, as a percentage (100 times the change in productivity, divided by the initial value).

(a) For how many firms does labor productivity go down? Why does it go down for these firms? For how many does it go up? Why does it go up for these firms?

(b) Now, take the average across firms of the growth rate of labor productivity. Is average productivity growth positive or negative?

(c) Compare your result to the effect on industry productivity computed in the previous problem. Does average firm productivity move in the same direction as industry productivity? If not, then why not?

REFERENCES

Bernard, Andrew B., and J. Bradford Jensen (1999). "Exceptional Exporter Performance: Cause, Effect, or Both?" *Journal of International Economics* 47, pp. 1–25.

Brainard, S. Lael (1997). "An Empirical Assessment of the Proximity-Concentration Trade-off Between Multinational Sales and Trade." *The American Economic Review*, 87:4 (September), pp. 520–544.

Feenstra, Robert C., John Romalis, and Peter K. Schott (2002). "U.S. Imports, Exports, and Tariff Data, *1989-2001."* NBER Working Paper 9387 (December).

Helpman, Elhanan (1981). "International Trade in the Presence of Product Differentiation, Economies of Scale, and Monopolistic Competition: A Chamberlin-Heckscher-Ohlin Approach," *Journal of International Economics* 11, pp. 305–340.

Helpman, Elhanan, and Paul Krugman (1987). *Market Structure and Foreign Trade: Increasing Returns, Imperfect Competition, and the International Economy.* Cambridge, MA: The MIT Press.

Helpman, Elhanan, Marc J. Melitz, and Stephen R. Yeaple (2004). "Export Versus FDI with Heterogeneous Firms," *American Economic Review* 94:1 (March), pp. 300–316.

Hervey, Jack L. (1978). "Canadian-U.S. Auto Pact—13 Years Afte." *Economic Perspectives* II:1 (January–February), pp. 18–23.

Melitz, M. J. (2003). "The Impact of Trade on Intra-industry Reallocations and Aggregate Industry Productivity." *Econometrica* 71:6, pp. 1695–1725.

Osborne, Martin J., and Ariel Rubinstein (1990). *Bargaining and Markets.* San Diego, CA.: Academic Press.

Trefler, Daniel (2004). "The Long and Short of the Canada-U.S. Free Trade Agreement." *The American Economic Review* 94:4 (September), pp. 870–895.

USITC (1976). *Canadian Automobile Agreement. United States International Trade Commission Report on the United States-Canadian Automotive Agreement· Its History, Terms, and Impact and the Ninth Annual Report of the President to the Congress on the Operation of the Automotive Products Trade Act of 1965.* Washington, DC: U.S. Government Printing Office.

4 Trade and Large Corporations: Kodak versus Fuji

John Wiley & Sons

A company with global reach: A shop advertises "Kodak products" in the town of Safranbolu, Turkey.

4.1 Big Players in the Game of Trade

Many antiglobalization activists argue that globalization is a process rigged in favor of large corporations, that the benefits accrue to powerful firms that effectively write the rules, and that ordinary workers or consumers are left out. One example, whose tone is typical of many others, is a comment by author James Bruges (2004, p. 102):

> *Three-quarters of all international trade is in the hands of multinational corporations. It enables them to drive down the cost of commodities (products in western shops become cheaper), to have more customers worldwide (they can take profit from customers in poor countries), and to locate their facilities where labour and environmental standards are low (if unions demand proper wages the MNC can move to another country). . . . Corporate free trade has seen a period of increasing poverty and social disintegration, alienation, breakdown of democracy, violent insurgency groups, environmental degradation and new diseases.*

Ralph Nader (1999) harbors a similar distrust:

> *The global corporatists preach a model of economic growth that rests on the flows of trade and finance between nations dominated by the giant multinationals— drugs, tobacco, chemical, oil, nuclear, munitions, biotechnology, autos, textile, banking, insurance and other services. . . . The global corporate model is premised on the concentration of power over markets, governments, mass media, patent monopolies over critical drugs and seeds, the workplace and corporate culture.*

This is a common theme: that multinational corporations can set the terms according to which international trade will be conducted and thus receive the lion's share of the benefits.

On the other hand, our large corporations sometimes take their turn claiming to be *victims* of globalization. Consider the Eastman Kodak Company, which has twice in the past claimed that its arch rival, Fujifilm of Japan, has acquired an unfair advantage over Kodak, and has tried to get governments to block Fujifilm's efforts to expand its sales in the United States, in effect protecting Kodak from globalization. In 1993, Kodak filed a complaint with the U.S. International Trade Commission (USITC) claiming that its arch rival was "dumping," or selling below cost in the United States, and in 1996 it filed another complaint alleging that Fuji was conspiring to keep Kodak film from being sold in Japan.

To analyze these questions of who wins in trade when it is dominated by large corporations, we need a theoretical framework that allows for *oligopoly*—a market with producers that are large enough that each has some substantial control over pricing. That will be the contribution of this chapter. Along the way, two very important ideas will emerge that will apply much more generally: First, *oligopoly is a reason for trade* in and of itself because we can construct an example of a market in which there would be no trade with perfect competition, but there is positive trade with oligopoly. Second, trade among oligopolists disproportionately benefits everyone *except* the oligopolists because *trade promotes competition, and competition is one thing that oligopolists do not want.*

4.2 Background on Kodak, Fuji, and the War

The world market for photographic film provides a good example of oligopoly in trade because it is dominated by two producers: Eastman Kodak, based in Rochester, New York, and the Japanese giant, Fujifilm.

Although Kodak first sold modest amounts of film in Japan as long as a century ago, the 1970s represented a new era of globalization in photographic film. The reason is that World War II completely stopped sales of U.S. film in Japan, and after the war the Japanese government prevented inward foreign direct investment (FDI) and tightly restricted imports of film. As the restrictions were lifted, Kodak's sales in Japan rose rapidly, from under 3% of the Japanese market in 1970 to a peak of 11% in 1981 (Tsurumi and Tsurumi, 1999, p. 818). Since then, Kodak has lost considerable ground in the Japanese market.

Fujifilm is a younger company, having been formed in 1934, but it has long held a dominant market position in Japan. In 1965, Fujifilm set up a marketing subsidiary in New York City, and from that point it put much effort into developing its sales in the United States. Fujifilm's U.S. market share rose from 0.3% in 1973 to 10% in 1984, increasing to 14% in 1994 and to 25% in 1997 (Tsurumi and Tsurumi, 1999, p. 823).

Much of the history of these two corporations is of Fujifilm outflanking Kodak in various ways. In 1976, Fujifilm introduced the first mass-marketed fast (ASA 400) color film. In the 1970s, the company pioneered the photoprocessing "mini-lab," which allowed one-hour processing of photos at a wide variety of locations such as drugstores and shopping malls, providing extra convenience to consumers. In the late 1980s, Fujifilm introduced single-use disposable cameras. All of these innovations proved extremely popular with consumers and contributed, together with a relentless public relations onslaught, to Fujifilm's progressive encroachment on Kodak's market. Kodak has tried to use anti-dumping law (a feature of international trade law that will be discussed in Chapter 8) to seek legal redress for what it has claimed were practices of unfair trade on Fujifilm's part. (See Fletcher, 1996, and Finnerty, 2000.)

Richard B. Levine/NewsCom

Fujifilm's presence over New York City. In the 1970's, Fujifilm began to pour resources into public relations, including high-profile sports sponsorships, to convince U.S. consumers that Fuji film was just as prestigious as Kodak film, so that they would be ready to buy whichever brand was offered at the lower price. It worked.

In later years, as Fuji's market share in the United States increased and the U.S. market share in Japan fell, Kodak endured some significant financial losses and reduced its workforce. With both firms increasingly moving toward digital photography, the market in the future will look quite different from what it has been in the past.

It is abundantly clear that this industry is not characterized by perfect competition. Both Kodak and Fuji generally capture about 70% of their respective home markets, and they certainly do not take price as given. Indeed, each firm's strategy includes huge expenditures to shape the market environment to its advantage, such as Kodak's attempts discussed above to use legal proceedings to shape the policy environment and both firms' extensive use of advertising, public relations, and promotions to mold public perceptions of their products (see *Brandweek,* 1998, for a description of this). Price-taking firms in a perfectly competitive market would not have an incentive to do those things. Thus, to analyze the effects of trade in the market for photographic film, we need to incorporate oligopoly into a model of trade. We will do that now.

4.3 Introducing Oligopoly

Do these two industry giants hog the benefits from the globalization of the market for photographic film? To analyze this question, we will look at this market through the lens of a model of oligopoly in trade that, although highly simplified and stylized, fits the key features of this market fairly well.[1]

The market for film in the United States is of course larger than that in Japan because the United States is a larger economy, but each is large enough to be an important market to the other country. So for simplicity let us postulate that they have the same demand curve, given by:

$$Q = \tfrac{1}{2}(11 - P)10^8,$$

where P is the price of a roll of film in U.S. dollars and Q is the quantity purchased per year. This is consistent with a market in which each household has a demand given by $\tfrac{1}{2}(11 - P)$ (so the average household would buy five and a half rolls of film per year if film was free, but only two per year if the price was $7 per roll), and there are 100 million households total. These numbers are about the right orders of magnitude.

Assume that Kodak is established as a manufacturer of film with production facilities in the United States, and Fujifilm is established with production facilities in Japan. We will assume that entry of other firms is not possible, either because of the fixed costs of setting up production facilities or because of the difficulty of establishing public trust in an unknown brand. This is a reasonable approximation, since no significant new competitor has ever entered this market.[2] Assume that both corporations have the same production technology and that both face a marginal production cost of $4 per roll.

---

[1] We will use the model of trade with oligopoly developed in a famous paper by Brander and Krugman (1983).

[2] The obvious exception is the new competition that has resulted from the rise of digital photography, which has profoundly changed this industry. We are focusing our attention on the pre-digital, silver halide era to focus on the effects of trade per se, rather than new technology.

4.4 Autarky

Initially, suppose that trade in film between the two countries is not possible, as was approximately the case in the mid-twentieth century, until the liberalizations of the 1970s (and before Fujifilm had its marketing subsidiary in the United States). In that case, which is of course autarky in the market for film, each corporation is a monopolist in its own market.

Look at Kodak's decision problem. The company must decide how to maximize profits selling only on the American market with no competition. The demand curve can be written as:

$$P = 11 - (2 \times 10^{-8})Q. \tag{4.1}$$

This implies a marginal revenue curve of:

$$MR = 11 - (4 \times 10^{-8})Q.$$

Setting this equal to the marginal cost yields:

$$11 - (4 \times 10^{-8})Q = 4,$$

or $Q = 175$ million rolls of film. Plugging this into the demand curve yields a price of $P = \$7.50$ per roll. This outcome is represented in Figure 4.1. The outcome in Japan with Fujifilm is identical.

Thus, under autarky, in each country the domestic producer sells 175 million rolls to domestic consumers, charging \$7.50 each. The resulting consumer surplus is represented by the dark blue triangle, equal to $\$(11 - 7.50)(1.75 \times 10^8)/2 = \$306.59$ million in each country, and the resulting profit per firm is represented by the light blue rectangle, equal to $\$(7.50 - 4)(1.75 \times 10^8) = \$612.50$ million.

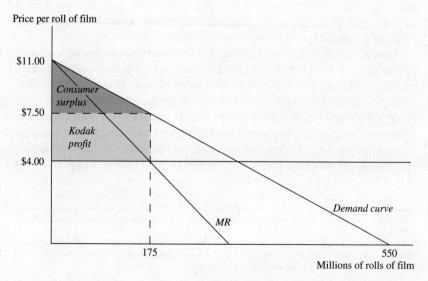

FIGURE 4.1
Autarky in the Market
for Photographic Film.

4.5 Trade

Now, we allow for trade between the two countries. We will maintain the assumption that from the point of view of consumers, Kodak and Fuji film are identical, so that if the two are not priced exactly the same, the consumers will buy only the cheaper brand. This is a fairly good approximation, since for amateur photography the technical properties of the two brands are essentially the same, and public perception of the two brands is very similar. This is the result of Fujifilm's public relations efforts in both countries to overcome Kodak's initial advantage in prestige, as documented, for example, in Tsurumi and Tsurumi (1999), resulting in what marketing specialists describe as the "commoditization of the market" (*Brandweek*, 1998). Thus, we will treat Kodak and Fujifilm as perfect substitutes, and the demand curve will be written as:

$$P^{US} = 11 - (2 \times 10^{-8})Q^{US} = 11 - (2 \times 10^{-8})(q_K^{US} + q_F^{US}),$$

where q_K^{US} denotes Kodak's sales in the U.S. market, q_F^{US} denotes Fujifilm's sales in the U.S. market, P^{US} denotes the price of film in the U.S. market, and $Q^{US} = q_K^{US} + q_F^{US}$ denotes total sales of film in the U.S. market.

Recall that in practice each firm typically sells much more in its home market than its competitor does. Indeed, since the earliest days of the globalized film market in the 1970s, the ratio of Kodak's share to Fujifilm's share in the United States has been between 3 and 7, and the ratio of Fujifilm's to Kodak's share in Japan has moved in a somewhat higher, but overlapping, range. This would not be the case if each firm did not have any advantage on its home turf; in that case, each firm would simply take half of the consumers in the other firm's home market. To allow the model to account for these differences in market shares, let us assume that each firm must pay a transport cost of $2 per roll of film sold in the foreign market. Thus, Kodak faces a marginal cost of $4 in the U.S. market but $4 plus $2 in Japan. Similarly, Fujifilm faces a marginal cost of $4 in Japan but $6 in the United States.

How do these two firms decide how much to produce, and what price to charge? We make the following assumptions: That (i) the two firms choose their quantities in both markets simultaneously; (ii) each firm makes a conjecture about how much the other firm will sell in each market; (iii) given that conjecture, each firm chooses its own quantities in the two markets to maximize its own profits, understanding how that choice will affect the product price; and (iv) (the tricky part) *each firm's conjectures about the other's sales levels are correct.* Assumption (iv) implies that the management of the two firms is rational and understands both the market and the thought process of the other firm. This approach was pioneered by French economist Augustin Cournot in a book published in 1838 and is still the most widely used framework for analyzing oligopolies of this sort. Accordingly, this is called *Cournot competition*, also sometimes called competition in quantities, since each firm makes an assumption about the other's quantities and chooses its own quantity accordingly.

Suppose, then, that Kodak has a conjecture about the quantity q_F^{US} that Fuji will sell in the United States. Then, holding that conjecture constant and varying its own quantity q_K^{US} to see the effect on the U.S. price of film, we derive Kodak's *residual demand curve*:

$$P^{US} = [11 - 2 \times 10^{-8} q_F^{US}] - 2 \times 10^{-8} q_K^{US},$$

The terms in square brackets are beyond Kodak's control, and so serve as a constant, or intercept, in the Kodak's residual demand curve. As a result, Kodak's marginal revenue in the United States is:

$$MR^{US} = [11 - 2 \times 10^{-8}q_F^{US}] - 4 \times 10^{-8}q_K^{US},$$

Equating this with the marginal cost of $4 per roll yields:

$$[11 - 2 \times 10^{-8}q_F^{US}] - 4 \times 10^{-8}q_K^{US} = 4, \quad \text{so}$$

$$q_K^{US} = 1.75 \times 10^8 - \tfrac{1}{2}q_F^{US}. \tag{4.2}$$

This is called Kodak's *reaction function* in the U.S. market, the function that shows how Kodak's optimal quantity depends on its conjecture of what Fujifilm's quantity will be. (The term *reaction function* is somewhat misleading, since the two firms move simultaneously and Kodak is really responding only to its conjecture of what Fujifilm will do, not what Fujifilm actually does.) Kodak's reaction function in the U.S. market is depicted in Figure 4.2. In this figure, Fujifilm's quantity in the United States is the independent variable, plotted on the vertical axis, and Kodak's is the dependent variable, plotted on the horizontal axis. Note that it is a downward-sloping curve with slope equal to 2 (because, from equation (4.2), Kodak's quantity falls by 1/2 whenever Fujifilm's expected quantity rises by 1) and with horizontal intercept equal to 175 million rolls, which is Kodak's monopoly quantity.

Repeating this for Fujifilm, which must make a conjecture of what Kodak will sell in the U.S. market and which faces a marginal cost of $6 in that market, we derive Fuji's reaction function in the U.S. market:

$$q_F^{US} = 1.25 \times 10^8 - \frac{1}{2}q_K^{US}. \tag{4.3}$$

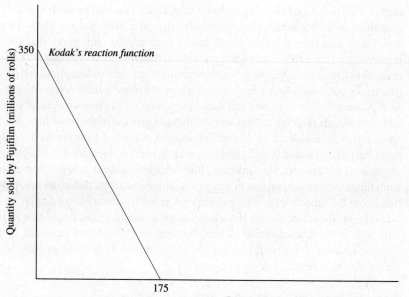

FIGURE 4.2
Kodak's Reaction
Function.

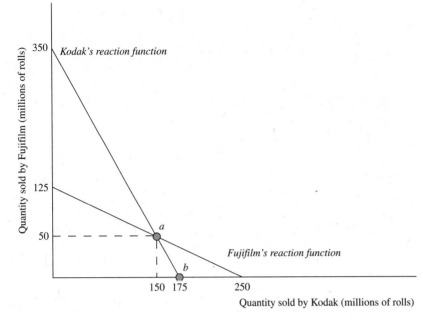

FIGURE 4.3
Equilibrium with
Trade.

The two conditions (4.2) and (4.3) must hold simultaneously, so this is a system of two linear equations in two unknowns. Solving them yields a value of 150 million for Kodak's sales in the United States and 50 million for Fuji's. Adding these quantities together yields total sales of 200 million rolls of film in the U.S. market, which from the demand curve (4.1) implies a price of $7 per roll of film. This outcome is the Cournot equilibrium and is depicted in Figure 4.3 as the intersection, *a*, of the two reaction functions. The equilibrium in Japan will be identical, with the roles of the two firms reversed.

Note that one quarter of world output of photographic film is now traded, with exports running in both destinations—despite our assumptions that the two countries are identical, the two companies' products are identical, and there are significant transport costs. Under perfect competition, there would be no trade in film at all; the price would be $4 per roll in either country, and no one would have any incentive to incur the $2 per roll cost to ship film from one country to another. We conclude that trade occurs here entirely because of oligopoly power, as each firm tries to grab some fraction of the other's oligopoly profits by acquiring customers in the other firm's home market. Thus, we see that *imperfect competition is itself a reason for trade.*

Note that in equilibrium, Kodak sells less in the U.S. market than it would under autarky: 150 million rolls instead of 175 million. However, U.S. consumers consume more than they would under autarky: 200 million rolls, because the price has been pushed down from $7.50 per roll to $7.00. Furthermore, note that although Kodak's domestic sales have gone down because of competitive pressure from Fujifilm, Kodak's total sales have gone up (from 175 million to 200 million rolls worldwide) because of its 50 million rolls exported to Japan. The welfare outcome is shown in Figure 4.4, which shows U.S. consumer surplus in dark blue and Kodak worldwide profits in light blue. Notice that there are two pieces to the profits: Profits on domestic sales, which amount to $3.00 per roll sold times 150 million rolls for a total of $450 million,

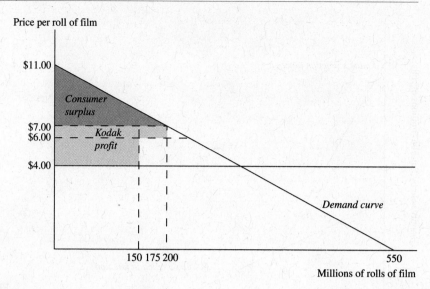

FIGURE 4.4
U.S. Welfare with Trade.

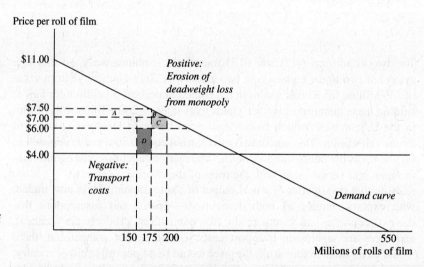

FIGURE 4.5
Net Welfare Effects of Trade in the Market for Photographic Film.

and are represented by the taller light blue rectangle; and profits on exports to Japan, which amount to $1.00 per roll sold times 50 million rolls for a total of $50 million, represented by the shorter light blue rectangle.

4.6 Winners and Losers

Having worked out the equilibrium with and without trade, we can analyze who benefits from trade, who is hurt by it, and by how much. The net effects on welfare are shown in Figure 4.5.

The first and easiest observation is that consumers of camera film in both countries benefit unambiguously. In both countries, trade has pushed the price of film down from $7.50 to $7.00, allowing consumer surplus to rise in Figure 4.5 by area $A + B$.

More complicated is the effect on the two film producers. Comparing profits in Figure 4.4 with profits in Figure 4.1, we see that Kodak has gained area C but lost area $A + D$. They sell at a lower price than they did under autarky, and they incur transport costs that were not an issue under autarky, but they both sell a larger quantity; it might appear that the effect of trade on their profits could be positive or negative. However, we can see, even without grinding through the numbers, that profits to both firms have *fallen* as a result of trade. First, note that under trade, both firms sell 200 million rolls of film at a price of $7.00 per roll. Under autarky, they both had the option of doing so (because that is a point on the demand curve), but chose not to, selling 175 million at a price of $7.50 instead. The reason must be that the higher-quantity-lower-price option was less profitable. Now, under trade, that same higher-quantity-lower-price option is even *less* profitable than it was under autarky, because a portion of the sales are made by export, which entails a transport cost that was absent under autarky.

This point needs to be underlined. In this market, *the oligopolists are the ones who lose from trade*, while everyone else gains. This is because trade forces the oligopolists to compete with each other — the one thing that oligopolists hate.

We might ask: Why do these firms trade, if trading lowers their profits? The answer is that each of them tries to grab some of the profits enjoyed by the other in the other firm's home market, and in doing so, they lower *both* firms' profits. It is thus an example of what game theorists call a Prisoner's Dilemma, a situation in which if each player takes the action that is optimal for itself, the result is an outcome that is worse for both than if neither was able to take that action. Consider the following table, which shows the two firms' profits under alternative decisions they might make. Each cell of the table shows two numbers, Kodak's profits first and Fujifilm's second, for a particular pair of decisions. The first row shows the profits resulting if Kodak chooses not to export to Japan, and the second row shows the results if Kodak does export to Japan. The first column shows the results if Fujifilm chooses not to export, and the second column shows the results if it does. For example, the upper left-hand cell shows the profits if neither firm exports, which is the same as the autarky profits. The upper-right hand cell shows profits if Fujifilm exports but Kodak does not, leaving Fujifilm its autarky monopoly profits of $612.5 m in Japan plus $50 m profits from exporting to the United States, while Kodak receives only $450 m from competition over its domestic market.

	Fujifilm does not export	Fujifilm exports
Kodak does not export	$612.5 m, $612.5 m	$450 m, $662.5 m
Kodak exports	$662.5 m, $450 m	$500 m, $500 m

Note that if Fujifilm is expected to leave the U.S. market alone, the optimal choice for Kodak is to export (since $662.5 m from the bottom left-hand corner is more than $612.5 m from the upper left-hand corner). At the same time, if Fujifilm is expected to export to the United States, the optimal choice for Kodak is still to export (since $500 m from the lower right-hand corner is more than $450 m from the upper right-hand corner). Therefore, no matter what

Fujifilm is expected to do, Kodak's optimal move is to export. Similarly, no matter what Kodak is expected to do, Fujifilm's optimal decision is to export. The result is that both firms export, but this brings them from the upper left-hand corner of the box, with its high profits, to the lower right-hand corner, with its low profits. This is the essence of what free trade does to this oligopoly.

The exact welfare effects of trade can be computed from Figure 4.5. Consumer surplus rises by $A + B$. The change in Kodak profits is equal to $C - A - D$, the new profits on exports (C) minus the drop in price on units that were sold in autarky (A) minus the rise in costs due to the transport cost paid on units that were sold domestically under autarky but now are exported (D). Working through the numbers, we see that consumer surplus has gone up by $93.75 million, while Kodak profits have fallen by $112.5 million.

In this model, U.S. social welfare is equal to consumer surplus plus Kodak's profits. Adding up the effects from the previous paragraph, the net effect of trade on U.S. social welfare is equal to $B + C - D$. This has a ready interpretation: The term $B + C$ is the reduction in the deadweight monopoly loss due to the fact that Kodak now must compete—the efficiency benefit of pushing price closer to marginal cost. The term D is the loss due to transport cost on what is in this context redundant and costly overseas shipments. There is in general no reason to expect the benefit from the trimming of deadweight loss to exceed the social loss from redundant shipping; indeed, in this case, the net effect of trade in film on U.S. social welfare is negative, with a loss of $18.75 million. The same loss is incurred in Japan. Another way of looking at it is that the corporation loses from trade, consumers benefit from trade; and the losses incurred by the corporation exceed the gains by the consumers. Whether or not that means it is a bad outcome is a political and ethical judgment, but at least in principle, in this model, Kodak would be willing to pay compensation to consumers to persuade them to reject trade.

4.7 Some Other Possibilities

Understanding the basic model, it is now easy to see how the analysis would change if we allowed for a number of alternative specifications.

(i) A market without transport costs. If we set transport costs equal to zero, then in the welfare diagram Figure 4.5, rectangle D would shrink to a zero height and hence a zero area. This would ensure that trade would be welfare-improving for both countries. In this case, the only effect of trade would be to remove the monopoly power of the two large firms by forcing them to compete with one another. In the photographic film case, this is not terribly realistic since it would also imply that Kodak and Fuji would have equal market shares in both markets while, as noted above, in practice each firm has had a much larger share in its home market than its competitor. However, it could be realistic for other industries. The more general point is that in the case of an international oligopoly, the lower are the transport costs, the more likely the consumer benefit of trade is to exceed the corporation's loss.

(ii) A Fujifilm advantage. For simplicity, we have assumed that both corporations face exactly the same production and transport costs. At one time that may have been a good approximation, but with Fuji's rising share of the U.S. market and Kodak's declining share in Japan's since the mid-1980s, it makes sense to ask how things change if Fuji has an advantage of some sort.

To take an extreme case, suppose that everything in the model above is unchanged except that Kodak's cost of selling in Japan is now prohibitively high. Then, the equilibrium in the U.S. market is unchanged, but Fuji is now effectively a monopolist in Japan, both under autarky and under trade. Under these conditions, Fujifilm *gains* from trade. It suffers no loss in price or sales in its home market, but picks up some additional sales and additional profits in the U.S. market. In addition, Kodak's loss from trade is greater than it was in the symmetric model, because it loses profits on its domestic sales and has no compensation from exports. Recall that we established previously that with the demand and cost conditions we have assumed, U.S. welfare falls with trade in the symmetric case studied in Sections 4.5 and 4.6; because Kodak failed to earn any profit in Japan, this asymmetric case is even worse for U.S. welfare.

In this asymmetric case, therefore, Japanese social welfare unambiguously rises from trade, while U.S. welfare unambiguously falls from it (at least with the demand and cost conditions we have assumed here). One interpretation is that when Fujifilm enters the U.S. market without a corresponding entrance of Kodak into Japan, two effects on U.S. welfare result: One, a rise in competition, which whittles away part of the deadweight loss from monopoly and is beneficial; the other, a transfer of oligopolistic rent from Americans to Fujifilm, which is a loss for U.S. welfare. In this case, the latter exceeds the former.

Finally, a note on trade and corporate profits: In Section 4.6, we found that in the symmetric model, both firms are hurt by trade. This asymmetric example illustrates that this finding is a consequence of the symmetry in the model. Again, symmetry is sometimes a realistic assumption, but not always

(iii) Product differentiation. In many oligopolistic industries, the automotive industry for example, every manufacturer's products are different from those of any other manufacturers, so trade allows each consumer to benefit from additional product variety as well as increased competition. This product differentiation can also result in the large corporations benefiting, on balance, from trade. Consider the extreme case in which Kodak and Fuji produce completely different types of film; for example, suppose Kodak film was useful only for snapshots, while Fuji film was useful only for X-rays. In that case, trade would extend Kodak's snapshot-film monopoly to Japan, and Fujifilm's X-ray-film monopoly to the United States. Both firms would benefit, and so would consumers, even though there would be no increase in competition.

(iv) Competition in prices. In this analysis, we have made Cournot's assumption: that each firm conjectures what the other's quantity will be and chooses its own optimal quantity accordingly, understanding how price would adjust. Suppose that, instead, each firm conjectures what the other's *price* will be and makes its optimal *price* decision accordingly, understanding how *quantities* will adjust. This is the assumption suggested by Joseph Bertrand in his 1883 critique of Cournot's book, and accordingly is called *Bertrand competition*, or competition in prices.[3] In this model, we will see that Bertrand competition implies that each firm will charge a price of $6.00 per roll (plus or minus one penny) and serve only domestic consumers. Thus, under Bertrand competition, the corporations are harmed and the consumers benefit as a result of trade (just as in the Cournot case), but there is no wasteful shipment of film

[3] A full analysis of the Bertrand model can be found in Tirole (1988, pp. 209–211, 234).

across the ocean. As a result, each country is guaranteed a social welfare benefit from trade.

We need two additional assumptions to complete the model. First, assume that firms must choose a price denominated in dollars and cents and cannot set a price in fractions of cents. Second, suppose that if a group of consumers faces a price for Kodak film that is the same as the price of Fuji film, half of those consumers choose Kodak and half choose Fuji.

Now, we will use an argument by contradiction to show that Fujifilm cannot charge any price above $6.01 in equilibrium in the U.S. market. To see this, pick any price above $6.01, say, $6.02. If Fujifilm charges $6.02 in equilibrium, then Kodak will undercut that price by one penny, or in other words charge $6.01. (This is more profitable for Kodak than matching Fuji's price of $6.02: Undercutting gives Kodak a profit margin of $(6.01 − 4.00) = $2.01 per roll of film, while matching Fuji's price gives the nearly identical profit margin of $(6.02 − 4.00) = $2.02. At the same time, undercutting gives Kodak the whole U.S. market, while matching Fuji's price gives each firm half of the U.S. market.) Thus, Kodak will set its price at $6.01. But that creates a contradiction: Knowing that Kodak will set its price at $6.01, Fujifilm will not choose a price of $6.02, because at that price it will make no sales, while if it matches Kodak's price of $6.01, it will get half the U.S. market and enjoy a slim but positive profit margin of $0.01 per roll. This argument by contradiction shows that it is not possible for Fujifilm to charge $6.02 in equilibrium. Identical logic can show that any other Fuji price above $6.01 is also not possible in equilibrium.

Following this type of reasoning, we see that there are only two possible equilibrium outcomes: Fujifilm charges $6.01 and Kodak charges $6.00, capturing the whole U.S. market; or Fujifilm charges $6.00 and Kodak charges $5.99, capturing the whole U.S. market.[4] The analysis is parallel in the Japanese market, with Fujifilm the market winner there. More generally, *in Bertrand models with constant marginal costs and identical products, in each market the equilibrium price is equal to the marginal cost of the higher-cost producer (to within a penny), and the market is captured entirely by the low-cost producer.*

In summary, in this Bertrand oligopoly, even under free trade, no actual imports occur: Kodak gets all of the U.S. consumers and Fujifilm gets all of the Japanese consumers. However, the *threat* of imports forces each firm to cut its prices from the monopoly price of $7.50 to $6.00 (plus or minus one cent). Thus, once again, the oligopolistic firms are hurt by trade and consumers benefit because trade allows for at least imperfect competition in place of pure monopoly.

---

[4] A purely technical note is in order here, for the technically minded. Strictly speaking, in a Bertrand equilibrium Fujifilm could charge any price between $5.99 and $4.01, with Kodak undercutting by one penny. For example, Fujifilm could charge $5.99 and Kodak $5.98. In this situation, Fujifilm does not hurt itself by pricing so low because, given the even lower Kodak price, no U.S. consumer will buy from Fujifilm anyway. We disregard these possibilities as uninteresting, since Fujifilm has no incentive to offer a price below its own marginal cost and take the risk that its conjecture about Kodak's price is wrong and it might accidentally make positive sales. Game theorists call such strategies "weakly dominated," and usually assume them away as unrealistic. From here on, we will simply assume that no firm ever offers a price below its marginal cost.

MAIN IDEAS

1. Cournot oligopoly is a model of imperfect competition in which each firm chooses its quantity, taking as given its conjecture about what quantity the other firm will choose.

2. Cournot oligopoly can produce international trade even when the oligopolists in different countries produce identical products, neither country has a cost advantage, and there are positive transport costs. The reason is that each firm wants to grab some of the others' customers, in order to grab some of the oligopolistic rents that go with them.

3. In a symmetric Cournot model, trade lowers the profits of oligopolists by forcing them to compete, but raises consumer surplus.

4. If transport costs are high enough, this can result in social welfare losses from trade, meaning that the benefit to consumers from enhanced competition is smaller than the loss in corporate profits.

5. If one country's oligopolist has a substantial cost advantage, trade can result in gains for that firm

and its country, but losses for the other firm and the other country. This is because one effect of trade in this case is the transfer of oligopolistic rents from the country without the cost advantage to the country with it.

6. If the products produced by oligopolists are not identical, then trade is more likely to raise oligopolists' profits and is also more likely to raise social welfare compared to the case of identical products.

7. Bertrand oligopoly is a model of imperfect competition in which each firm chooses a price, taking as given its conjecture about what price the other firm will choose.

8. Bertrand oligopoly *cannot* produce international trade if the oligopolists produce identical products, neither country has a cost advantage, and there are positive transport costs. However, in this case the *threat* of trade has a substantial effect in each country, lowering prices and increasing social welfare.

WHERE WE ARE

We have added two kinds of oligopoly model to our inventory of trade theories, Cournot models and Bertrand models.

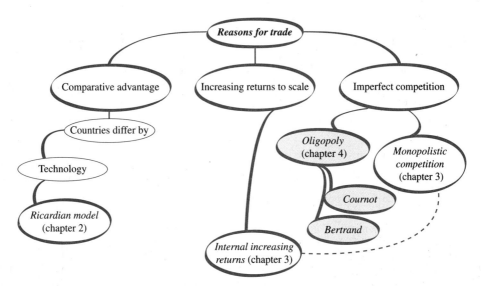

The other important category of imperfect competition model, monopolistic competition, was introduced in the previous chapter.

QUESTIONS AND PROBLEMS

1. Identify one industry that is best thought of as perfectly competitive, one that is best thought of as monopolistic competition, and one that is best thought of as an oligopoly (staying away from examples discussed in the text). Explain your reasoning.

2. Think of what we know about trade and imperfect competition in the variants we have seen— monopolistic competition versus oligopoly, symmetric versus asymmetric oligopoly, and homogeneous versus differentiated products. Under which of these conditions would we be most likely to see serious political opposition to a trade agreement that opens an industry to free trade? And which party would be opposed?

3. Consider a model with two countries called France and Germany. France has one automaker, called Citroen. Germany has a competitor company, called Volkswagen. Citroen can produce cars at a constant marginal cost of $1,000 each. VW can produce cars at a constant marginal cost of $2,000 each. Within each country, the demand for cars is given by the same demand curve:

$$Q = (18 - P) \times (10,000),$$

where Q is the number of cars demanded in that country per month and P is the price per car in that country, in thousands of dollars. Assume that no one other than Citroen or VW can transport cars between the two countries, so it is possible for the price of cars in the two economies to be different.

(a) Suppose initially that both economies are in autarky. What will be the price and the quantity sold in each country?

(b) Suppose that we now have free trade between the two economies. There is no cost to transporting the cars across borders for either firm. Suppose that the two corporations set their quantities in each market simultaneously. For any given quantity q_F^V that Citroen expects VW to sell in the French market, find the profit-maximizing quantity q_F^C that Citroen will sell in the French market. Using your answer, draw Citroen's reaction function for the French market.

(c) Using logic parallel to (b), draw VW's reaction function for the French market on the same diagram.

(d) Assume that each firm correctly guesses how much the other will produce in each market. What will be the price charged and the quantity sold in each market?

(e) Analyze diagrammatically the effect of trade on the profits of the two firms, on consumer welfare in the two countries, and on overall social welfare. Do the two countries benefit from trade? Does anyone lose from it?

4. In the main Kodak-Fuji model of Sections 4.3 to 4.6, we have assumed that the marginal cost of producing film is $4. Suppose that this marginal cost arises because each roll of film requires 1 hour of unskilled labor to produce, and the market wage for unskilled labor is $4 per hour. Suppose that this market wage is unaffected by whatever happens in the film industry, and that workers can easily find a job in the other industries at that wage.

(a) If Kodak simply pays its workers their opportunity wage of $4 per hour, then do Kodak workers benefit from, lose from, or remain indifferent to the opening of trade in the film industry?

(b) Now, suppose that Kodak workers are unionized, so that in addition to receiving their opportunity wage they bargain to receive a fraction of the economic rents the company generates. Assume for simplicity that the existence of the union does not affect the firm's output and pricing decisions.[5] Will your answer to the question in (a) be different?

(c) Consider the political incentives of Kodak workers to support or oppose free trade in film. Will those political incentives be more closely aligned with the political incentives of management if the workers are unionized or if they are not unionized? Explain.

5. Recall the discussion in Section 4.7, part (ii), of trade in which Fujifilm has a cost advantage. Draw a diagram showing the effect of trade on U.S. consumer surplus, Kodak profit, and U.S.

---

[5] The same reasoning applies as in Question 3 of Chapter 3. For example, a Nash bargaining model in which union and management bargain over how much film will be produced for both markets, and the hourly wage, w, that will be paid to Kodak workers will imply that the firm's output and pricing decisions will be the same as they would have been with no union and a marginal cost of $4.

social welfare in this case. Interpret the welfare effect in terms of a competition effect, which is beneficial, and a rent-transfer effect, which is a loss for the United States. Mark these two effects clearly on the diagram.

6. Consider a market for CDs in a country called Home that has only one producer, Music, Inc. Suppose that the demand curve is given by:

$$Q = 100 - P,$$

where Q is the number of CDs demanded in that country per month and P is the price per CD in that country. The marginal cost of producing a CD is $6.

   (a) Work out the price, quantity, Music, Inc.'s profit, and consumer surplus under autarky.

   (b) Now, suppose that although Music, Inc. is still unable to reach any export markets, a foreign producer is now able to sell in Home. Initially, the foreign producer sells 2 units in Home. Assuming that consumers view the foreign CDs as perfect substitutes for Music, Inc.'s CDs, and assuming that Music, Inc. takes as given that the foreign producer will sell 2 units in the Home market, compute Music, Inc.'s residual demand curve and equilibrium price, quantity, profit, and consumer surplus. Has Home's social welfare gone up or down? Interpret with a welfare diagram, explaining in terms of a competition effect and the rent transfer effect.

   (c) Now, repeat part (b) under the assumption that the foreign producer will sell 90 units in the Home market. Do you get a different answer compared to part (b)? If so, why?

7. Recall the discussion of equilibrium in the Bertrand model of Section 4.7, part (iv). Draw a well-marked diagram of the welfare effects of trade in this model. Is trade necessarily welfare-improving in this case? Why or why not?

8. In the Citroen-Volkswagen model of question 3, what would the trade equilibrium be if competition was in prices instead of quantities? Compute equilibrium prices, quantities, profits, consumer surplus, and social welfare in both countries. Is trade beneficial to both countries?

REFERENCES

Brander, James A., and Paul Krugman (1983). "A 'Reciprocal Dumping' Model of International Trade." *Journal of International Economics*, 15:3/4 (November), pp. 313–321.

Brandweek (1998). "Momentous Shifts—Fuji Bites into Kodak's Market Share." June 1, 1998.

Bruges, James (2004). *The Little Earth Book*. New York: The Disinformation Company.

Finnerty, Thomas C. (2000). "Kodak vs. Fuji: The Battle for Global Market Share." New York: Pace University.

Fletcher, Matthew (1996). "Film Fight: Fuji vs. Kodak." *Asiaweek*, July 5, 1996.

Nader, Ralph (1999). "Seattle and the WTO," from *In the Public Interest*, syndicated column, December 7.

Tirole, Jean (1988). *The Theory of Industrial Organization*. Cambridge, MA.: The MIT Press.

Tsurumi, Yoshi, and Hiroki Tsurumi (1999). "Fujifilm-Kodak Duopolistic Competition in Japan and the United States." *Journal of International Business Studies* 30:4, pp. 813–830.

5

Why Did the North Want a Tariff, and Why Did the South Call It an Abomination?

North Wind Picture Archives/The Image Works

A New England textile mill, c.1819.

5.1 A Cold War before the Hot War

The nightmare of the American Civil War (1861–1865) was foreshadowed by seven decades of increasing tension between the states of the North and those of the South. Some of the points of conflict are well known from standard American history textbooks: The Southern economy was based on slavery, which was banned in the North. Northerners wanted slavery to be banned in new states and territories, while Southerners wanted it legal there. Northerners wanted to protect fugitive slaves who made it to the North, while Southerners wanted to impose rules preventing such protection. Overall, political currents in the North ran increasingly toward antislavery sentiments; although Abraham Lincoln promised he would not try to end slavery in the South when he was elected president in 1860, many Southerners did not believe him, and his strong stand on fugitives and on slavery in the territories convinced many of them to support succession.

These tensions springing from the issue of slavery are well known. However, another important source of conflict between North and South is much less familiar: tariff policy. During the early nineteenth century, Congress several times established high import tariffs, which Northern politicians supported and Southern politicians bitterly opposed. This disagreement over tariff policy resulted in a constitutional crisis of its own, with the state of South Carolina at one point in 1832 threatening to violate the tariff law and even perhaps to secede over the issue. Here we will analyze some of the key economic features of this dispute, showing how it is fairly easy to understand within a comparative-advantage framework. In order to do so, we need to add one important element to the model we already have.

The Granger Collection, New York

TOBACCO PLANTATION.

First, some background. The early U.S. economy was agricultural, and Americans imported virtually all of their manufactured goods from Europe, especially England. During the early 1800s, particularly in New England, entrepreneurs experimented with manufacturing, with cotton textiles and later woolen textiles as the key products. Taussig (1914, p. 27) reports that as of 1803 there were *four* cotton textile factories in the United States. From this tiny base, the industry grew rapidly, although by 1840 the share of the New England labor force employed in large-scale manufacturing was still not quite 15%. Most manufactures, including textiles and apparel, were still imported, but now there were a substantial number of U.S. manufacturers competing with the imports. These competing firms were concentrated in the Northern states, and particularly in New England. The country's exports were mostly agricultural commodities such as cotton and tobacco—both produced exclusively in the South. Thus, it was a thoroughly comparative-advantage economy, exporting agricultural commodities and importing manufactures. (Put differently, it resembled the model of Chapter 2 more than the models of Chapter 3 or 4.)

Congress first established import tariffs in the earliest years of the republic, with the tariff bill of 1789 (Taussig, 1914, pp. 14–15), which put most import duties at 5%. Tariff levels remained at modest levels until the 1820s. Following disruptions in imports from England due to the War of 1812 that led to a rapid expansion of U.S. manufactures in the mid-1810s, New England industrialists began to apply pressure for protection. Congress passed bills to increase tariffs in 1816 (to 25% for cotton textiles, for example; Taussig, pp. 29−30), and then again in 1820 and 1824. Starting with the 1820 bill, members of Congress from the South began to resist tariffs, and Northern manufacturers began to organize to be ever more aggressive in seeking protection. In 1826, a coalition of manufacturers of woolen products met in Boston to work out a political strategy to increase their trade protection, enlisting the aid of Massachusetts Senator Daniel Webster—previously a staunch free-trader. A delegation of manufacturers traveled from Boston to Washington to plead their case before congressional committees. In 1827, after a new tariff bill narrowly failed to pass, a broad coalition of manufactures and allies met in Harrisburg, Pennsylvania, to draft a more aggressive tariff bill and work out a strategy for its passage.[1]

These moves led to the most protective bill ever enacted in the United States: the tariff bill of 1828. It raised tariffs sharply on a wide variety of manufactured imports as well as some imported raw materials. Figure 5.1 illustrates the effect clearly. The graph plots the average tariff on dutiable imports from 1790 to 1836, shown as revenue per dollar of dutiable import as well as per dollar of all imports. Note that tariffs rose steadily through the 1820s, as the protectionist movement gained strength, but increased sharply with passage of the 1828 bill, to a striking average of above 50%—a higher rate of average tariff than the country has seen before or since.

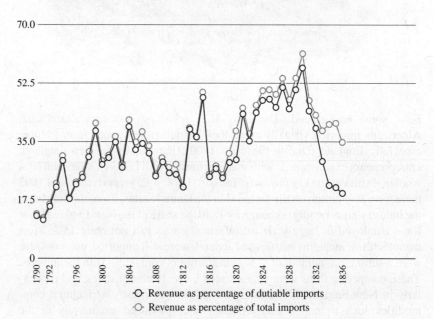

FIGURE 5.1
Average U.S. Tariffs:
1790−1836.

-O- Revenue as percentage of dutiable imports
-O- Revenue as percentage of total imports

Source: Irwin (2003). For 1820, there are no data available for the tariff as a fraction of all imports. For this one data point, the figure uses a linear interpolation of the two adjacent dates.

[1] Taussig (1888) (pp. 20−28) provides a detailed account of this maneuvering.

The 1828 tariff created a sharp split. Until the 1820s, Southern members of Congress had been willing to go along with tariffs, but they fought hard against the 1828 bill. Voting on the bill was strongly correlated with region, with Northern members of Congress voting overwhelmingly for the bill and Southern congressmen voting overwhelmingly against it (Irwin, 2008, pp. 7, 32–33). Not only was the voting split, but there was a terrible political fallout from the bill—which Southerners took to calling the Tariff of Abominations. In 1832, the government of South Carolina threatened to "nullify" the tariff, or to declare it invalid and unconstitutional, and to allow import of foreign goods into the state without paying any of the duty required by the law. This action prompted President Andrew Jackson to repudiate the states' ability to nullify U.S. law, and the U.S. Congress to pass the "Force Act," authorizing the use of military force to ensure that any recalcitrant state would enforce federal tariffs. Because of this episode, called the nullification crisis of 1832, it is conceivable that armed hostilities could have broken out in at least some of the states as early as 1832.[2] The crisis was defused with a compromise that brought tariffs down, and tariffs stayed low for several decades.

Can we make sense of this conflict economically? The U.S. economy was at the time a comparative-advantage economy, exporting cotton, tobacco, and assorted agricultural commodities, and importing manufactures. In a simple comparative-advantage model of the Ricardian type such as we saw in Chapter 2, everyone gains from trade, and further, within each country everyone is affected by trade policy in the same way. For example, in the simple model of Nigerian trade, every Nigerian had the same budget line, so anything the government might do to benefit one citizen by shifting her budget line outward would equally benefit all citizens by shifting all of their budget lines outward. There could be no disagreement or conflict over trade policy. Clearly, the model needs to be modified to explain the intense conflict surrounding the tariff of 1828. In this chapter, we will add *specific factors* to the model in order to understand this type of political conflict over trade policy. A specific factor is a factor of production that can be used in only one industry. A simple example is a machine that is designed to produce one product and cannot be used to produce anything else, such as the giant auto-body stamps that are used to make an automobile body out of a sheet of metal and that are useless for any other purpose. Another example is human capital; a highly-skilled worker's training is often specialized to one industry (a medical degree is not useful in growing cotton). A slightly more subtle example is a worker who has geographic constraints. If the shrimping industry is located in one part of the country and a worker is constrained by personal circumstance to live in a different part of the country, that worker is unable

---

[2] Some authors have gone as far as to try to argue that tariffs were the real cause of the Civil War; that longstanding bitterness over the issue flared up with a new tariff bill in 1860, and when that bill passed, Southerners decided to leave the Union (see Scruggs, 2005 for an example of this line of argument). As tempting as it may be for a trade economist to try to explain everything that happens in the world by trade or trade policy, this is surely pushing the argument too far. It is more plausible that trade policy was one of a number of major irritants that brought about the war, important but not as important as the slavery issues. The four states whose legislatures promulgated reasons for secession, for example, all dwelled at length on slavery issues; only one, Georgia, explicitly discussed tariffs, and even that declaration spent more time on slavery issues. But the tariff is still crucial to understanding nineteenth-century U.S. politics, and North–South relations in particular.

to work in the shrimping industry and so effectively becomes a kind of specific factor.

We now add specific factors to our comparative-advantage model of trade and show how they create a pattern of political conflict over trade policy very similar to the situation in 1828. We first look at the simplest case, a *pure specific-factors model*, one in which every factor of production is specific. This has the virtue of being the easiest form of specific-factors model to analyze. Then we allow one factor to be perfectly mobile, producing a *mixed specific-factors model*, often called the *Ricardo-Viner* model. In the real world, labor is neither perfectly immobile as in the pure specific-factors model, nor perfectly mobile as in the mixed version, so both models should be regarded as somewhat extreme, but useful, special cases.

Specific-factors models are useful far beyond the historical example that is the focus of this chapter. Indeed, a huge research literature uses specific-factors models to analyze the political forces behind trade policy (as pioneered, for example, in an influential paper by Grossman and Helpman, 1994; this topic will be discussed in some detail in Chapter 7). Specific-factors models have been quite helpful in understanding the effects of trade policy on income distribution; Kovak (2011), for example, shows that it helps understand the differential impact of trade reform on different workers in Brazil. These models are a good tool to have in the applied trade economist's toolkit.

5.2 A Pure Specific-Factors Model

We start by simplifying the U.S. economy of 1828 so that there are only two goods: cotton textiles (C) and tobacco (T). Suppose that manufacturers produce cotton textiles from capital and labor using a production function f^C with constant returns to scale, so that:

$$Q^C = f^C(L^C, K^C),$$

where L^C and K^C denote, respectively, labor and capital used to produce cotton textiles, and Q^C denotes the output produced. Assume that all manufacturers of cotton textiles have the same production function. Suppose further that Southern farmers produce tobacco by using labor and land with a production function f^T with constant returns to scale, so that:

$$Q^T = f^T(L^T, A^T),$$

where L^T and A^T denote, respectively, labor and land used to produce tobacco and Q^T denotes the output produced. Assume that all tobacco farmers have the same production function, and that all capital is equally productive, all workers are equally productive, and all land is equally productive.

Assume that all of the capital for producing textiles is in the North and all of the land for tobacco production is in the South.[3] In this model, all three factors

---

[3] This assumption means, among other things, that the North was entirely dependent on manufactures for employment. In fact, at this time most workers in the North were still engaged in agriculture. However, for the most part they did not produce crops for export, unlike farmers in the South. This difference is key for the discussion in this chapter.

are specific. Capital is not useful for producing tobacco, land is not useful for producing cotton textiles, and each worker is constrained to work in his or her own industry—not least because switching industries would require moving to another part of the country. On the other hand, assume that within the North, labor can move freely from employer to employer so that all Northern employers will pay the same wage in equilibrium, and any machine can be rented by one manufacturer to any other, so every piece of capital will earn the same return no matter where it is used. Similarly, setting aside slaves (who will be discussed later), workers in the South will all be paid the same wage in equilibrium, and all land will earn the same return. For this discussion, let us assume that the prices of tobacco and cotton textiles are determined on world markets and not affected by what happens in the U.S. economy. In other words, the United States is a small country for our purposes, and we can take the product prices as fixed parameters. That is a fairly reasonable assumption for this stage of U.S. economic development; at any rate the main points about the effects of the tariff do not rely on it.

Courtesy Lowell Historical Society

The Merrimack Manufacturing Company factory, in Lowell, MA.

Suppose that in the North there are K^N units of capital and L^N workers, while in the South there are A^S acres of land and L^S workers. These factor supplies are fixed and exogenous. All suppliers of factors, employers, and consumers take prices as given, and prices adjust to clear the market. We represent the wage in the North and South by w^N and w^S, respectively, and the rental price for capital in the North and land in the South by r^N and r^S, respectively.

Consider one cotton textile manufacturer, the Merrimac Manufacturing Company, which established its main factory in 1822 in what would become Lowell, Massachusetts (Taussig, 1914, p. 32; Dublin, 1981). This factory was one of the first of a wave; the Merrimac River in the northern part of the state provided power that led to a blossoming of manufacturing and employment for thousands of women, with accompanying economic and social transformation (Dublin, 1981).

Suppose that Merrimac has K^M units of capital, which it can rent out to another manufacturer or use in its own factory in Lowell. The company must choose its labor input, L^M, to maximize its profit:

$$p^C f^C(L^M, K^M) - w^N L^M, \qquad (5.1)$$

where p^C is the price of cotton cloth and w^N is the wage in the North, both of which Merrimac takes as given. The optimal choice of L^M involves setting the marginal value product of labor equal to w^N. With a constant-returns-to-scale production function, the marginal product of labor is determined by the ratio of labor used to the other factor, so we can write:

$$w^N = p^C MPL^C(L^M/K^M),$$

where MPL^C denotes the marginal product of labor in cotton textile production, which is a decreasing function of L^M/K^M. This equation, then, determines the labor-capital ratio for the Merrimac Manufacturing Company as a function of the wage w^N and the product price p^C.

Importantly, since all other cotton textile manufacturers in the North face the same wage and product price, and since they have the same production function, they will all choose the same labor-capital ratio. Therefore, the market will not be in equilibrium until the wage adjusts so that every manufacturer chooses a labor-capital ratio equal to L^N/K^N, the aggregate labor-capital ratio in the North. This implies:

$$w^N = p^C MPL^C(L^N/K^N). \tag{5.2}$$

Similarly, since the opportunity cost of Merrimac's capital is the rental price r^N, it will also set the marginal value product of capital equal to this value:

$$r^N = p^C MPK^C(L^N/K^N), \tag{5.3}$$

where MPK^C denotes the marginal product of capital, an increasing function of (L^N/K^N). In an equilibrium with constant returns to scale and perfect competition, we must have zero economic profits, so that Merrimac makes the same income by using its capital in its Waltham factory as it would if it simply rented it out. Therefore, equation (5.3) is Merrimac's equilibrium income per unit of capital.

Note that with (L^N/K^N) fixed, equations (5.2) and (5.3) are both proportional to p^C. This conclusion is important: *The incomes of specific factors are increasing in the prices of the output for the industry to which they are specific.*

The analysis of equilibrium in the South is parallel to the analysis of equilibrium in the North, with the important exception that some of the tobacco farmers have access to coerced labor. (The main point of this discussion, which is about the role of specific factors in conflict over trade policy, does not depend on this issue of coerced labor, but it would be unseemly to ignore slavery in any discussion of tobacco production in the 1820s.) Suppose that among the South's L^S workers are L' who are constrained to work without pay, and suppose that every tobacco farmer who has slaves also hires some free workers (meaning nonslave, wage-earning workers; indeed, a large portion of the Southern workforce was made up of free workers).[4] Then, in equilibrium, each tobacco farmer hires free labor at the wage w^S (where the superscript S stands for South) until the marginal value product of labor is equal to the wage, resulting in the same labor-land ratio for each tobacco farm

---

[4] If a farmer had an unusually large ratio of slaves to usable land, the marginal product of labor on that farm would be less than the market wage, and the farmer would not hire any free workers. We ignore this possibility for simplicity.

(where the labor-land ratio is the ratio of *total* labor, coerced and free, to land). Market clearing requires that this ratio be equal to the aggregate labor-land ratio L^S/A^S. This implies that the wage for free labor is given by:

$$w^S = p^T MPL^T (L^S/A^S), \tag{5.4}$$

where p^T is the price of tobacco, and income to tobacco farmers is equal to:

$$r^S A^S + w^S L' = p^T [MPA^T (L^S/A^S)A^S + MPL^T (L^S/A^S)L'], \tag{5.5}$$

where MPA^T denotes the marginal product of land in tobacco. Note that in equation (5.5) we include earned income on land $r^S A^S$ in parallel with equation (5.3), and also unearned income on coerced labor $w^S L'$.[5] Once again, note that, with A^S, L^S, and L' all fixed, equations (5.4) and (5.5) are proportional to the output price, p^T.

5.3 The Tariff

Now, to analyze the effect of trade policy. Assume that the price of cotton cloth set in world markets is 10¢ per yard and the price of tobacco is 25¢ per pound. These are roughly in the range of prices paid for cotton textiles and for retail tobacco in this period (Taussig, 1914, p. 30; Norris, 1962, p. 457).

Assume that at these prices, domestic U.S. demand for cotton cloth is much greater than domestic production, and domestic U.S. demand for tobacco is well below domestic production, so that the U.S. exports tobacco and imports cotton cloth.

Initially, trade is free, but now suppose that the government imposes a 50% tariff on imports of cloth, which is about the size of the tariff on cloth in the 1828 tariff bill. (The bill actually established complicated tariff schedules for each commodity, in which the rate paid varied with the value imported; see Taussig, 1888, pp. 32–36 for a description.) With the tariff in place, if an importer imports $1.00 worth of cloth into the United States (after converting into U.S. currency, if needed), then the importer must pay $0.50 to the U.S. Customs Service at the port of entry. This applies for any unit of cloth imported into the United States, regardless of where it enters the country and where it winds up in the country. As a result, any U.S. consumer wishing to purchase a unit of imported cloth will pay $0.15 under the tariff: $0.10 to the foreign supplier and $0.5 to U.S. Customs.

If domestic producers such as the Merrimac Manufacturing Company did not raise their own prices in response to the tariff, domestic consumers would then turn to the domestic producers to satisfy their demand; but this would create an excess demand because domestic supply is not sufficient to meet domestic demand. As a result, we conclude that domestic producers *do* raise their price, and the equilibrium outcome is an increase in the domestic

---

[5] Put differently, in the absence of slavery, the farmer's income would be $r^S A^S = p^T MPA^T (L^S/A^S)A^S$, exactly parallel to the capitalist's income in the case of the cotton cloth industry. This is net of payments to workers. If, on the other hand, there are L' workers who do not need to be paid, the farmer thereby saves $w^S L'$ on wages and thus has a net income that is $w^S L'$ higher. This produces the expression in equation (5.5).

price for cloth to 15¢ per yard for every U.S. consumer and producer. At that price, U.S. consumers are indifferent between buying from domestic firms and importing.

Consider the budget line of a Northern worker. The cotton cloth intercept is w^N/p^C, which equals $MPL^C(L^N/K^N)$ by equation (5.2). This intercept is not affected by the tariff. The tobacco intercept is $w^N/p^T = (p^C/p^T)MPL^C$ (L^N/K^N) by equation (5.2), which has now increased by 50%. (The value (p^C/p^T) was equal to $(0.10/0.25) = 0.4$ without the tariff, and $(0.15/0.25) = 0.6$ with the tariff.) Thus, the Northern worker's budget line has pivoted outward as a result of the tariff, clearly benefiting the Northern worker. The analysis for the Northern capitalist, such as the owners of the Merrimac Manufacturing Company, is identical: All Northerners benefit from the tariff.

Now, consider the Southern free worker's budget line. The cloth intercept is w^S/p^C, which equals $(p^T/p^C)MPL^T(L^S/A^S)$ by equation (5.4). Since (L^S/A^S) is unchanged, but (p^T/p^C) has fallen (from $0.25/0.10 = 2.5$ to $0.25/0.15 = 1.67$), this intercept shifts inward because of the tariff. The tobacco intercept is w^S/p^T, which equals $MPL^T(L^S/A^S)$ by equation (5.4), and is unchanged by the tariff. Therefore, the Southern worker's budget line pivots inward as a result of the tariff. The analysis of the tobacco farmer's budget line is parallel, yielding the conclusion that all free Southerners are hurt by the tariff.[6]

The conclusion is that some Americans are hurt by the tariff and some benefit, giving rise to the potential for political conflict over trade policy. This is a direct result of specific factors. The pattern of political conflict is very clear: People are aligned *according to which industry they are in.* All owners of specific factors in textile manufacturing, capitalists and workers alike, have an incentive to support the tariff, while all owners of factors specific to tobacco, landowners and free workers alike, have an incentive to fight the tariff. In this case, the geographic pattern of economic activity was such that manufacturing was concentrated in the North and tobacco and related export crops were concentrated in the South. Thus, the specific factors model explains why Northern politicians voted overwhelmingly for the tariff while Southern politicians voted overwhelmingly against it—and why they might be inclined to call it an "abomination."

One important omission in this discussion is the tariff revenue. Under the tariff, every yard of cloth imported yields the government 5¢ of revenue. In the 1820s, this added up to a considerable amount of funds, and the analysis of who benefits and who loses from the tariff could be very much affected by how these funds are used. In practice, the revenues were largely used for infrastructure investments such as road improvements, and the Northern states tended to receive about half of those expenditures, with the South receiving only a fifth (and half as much as the North in per capita terms) (Irwin, 2008). By far the largest recipient of federal funds for infrastructure on a per capita basis was the block of Western states, consisting of Ohio, Michigan, Illinois, Kentucky, and Missouri (they were Western at the time; of course, the meaning of "Western" shifts over time). These were the states that were most in need of good roads to allow them to connect with the world market, and representatives from these states voted for the tariff of 1828 essentially on the understanding that they would receive a big share of the tariff revenues

---

[6] We will assume that the plight of the slaves is unchanged.

for exactly this purpose. In fact, this grand bargain—Western states voting for protection for Northern manufactures in return for funds for infrastructure—had a name: It was the "American system," envisioned by Senator Henry Clay of Kentucky.[7]

5.4 A Constitutional Error, and the Lerner Symmetry Theorem

A corollary emerges from the previous discussion. Suppose that instead of a 50% tax on imports, Congress had imposed a tax on *exports* equal to one-third of the value of exports. Then tobacco farmers selling their crop to foreign purchasers would need to pay $25¢ \div 3 = 8.33¢$ per pound to U.S. Customs, resulting in net revenue to the farmer of only $(25 - 8.33)¢ = 16.67¢$ per pound. This will result in the price of tobacco for all Americans falling to $16.67¢$. To see this analysis more clearly, note that if the price U.S. consumers pay for tobacco did not change, Southern tobacco farmers would prefer to sell only to domestic consumers; but if they all sold only to U.S. consumers, there would be an excess supply of tobacco on the U.S. market, since U.S. consumer demand is not sufficient to absorb U.S. supply. As a result, the price of tobacco would be pushed down for everyone in the United States, until it would come to rest at the value $16.67¢$ per pound. At this point, domestic producers are indifferent between selling domestically and exporting.

Thus, under the export tax, the price of cotton cloth is still $10¢$ per yard, but the price of tobacco, for producers and consumers in the United States, is equal to $16.67¢$. We can use this information to see how the export tax changes the budget line of a Northern worker, a Northern capitalist, a Southern free worker, and a Southern tobacco farmer just as with the tariff. The details are left as an exercise, but it can be verified quickly that the *effect on everyone's budget line is exactly what it was under the tariff.* This is because the value of (p^C/p^T), namely, $(0.10/0.1667) = 0.6$, is exactly what it was under the tariff.

In other words, a 50% import tariff is equivalent to a 33.3% export tax. More generally, for *any* import tariff, there is an export tax that has exactly the same effects. This proposition is known as the *Lerner symmetry theorem*, and it holds in any comparative-advantage model.[8]

In negotiations over drafting the U.S. Constitution in the Constitutional Convention 1787, representatives of the Southern states had insisted that export taxes be banned, and they were. As a result, taxes on exports are—to this day—unconstitutional in the United States. However, those same representatives did not hold such a hard line on tariffs; although they proposed banning tariffs, they finally agreed to a constitution without a tariff ban in return for some other concessions. As we have seen, however, a ban on export taxes without a ban on import tariffs is meaningless.

Evidently, the Southern representatives did not understand the Lerner symmetry theorem. (In fairness, it would be another century and a half before

---

[7] Irwin (2008) has an extensive analysis of this system and the breakdown of this bargain in the 1830s; see especially his Table 3.

[8] An exception occurs when foreign direct investment is added to the model, as shown in Blanchard (2009).

economist Abba P. Lerner (1936) would write it down and prove it.) It is natural to ask: If they had, would there have been a United States of America?

5.5 A Mixed Model

Recall that we have assumed that labor is sector specific along with land and capital. This assumption might be too extreme. Free workers could, after all, move from the North to the South or vice versa if they wanted to badly enough. More to the point, there was a lot of agriculture in the North, so workers there had at least some alternatives if the wages in manufacturing fell. As a result, we will look at a version of the model in which land and capital are still specific, but free labor is mobile across industries.[9] We will call this a *mixed specific-factors model*, and it is also often called a *Ricardo-Viner model*. (Some trade economists call this model "*the* specific-factors model.")

With labor mobile, employers in both sectors must pay the same wage (or else all of the free workers will move to the sector with the higher wage). Thus, rather than keeping track of a wage w^N in the North and w^S in the South, we will have one wage, w, that applies to the whole country. Each Northern manufacturer will hire workers until the marginal value product of labor equals w, and each Southern tobacco farmer will do the same. This results in a total nationwide demand for labor; the wage, w, must then adjust so that this demand is equal in equilibrium to the total nationwide supply of labor. This can be represented in Figure 5.2.

The figure shows labor demand from the cotton textile industry, labor demand from tobacco farming, and total labor supply. Labor demand in cotton textiles is measured from the leftmost axis rightward. The horizontal distance

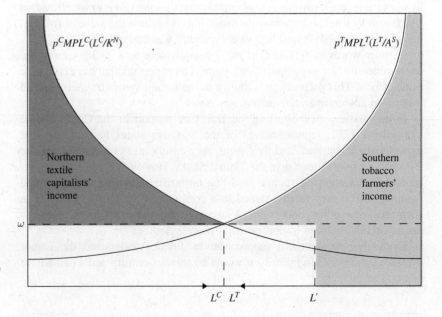

FIGURE 5.2
Equilibrium with the
Mixed Specific-
Factors Model.

---

[9] Readers who want to learn about this model in greater depth can turn to the pioneering paper: Jones (1971).

from the leftmost axis is the quantity of labor employed in cotton textiles, and for each quantity of labor the height of the downward-sloping curve extending from that axis is the marginal value product of labor in cotton textiles. Thus, for any value of w, the number of workers demanded by the cotton textile manufacturers is equal to the horizontal component of the point on that curve with height w. Labor demand in tobacco is measured from the rightmost axis *leftward*. The horizontal distance from the rightmost axis is the total quantity of labor employed in tobacco, and for each quantity of labor the height of the upward-sloping curve extending from that axis is the marginal value product of labor in tobacco. (It is the mirror-image of how we would usually draw the demand curve for labor in the tobacco sector, and that is why it slopes upward. The marginal product of labor in tobacco falls as we increase labor used in tobacco—in other words, as we move leftward in the diagram.) Thus, for any value of w, the total number of workers demanded by the tobacco farmers is equal to the horizontal component of the point on that curve with height w.

Therefore, we can find the total demand for workers in the economy for any given value of w as the sum of the quantities given by these two curves. Note that the box has been drawn with a length equal to the total amount of labor in the economy, L. (This distance includes both free labor and the labor that is coerced, which is labeled L' as before.) Therefore, the equilibrium wage is the value of w such that demand for labor in the two sectors adds up to the length of the box. In other words, the equilibrium point is the intersection of these two curves. This intersection shows the equilibrium allocation of labor to cotton textiles, L^C, the equilibrium total allocation of labor to tobacco, L^T, and the equilibrium wage, w.

Recall that the area under the marginal product of labor curve up to the employment point is equal to the amount produced. As a result, the area under the marginal *value* product of labor curve for cotton textiles up to L^C is equal to $p^C Q^C$, the total value of cloth produced by the cotton textile industry. Subtract from that the payments made to workers in that industry, wL^C, and the result is the net income to owners of capital in the cotton textile industry, represented by the shaded region under the cotton textile marginal value product of labor curve in Figure 5.2. Similarly, the shaded region under the tobacco marginal value product of labor curve is the net income to the tobacco farmers. (The difference in this case is that some portion of their labor is obtained at a zero wage because it is coerced; thus the payments to labor in tobacco are equal to $w(L^T - L)$ instead of wL^T. For this reason the shape of the shaded region for tobacco is different from the shape of the shaded region for cloth.)

How is all of this changed by the tariff? Recall that the tariff raises the domestic price of cloth by 50%, from 10¢ a yard to 15¢ a yard, and it shifts the value marginal product of labor curve for cloth up by 50% everywhere, as shown in Figure 5.3. This shift implies an increase in the labor allocated to cloth and a reduction in the labor allocated to tobacco because the new equilibrium (at point C) is farther to the right than the original equilibrium (at point A). Therefore, the tariff has increased production of cotton cloth and reduced production of tobacco.

The new equilibrium also implies an increase in the wage—at least in nominal terms. The new equilibrium wage is denoted w'. It is important to observe that the increase in the wage is less than 50%—less than the tariff and less than the proportional rise in the price of cloth. We can see this because a

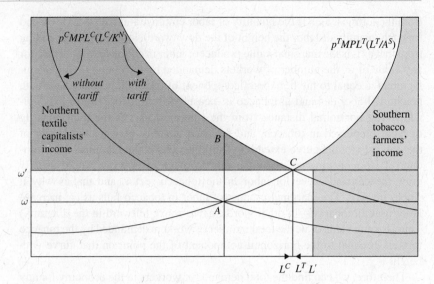

FIGURE 5.3
Effect of the Tariff.

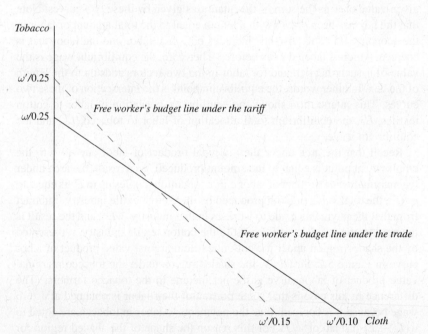

FIGURE 5.4
The Effect of the Tariff on Workers' Budget Lines.

50% increase in the wage would move it up from point A in the figure to point B, but point B is not the equilibrium; the equilibrium, C, is down and to the right along the cloth labor demand curve compared to B. Therefore, the increase in the wage is less, proportionally, than the increase in the price of cloth.

This conclusion is important because it affects how workers' budget lines are changed by the tariff. Figure 5.4 shows a typical free worker's budget line before and after the tariff. The solid line shows the budget line under free trade, and the broken line shows the budget line as it is affected by the tariff. The price of tobacco has not changed, so the tobacco intercept w'/p^T under the tariff is greater than the tobacco intercept w/p^T under free trade. On the other hand, the (domestic U.S.) price of cotton cloth *has* gone up by 50%, while the wage has gone up by *less than* 50%, so the cotton cloth intercept w'/p^C under

the tariff is *smaller* than the cotton cloth intercept w/p^C under free trade.[10]
Therefore, the tariff-affected budget line and the free-trade budget line cross
each other, and it is possible that free workers have either higher or lower utility
as a result of the tariff. The more important clothing is in their consumption
bundle, the more likely it is that they are worse off. The more important tobacco
is in their consumption bundle, the more likely it is that they are better off.

One thing that we do know about the effect of the tariff on the wage is that
whatever the effect is, positive or negative, it is shared by *all* free workers, no
matter where they live and no matter what sector of the economy they work in.
This is because the mobility of workers across sectors means that all workers
will earn the same wage, both before and after imposition of the tariff.

Now consider the welfare of the specific-factor owners. From Figure 5.3,
we can see that the upper boundary of the area representing the income of
Northern capital owners has shifted up (by 50%), and the lower boundary has
also shifted up (by less than 50%). If both boundaries had shifted up by 50%,
then the area would have increased by 50%, and the capitalists' income would
have risen by 50%. However, since the lower bound has shifted up by less than
that, the whole area has increased by *more* than 50%. Therefore, if we denote
the income of those Northern capitalists by $r^N K^N$, we find that $r^N K^N/p^C$ has
increased (since the numerator has increased by more than 50% but the
denominator has increased by only 50%). Of course, since p^T has not changed,
$r^N K^N/p^T$ has also gone up. Therefore, the budget line of a typical Northern
capitalist has shifted outward, as shown in Figure 5.5.

Similarly, Figure 5.3 also shows the effect of the tariff on Southern tobacco
farmers. The increase in the wage shrinks the area that represents their income,

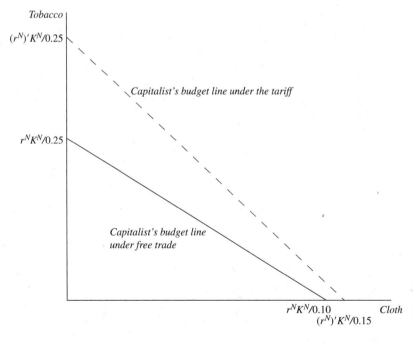

FIGURE 5.5
The Effect of the Tariff
on the Budget Line of a
Northern Capitalist.

---

[10] Another way to look at this is to recall that $w = p^C MPL^C(L^C/K^C)$; since L^C has gone up, we know
that $MPL^C(L^C/K^C)$ has gone down. Therefore, w/p^C has gone down as well.

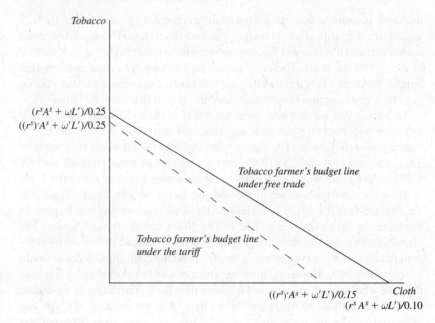

FIGURE 5.6
The Effect of the
Tariff on the Budget
Line of a Southern
Tobacco Farmer.

so that $r^S A^S + wL'$ falls. As a result, since the price of cloth has gone up while the price of tobacco is unchanged, the tobacco farmers' incomes have fallen in terms of both goods, so that their budget line shifts in, as indicated in Figure 5.6.

In summary: (i) Owners of factors specific to the export sector (such as tobacco land) are unambiguously hurt by the tariff. (ii) Owners of factors specific to the import-competing sector (such as capital in the textile industry) unambiguously benefit from the tariff. (iii) Owners of factors that are mobile across industries (such as free labor in this model) may be helped or hurt by the tariff—but whether they are helped or hurt does not depend on the industry in which they happen to be located.

Thus, we can still explain the basic politics of the tariff of 1828 with a mixed specific-factors model, with Southern landowners opposing the tariff and Northern capitalists supporting it. The major change is in the incentives of free workers to present a united front, either for or against, rather than identifying with their region.

The two models present stark assumptions for labor mobility, with reality likely somewhere in between. For example, the pure specific-factors model implies that there will be no supply response to the tariff; the quantities of cloth and tobacco produced are fixed by the supplies of factors specific to the sectors and will not change in response to the tariff. However, historians generally believe that cotton textiles output increased a great deal as a result of the tariff (see Zevin, 1971, for an extensive analysis). Thus, the pure specific-factors model is not consistent with the data. On the other hand, perfect mobility is not realistic either. Research by Artuç, Chaudhuri, and McLaren (2010) has provided evidence of quite large costs faced by workers in the modern U.S. economy when they switch industries, making large and persistent differentials in wages possible, and there is no reason to think that this was not also the case in the nineteenth century. The most realistic model would allow for costly, imperfect labor mobility across industries, which is more complicated and less elegant than the models presented in this chapter.

5.6 Specific Factors in Trade More Generally

So far in this chapter, we have explored specific-factors models only for their implications for the effects of trade on income distribution (and therefore for political conflict). However, they can be used to look at trade more generally. Here, we complete the model by introducing a second country, called Europe, with which the U.S. economy developed in this chapter can trade. We will see that the basic principles of comparative advantage and the gains from trade work in this model just as in the Ricardian model of Chapter 2.

We will use the mixed-specific-factors model of Section 5.5 but will drop the assumption that the United States is a small economy. To make the example as simple as possible, assume that Europe is just the same as the United States in every way, including the amount of land, labor, and capital and the technology of production, except that Europe's land is not as suitable for growing tobacco as the land in the United States. Consequently, for any given allocation of labor between the two sectors, the marginal product of labor in tobacco growing will be lower in Europe than in the United States. This assumption will ensure that the United States has a comparative advantage in tobacco and that Europe has a comparative advantage in cloth, as is illustrated in Figure 5.7, which shows the labor-allocation box corresponding to Figure 5.2 for both countries simultaneously. The figure shows the marginal value product of labor in cloth in each country as a function of the labor L^C and capital K^C used in the sector; this curve is the same for both countries. It also shows the marginal value product of labor in tobacco as a function of the labor L^T and land A^T used in the sector, but the curve for the United States is drawn in black and lies everywhere above the curve for Europe, which is drawn in blue. The allocation of labor is shown as point A for the United States and point B for Europe, with wages respectively equal to w^{US} and w^E; for given product prices, the United States allocates more labor to tobacco and less to cloth than does Europe.

The equilibrium condition for the allocation of labor within each country is:

$$p^C MPL^C(L^C/K^C) = p^T MPL^T(L^T/A^T). \qquad (5.6)$$

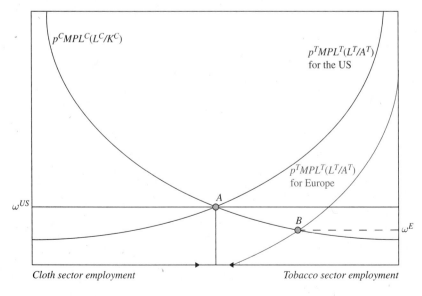

FIGURE 5.7
The Labor Market in the U.S. and Europe.

Recall that in each country the total capital for cloth making, K^C, and total land for tobacco, A^T, are given, so equation (5.6) merely governs the division of labor between the two industries. The allocation of labor that satisfies this for any given value of p^C and p^T will continue to satisfy it if we double p^C and p^T, so the allocation of labor depends only on the ratio of the two prices, p^C/P^T, and not on their absolute level. As a result, we can write the labor input for tobacco in each country as a function of the relative price of cloth, p^C/P^T. A rise in p^C holding P^T constant will shift the demand for labor in cloth upward, reallo-cating labor from tobacco to cloth and increasing the amount of cloth produced, Q^C, as it reduces the amount of tobacco produced, Q^T. Consequently, a rise in p^C/p^T raises the quantity of cloth produced divided by the quantity of tobacco produced—the relative supply of cloth. Therefore, each country's relative supply curve for cloth is upward sloping, as depicted in Figure 5.8, in which the vertical axis measures the relative price of cotton and the horizontal axis measures the relative quantity of cotton. The relative supply curve for the United States is labeled RS^{US}, and the curve for Europe is marked RS^E.

By assumption, the labor-demand curves for manufacturing for both countries are identical, but the labor-demand curve for manufacturing for the United States lies above that for Europe. As a result, for any given product prices, more labor will be allocated to tobacco in the United States, and so more tobacco and less cloth will be produced in the United States than in Europe, resulting in a greater relative supply of cloth in Europe than in the United States. This is why RS^E is drawn to the right of RS^{US}.

Assume that the relative demand for cotton is the same for all consumers in either country and is depicted as RD in Figure 5.8. We can put this together with the relative supply curves for the two countries to find the autarky prices for each country. (Recall from Chapter 2 that autarky is a hypothetical condition in which no trade is possible.) The relative prices are marked as P^{US} and P^E for the United States and Europe, respectively. Note that $P^E < P^{US}$, which makes sense because the European economy is very poor at producing tobacco. Thus, in autarky tobacco is very expensive in Europe relative to cloth (which is the same thing as saying that cloth in Europe is very cheap relative to tobacco).

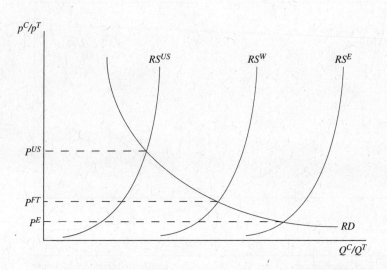

FIGURE 5.8
Relative Supply,
Relative Demand,
and Equilibrium.

Now, what happens when we open up trade? Assume that neither country uses any tariffs or other trade impediments, and that there are no transport costs. As with the model in Chapter 2, for any given relative price we can put together the quantities of cloth produced in both countries and divide that sum by the total quantity of tobacco produced by both countries to obtain the *world* relative supply curve, marked in Figure 5.8 as RS^W. The world relative supply curve lies, as always, between the two country relative supply curves. Putting this world relative supply curve together with the relative demand curve provides the free-trade equilibrium, with price indicated as P^{FT}. This relative price lies between the two autarkic prices, so trade raises the relative price of cloth for Europe and lowers the relative price of cloth for the United States. Note that at the free-trade price P^{FT}, Europe's relative supply of cloth is greater than its relative demand, implying that it exports cloth and imports tobacco, while the reverse is true for the United States. Thus, just as in the Ricardian model, trade lowers the relative price of each country's imported good and raises the price of each country's export good.

We can examine the effect of trade on each country's aggregate welfare with the help of Figure 5.9, which shows the production possibilities frontier (PPF) for Europe. In autarky, Europe produces at point A, where the slope of the PPF is equal to minus 1 times the autarkic relative price of cloth in Europe, $-P^E$. Imagine for the sake of argument that Europe is made up of millions of individuals, each one of whom is a worker but also owns some capital and some land, and suppose that all Europeans own exactly the same amount of each of these resources. Then each European will have the same consumption, and we can speak of a "typical" citizen of Europe. In that case, the typical European's budget line under autarky will look like the solid black line in Figure 5.9 (scaled up by the size of the population). It is a straight line with a slope equal to minus 1 times the relative price of cloth, or $-P^E$, that passes through the economy's autarkic production point (because the value of Europe's consumption must be equal to the value of Europe's production). This budget line must also be tangent to the consumption point. Since under autarky each country consumes what it produces, A is also the

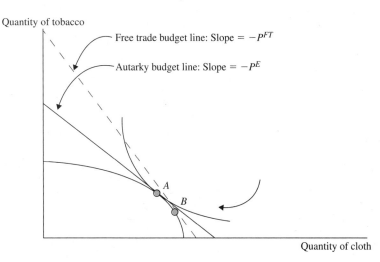

Quantity of tobacco

Free trade budget line: Slope $= -P^{FT}$

Autarky budget line: Slope $= -P^E$

A

B

Quantity of cloth

FIGURE 5.9
The Gains from Trade in
Europe.

consumption point, so an indifference curve is tangent to the budget line at point *A*.

Now, when trade is opened up, the relative price of cloth seen by Europeans rises to P^{FT}, and the production point moves to *B*, with more cloth and less tobacco produced than under autarky. As a result, the typical European's budget line changes to the broken blue line, with a slope equal to the new relative price of cloth and passing through the new production point. It is clear that the new budget line passes strictly above the autarky consumption point *A*, making possible a range of consumption possibilities on an indifference curve above the autarky indifference curve. Therefore, Europeans attain higher utility with trade than without.

We conclude that, just as in the simple Ricardian model of Chapter 2, we have gains from trade in this specific-factors model. However, if we drop the egalitarian assumption that each European owns the same bundle of resources and adopt the more realistic assumption that each European is either a worker, a landowner, or a capital owner, then it is no longer the case that each individual European will benefit from trade. Rather, the analysis of Section 5.5 shows that each capital owner will benefit (as the owner of the factor specific to the export sector); each landowner will be hurt (as the owner of the factor specific to the import-competing sector); and workers could go either way. What the gains-from-trade finding of Figure 5.9 shows is that *even though some individuals are hurt by trade, the gains to those who benefit are large enough that the winners could compensate the losers, making everyone better off*. There are enough gains to spread around so that trade could, in principle, be Pareto-improving.

The analysis for the United States is parallel and is shown in Figure 5.10. The autarky production point is shown on the U.S. PPF as point *C*. Trade leads the U.S. economy to produce more tobacco and less cloth, at point *D*. The autarky budget line is shown as a solid black line, tangent to an indifference curve at point *C*. The new budget line after trade is opened is broken blue and clearly passes above point *C*, making possible consumption choices on a higher indifference curve. As in Europe, trade leads to aggregate gains

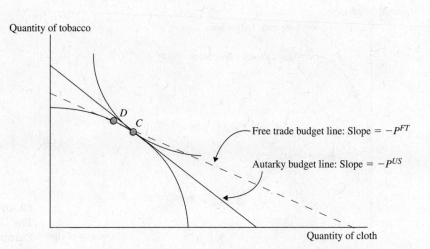

FIGURE 5.10
The Gains from Trade
in the U.S.

from trade, which implies that the winners from trade would be able to compensate the losers and still be better off.

Thus, in this model, although it is much richer and more complex than the Ricardian model, a number of the main findings from the Ricardian model still hold true. Each country exports the good that was relatively cheap in that country under autarky; the relative price of the export good in each country rises as a result of trade; and the relative price of the import good in each country falls as a result of trade. Furthermore, each country gains from trade in the aggregate. However, there are important differences introduced by specific factors. Unlike in a Ricardian model, even in trade there is no reason to expect either country to specialize completely (in other words, ordinarily both countries produce both goods), and there will be some individuals in each country who will be made worse off due to trade if there is no compensation.

It should be mentioned that the idea of autarky in the early-nineteenth-century U.S. economy is not a mere thought experiment: It actually was experienced, in the years 1807–1809. When the British Navy boarded U.S. merchant vessels bound for France while Britain and France were at war, President Thomas Jefferson protested by cutting off all trade with Britain and all its colonies. Since at the time almost all U.S. trade was with Britain and British colonies, this action plunged the U.S. economy into a state closely approximating autarky, which lasted for a year and a half. As the model we have examined here would predict, the prices of exports such as tobacco (as well as cotton, flour, and rice) fell relative to the prices of imported goods. By the end of the autarky episode, the drop in domestic relative prices of exports reached more than 60%. Irwin (2005) estimates that the loss of trade reduced real GNP by 4 to 6%, and notes that contemporary accounts blamed the loss of trade for "paralysis," "depression," and "severe distress." Clearly, this implies that the gains from trade were substantial.

(Fortunately, Mr. Jefferson had other accomplishments.)

MAIN IDEAS

1. A specific factor is a factor of production that cannot be reallocated from one industry to another. A model in which some or all factors of production are specific is called a specific-factors model.

2. Generally, the real income earned by factors specific to an export sector increases with trade liberalization, and the real income earned by factors specific to an import-competing sector is reduced by trade liberalization.

3. Factors of production that are not specific, but are freely mobile across sectors, can be made better off or worse off by trade liberalization.

For example, workers in a Ricardo-Viner model are assumed to be perfectly mobile across industries, and they benefit from trade liberalization if they consume a lot of the import-competing good, but they are worse off if they consume a lot of the export good. The one thing we know is that *all* workers in that model, regardless of what industry they work in, will have the *same* experience of trade liberalization.

4. In general equilibrium, the effects of an import tariff can be replicated by a tariff on exports. This is called the Lerner symmetry theorem.

WHERE WE ARE

We have introduced specific factors to comparative-advantage models.

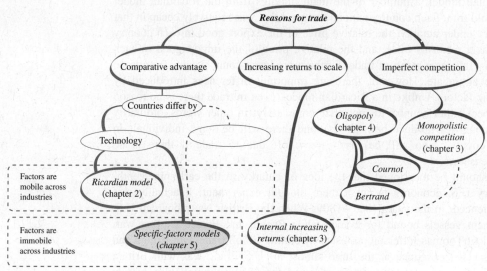

The Family Tree of Trade Models.

QUESTIONS AND PROBLEMS

1. Identify an occupation that requires sector-specific skills and another whose skills are not sector-specific. For each, explain your reasoning. Do these differences in the mobility of skills change the way workers in both occupations are likely to be affected by a reduction in tariffs?

2. Consider the following thought experiment regarding foreign direct investment and specific factors.

   (a) In the pure specific-factors model in the text, suppose that a wave of foreign direct investment suddenly increases the availability of capital in the cotton cloth sector. How would that affect the distribution of income in the United States? Specifically, what would it do to the real incomes of U.-S. workers and capitalists in the cotton cloth industry, and workers and farmers in the tobacco sector? How would it affect the distribution of income between workers in the North and in the South?

   (b) Now, answer the same question for the mixed specific-factors model, explaining the reason for any differences from the answer in (a).

3. Suppose that we have data on wages for workers in hundreds of Brazilian industries at two dates. We also have data on each industry's import tariff at each date. Suppose that tariffs change between the two dates for a number of industries, and this is the only exogenous change in the economy during those two dates. We plot the data on a scatterplot, with the change in industry tariff on the horizontal axis and the change in industry wage on the vertical axis. (In other words, each dot of the scatterplot shows, for one Brazilian industry, the change in tariff and the change in average industry wage.)

   (a) Suppose that the Brazilian economy is a pure specific-factors economy, such as the one in Section 5.2. What will the scatterplot look like? Sketch an example and describe its key features in words, explaining the economic reasoning.

   (b) Now, suppose the Brazilian economy is a mixed specific-factors, or Ricardo-Viner, model, such as the one in Section 5.5. Answer the same question, explaining the reason for any differences from the answers in part (a).

4. Consider an economy that produces tea and rice. Each requires a different type of land, so the flat, low-lying flood land used for rice is a factor

specific to rice and the hilly land used for tea is specific to tea. However, labor can move freely between the two sectors, so that the wage paid to labor in both sectors is the same. Suppose the marginal product of labor in the tea sector is given by $120 - L^T$, where L^T is the number of workers in the tea sector, and the marginal product of labor in the rice sector is given by $120 - L^R$, where L^R is the number of workers in the rice sector. Suppose that there are 120 workers, 100 rice farmers, and 100 tea growers in the economy. Assume that the economy is a net importer of rice.

(a) If the world price of tea and the world price of rice are both $1 per unit, and if the country has a free-trade policy so that the domestic price of each good is equal to the world price, find the equilibrium allocation of labor to each sector, the quantity of each good produced in this economy, and the wage.

(b) Now, suppose the government imposes a 100% *ad valorem* tariff on rice imports, doubling its domestic price to $2. Repeat the analysis of part (a).

(c) Derive budget lines for workers, rice farmers, and tea growers, before and after the tariff. Disregarding tariff revenue, who benefits from the tariff? Who is hurt? Is there any group for which you cannot tell?

(d) Suppose we added one more piece of information: All consumers in this economy have Leontieff preferences, so that they always consume 4 units of rice for every unit of tea that they drink. Does that change your answer to (c)?

5. In the model of question 44, suppose that instead of an import tariff, the government had imposed a 50% tax on exports of tea. Repeat the analysis. How do the outcomes compare with the case of the tariff?

REFERENCES

Artuç, Erhan, Shubham Chaudhuri, and John McLaren (2010). "Trade Shocks and Labor Adjustment: A Structural Empirical Approach." *American Economic Review* 100:3 (June), pp. 1008–1045.

Blanchard, Emily J. (2009). "Trade Taxes and International Investment." *Canadian Journal of Economics*, 42:3, pp. 882–899 forth coming.

Dublin, Thomas (1981). *Women at Work: The Transformation of Work and Community in Lowell, Massachusetts, 1826–1860.* New York: Columbia University Press.

Grossman, Gene M., and Helpman, Elhanan (1994). "Protection for Sale." *American Economic Review* 84:4, pp. 833–850.

Irwin, Douglas A. (2003). "New Estimates of the Average Tariff of the United States, 1790–1820." *The Journal of Economic History*, Vol. 63:, No. 2 (June 2003), pp. 506–513.

_____ (2005). "The Welfare Cost of Autarky: Evidence from the Jeffersonian Trade Embargo, 1807–1809." *Review of International Economics* 13 (September), pp. 631–645.

_____ (2008). "Antebellum Tariff Politics: Coalition Formation and Shifting Regional Interests." *Journal of Law and Economics* (November), pp. 715–742.

Jones, Ronald I. (1971). "A Three-Factor Model in Theory, Trade, and History," in J.N. Bhagwati, R.W. Jones, R.A.

Mundell, and J. Vanek (eds.), *Trade, Payments and Welfare, Papers in Economics in Honor of Charles P. Kindleberger.* Amsterdam: North-Holland.

Kovak, Brian K. (2011). "Local Labor Market Effects of Trade Policy: Evidence from Brazilian Liberalization." Working Paper, Carnegie Mellon University.

Lerner, A. P. (1936). "The Symmetry between Import and Export Taxes." *Economica* (New Series), 3:11, pp. 306–313.

Norris, James D. (1962). "One-Price Policy among Antebellum Country Stores." *The Business History Review*, 36:4. (Winter), pp. 455–458.

Scruggs, Mike (2005). *The Un-Civil War: Truths Your Teacher Never Told You.* Asheville, NC: Published by the *Asheville Tribune.*

Taussig, F. W. (1888). "The Early Protective Movement and the Tariff of 1828." *Political Science Quarterly*, 3:1 (March), pp. 17–45.

_____ (1914). *The Tariff History of the United States* (6th ed.). New York: G.W. Putnam's Sons.

Zevin, Robert Brooke (1971). "The Growth of Cotton Textile Production Aafter 1815," in R. W. Fogel and S. L. Engerman, (eds.), *The Reinterpretation of American Economic History* (New York, 1971), pp. 122–124.

6

Is Free Trade a Rip-off for American Workers?

Lynn Johnson/National Geographic/Getty Images, Inc.

An American steel worker in Pittsburgh, PA. The U.S. steel industry has been battered by intense foreign competition for a quarter century.

6.1 The Charges

Consider the following three facts on the experience of U.S. workers, which are often used as a bill of indictment against globalization.

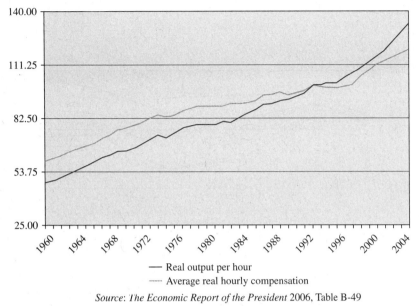

FIGURE 6.1
Output per Hour
and Real Hourly
Compensation.

— Real output per hour
---- Average real hourly compensation

Source: The Economic Report of the President 2006, Table B-49

FACT 1. Despite sharply rising productivity per head—and unlike what has happened in the past—real wages and real compensation have stagnated for the last 30 years.

Historically, U.S. wages have approximately kept pace with labor productivity, allowing for steady increases in living standards for workers generation after generation. However, for some reason this process appears to have become stuck sometime after the 1970s. Figure 6.1 illustrates this stagnation by plotting real hourly compensation for U.S. workers against real output per worker over several decades. "Compensation" includes not only wages and salaries but also employer contributions to pensions and health insurance. Notice that up to the 1970s the two plots are parallel, but after that compensation slows down considerably even as productivity marches on.

FACT 2. Inequality in wages has increased substantially since the 1970s.

Consider Figure 6.2, which shows the evolution of the distribution of real wages for U.S. men[1] since 1970 by deciles, labelled 10 for the first decile through 90 for the top decile and normalized so that all variables take a value of 100 in 1973. The median (50th percentile) wage takes approximately the same value at the end of the data that it did 32 years earlier.[2] At the same time, the wages at the high end of the distribution have increased significantly, and the wages at the low end have fallen significantly. For example, the 90th percentile wage has increased by about 30%, while the 20th percentile wage has dropped by about 8%. Half of the workforce has actually lost ground.

FACT 3. The U.S. economy has become much more integrated with the world economy since the 1970s.

---

[1] Women's wages show a somewhat more optimistic picture, but analysis of women's wages is more complicated since they are likely affected by the huge changes in labor force participation and educational attainment for women during this period.

[2] This figure does not include benefits such as health care premiums paid by employers, but including them does not change the story much. See, for example, Mishel, Bernstein, and Allegretto (2007), Figure 3N.

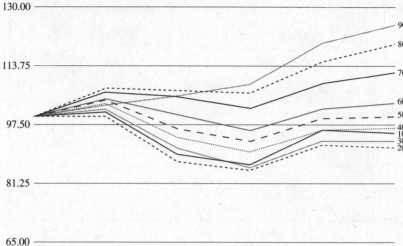

FIGURE 6.2
Male Wage Growth
by Percentile,
1973–2005.

Constructed from Table 3.6 and Figure 3D of Mishel, Bernstein, and Allegretto (2007),
The State of Working America 2006/2007.

This fact, of course, was observed and documented in Chapter 1, as part of the second wave of globalization.

If we put these facts together, we observe that wages started lagging behind productivity, and low-end wages began to slide backward, at around the same time as the wave of globalization hit. It is natural to ask: Are these phenomena related? In particular, did globalization *cause* the stagnation in wages and the backward slide in incomes of low wage workers? Many observers answer in the affirmative—an answer that is full of implications for policy.[3]

Causation is very difficult to prove in economics. Once again, a *post-hoc* argument needs to be used with care, as it is possible that both the globalization and the labor market problems were caused by different factors, or by a common factor, as opposed to the former causing the latter. But trade economists have identified a tool that may be useful in determining the lines of causation in this case: a theoretical setup known as the Heckscher-Ohlin model. This is probably the simplest model that predicts the sort of labor-market problems we have been discussing as a result of globalization. We will examine that model and then identify telltale signs that, if seen in the data, would be evidence that the mechanisms of the model are at work, generating the labor-market paradoxes in question. Finally, we will turn to the data to see if those telltale signs can be observed. This chain of logic allows us to come to a judgment as to whether or not globalization is the culprit.[4]

---

[3] This argument is used often in political discourse; for example, President Obama, in an interview with the *Washington Post* editorial board on January 15, 2009, argued that globalization is one reason that "wages and incomes have flatlined" (transcript available on www.washingtonpost.com).

[4] The Heckscher-Ohlin model is actually much older than this debate about trade and wages, but this is a good use for it. For more on the model and its various empirical applications, see Feenstra (2004, pp. 4–29 and Chapters 2 and 3).

6.2 The Model with Fixed Coefficients

The Heckscher-Ohlin model is a type of comparative-advantage model and therefore is a theory of trade based on differences between countries. The particular differences it focuses on are differences in relative factor endowments: land per worker, capital per acre of land, and so on. Here, to see the basic logic of the model, we will examine a two-country, two-good, two-factor version of the model. Suppose, for concreteness, that the world is made up of two countries, the United States and China; that the only two goods to be produced and consumed are apparel (A) and plastics (P); and that the two factors required to produce these goods are skilled labor (L^S) and unskilled labor (L^U), which we will interpret as roughly meaning workers with and without a college degree.[5] The terms *skilled* and *unskilled* are somewhat misleading, since there are so many ways to learn a skill aside from college; *blue collar* and *white collar* could be used as less loaded terms, but we will use the terms that are traditional in this research area. Importantly, we will assume that both kinds of labor are perfectly mobile across industries (there are no specific factors), so that there is one unskilled wage and one skilled wage for the whole economy. All owners and employers of factors and all consumers take prices as given.

The two kinds of labor combine to produce the two outputs with constant-returns-to-scale production functions. We will consider two different assumptions on this. First, we will assume fixed-coefficients production functions (or Leontieff technology) because the model is simplest to analyze with this type of technology. Then it will be easy to analyze the case of general technology with variable proportions.

To have a concrete example, suppose that to produce one unit of apparel in either country requires 1 unit of skilled labor and 2 units of unskilled labor. At the same time, to produce one unit of plastics requires 3 units of skilled and 3 units of unskilled labor. These coefficients are the same for both countries, and no other factors of production are required. (Since generally between two-thirds and three-quarters of GDP goes to labor costs, that may not be too terrible an approximation for our purposes.)

Note that the unskilled-labor-to-skilled-labor ratio in the apparel sector will always be greater than that in the plastics sector (the ratio is 2 and 1, respectively, in the two industries). We say that apparel is *unskilled-labor intensive*, and plastics are *skilled-labor intensive*. Note that these are relative terms: One unit of plastics output requires more unskilled labor than one unit of apparel, but it is still not unskilled-labor intensive because of its low *ratio* of unskilled to skilled workers used.

Suppose that the U.S. economy has 72 million unskilled and 60 million skilled workers, and that China has 540 million unskilled and 300 million skilled workers. Since the skilled-labor-to-unskilled-labor ratio is higher in the U.S. than in the Chinese economy, we will say that the United States is *skilled-labor abundant* relative to China, and *unskilled-labor scarce*. Similarly, China is unskilled-labor abundant and skilled-labor scarce. Note that these are relative terms; in this example, China has far more skilled labor than the United

---

[5] We will be using this as an illustrative model, but the two goods have been chosen because apparel is a major Chinese export to the United States, and plastics are the largest manufactured U.S. export to China.

States, but is still skilled-labor scarce because it has a low *ratio* of skilled to unskilled workers.

First, we will discuss how factor markets work in this model, and then we will analyze goods markets.

6.3 Supply, Demand, and Equilibrium

Focus first on the U.S. economy. In order for the factor markets to be in equilibrium, it is necessary that the demand for each type of labor be equal to its supply. For unskilled labor, this means:

$$2Q^A + 3Q^P = 72 \text{ million}, \tag{6.1}$$

where Q^A denotes the amount of apparel produced and Q^P denotes the amount of plastics produced. We can call this equation the *unskilled-labor resource constraint*. The amount of unskilled labor demanded by the apparel sector is equal to $2Q^A$, and the amount demanded by the plastics sector is equal to $3Q^P$. The right-hand side of the equation is the total supply of unskilled labor available. Similarly, for skilled labor the equilibrium condition is:

$$Q^A + 3Q^P = 60 \text{ million}. \tag{6.2}$$

This is the *skilled-labor resource constraint*. Putting these together provides us with two linear equations in two unknowns, Q^A and Q^P. Solving yields:

$$Q^A = 12 \text{ million}$$

$$Q^P = 16 \text{ million}.$$

This is the only output pair consistent with full employment of both factors in the U.S. economy and is therefore the supply produced by the U.S. economy. Figure 6.3, which measures the quantities of the two industries' output on the

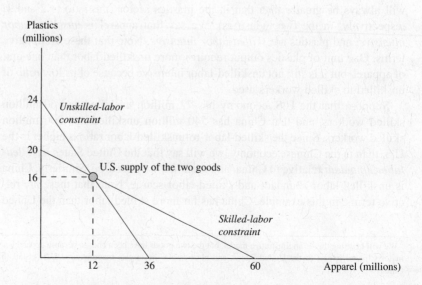

FIGURE 6.3
Production in the U.S. Economy.

two axes, shows the two constraints and their unique solution. The steeper straight line shows the unskilled-labor resource constraint (6.1), and the flatter one shows the skilled-labor resource constraint (6.2). The output point is the intersection of the two. Notice that the relative supply of apparel produced by the U.S. economy is equal to:

$$Q^A/Q^P = 0.75$$

regardless of the output prices. Therefore, if we draw the U.S. relative supply curve in a diagram with the relative price on the vertical axis and relative quantities on the horizontal axis, the result is a *vertical* line, as shown in Figure 6.4.

Note two more points about supply. First, if we were to double the amount of both skilled and unskilled labor, then the output of both goods would double and relative supply would be unchanged. (In other words, if we double the right-hand sides of (6.1) and (6.2) and also double Q^A and Q^P in the left-hand side, the equations will still be satisfied.) Therefore, the absolute level of L^S and L^U does not matter for relative supply, only their ratio, and so we can write the relative supply as a function of L^U/L^S.

Second, what would happen if we increased the endowment of unskilled labor without changing the supply of skilled labor? That would shift the unskilled-labor resource constraint line out, as shown in Figure 6.5, which implies an increase in apparel output and a *decrease* in plastics output. (The broken blue line indicates the unskilled labor constraint after the endowment of unskilled labor has been increased.) The latter effect might be surprising— adding another resource to the economy, of a type used to make plastics as well as apparel, might be expected to increase the output of both goods. The drop in plastics output results from the fact that any increase in apparel output requires the transfer of some skilled labor from plastics to apparel to work with the new unskilled labor. Given the fixed-proportions technology, this implies a reduction in plastics output. This observation applies to all Heckscher-Ohlin models and is known as *the Rybczynski theorem*. More generally, the Rybczynski theorem says that (holding output prices constant) an *increase in the supply of one factor will increase the output of the good that is intensive in that factor, and a reduction in the output of the other good.*

These two points imply that the relative supply of apparel is an *increasing* function of L^U/L^S. As a result, China, with a higher unskilled/skilled ratio,

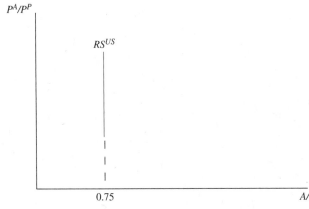

FIGURE 6.4 The U.S. Relative Supply Curve.

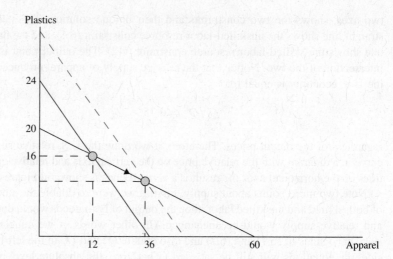

FIGURE 6.5
The Effect of a Change
in Factor Supplies.

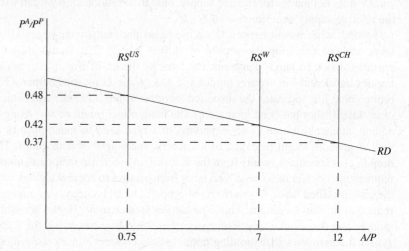

FIGURE 6.6
Relative Supply, Relative
Demand, and Equilibrium.

should also have a higher relative supply of apparel. Working out the analogue to equations (6.1) and (6.2) with 540 million unskilled workers and 300 million skilled workers on the right-hand sides, respectively, we find that China produces 240 million units of apparel and 20 million units of plastics, for a relative supply of 12. Both countries' relative supply curves are shown in Figure 6.6, marked RS^{US} and RS^{CH}, respectively. (Note that they are both vertical because they do not respond to price changes, and China's relative supply lies to the right of the American relative supply because of the Rybczyinski theorem.)

If we assume that all consumers in both countries have the same relative demand curve, we can then solve for autarky equilibrium in both countries. To complete our example, suppose that the relative demand curve is the line marked as RD in the figure, and the autarky relative prices of apparel for the United States and China are given by 0.48 and 0.37, respectively.[6]

---

[6] To be really complete, we would derive the relative demand curve from consumers' utility functions, but we will avoid that complication here because it is not essential to the main argument. In this illustrative example, the relative demand curve is given by the equation $RD = 49 - 100(P^A/P^P)$.

All that is needed to compute the free-trade equilibrium is the *world* relative supply curve, and that can be obtained readily from the individual countries' supplies. World supply of apparel is $(12 + 240)$ million, and world supply of plastics is $(16 + 20)$ million, so world relative supply of apparel is $252/36$, or 7. This is also depicted in Figure 6.6 as RS^W, along with its equilibrium relative price of 0.42. Trade raises the relative price of apparel in China (from its autarky value of 0.37 to its free-trade value of 0.42), but lowers the relative price of apparel in the United States (from its autarky value of 0.48 to its free-trade value of 0.42). This is understandable because the United States is the unskilled-labor-scarce country, and so the unskilled-labor-intensive good, apparel, is expensive there compared to the unskilled-labor-abundant country, until trade equalizes prices across the two countries.

Note that at the free-trade equilibrium, China's relative supply of apparel (12) exceeds its relative demand for apparel (7), so it exports apparel and imports plastics. The United States' relative demand for apparel (7) exceeds its relative supply (0.75), so it imports apparel and exports plastics.

One way to summarize this outcome is that *each country exports the good that is intensive in the factor in which it is abundant*. The United States is abundant in skilled labor, and it exports plastics, which are intensive in skilled labor. China is abundant in unskilled labor and exports apparel, which is intensive in unskilled labor. This feature of the trade equilibrium is a general feature of Heckscher-Ohlin models and is in fact called *the Heckscher-Ohlin theorem*.

6.4 Trade and the Distribution of Income

The important question is what all of this does to people's real incomes.

First, what happens to *aggregate* income? Consider the following thought experiment. Suppose income in the United States is shared on an egalitarian basis; people take their hard-earned wages and put them into a pot and divide them up. In that case, everyone has the same budget line and everyone chooses the same consumption. Slightly less fancifully, we could imagine that every household is made up of some skilled and some unskilled workers, in the same proportions as the aggregate numbers, and within each household people share their incomes equally.

Figure 6.7 then shows us the effect of trade. Point *A* is the output of the economy, as derived above. Under autarky, this also must be the consumption point, so the indifference curve for the representative consumer must be tangent to the autarky budget line at that point. That budget line is shown as the solid line in the figure; it must pass through the production point and have a slope equal to minus 1 times the autarky relative price of apparel in the United States under autarky, which is 0.48. Now, under free trade, the new budget line, drawn as a broken blue line in the figure, must still pass through the production point (which is not changed by trade) and must have a slope equal to minus 1 times the free-trade relative price, or 0.42. Note that *the new budget line necessarily cuts through the autarky indifference curve*, making higher-utility points available to the representative consumer. Specifically, the range of consumption points on the new budget line just to the right of point *A* is superior to the original consumption point. This guarantees that the representative consumer will choose consumption on a higher indifference curve

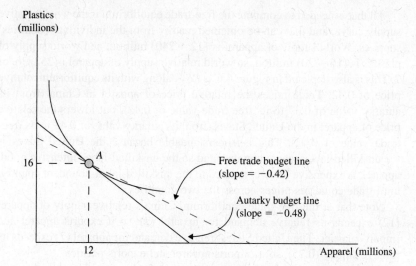

FIGURE 6.7
The Gains from Trade
in the U.S.

under free trade than under autarky. As a result, we can conclude that total U.S. welfare is higher under free trade than under autarky.

But this means that real U.S. GDP is higher under free trade than under autarky—or, put differently, that the United States as a whole gains from trade.

Now, abandon the egalitarian thought experiment and return to the model in which each worker's income is his or her wage. What does trade do to the real income of each class of worker? Once again, what really matters is each worker's budget line. We can figure out the intercepts for each budget line from the following trick. First, note that equilibrium requires zero profits in each industry, due to perfect competition and constant returns to scale.[7] This implies that:

$$2w^U + w^S = P^A, \text{ and} \qquad (6.3)$$

$$3w^U + 3w^S = P^P, \qquad (6.4)$$

where P^A is the price of apparel, P^P is the price of plastics, w^U is the unskilled wage, and w^S is the skilled wage. The left-hand side of (6.3) is the unit cost of production in the apparel industry, which includes the cost of hiring the 2 units of unskilled labor and the 1 unit of skilled labor needed to produce one unit of apparel. The right-hand side of (6.3) is the revenue per unit of apparel sold, so (6.3) is the condition for zero profits in apparel. Similarly, (6.4) is the zero-profit condition for plastics.

---

[7] Think of it this way. If a plastics maker could make $1 of profit per unit of plastics produced, then she could make $1 million profit by hiring enough workers to make 1 million units, but she could make $2 million profit by hiring twice as many and $4 million profit by hiring twice as many as that. This would be true of all plastics makers, so the demand for both kinds of labor would be infinite. That is clearly not an equilibrium. The only way plastics makers would be content hiring a finite amount of labor is if the profit per unit is $0 per unit. Note that that does not mean that plastics makers are starving. We could think of the management of a plastics firm as the skilled workers who hire the unskilled workers to produce output and sell it. The technology requires one unskilled worker per skilled manager, producing 1/3 of a unit of output per manager. The income of the firm's management is then $(1/3)P^P - w^U$ per manager, which in equilibrium must be the same as the managers' opportunity income, w^S.

To derive each worker's budget line, we need each wage divided by the two product prices, so we will divide (6.3) and (6.4) by P^A and P^P in turn. First, dividing by P^A yields:

$$2(w^U/P^A) + (w^S/P^A) = 1, \text{ and} \tag{6.5}$$

$$3(w^U/P^A) + 3(w^S/P^A) = P^P/P^A \tag{6.6}$$

This is a system of two equations in two unknowns, namely, the apparel-axis intercept (w^U/P^A) of the unskilled workers' budget line and the apparel-axis intercept (w^S/P^A) of the skilled workers' budget line. Given that for each country's autarky and for free trade we know the value of P^P/P^A, we can solve this system for those intercepts. For example, for U.S. autarky, the autarky relative price of apparel equals 0.48, so P^P/P^A must be equal to the reciprocal of that, or 2.1. Solving (6.5) and (6.6) with this value on the right-hand side of (6.6) implies that $(w^U/P^A) = 0.3$ and $(w^S/P^A) = 0.4$ under autarky.

To get the plastics-axis intercepts, we divide (6.3) and (6.4) by P^P. This gives us:

$$2(w^U/P^P) + (w^S/P^P) = P^A/P^P, \text{ and} \tag{6.7}$$

$$3(w^U/P^P) + 3(w^S/P^P) = 1. \tag{6.8}$$

Once again, we can solve this for the budget-line intercepts once we fill in the equilibrium value of P^A/P^P in (6.7), which we recall from Figure 6.6 is equal to 0.48 for U.S. autarky. (Or, more easily, we can take the values we got above for (w^U/P^A) and (w^S/P^A) and multiply them by P^A/P^P!) This calculation shows us that $(w^U/P^P) = 0.14$ and $(w^S/P^P) = 0.19$ under autarky.

This gives us our budget lines under autarky. How does trade change them? We can solve the equations again readily with the free-trade relative goods prices, but first we can see quickly in what direction things will move with a simple picture. Figure 6.8 shows the equations (6.5) and (6.6) depicted as solid straight lines. The absolute value of the slope of the line

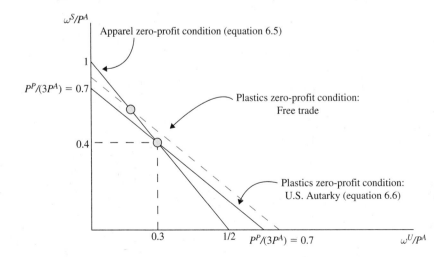

FIGURE 6.8
Equilibrium
Real Wages.

depicting the apparel zero-profit condition (6.5) is 2, the unskilled-to-skilled labor ratio for the apparel sector. The absolute value of the slope of the line depicting the plastics zero-profit condition (6.6) is 1, the unskilled-to-skilled labor ratio for the plastics sector. *The apparel line is steeper than the plastics line because apparel is labor intensive.* This is crucial for understanding the effects of trade on income distribution, as will be seen in a moment.

Now note the crucial point: *when trade is opened up, the relative output price P^A/P^P in the United States falls* (recall Figure 6.6) since the United States can now import cheap apparel from China. That means that P^P/P^A must rise, so from (6.6) the zero-profit line for the plastics industry in Figure 6.8 shifts *out*, as shown by the broken blue line, while the other line is unchanged. Clearly, this results in an increase in (w^S/P^A) and a decrease in (w^U/P^A). Something similar occurs in the plastics-axis intercepts, as shown in Figure 6.9. There, trade shifts the apparel line inward for the United States, which implies that (w^S/P^P) rises and (w^U/P^P) falls.

The outcome is that in the United States the skilled worker's budget line has been shifted outward by trade, with both intercepts (w^S/P^P and w^S/P^A) rising, while the unskilled worker's budget line shifts *in*, with both intercepts $(w^U/P^A$ and $w^U/P^P)$ *falling*. These changes are driven by the fall in the relative price of apparel seen in the U.S. economy when trade opens, as shown in Figures 6.6 and 6.7. On the other hand, when China opens up to trade, it sees a *rise* in the relative price of apparel, so the zero-profit lines in Figures 6.6 and 6.7 shift in the opposite direction compared to what happens with the United States, and so the unskilled workers' budget lines shift *out* while the skilled workers' budget lines shift *in*. This is another feature of equilibrium in all Heckscher-Ohlin models: *In each country, the scarce factor's income falls when trade opens in terms of both goods, and the abundant factor's income rises in terms of both goods.* This is called *the Stolper-Samuelson theorem.*

Put differently, in each country any rise in the relative price of the unskilled-intensive good raises the income of unskilled workers in terms of both goods and lowers the income of skilled workers in terms of both goods. Given that trade lowers the relative price of unskilled-intensive goods in the

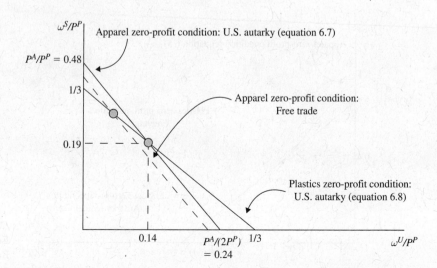

FIGURE 6.9
Equilibrium Real
Wages.

United States and raises it in China, the effect on the different workers in the different countries follows.

Of course, in both countries skilled workers make more money than unskilled workers, so when unskilled real wages fall in the United States due to trade as skilled real wages are rising, income inequality rises. This is in contrast to what happens in China, where when unskilled real wages rise as skilled wages are falling, inequality *falls*.

A last point to make about the wages in equilibrium: They are the same, under free trade, for both countries. This is because equations (6.3) and (6.4) apply equally to both countries, and product prices are identical in both countries. This is a general finding in Heckscher-Ohlin models: If both countries produce both goods under free trade, then factor prices (such as wages) will be equalized across countries by trade. This property is (naturally) called *factor price equalization*.

But the main point for our purposes is that the facts we discussed at the beginning of the chapter are mimicked by the model, with a clear causal mechanism in place: in this model, opening the United States to trade with China raises U.S. real income (the gains from trade displayed in Figure 6.7), but lowers the wages of low-wage workers even as it raises the wages of high-wage workers (the Stolper-Samuelson effect), increasing U.S. income inequality. It thus provides a plausible theory as to why globalization could be behind the labor-market phenomena observed in the data.

Next, we will see briefly how this model works when we relax the assumption of fixed-proportions technology, which will then show how this allows us to test this model to see if it is the *right* explanation.

6.5 Allowing Substitutability—and the Telltale Signs

Now, suppose that apparel and plastics are both produced from skilled and unskilled labor by constant-returns-to-scale production functions that allow for substitution of the two kinds of labor and that therefore have isoquants as pictured in Figure 6.10. The figure shows *unit isoquants* for the two industries—in other words, combinations of skilled and unskilled labor required to produce one unit of output. For a given pair of unskilled and skilled wages w^U and w^S, the cost-minimizing choice of labor inputs to produce

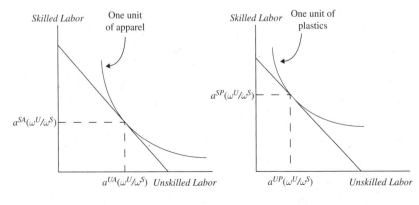

FIGURE 6.10
The Case with
Substitutable Labor.

one unit of output are denoted by $a^{UA}(w^U/w^S)$ and $a^{SA}(w^U/w^S)$ for apparel and $a^{UP}(w^U/w^S)$ and $a^{SP}(w^U/w^S)$ for plastics. These are found at the point of tangency between the isoquant and the isocost line with slope equal to $-(w^U/w^S)$. Of course, any increase in the relative cost of unskilled labor (w^U/w^S) will result in a movement up and to the left along the isoquant, or a rise in the ratio of skilled labor to unskilled labor used in both industries.

We will assume that for any value of w^U/w^S the cost-minimizing skilled-to-unskilled ratio will be higher for plastics than for apparel, or $a^{SP}(w^U/w^S)/a^{UP}(w^U/w^S) > a^{SA}(w^U/w^S)/a^{UA}(w^U/w^S)$—as shown in Figure 6.10. This is the variable-proportions version of the assumption that plastics is skilled-labor intensive.

The model with substitutability works like the model with fixed proportions, but with small changes along the way. First, we can write the zero-profit conditions as follows:

$$w^U a^{UA}(w^U/w^S) + w^S a^{SA}(w^U/w^S) = P^A \quad \text{for apparel, and}$$

$$w^U a^{UP}(w^U/w^S) + w^S a^{SP}(w^U/w^S) = P^P \quad \text{for plastics.}$$

These are analogous to (6.3) and (6.4) for the fixed proportions case. Again, these equations can be used to find the workers' budget-line intercepts by dividing through by P^A and P^P to obtain equations analogous to (6.5), (6.6), (6.7), and (6.8). These can be graphed similarly, the only difference being that instead of straight lines they are strictly convex curves, as shown in Figure 6.11, the analogue to Figure 6.8. Once again, the steeper of the two curves is the curve for apparel because it is unskilled-labor intensive. As a result, if P^A/P^P goes up, the plastics curve shifts out, just as in Figure 6.8, raising the intercept for the skilled worker and lowering it for unskilled workers. The analogue for Figure 6.9 works similarly.

One consequence of this change in factor prices is that, unlike in the fixed-proportions model, a change in relative output prices produces a change in output. This can be seen by writing the resource constraints as:

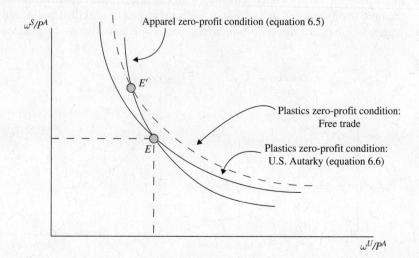

FIGURE 6.11
Equilibrium Real
Wages with Labor
Substitutability.

$$a^{UA}(w^U/w^S)Q^A + a^{UP}(w^U/w^S)Q^P = 72 \text{ million, and}$$

$$a^{SA}(w^U/w^S)Q^A + a^{SP}(w^U/w^S)Q^P = 60 \text{ million.}$$

These are analogous to (6.1) and (6.2), but of course the unit labor demands are variables, not fixed numbers. This gives rise to a diagram analogous to Figure 6.3. The difference is that when the relative price of apparel P^A/P^P falls, then as shown in Figure 6.11, w^U/w^S will fall through the Stolper-Samuelson effect, so by cost minimization a^{UA} and a^{UP} will rise and a^{SA} and a^{SP} will fall, as shown in Figure 6.12. (In that figure, the autarky unit isocost line is shown as a solid black line, while the free-trade unit isocost line is a broken blue line.) As a result, in the analogue to Figure 6.3 the skilled-labor resource constraint will shift out and the unskilled-labor resource constraint will shift in, resulting in a new intersection up and to the left compared to the old one. As a result, production of apparel will go down and production of plastics will go up, so the drop in P^A/P^P has caused a drop in the relative supply of apparel. In other words, with variable coefficients, the relative supply of apparel curve slopes *up*, unlike the vertical relative supply curves of Figure 6.6.

The big picture, however, is the same as in the fixed-proportions case. Because of the Rybczynski effect, the relative supply curve for China lies to the right of the relative supply curve for the United States, just as in Figure 6.6, and the world relative supply curve lies in between the two. Therefore, when trade is opened up, the relative price of apparel falls in the United States and rises in China, and China exports apparel while the United States exports plastics. Because of the movement in relative prices in each country, real wages rise for skilled labor in the United States and unskilled labor in China and fall for unskilled workers in the United States and skilled workers in China. Finally, just as before, both countries gain from trade in the aggregate, so real GDP goes up in both countries. This final point can be seen in Figure 6.13, which is the analogue to Figure 6.7 with substitutable factors. Once again, the autarkic production and consumption point is labeled as A, and the autarkic budget line goes through A tangent to the autarkic indifference curve. Now, however, the country has a concave production possibilities frontier, and with trade the production point moves from A to B. The free-trade budget line is the broken blue line, which cuts through the autarkic indifference curve, allowing higher utility.

Thus, either version of the model, with fixed or variable proportions, provides the same basic interpretation of the three facts discussed at the beginning

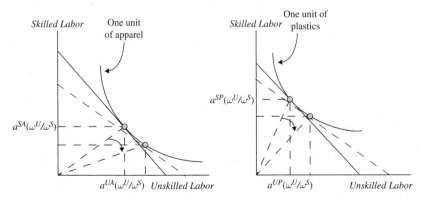

FIGURE 6.12
The Effect of Trade
on Skilled/Unskilled
Labor Ratios.

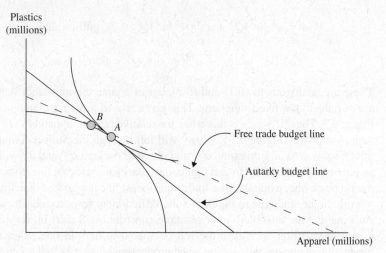

FIGURE 6.13
The Gains from Trade in the
U.S. with Substitutable
Factors.

of the chapter: Opening up trade causes real GDP per worker to go up but also causes increased U.S. income inequality, increasing real wages for high-wage workers and reducing them for low-wage workers.

However, they also make a number of additional predictions—which can be tested. Here are three of the most important.

Prediction 1. The increase in skilled-to-unskilled wage ratios in the United States is accompanied by a drop in the relative employment of skilled labor in each industry in the United States. This, of course, does not occur in the version with fixed proportions, but it is an inevitable result of the fact that trade makes skilled workers relatively more expensive in the United States, as shown in Figure 6.12.

Prediction 2. The increase in skilled-to-unskilled wage ratios in the United States is accompanied by a fall in the relative price of unskilled-labor-intensive goods. In fact, the fall of P^A/P^P in the U.S. economy is what drives the rise in w^S/w^U, as seen from Figures 6.8, 6.9, and 6.11.

Prediction 3. As globalization proceeds, income inequality rises in skill-abundant countries, which are also the countries with high per capita income; but income inequality falls in skill-scarce countries, which are also countries with low per capita income. This is an immediate consequence of the fact that the relative price moves in opposite directions in both countries when trade is opened, as demonstrated in Figure 6.6. Where the skilled-to-unskilled wage ratio rises, income inequality increases, and vice versa.

These can be taken as telltale signs that the Heckscher-Ohlin mechanism is what is driving developments in the labor market. Now we will ask if these signs are there in the data.

6.6 Testing the Theory

Evidence on the first two of these telltale signs can be found in a famous paper by Robert Lawrence and Matthew Slaughter (1993). They gathered data on wages and employment by "production" workers and "nonproduction" workers for U.S. manufacturing. Production workers include all workers directly involved in producing output, such as operating a machine on an assembly line. Nonproduction workers include all other workers, such as supervisors, management, engineering, accounting, office help, and custodial. This is a crude way of dividing the data into skilled and unskilled workers, which is conveniently available in some data sets in which actual skill and qualifications are not recorded. It roughly correlates with a true division by skill because most of the workers in the nonproduction category require more formal qualifications than most of the workers in the production category, and the average nonproduction worker's wage is always higher than the average production worker's wage.

The Lawrence and Slaughter study focuses on the 1980s, a period of rapid globalization across the board. For each U.S. manufacturing industry, Lawrence and Slaughter studied the behavior over the 1980s of the ratio of the nonproduction wage to the production wage, which we can call the "relative wage" for short, and is a rough proxy for w^S/w^U in the notation above. They correlated this with the ratio of the number of nonproduction employees to production employees in each industry, which we can call "relative employment" and is a rough proxy for a^{SA}/a^{UA} and a^{SP}/a^{UP} in the notation above. Their Figure 7, reconstructed here as Figure 6.14 using data from the NBER-CES Manufacturing Industry Database, shows a scatterplot for the change in relative wages against relative employment over the 1980s for all U.S. manufacturing industries. The classification is by the 1972 4-digit Standard Industrial Classification (SIC) system; to illustrate, this includes the robes and dressing gowns industry, the buttons industry, and the tanks and tank parts industry, along with 442 others.[8] The horizontal axis measures the percentage change in relative employment over the 1980s for each industry (so, for example, if an industry had 10% more nonproduction employees than production employees in 1980 but 21% more nonproduction employees than production employees in 1990, then this number would be $((1.21 - 1.1)/1.1) \times 100\% = 10\%$). The vertical axis

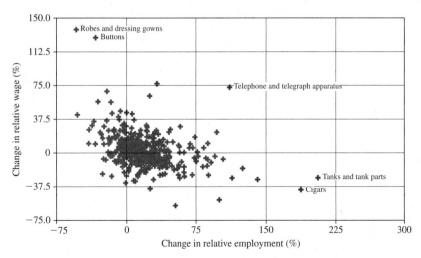

FIGURE 6.14 Changes in Relative Wages and Employment, 1979–89, by Industry.

[8] Research assistance by Gihoon Hong is gratefully acknowledged. Two industries have been dropped due to missing data. In addition, the "primary lead" industry was dropped as an outlier, with its rise in relative employment above 1000%. If that industry were included, the point made here would be all the stronger.

measures the percentage change in relative wage over the 1980s for each industry (so if in 1980 the average nonproduction worker in an industry earned 10% more than the average production worker in that industry, but in 1990 the non-production worker earned 21% more, this number would again be 10%).

A glance at the figure shows the story: The great majority of industries are represented by dots above the horizontal axis, indicating that their relative wage increased over the 1980s, consistent with the facts presented at the beginning of the chapter. At the same time most of the dots lie *to the right of the vertical axis*, therefore indicating a *rise* in the relative skilled employment, which stands in *contradiction* to Prediction 1 listed above. According to the model, every point should be in the upper-left quadrant, with increases in the relative wage and decreases in relative employment, but in fact *three-quarters* of the industries lie in the right-hand quadrants. We conclude that Prediction 1 is violated by the data.

A second line of inquiry by Lawrence and Slaughter concerned output prices. Recall that Prediction 2 was that the prices of unskilled-labor intensive products would fall in the United States relative to the prices of skilled-labor intensive products. Lawrence and Slaughter examined data on import prices and computed the percentage change in import price for each industry over the 1980s. They correlated this with the initial relative employment (again the ratio of nonproduction workers to production workers) across industries. If Prediction 2 is correct, we should see a clear *positive* correlation between these two variables, as the prices of skilled-intensive products rise relative to the prices of unskilled-intensive products as globalization progresses. In fact, there was only a very weak relationship between these variables, and what relationship existed was *decreasing*, not increasing. Prices of skilled-intensive goods in the United States *fell* slightly relative to the prices of unskilled-intensive goods. Therefore, Prediction 2 is very sharply rejected by the data.

Prediction 3 can be addressed by data on income inequality across countries, following an approach by Berman, Bound, and Machin (1998). Figure 6.15 shows data from the University of Texas Inequality Project, which has compiled measures of inequality over time for a wide range of countries.[9] For each country, the vertical axis measures the change in inequality from 1980 to 1990, and the horizontal axis measures the 1980 income per capita. Therefore, the countries are lined up from the poorest on the left to the richest on the right. Note that the great majority of the data points lie above the horizontal axis, meaning that in the great majority of countries income inequality rose. Since this was a period of rapid globalization worldwide, Prediction 3 calls for a positive relationship between the two variables, as higher-income countries should be more likely to see an increase in inequality than low-income ones. However, there is no such positive relationship in the figure. In fact, the two variables show a *negative* correlation (-0.35), and a linear best-fit to the scatterplot, shown as a black line, shows a negative slope. For countries at the lowest income levels, such as Cameroon and Bangladesh, income inequality was much more likely to go up than down. We can conclude that the data reject Prediction 3 as well. [10]

---

[9] The data can be found at http://utip.gov.utexas.edu. The income inequality measure is the Theil index, and the method of calculation is described in detail in Galbraith (2009).

[10] The original study by Berman, Bound, and Machin (1998) focused on the wage premium for skilled workers rather than overall income inequality, but found similar results to those reported here. See, in particular, their Figure IV.

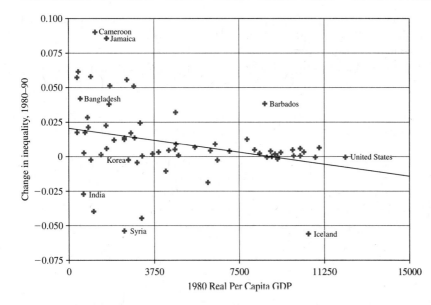

FIGURE 6.15
Changes in Income
Inequality, and Initial
GDP per Capita,
1980–90.

Thus, although superficially the Heckscher-Ohlin model appears to provide a plausible explanation of the U.S. labor-market experience since the 1970s as a consequence of trade, in fact the data rejects that theory quite decisively.

6.7 The Upshot—with an Important Qualification

We have documented some problems of the U.S. labor market and shown a plausible—and influential—theory of how this may have been caused by freer trade, the Heckscher-Ohlin model. We then saw that this explanation does not fit the data, in a number of crucial ways, so if trade is the culprit it must work through some other mechanism.

Economists mostly agree that the wage performance of the U.S. economy has been disappointing in the era of the second wave of globalization, but most do not ascribe very much of this performance to trade. There is no consensus on a single cause, but different authors emphasize changes in technology, declines in unionization, immigration, and deterioration in the real value of minimum wages—each hotly contested. A useful survey of a fairly substantial literature on this issue is found in Freeman (1995).

We should point out two theories that are particularly prominent. First, many researchers believe that the explanation lies in *skill-biased technical change*, meaning a change in technology, possibly due to the rise of computers and automation, that results in a higher ratio of skilled labor to unskilled labor chosen by each firm for any given wages. This explanation is forcefully argued by, for example, Berman, Bound, and Machin (1998), and can help explain why the ratio of skilled to unskilled workers employed has gone up throughout the economy in many countries even as skilled labor has become relatively more expensive. Second, in recent decades there has been a swing in demand toward services, resulting in increases in their prices. Since, at least in the United States and other high-income countries, services are on average very much more skilled-labor intensive than goods sectors, this can result in increases in the skilled wages relative to unskilled wages. Harrigan (2000) and Reshef (2009) show that this explanation fits the data very well.

One conclusion that we *cannot* take from this exploration, however, is that trade has no distributional costs. Workers in import-competing industries typically lose income from an increase in import competition (see Kletzer, 2002, for a survey of evidence). The point is that the expectation that *blue-collar workers as a whole are hurt by trade* is not well supported by the data. It appears that workers face substantial costs of switching industries, as documented, for example, by Artuç, Chaudhuri, and McLaren (2010), so that in some respects the economy functions like the specific-factors model of Chapter 5. (It is not so easy to leave one's job making buttons one day and begin making tanks and tank parts the next.) Thus, the pattern of gains and losses from import competition is different than the Heckscher-Ohlin pattern; rather than a class-based pattern of white-collar gains and blue-collar losses from globalization, an *industry*-based pattern of losses for less-mobile (particularly older) workers in import-competing industries—and gains for everyone else—may be closer to the truth.

Finally, there are indications that the earlier methods of looking for a relationship between trade and inequality may have missed much of what is going on, perhaps by looking at aggregate data. An important strain of research looks at data at the level of individual plants. Bernard, Jensen, and Schott (2006) show that imports from low-wage countries are correlated with an increased rate of plant closings for low-skill intensive plants in the United States, which suggests that within each industry the products exported by low-wage countries are different from those exported by high-wage countries, and that low-wage imports could drive U.S. wage inequality to some degree even within each industry. An important consequence of the finding that rich and poor countries produce different goods is explored by Zhu and Trefler (2005). They show that if skill-abundant countries produce skill-intensive goods and skill-scarce countries produce less skill-intensive goods and there is a cutoff good that marks the boundary between the two, a rise in productivity in skill-scarce countries will shift that boundary, transferring production of some goods from skill-abundant countries to skill-scarce countries. The goods thus moved were the least skill-intensive goods in the skill-abundant countries but they are now the most skill-intensive goods in the skill-scarce countries. Therefore, the rise in skill-scarce country productivity can increase the relative demand for skilled labor in every country at once. This theory explains many features observed in globalization in practice, including a rise in income inequality in all regions at once.

This is an active area of inquiry and debate. A number of strands of ongoing research seem to point to a role for trade in increasing wage inequality; see Harrison, McLaren, and McMillan (2011) for an overview.

MAIN IDEAS

1. A model in which trade is driven only by differences in factor endowments across countries, and in which factors are perfectly mobile across industries, is called a Heckscher-Ohlin model. This is a form of comparative-advantage model in which technology and consumer preferences are assumed to be the same across countries, leaving only differences in factor supplies as a reason for trade.

2. In such a model, each country exports the good intensive in the factor in which it is relatively abundant (a result called the Heckscher-Ohlin theorem). This is also the good that was relatively

cheap in that country under autarky, so in each country trade raises the relative price of the good that is intensive in the factor that is relatively abundant in that country.

3. In a Heckscher-Ohlin world, factor prices are determined by output prices through each industry's zero-profit condition. A rise in the price of a good raises the real income of the factor that is intensive in the use of that good and lowers the real income of the other factor.

4. As a result, in such a model, trade raises the real income of each country's abundant factor and lowers the real income of each country's scarce factor. This is known as the Stolper-Samuelson theorem.

5. Therefore, if each person owns only one factor of production, then in each country, one group of people will be hurt by trade and one group will benefit. On the other hand, if ownership of factors is evenly spread out, everyone will benefit from trade.

WHERE WE ARE

We have added the final form of comparative-advantage model, the Heckscher-Ohlin model, distinguished by its use of factor endowments as a reason for trade and by its assumption of perfect factor mobility across industries.

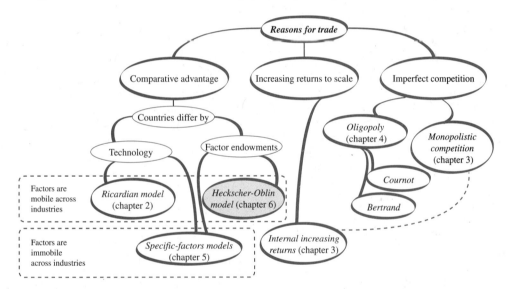

QUESTIONS AND PROBLEMS

1. *Political economy effects.* Consider an economy in which two factors of production, labor and capital, produce two goods, capital-intensive pharmaceuticals and labor-intensive clothing. Suppose that both factors of production are freely mobile across both industries and that all producers, consumers, capitalists, and workers are price-takers. Suppose that there are currently steep tariffs on all imported goods, but there is a bill before Parliament to eliminate those tariffs, and the government has invited citizen representatives of workers and capitalists to express their opinions on the matter. Suppose that all citizen representatives understand the consequences of eliminating the tariffs, and suppose as well that

each representative simply wants to maximize his or her real income. The parliamentary hearing takes testimony from four groups, representing workers in the clothing industry, capitalists in the clothing industry, workers in the pharmaceuticals industry, and capitalists in the pharmaceuticals industry, respectively.

(a) If this economy is capital-abundant relative to the rest of the world, which of these four groups do you expect to support the tariff-elimination bill, and which do you expect to oppose it? Why?

(b) Now, suppose that the country is labor-abundant relative to the rest of the world, and answer the same question, explaining any differences there might be with the previous answer.

(c) How would your answer now change if, instead of being freely mobile, we assumed that both labor and capital were sector-specific?

(d) Comment on how the mobility or immobility of factors across industries affects the nature of political conflict we can expect to see over trade policy.

2. To the model of U.S.-China trade presented in Section 6.2, add a third country, called Colombia. Suppose that the Colombian economy has 90 million unskilled workers and 60 million skilled workers, and the same technology and preferences as China and the United States, and that both kinds of labor are freely mobile across industries just as in those two countries.

(a) Suppose that Colombia opens up trade with the United States at a time when trade is not possible between either China and Colombia or China and the United States. What will happen to wages and the distribution of income within Colombia as a result of the opening of trade? (Answer qualitatively; no computation is necessary, although a diagram may help you explain your reasoning.)

(b) Now, suppose that Colombia opens up trade with the United States after the United States has opened up free trade with China. Will the effect of trade on wages and on the distribution of income in Colombia be different than it was in Question (a)? Why or why not?

3. *More political economy.* Suppose the world is a Heckscher-Ohlin model with two factors of production, skilled and unskilled labor, and many countries that differ in their ratio of skilled to unskilled workers. Suppose that in each country trade policy is determined by the need to keep unskilled workers happy, because in each country unskilled workers form a majority of the population and as a result only politicians who do what unskilled workers want will win an election. Each country's government must choose between free trade and protectionism. Assuming that each voter votes for the politician whose policies will give that voter the highest real income, which countries will have protectionist policies? Which will have free trade?

4. Home and Foreign both produce cars and food using labor and capital. In each country, both labor and capital are freely mobile across industries. It takes 5 units of labor and 3 units of capital to produce 1 unit of food, and 4 units of labor and 4 units of capital to produce 1 car. Home has 600 units of labor and 400 units of capital, while Foreign has 600 units of labor and 500 units of capital. Each country has the same relative demand curve, given by $P^F/P^C = 1.1 - (0.075)Q^F/Q^C$, where P^j is the price of good j and Q^j is the quantity of good j.

(a) Which country is labor abundant? Labor scarce? Which good is labor intensive? Capital intensive?

(b) How much of each good will each country produce?

(c) For Home, find the relative price of food, the wage, and the rental price of capital in autarky. Draw the budget line for a Home worker and for the owner of 1 unit of Home capital.

(d) Do the calculation of (c) for free trade. Draw the budget lines on the same diagram as you used for (c).

(e) Who in Home benefits from trade? Is it the scarce factor or the abundant factor? Who loses? The scarce factor or the abundant factor?

5. *Production with factor substitution.* Suppose that an economy produces apparel and plastics with skilled and unskilled labor. The economy has 120 units of unskilled labor and 100 units of skilled labor. Under the initial conditions, the relative price of apparel is equal to $P^A/P^P = 1.2$, factor prices are such that apparel producers use 2.2 units of unskilled labor and 1 unit of skilled labor for each unit of output, and plastics producers use 1 unit each of skilled and unskilled labor. However, when trade is opened, the relative price of apparel rises to $P^A/P^P = 1.4$, so the relative unskilled wage rises, and both industries substitute toward skilled labor. Suppose that after the change, apparel producers use 2 units of unskilled labor and 1.2 units of skilled labor for each unit of output, and plastics producers use 0.6 units each of unskilled labor and 1.2 units of skilled labor.

(a) Show the factor-use points given on a unit-isoquant diagram as in Figure 6.12. Do not worry about wages or the isocost lines. Sketch what the whole isoquant might look like for each industry, based on the two points for which you have data.

(**b**) Compute the output of each industry before and after trade has opened up.

(**c**) Use the information you have derived in (b) to compute the relative supply of apparel before and after trade, and plot those two points on a graph with the relative supply of apparel on the horizontal axis and the relative price of apparel on the vertical axis. Sketch what the rest of the relative-supply curve might look like, based on the two points for which you have data.

REFERENCES

Artuç, Erhan, Shubham Chaudhuri, and John McLaren (2010). "Trade Shocks and Labor Adjustment: A Structural Empirical Approach." *American Economic Review* 100:3 (June), pp. 1008–1045.

Berman, Eli, John Bound, and Stephen Machin (1998). "Implications of Skill-Biased Technical Change: International Evidence." *Quarterly Journal of Economics*, November 1998., pp. 1245–1280.

Bernard, Andrew B., J. Bradford Jensen, and Peter K. Schott (2006). "Survival of the Best Fit: Exposure to Low-wage Countries and the (Uneven) Growth of U.S. Manufacturing Plants." *Journal of International Economics* 68, pp. 219–237.

Feenstra, Robert C. (2004). *Advanced International Trade*. Princeton, NJ: Princeton University Press.

Freeman, Richard B. (1995). "Are Your Wages Set in Beijing?" *The Journal of Economic Perspectives* 9:3 (Summer), pp. 15–32.

Galbraith, James K. (2009). "Inequality, Unemployment and Growth: New Measures for Old Controversies." *Journal of Economic Inequality* 7:2, pp. 189–206.

Harrigan, James (2000). "International Trade and American Wages in General Equilibrium, 1967–1995", in *The Impact of International Trade on Wages*, Robert C. Feenstra (ed.), pp. 171–193. Chicago: University of Chicago Press for the NBER.

Harrison, Ann, John McLaren, and Margaret McMillan (2011). "Recent Findings on Trade and Inequality." *Annual Reviews of Economics*, Volume 3 (September).

Kletzer, Lori G. (2002). *Imports, Exports and Jobs: What Does Trade Mean for Employment and Job Loss?* Kalamazoo, MI: W. E. Upjohn Institute for Employment Research.

Lawrence, Robert Z., and Matthew J. Slaughter (1993). "International Trade and American Wages in the 1980s: Giant Sucking Sound or Small Hiccup?" *Brookings Papers on Economic Activity* (Microeconomics 1993).

Mishel, Lawrence, Jared Bernstein, and Allegretto, Sylvia (2007). *The State of Working America 2006/2007. An* Economic Policy Institute book. Ithaca, NY: ILR Press, an imprint of Cornell University Press.

Reshef, Ariell (2009). "Is Technological Change Biased Towards the Unskilled in Services? An Empirical Investigation." *Working Paper*, University of Virginia.

Zhu, Susan Chun and Daniel Trefler (2005). "Trade and Inequality in Developing Countries: A General Equilibrium Analysis." *Journal of International Economics* 65, pp. 21–48.

7

Why Doesn't Our Government Want Us to Import Sugar?

John Wiley & Sons, Inc.

LifeSavers candy: As the label says, now made in Canada.

7.1 Sinking LifeSavers

For 35 years, a factory in Holland, Michigan, produced every LifeSavers candy sold in the United States, but in the fall of 2003, the plant closed its doors, eliminating 600 local jobs. Production of LifeSavers was transferred to a factory in Montreal, Quebec, owned by Kraft foods, the brand owner. Many factors were involved in the decision to move, but one factor cited by most observers is the cost of the principal ingredient: sugar (see Belsie, 2002 or *USA Today,* 2002). Wholesale prices of sugar are substantially higher in the United States than they are in Canada—often *twice* as high, which obviously will have an effect on the cost of production for a product that is almost entirely sugar. Sugar prices are also a factor in the closing of a large Brach's candy plant in Chicago, with production moved to Argentina and Mexico, and in the decision of a number of other U.S. candy manufacturers to move production out of the country (see Jusko, 2002).

A natural question is, then, *why* is sugar expensive in the United States? In particular, why is wholesale sugar so much more expensive than it is in Canada, a country with no cane sugar capacity at all (only sugar beets in Ontario and Alberta), than in the United States, with abundant cane production capability in Florida, Louisiana, Hawaii, and Texas, as well as beet sugar in the north?

The principal reason appears to be, very simply, that the U.S. government has, for decades, made it very difficult to import sugar from the rest of the world, while the Canadian government has not. This import restriction policy has had wide ramifications, from the discouragement of domestic candy production to the creation of a huge corn-syrup industry that otherwise likely would not exist, to a rise in sugar and candy prices for U.S. consumers. We will try to figure out exactly what the government is trying to do with this program. The first step will require us to understand how it works.

U.S. sugar import restrictions take the form of a *tariff-rate quota* (TRQ). This is a variant of a tariff (recall from Chapter 5 that a tariff is a tax on imports). With a TRQ, the government allows a certain quantity of imports of the commodity in question at a low tariff rate, but assesses a higher tariff rate on imports above that level. For example, in 2002, the U.S. policy charged 0.625 cents per pound of sugar for the first 1.29 million tons imported, and 15.36 cents per pound for any imports beyond that (see Elobeid and Beghin, 2006, for a summary of world sugar policies). The 0.625¢/lb rate is called the in-quota tariff, and the 15.36¢/lb rate is called the out-of-quota tariff. Note that the out-of-quota rate is much higher than the in-quota rate; this is generally the case with TRQs. Since world raw sugar prices generally fluctuate around 10 cents per pound, the out-of-quota rate for the U.S. sugar policy is a very steep disincentive to imports beyond the quota threshold.

In fact, the U.S. sugar import policy is a hybrid that combines elements of a tariff and a related policy called a *quota*. Under a quota, a government declares some quantity of imports of a commodity that it will permit, with imports beyond that quantity simply prohibited. For our purposes, the main effects of the sugar policy can be well understood by approximating the more complicated TRQ by a simple quota or tariff, and that is the approach we will pursue here. Once we understand how one of these simpler policies works, it will be easy to see how the more complicated TRQ works (and it will also be clear that it does essentially the same things).

In general, any policy of restricting imports by any of these means is often called *protectionism* because it has the effect of protecting domestic producers from foreign competition. An analysis of the government's motivation for sugar protectionism can reveal tools that can be used to understand protectionist policies more generally. There are two main candidate explanations for why the U.S. government severely restricts sugar imports. The first is that by doing so it can force the world price of sugar down, which tends to raise real U.S. incomes because the United States is a net importer of sugar. Since this amounts to an improvement in the U.S. terms of trade, it is often called the *terms-of-trade motive* for protectionism. Note that under this hypothesis, the United States as a whole is made richer by the protectionism, although some groups of Americans might be hurt. The second hypothesis is that the import restrictions make Americans as a whole poorer, but benefit some group within the country that has disproportionate influence on the political process. This is the *interest-group motive*. We will look at these two explanations in turn.

7.2 Hypothesis I: The Terms-of-Trade Motive

7.2.1 A Partial-Equilibrium Model

To get started, we need a model of world sugar trade. In analyzing trade policy, we always need to be clear about the kind of trade we are looking at; trade policy in a comparative-advantage setting can have very different effects compared to trade based on increasing returns or imperfect competition. Note that trade in sugar is driven by comparative advantage; the reason that Brazil and the Dominican Republic are major exporters, for example, is that climate and soil conditions there favor the production of sugar cane, unlike colder and drier locations. Since sugar, as other agricultural commodities, is produced by a large number of growers with no single grower dominating, it makes sense to use a competitive model with all producers as price-takers. Further, since sugar is both a small part of the U.S. economy and a small portion of consumers' budget sets, a partial-equilibrium approach is appropriate. Here, we will adopt a very simple approximation of the model constructed by the U.S. General Accounting Office (GAO) in collaboration with a team of economists from the University of Iowa for its June 2000 report on U.S. sugar polices, a report commissioned by Congress that is probably the most influential study of U.S. sugar policies available (General Accounting Office, 2000).

We will use the following approximation to the supply relationship for sugar in the United States (including both sugar from cane and sugar from beets):

$$S^{US} = 1.48 \times 10^{10} + 5.44 \times 10^{7} P, \tag{7.1}$$

where S^{US} is the U.S. quantity supplied in pounds and P is the price in cents per pound. The following will approximate the U.S. consumer demand relationship:

$$D^{US} = 2.56 \times 10^{10} - 2.79 \times 10^{8} P, \tag{7.2}$$

where D^{US} is the U.S. quantity demanded, in pounds. For any given price, the difference between the U.S. quantity demanded and the U.S. quantity supplied provides the U.S. import demand for sugar, so the difference between (7.2) and (7.1) yields the U.S. *import* demand curve:

$$MD^{US} = 1.08 \times 10^{10} - 3.33 \times 10^{8} P, \tag{7.3}$$

where MD^{US} denotes the quantity of sugar demanded by the United States, in pounds.[1] These three relationships are denoted in Figure 7.1. Note that the import demand MD^{US} at any given price is the horizontal difference between

---

[1] These parameters come from approximating the GAO (2000) model linearly. Table 7 (p. 25) of the GAO report lists predictions of the model, with and without the sugar program in place. The parameters of the U.S. supply and demand equations given here, (7.1) and (7.2), are chosen to replicate the quantities in that table, given the domestic price. The parameters for the rest-of-world export supply (7.5) are chosen to match the predicted export quantities, given the world price, and then are broken into supply and demand curves for the rest of the world by assuming that the United States and rest-of-world supply curves have the same slope—an assumption that is immaterial to the policy questions at hand.

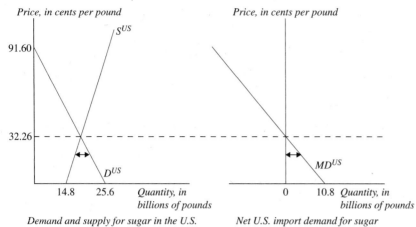

FIGURE 7.1
The Market for Sugar
in the U.S.

the domestic demand D^{US} and the domestic supply S^{US}, as indicated by the two-headed arrow, which has the same length in both panels of the figure.

Similarly, let the rest of the world's sugar supply relationship be approximated by:

$$S^{ROW} = 3.00 \times 10^{11} + 5.44 \times 10^{7} P, \qquad (7.4)$$

where S^{ROW} denotes the quantity of sugar produced in the rest of the world (henceforth denoted by ROW), and let the rest of the world's sugar demand relationship be approximated by:

$$D^{ROW} = 3.21 \times 10^{11} - 2.45 \times 10^{9} P, \qquad (7.5)$$

where D^{ROW} denotes the quantity of sugar consumed by the rest of the world. For any given price, the rest-of-world supply minus the rest-of-world demand amounts to the rest-of-world export supply (to the United States), so subtracting (7.5) from (7.4) yields the rest-of-world export supply curve:

$$XS^{ROW} = -2.08 \times 10^{10} + 2.5 \times 10^{9} P, \qquad (7.6)$$

where XS^{ROW} represents the rest of the world's sugar exports to the United States. This is depicted in Figure 7.2.

Consider an equilibrium with free trade—in other words, with no trade barriers or transport costs, so that the price of sugar is the same everywhere. Market clearing requires that the U.S. import demand equal the rest of the world's export supply, so to find the equilibrium we need to set the right-hand-sides of (7.3) and (7.6) equal to each other and solve for the world price, P. This implies a world price of 11.14 cents per pound, as shown in Figure 7.3, and 7.04 billion pounds of sugar imported by the United States.[2]

---

[2] Alert students duplicating this algebra on their own will notice small discrepancies between the reported values and the equilibrium values they compute from the export supply and import demand equations. That is due to the rounding used to report the export supply and import demand equations. The world price reported here is computed without rounding and can be obtained from the accompanying spreadsheet, *optimal tariff.xls*.

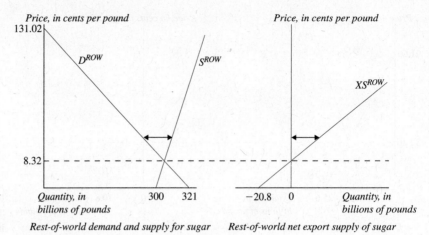

FIGURE 7.2
The Market for Sugar in the Rest of the World.

Rest-of-world demand and supply for sugar   Rest-of-world net export supply of sugar

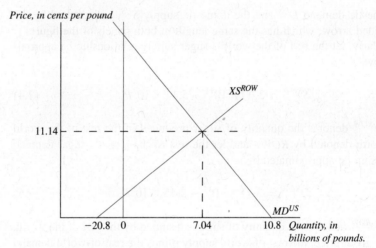

FIGURE 7.3
The World Market for Sugar.

Now, we impose the U.S. trade restrictions. We will approximate the U.S. policy first with a tariff and then with a quota.

7.2.2 The Effects of a Tariff

It turns out that the effects of the U.S. sugar policy are well approximated by a tariff set at 12.38 cents per pound on every unit imported. This is an example of a *specific tariff*, meaning a tariff that is charged per unit of quantity imported. (By contrast, a tariff charged per unit of value is an *ad valorem tariff*. An example would be a tariff that requires payment of customs duty equal to 5% of import invoice value.)

A specific tariff of 12.38¢/lb would then change the U.S. import demand curve as follows (the details are laid out in Figure 7.4). We need to derive how much sugar the United States will now import for any given world price, and we can do that in four steps. ① First pick a value for the world price, say, 10 cents per pound. ② Then add the 12.38¢/lb tariff to that 10¢/lb to find the domestic U.S. price of sugar that implies: 22.38¢/lb. The reason that the domestic U.S. price would be increased in this way is straightforward: U.S. consumers now need to pay the world price plus the tariff for any

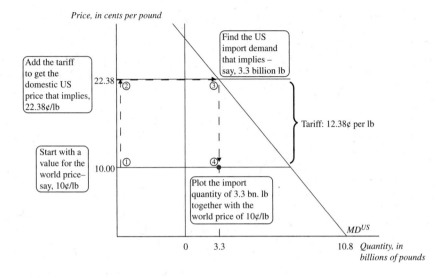

FIGURE 7.4
A Tariff Changes the
U.S. Import Demand
Curve.

imported sugar they will buy, so the price they face for foreign sugar is
22.38¢/lb. If the price of domestically produced sugar in the United States did
not also rise, then U.S. consumers would buy only domestically produced
sugar; but (as Figure 7.1 shows), at 10¢/lb, domestic U.S. supply is less than
domestic U.S. demand, so there would be an excess demand for sugar in the
United States. This would drive the domestic U.S. price up, until it would
reach a point at which U.S. consumers are once again ready to import sugar—
in other words, 22.38¢/lb. ③ Now that we know the domestic U.S. price
implied by a world price of 10¢/lb, we can find out the quantity of U.S. import
demand this implies by reading it off of the original U.S. import demand curve
at the new U.S. domestic price. ④ We now have a U.S. import demand
quantity (3.3 billion pounds) associated with the hypothetical world price of
10¢/lb, and we can plot this price/quantity pair as the blue dot in the figure.
Note that it is below the original MD^{US} curve by exactly 12.38¢/lb, the amount
of the tariff.

We can repeat the logic now for *any* hypothetical value of the world price, and
doing so traces out the new U.S. import demand curve, shown as the blue curve
$MD^{US,\,tariff}$ in Figure 7.5. In this figure, the vertical axis measures the world price
of sugar, which we have seen will now be different from the domestic U.S. price.
The new U.S. import demand curve lies below the original import demand
curve, at each point, by exactly 12.38¢/lb, the amount of the tariff. Obviously,
this implies that its intersection with the rest of the world's export supply
schedule occurs below and to the left of the original equilibrium, implying a
lower world price of sugar and lower U.S. sugar imports as a result of the tariff.
(The XS^{ROW} curve is not affected by the U.S. tariff.) Algebraically, the new
$MD^{US,\,tariff}$ equation is found simply by replacing P in equation (7.3) with
$(P + 12.38)$, because the domestic U.S. price and not the world price determines
domestic U.S. supply and demand, and hence U.S. import demand. This
replacement yields a new U.S. import demand schedule:

$$\begin{aligned} MD^{US,\,tariff} &= 1.08 \times 10^{10} - 3.33 \times 10^8 (P + 12.38) \\ &= 6.68 \times 10^9 - 3.33 \times 10^8 P, \end{aligned} \tag{7.7}$$

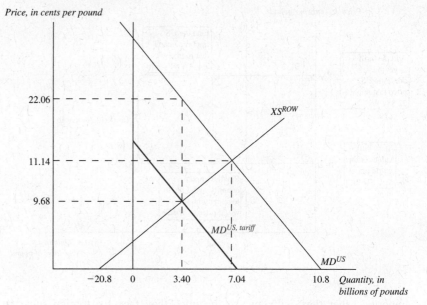

FIGURE 7.5
The Effect of the
Tariff on the World
Market.

where $MD^{US, tariff}$ denotes the U.S. import demand as affected by the tariff, in pounds, and where P denotes the *world* price of sugar. To find equilibrium, we need a world price P such that the ROW export supply (7.6) is equal to the U.S. tariff-affected import demand, (7.7); we therefore set the right-hand sides of (7.6) and (7.7) equal to each other and solve for P. This yields a world price of exactly 9.68¢/lb (compared to the free-trade price of 11.14¢/lb) and a new quantity of 3.4 billion pounds imported by the United States (compared to the free-trade quantity of 7.04 billion).[3]

The point is that the U.S. tariff has made it harder for foreign producers to get into the U.S. market, with the result that a larger fraction of their output is sold on the rest of the world market, depressing the world price. At the same time, the tariff makes sugar more scarce in the United States, raising the U.S. domestic price.

The effects of the tariff within the United States can be seen from Figure 7.6, which re-creates the U.S. supply and demand curves from Figure 7.1, but with the relevant part of the picture magnified. We will evaluate the welfare effect in terms of three pieces. First, there is the effect on *consumer surplus*, which we used in Chapter 4, and is the net benefit of the commodity to consumers, and is measured as the area between the demand curve and the horizontal line marking the price that consumers pay. Second, there is *producer surplus*, which measures the net income to sugar producers from sugar production and is measured as the area between the supply curve and the horizontal line marking the price that producers receive. Finally, there is the *tariff revenue*, which is the income the government receives from collecting the import tariff.

The original price under free trade, the new, lower world price with the tariff, and the new domestic U.S. price (9.68¢/lb plus the 12.38¢/lb tariff equals 22.06¢/lb) are all shown in Figure 7.6. Under the tariff, American production of sugar rises and American consumption of sugar falls. U.S.

---

[3] The comments about rounding error made in footnote 2 apply here as well.

Price, in cents per pound

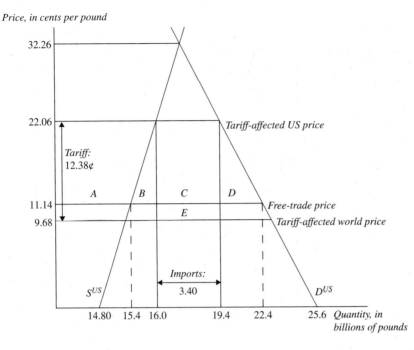

FIGURE 7.6
The Effect of the Tariff
in the U.S.

consumer surplus under free trade was equal to the area under the demand curve above the price of 11.14¢/lb, but under the tariff it is the area above the price of 22.06¢/lb and is therefore smaller by areas $A + B + C + D$. U.S. consumers of sugar are hurt by the tariff. Under free trade, U.S. sugar producer surplus was given by the area above the supply curve below the price of 11.14¢/lb, but with the tariff it is equal to the area below the price 22.06¢/lb and is therefore larger by area A.

The third important welfare effect is the tariff revenue: The U.S. government collects 12.38 cents per pound of sugar imported, which goes into the government coffers to be used for whatever expenditures the government requires. It can also be used to reduce all Americans' income taxes, without changing expenditures. We will assume for now that a dollar of tax revenues in the U.S. Treasury has the same value for social welfare calculations as a dollar of personal income. Tax revenues in this example are equal to the 12.38 cent-per-pound tariff times 3.4 billion pounds imported, or areas $C + E$ in Figure 7.6.

To sum up the effects of the tariff on Americans, add the change in consumer surplus $-(A + B + C + D)$ to the change in producer surplus (A) and the tariff revenue $(C + E)$ to get the total change in U.S. social welfare, $(E - B - D)$, as depicted in Figure 7.7.

We can make sense of this figure quite easily.

- First, the United States benefits any time the world price of a commodity it imports falls. That benefit is measured here by the rectangle E, whose area is the reduction in the world price due to the tariff (the height of the rectangle, or the amount that the United States saves per unit imported), times the number of units imported (the length of the rectangle). This is the simple cost savings to the United States due to the terms-of-trade effect of the tariff; accordingly it is called the *terms-of-trade benefit* of the tariff.

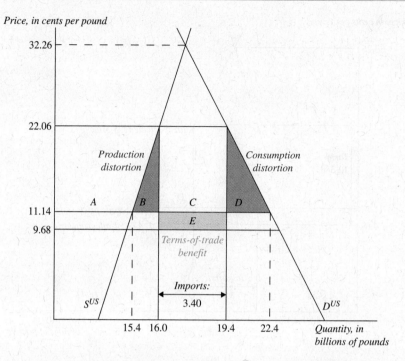

FIGURE 7.7
Welfare Effects.

- Second, the area *B* is the gap between the world free-trade price and the U.S. supply curve, added up over the range of increased U.S. sugar production caused by the tariff. The height of the supply curve at any point is the marginal cost of producing sugar in the United States; if we interpret the original free-trade world price as the true social marginal cost of procuring sugar, then the gap between the two is the additional marginal social cost of producing a pound of sugar in the United States rather than buying it on the world market. Thus, the area *B* is the inefficiency from producing too much sugar in the United States and is accordingly called the *production distortion* from the tariff.

- Finally, the area *D* is the gap between the world free-trade price and the U.S. demand curve, added up over the range of decreased U.S. sugar consumption due to the tariff. The height of the demand curve at any point is equal to the marginal consumer benefit of one more pound of sugar, so the gap is the extent to which each pound of sugar not consumed because of the tariff had a marginal utility higher than its true marginal social cost. Thus, the area *D* is the inefficiency from consuming too little sugar in the United States and is accordingly called the *consumption distortion* from the tariff.

The tariff leads to overproduction and underconsumption of sugar in the United States, both of which are social welfare costs to the United States (dark blue in Figure 7.7), but it also lowers the cost of sugar on the world market, which is a social welfare benefit to the United States (light blue in Figure 7.7). If the light blue area in Figure 7.7 is greater than the dark blue areas, then the tariff is beneficial to U.S. social welfare—and the terms-of-trade motive is sufficient to justify the tariff. Note that in practice "consumers" of sugar include individuals buying one-pound bags at the supermarket as well as candy manufacturers buying it in bulk as an input. If you go into the kitchen and examine the ingredients list of supermarket items, whenever you see high-fructose corn syrup, you are likely looking at a portion of triangle D, because the corn syrup is probably being used instead of sugar, due to the high domestic price of sugar.

In general, the effect of the tariff on U.S. welfare could be positive or negative depending on elasticities of supply and demand and the size of the tariff. In this particular case, the area of the right-angled triangles and rectangles of Figure 7.7 can be readily computed to show that the terms-of-trade benefit is not close to being large enough to outweigh the consumption and production distortions, so in this case the effect on U.S. welfare is negative.[4]

This is due to the fact that the tariff is extremely high—roughly doubling the domestic U.S. price, and thus creating huge domestic consumer and producer distortions—together with the fact that foreign export supply is quite elastic, so that the terms-of-trade effect is modest. The policy pushes down the world price by only about a penny per pound, after all.

The welfare analysis for the rest of the world is simpler, as shown in Figure 7.8. Consumer surplus rises by A' as a result of the tariff, and producer surplus falls by $(A' + B' + C' + D')$, both due to the fall in the world price. There is no tariff revenue, so the net effect is simply equal to $-(B' + C' + D')$, the blue area of social welfare loss in the figure. The rest of the world simply

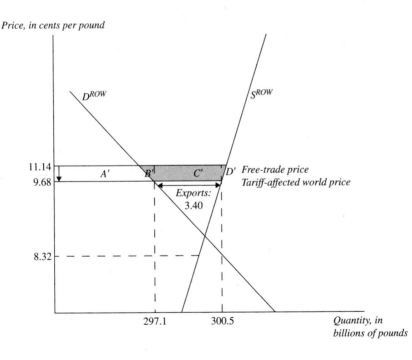

FIGURE 7.8
The Effects of the
Tariff on the Rest of
the World.

---

[4] The height of B is $(22.06 - 11.14)$. The base is $(16.0 - 15.4)$ (since at the free-trade price of 11.14¢, U.S. producers would produce 15.4 billion pounds). The area is, then, half the base times the height, or $B = (22.06 - 11.14) \times (16.0 - 15.4)/2 = 3.28$. The height of D is also $(22.06 - 11.14)$. The base is $(22.4 - 19.4)$ (since at the free-trade price of 11.14¢, U.S. consumers would consume 22.4 billion pounds). The area is, then, half the base times the height, or $D = (22.06 - 11.14) \times (22.4 - 19.4)/2 = 16.38$. The height of E is $(11.14 - 9.68)$, and the base is 3.40 billion pounds. The area is, then, $E = (11.14 - 9.68) \times 3.40 = 4.96$.

In summary, denoting values in billions of cents, we get $B = 3.28$, $D = 16.38$, and $E = 4.96$. Thus, D alone vastly exceeds the terms-of-trade effect, so the net effect of the policy on U.S. welfare is negative.

suffers production and consumption distortion plus an uncompensated terms-of-trade loss. Note as well that area C' of Figure 7.8 is identical to area E of Figure 7.7: *The terms-of-trade gain to the United States from the tariff is exactly equal to the terms-of-trade loss of the rest of the world.*

7.2.3 The Effects of a Quota

It is now easy to see that the same conclusion follows if we approximate the policy with a quota instead of a tariff.

Suppose that the U.S. government charges no tariff on imported sugar, but instead declares that no one can import sugar into the United States without a license. It then prints up licenses, each of which entitles the bearer to import a given quantity of sugar into the United States, and whose quantities all together add up to 3.4 billion pounds. This is the same level of imports as came in under the equilibrium with the tariff, and it is also the actual historical level of imports in 2000.[5] Suppose the government then distributes these licenses to private-sector traders somehow (we will shortly discuss how these are distributed) and instructs the customs service to inspect incoming shipments to be sure that each sugar shipment has its required license.

This changes the world equilibrium, as shown in Figure 7.9. Once again, it is useful to think of the vertical axis as measuring the *world* price. The U.S. import demand curve takes the form of the blue curve $MD^{US,Quota}$, which is the same as the free-trade import demand curve for high prices but then hits a brick wall at the quota quantity of 3.4 billion pounds. No matter how low the world price goes, U.S. imports under the quota cannot exceed this value.

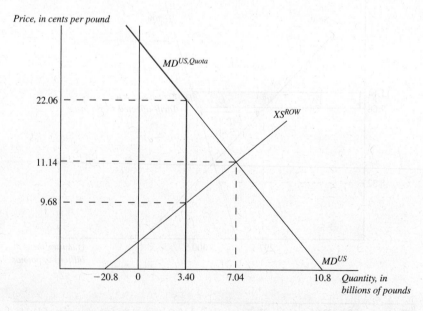

FIGURE 7.9
The Effect of a Quota on the World Market.

---

[5] The alert reader may notice that the actual quantity imported in 2000 exceeds the TRQ quota, despite the fact that the difference between the domestic U.S. price and the world price was less than the out-of-quota tariff. This is explained by the fact that the sugar TRQ is more complicated than described here, with different quotas for different types of sugar, while we have lumped all types together for simplicity. The GAO (2000) model takes account of heterogeneous sugar types, along with other complications we are ignoring in this chapter.

Clearly, the new world equilibrium is below and to the left of the original equilibrium, with a lower quantity imported and a lower world price. In fact, since the quota quantity is the same as the imported quantity under the tariff; and since the new equilibrium must be on the rest of the world's export supply curve—as in the case of the tariff—and this export supply curve has not changed—the equilibrium world price must be the same as it was with the tariff. Further, the domestic U.S. price must again be above the world price, since otherwise there would be an excess demand for sugar in the United States, and further, it must rise to exactly the level at which U.S. consumption demand exceeds U.S. production by 3.4 billion pounds—but this is 22.06¢/lb, just as it was with the tariff. Therefore, *the world price, the domestic U.S. price, traded quantities, and every agent's consumer and producer surplus are exactly as they were with the tariff.* This point is general to comparisons of tariffs and quotas with perfect competition and is known as *the equivalence of tariffs and quotas.*

One important difference with the tariff, however, is that the quota generates no government revenue, as long as the government gives the licenses away rather than selling them. Instead of revenue accruing to the government, the quota creates profits for license-holders, who can buy sugar at the artificially low world price of 9.68¢/lb and sell it in the United States at the artificially high U.S. price of 22.06¢/lb. It is clearly a *very* valuable thing to own an import license, and we should include those profits in our social welfare calculation. Call the profits that accrue to license holders *quota rents.* The total quota rents generated by the system are equal to the price differential, $(22.06 - 9.68)$¢/lb $= 12.38$¢/lb, times the number of pounds of imports permitted, 3.4 billion. This is exactly the area $(C + E)$ in Figures 7.6 and 7.7; in other words, it is exactly the same as tariff revenue, except that it is captured by license-holders and not the government.

Now, it makes a large difference how the government distributes the import licenses. If it gives them to American traders, then the quota rents are simply added to U.S. social welfare in the same way that tariff revenue was in the case of the tariff, and the welfare diagrams are exactly the same as in Figures 7.7 and 7.8. However, if the government gives the licenses to foreign traders, then none of the quota rents are captured by Americans. Adding up the social welfare effects in that case produces Figure 7.10 for the United States and Figure 7.11 for the rest of the world. Once again, dark blue denotes social welfare losses and light blue social welfare gains. From Figure 7.10, we can see that the United States is unambiguously worse off due to the quota when foreigners capture the quota rents; there is no terms-of-trade benefit to compensate for the consumption and production distortions because all of that benefit is given away to foreign traders in the form of quota rents. For the rest of the world, the huge light blue rectangle driven by quota rents counteracts the dark blue terms-of-trade loss and production and consumption distortions, and (in this case, with this policy) completely overwhelms them. Whether or not the rest of the world benefits from a quota in this way will in general depend on elasticities of supply and demand and on how restrictive the quota is, but in this case we have the somewhat ironic finding that the United States is hurt from the U.S. sugar policy and the rest of the world benefits from it.[6]

---

[6] It should be emphasized that the quota rents are not captured by foreign farmers, but by traders, middlemen, import–export corporations, and the like, some of which may be state-owned. The incomes of sugar producers themselves, unless they are directly involved in export and can get hold of a license, are likely to be depressed by the policy.

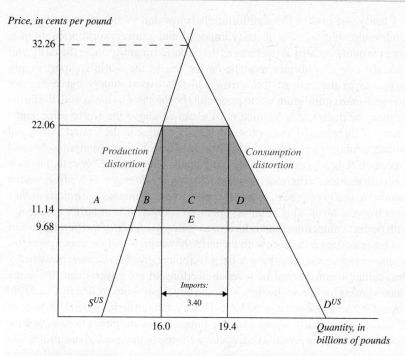

FIGURE 7.10
Effects of the Quota
on U.S. Welfare if
Foreigners Capture
the Quota Rents.

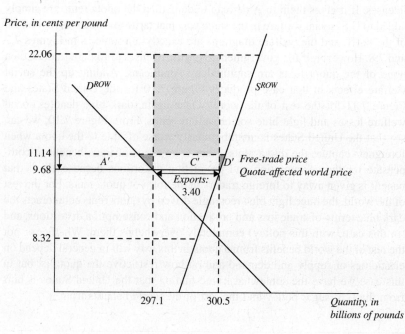

FIGURE 7.11
The Effects of the
Quota on the Rest
of the World if
Foreigners Capture
Quota Rents.

NG Image/NG Image Collection

**Unlikely to receive any quota rents: Cane workers in the Dominican Republic.
U.S. sugar policy most likely lowers the income of these workers by pushing down
producer's prices for sugar.**

In fact, the actual sugar policy is intermediate between these two cases. Each
exporting country is assigned a quota allocation by the U.S. government, and
the exporting-country government provides licenses totaling the required
amount to its own traders (see USITC, 2001, pp. 37–48, for a fuller discussion
of the implementation of the policy). As a result, the United States does not
capture the quota rents; foreign traders do. However, since it is a TRQ scheme
rather than a pure quota scheme, not all of the $(C + E)$ rectangle takes the form
of quota rents; a portion of that rectangle is captured by the U.S. government in
the form of tariff revenues. As a result, the rent/revenue rectangle $(C + E)$ is
captured partly by Americans and partly by foreigners. What is clear is that if
any of the rectangle is captured by foreigners, the TRQ is even worse for U.S.
social welfare than the equivalent tariff would be.

7.2.4 Evaluation: Is the Terms-of-Trade Motive Sufficient?

It should be clear by now that the terms-of-trade motive is not sufficient to
explain the U.S. sugar policy. Approximating the policy with a tariff, the
terms-of-trade effect its dwarfed by the consumption and production distortions; approximating with a quota, once we note that a large portion of the
quota rents is captured by foreigners, the effect is even more negative because
the terms-of-trade benefit is given away as a gift to foreign traders. Note that
the tariff and the quota do essentially the same thing, except for the question of
who receives the tariff revenue/quota rent rectangle, and remember that the
actual tariff-rate-quota policy is a hybrid of the two, with effects that lie
somewhere in between. In other words, the sugar TRQ policy gives a bit of
tariff revenue to the U.S. government and a lot of quota rent to foreign
traders. The upshot, as found in a much more exhaustive analysis by the GAO
report (GAO, 2000), is that the sugar policy makes the United States as a
whole a slightly poorer country, even after taking full account of terms-of-
trade effects.

Cliff Lipson/CBS/Landov LLC

The winners: Technically, Jimmy Smits and Nestor Carbonell are not Florida sugar producers; they merely played that role in the CBS drama *Cane*. But their real-world counterparts certainly are a political interest group that shapes and gains from U.S. sugar policies.

Why, then, would a government ever embark on, and persist with, a policy that makes its country a little bit poorer? To find out, we will have a look at the second hypothesis.

7.3 Hypothesis II: Interest Groups

Up to now, we have assumed that the decision process of the U.S. government puts equal weight on all Americans (and no weight on foreigners). Perhaps this is an error. The reason for the sugar policy may be that for some reason the domestic beneficiaries of the policy are given more weight in the political decision process than other Americans.

In particular, sugar producers do seek favorable treatment, in large part by making campaign contributions to politicians. This is documented and analyzed in Gökçekuş et al., (2003). By their calculations, between 1989 and 2002, individuals in the sugar business and in Political Action Committees representing sugar interests donated approximately $1.5 million annually in campaign contributions to members of the U.S. Congress. The donations were strategically allocated: They went disproportionally to members of Congress who had a position on the relevant subcommittees that oversee agricultural policy, and they went disproportionally to members who belonged to the majority party, which can set the agenda and thus have much more control over resulting legislation than members of the minority party. Gökçekuş et al. (2003) provocatively estimate that U.S. sugar policies provided approximately $1 billion of benefit to sugar producers per year, so that if one assumes that they are all due to sugar-industry campaign contributions, sugar producers received $714 in benefit for each dollar invested in the political process.

A less obvious place to look for political influence over sugar policy is the agro-processing sector. Archer Daniels Midland (ADM) is a large corporation offering a wide range of products to the industrial agriculture and food processing sectors, and has a history of aggressive political activism in favor of the policies it desires; it is known for extraordinary generosity to politicians of both parties. As a particularly bold example, the CEO allegedly once attempted to deliver $100,000 in an unmarked envelope to Richard Nixon at the White House (Bovard, 1995). In 1974, the company made a large ($80 million) and risky investment in technology to produce high-fructose corn syrup, a sugar substitute, from surplus corn (*Business Week*, 1976). For a while this appeared to be a disastrous move, as sugar prices fell below what the company needed to break even on its corn syrup. However, the company saw its salvation in policies to keep domestic sugar prices high, continued to spend heavily on campaign contributions to both parties, and has subsequently benefited from the restrictive policy we have today, which has ensured high U.S. sugar prices and profitable corn syrup operations for ADM.

One way of interpreting the effects of these influence activities is that they induce government decision makers to maximize not social welfare, but *weighted* social welfare—social welfare calculated with additional weight placed on the group that is paying for influence. This approach was popularized in international economics, for example, in a famous paper by Gene Grossman and Elhanan Helpman (1994) who suggested that the process could be well approximated by a kind of auction in which the government "sells" protection to interest groups that bid against each other. If the government values social welfare but also values money from campaign contributors, it chooses policy to maximize social welfare, with extra weight put on the interest groups that are bidding. More generally, there are many reasons a group of citizens might get extra weight in the policy decision process. The government might, for example, put more weight on citizens who are perceived to be needy (a portion of the population with a high poverty rate, for example), or a group that are perceived as a "swing" voting bloc who might base their vote in the next election on trade policy for their industry.

For our purposes, let us for simplicity suppose that the government sets its tariff policy to maximize the following weighted welfare function:

$$A^{cons}CS(P^{US}) + A^{prod}PS(P^{US}) + A^{tax}TR(P^{US}, P^{world}), \qquad (7.8)$$

where $CS(P^{US})$ and $PS(P^{US})$ are consumer and producer surplus in the sugar sector, respectively, as a function of the domestic price of sugar; $TR(P^{US}, P^{world})$ is revenue from the tariff, as a function of the domestic and world price (of course, the tariff rate is just the difference between the two); and the A^i's are positive weights on consumer surplus, producer surplus, and tax revenues, respectively, that show the government's bias if any. If $A^{cons} = A^{prod} = A^{tax}$, then the government will set the tariff to maximize social welfare. If $A^{prod} > A^{cons} = A^{tax}$, then the government is biased toward sugar producers, a bias that might be generated by their history of campaign contributions.

It is straightforward to confirm, for example, by working out the areas of the triangles and rectangles of Figure 7.6, that if $A^{cons} = A^{tax} = 1$ and $A^{prod} = 1.17$, then the bias toward sugar producers is sufficient to explain the tariff policy or a quota policy that gives the quota rents to Americans (meaning that weighted welfare (7.8) is higher with the tariff or quota than with free trade), but the bias is not big enough to rationalize a quota policy that gives the rents to foreigners. However, if $A^{cons} = A^{tax} = 1$ and $A^{prod} = 2$, then the political bias toward sugar producers is sufficient to explain either policy.

To sum up, it is difficult to rationalize the U.S. sugar policy on the basis of the terms-of-trade motive, but easy to rationalize it as the outcome of interest-group politics.

7.4 Additional Observations

7.4.1 The Optimal Tariff

It should quickly be pointed out that even if a tariff of 12.38 cents does not raise U.S. welfare, that does not imply that there is no level for the tariff that *would* raise U.S. welfare. Indeed, in general whenever a country has some control over its terms of trade there is a strictly positive tariff that will improve its welfare. The level of the tariff that raises social welfare for the country that imposes it is called the "optimal tariff," and it can be analyzed as follows.

In order for a given tariff level to be optimal for the country that imposes it, it must be the case that the marginal benefit of a small increase in the tariff is equal to the marginal cost. Figure 7.12 shows what this looks like. If we increase the tariff by a small amount, say Δt, then the world price falls a bit, the domestic price rises a bit, the domestic consumption level falls a bit, and the domestic production level rises a bit. This slightly increases the height of the terms-of-trade effect (area E of Figure 7.7) but slightly reduces its length, and at the same time adds a bit of area to the production and consumption distortions (areas B and D of Figure 7.7). This results in an increase in U.S. social welfare given by the light blue area of Figure 7.12, the marginal benefit of raising the tariff, and a decrease in social welfare indicated by the dark blue areas in Figure 7.12, the marginal cost of raising the tariff. For the level of the tariff to be optimal, those two effects must cancel each other out, so

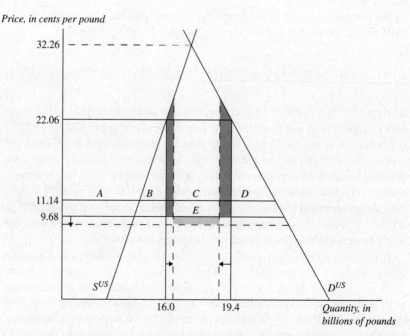

FIGURE 7.12
An Increase in the Tariff, and the Optimal Tariff.

the dark blue and light blue areas must be equal. The light blue area is equal to the change in the world price, which we can denote by ΔP^{ROW}, times the level of imports, which we can denote as $XS^{ROW}(P^{ROW})$, since U.S. imports must equal the rest of the world's exports in equilibrium. The area of the two combined dark blue areas is equal to the change in imports times the level of the tariff, t. Therefore, for the tariff to be optimal, we must have:

$$\Delta P^{ROW} XS^{ROW}(P^{ROW}) = [XS^{ROW}(P^{ROW} + \Delta P^{ROW}) - XS^{ROW}(P^{ROW})]t.$$

Rearranging slightly and dividing both sides by the world price yield:

$$\frac{t}{P^{ROW}} = \frac{\Delta P^{ROW} XS(P^{ROW})}{P^{ROW}[XS(P^{ROW} + \Delta P^{ROW}) - XS(P^{ROW})]}$$

The left-hand side is the ad valorem tariff, or the tariff expressed as a fraction of price. For example, in the tariff model analyzed in Section 7.2.2, the tariff was 12.38 cents per pound, and the world price was 9.68 cents per pound, so the ad valorem form of the tariff is 12.38/9.68 or 128%. The right-hand side is the proportional change in the world price ($\Delta P^{ROW}/P^{ROW}$), divided by the proportional change in the rest of the world's exports to the United States ($\Delta XS^{ROW}/XS^{ROW}$). In other words, the right-hand side is the reciprocal of the rest of the world's export supply elasticity. Thus, the condition for the optimal tariff can be written:

$$\tau = \frac{1}{\varepsilon},$$

where τ denotes the *ad valorem* tariff and ε denotes the elasticity of rest-of-world export supply. This is known as the 'inverse elasticity formula' for the optimal tariff (although it is not really a formula, in the sense that one can plug parameter values into the right-hand side to compute the value on the left-hand side; the elasticity takes different values at different points along the export supply curve, so the right-hand side actually depends on the tariff).

It is easy to understand why the more elastic is the rest of the world's export supply, the lower is the optimal tariff, because the more elastic is the export supply, the flatter is the rest of the world's export supply curve and the harder it is to manipulate the world price by use of a tariff.

This goes hand in hand with an important observation on tariffs in comparative-advantage trade:

7.4.2 The Optimal Tariff for a Small Country Is Zero

For our purposes, a *small country* is one that has no influence on the world prices it faces. When we call a country "small" within the context of trade policy, we are not commenting on size per se but elasticity. In the sugar model studied here, for example, the United States would be called a small country in the sugar market if it faced a horizontal, hence an infinitely elastic, export supply curve. On the other hand, Madagascar, for example, is a small country in most respects, but in the vanilla market it is a major supplier with considerable power over world prices and would consequently be called a large country.

Recalling Figure 7.7, a small open economy would incur the production and consumption distortions B and D from a tariff, but would receive no terms-of-trade benefit. Therefore, it is better off sticking with free trade. Alternatively, we can look at the reciprocal-elasticity "formula" for the optimal tariff just derived above, and note that for a small country ε is infinite—it faces a horizontal export supply curve and takes the world price as given—so the only value for a tariff consistent with the equation is zero.

7.4.3 Voluntary Export Restraints

In the quota policy studied in Section 7.2.4, under the assumption that the quota licenses were handed to foreign traders, we arrived at a paradoxical conclusion: that the rest of the world as a whole would *benefit* from U.S. sugar import restrictions, provided that they were administered in that way, while the United States as a whole would be made poorer. This implies that if the U.S. government wanted to do a favor to its own sugar producers and wanted as little resistance from foreign governments as possible, this could be a way of receiving the consent of foreign sugar-exporting countries. This phenomenon, as it turns out, is not uncommon in practice and is indeed the basis of what is called a *voluntary export restraint* (VER).

A VER is a quota restricting exports of some product from one country to a second country, agreed to by mutual consent of the two governments, in which the importing country compensates the exporting country for its terms-of-trade loss by allowing the exporting country to award the import licenses (and hence the quota rents) to its own citizens. In the 1980s, VERs were implemented between the United States and Japan on computer memory chips and cars, as we will discuss in Chapter 10, and from the 1960s to 2004, industrial countries restricted textile and apparel imports from developing-country sources with a complicated system of VERs called the Multifibre Arrangement (MFA).

7.4.4 Equivalence of Tariffs and Quotas (and How It Can Break Down)

Recall that in the example we have been discussing, a tariff and a quota had exactly the same effects—the same effects on the world price, on the domestic price, on the quantities traded, on producer and consumer surplus in each country—except for the question of who captures the tariff revenues/quota rents. This principle is called *the equivalence of tariffs and quotas*. It is a general principle in models of this type, but it should be pointed out that it breaks down under a number of important circumstances.

1. *Uncertainty*. If, after the government sets the level of the tariff or quota, unpredictable random shocks shift the demand and supply curves, the equilibrium will be affected in different ways in the case of a tariff compared to a quota. For example, under a tariff, the quantity imported will generally change as supply and demand curves shift, but under a quota it will be unchanged (and domestic prices will generally be more volatile under a quota as a result).

2. *Rent Seeking*. Under a quota, ownership of an import license is valuable because it allows the bearer to buy the good at an artificially low world

price and sell it at the artificially high domestic price. As a result, if a firm can increase its allocation of these licenses by undertaking some action, even if that action is costly, it may be a worthwhile investment to do so. This is called *rent seeking*; more generally, rent seeking denotes any use of otherwise potentially productive resources to increase one's share of an economic rent such as a quota rent. The phrase was coined in a famous analysis by Krueger (1974), who argued that such competition for quota rents was an argument for preferring tariffs over quotas. For example, a firm might hire a team of *lobbyists*, professionals who specialize in persuading government decision-makers, to go to the trade ministry and convince the bureaucrats there that the firm deserves a larger share of the quota licenses than other firms. If all firms do this, and there is free entry into rent seeking, then zero profits will result, meaning that the quota rent each firm receives will be equal to that firm's spending on lobbyists. Adding this up implies that total spending on lobbyists is equal to the total quota rent—and the welfare effect on the United States is exactly the same as in Figure 7.10. Assuming that lobbyists could have done something productive with their lives, the allocation of a portion of the educated workforce to this activity is a waste of resources that afflicts quotas but not tariffs.

3. *Domestic Monopoly.* For a period in the 1990s, the government of Tanzania protected its struggling domestic matchstick industry with an import quota. Importantly, there was only one manufacturer of matchsticks in the country. In a famous paper, Bhagwati (1965) pointed out that in those circumstances—only one domestic provider of the good or service in question, or in other words *domestic monopoly*—a tariff and a quota can have profoundly different effects. The reason can be seen from Figure 7.13. The vertical axis measures the price P of matches, priced per

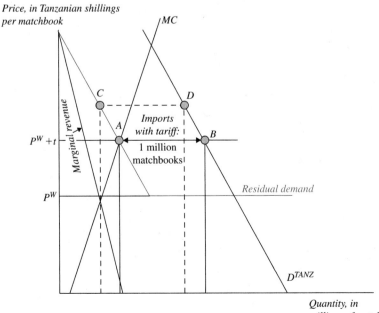

FIGURE 7.13
Tariffs vs. Quotas
with a Domestic
Monopoly.

matchbook, and the horizontal axis measures the quantity. The demand curve for matches in Tanzania is indicated as $D^{TANZ}(P)$, and the marginal cost of the local manufacturer is marked MC. The world price of matches is P^W. Assume that Tanzania is a small country in the market for matches. If the government protects the domestic firm with a specific tariff, t, on all imported matches, then the domestic firm will not be able to make any sales at a price above $P^W + t$, so it maximizes its profit by increasing its output until its marginal cost equals $P^W + t$. The domestic firm therefore produces at point A, and domestic consumers import and consume at point B. In other words, with the tariff, both for the domestic manufacturer and for domestic consumers, the price of matches is effectively taken as given and equal to $P^W + t$. For concreteness, suppose that the quantity of matches imported in that situation—the horizontal distance between points A and B—is one million matchbooks.

Now, suppose that instead of the tariff, the government imposes a quota that restricts imports to exactly the same level as occurred under the tariff—one million matchbooks. Now, the domestic manufacturer knows that it can sell as much as it wants at the world price, but if it charges any price P above the world price, it will be able to sell only the local demand, $D^{TANZ}(P)$, minus the one million units that consumers are permitted to import. As a result, for prices above the world price the domestic manufacturer will face a residual demand curve, or the demand curve that is left over after competing sources of supply have been exhausted, that is the same as the domestic demand curve shifted to the left by one million matchbooks. This residual demand curve is depicted in Figure 7.13 as the blue hockey-stick shape, which is bounded below by P^W because the domestic manufacturer can sell as much as it wishes at that price (including exporting, if need be).

Since this is a downward-sloping residual demand curve, the domestic manufacturer maximizes profit by finding its marginal revenue, here marked as a solid black line, and by setting it equal to marginal cost. This gives optimal production and pricing at point C, while domestic consumers consume at point D. Note that, although the tariff and quota examined here, by construction, allow exactly the same level of imports, under the quota domestic matchbook production and consumption are both strictly lower than they were under the tariff, and the price under the quota is strictly higher than it was under the tariff. That is because the quota allows the domestic monopolist to control the price, which it could not do under a tariff. With a tariff, it took price as given at the value $P^W + t$, and so it had no incentive to lower output in order to increase the price, but with a quota, it does have such an incentive. Put differently, *trade robs a domestic monopolist of its monopoly power; a quota gives some of it back, but a tariff does not.* For that reason, with a domestic monopoly (or oligopoly), tariffs are actually welfare superior to quotas.

7.4.5 Nonoptimality of Export Subsidies

Having understood how import tariffs work in a model like this, we can easily see how export subsidies would work—and why they would always be undesirable, if the goal is to maximize national social welfare. Recalling Figure 7.5, an import tariff shifts the importing country's import demand curve

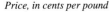
Price, in cents per pound

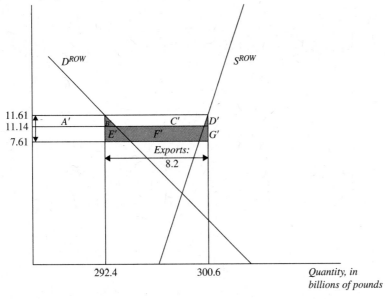

FIGURE 7.14
The Effects of the
Export Subsidy on the
Rest of the World.

*Quantity, in
billions of pounds*

down by the amount of the tariff. Following exactly parallel logic, an export subsidy imposed by the exporting country would shift the *export supply* curve down by the amount of the subsidy. This would lower the world price for the exported good by somewhat less than the subsidy, raising the domestic price in the exporting country so that it is higher than the world price by the amount of the subsidy. Figure 7.14 illustrates the welfare analysis and shows that the exporting country suffers from a consumption and production distortion (B' and D', respectively), and in addition a terms-of-trade loss ($E' + F' + G'$). After all, the export subsidy pushes the price of the good on world markets *down*, which is a drawback for the country that *sells* it on world markets. For this reason, a country in a perfectly competitive trade model can never improve its social welfare with an export subsidy. The subsidy does, however, raise domestic producer surplus by raising the domestic price, so there could be an interest-group motivation for it.

7.4.6 The Argument in General Equilibrium

The whole discussion to this point has been framed in partial equilibrium, but none of the main points depends on that. To sketch how the analysis plays out in general equilibrium, consider the Heckscher-Ohlin model with Apparel and Plastics, produced by skilled and unskilled labor, from Chapter 6. Consider the version of that model with variable-proportions technology, and for the moment assume that within each country each household has the same number of skilled and unskilled workers as all other households, so that we can speak in terms of a "typical" or "representative" household.

The production possibilities frontier has the appearance shown in Figure 7.15, with a concave shape. Consider the case of a small open economy, which faces a world relative price for apparel equal to P^W. Under free trade, it produces at point A, where the marginal rate of transformation is equal to P^W, and the typical household's budget line is the straight line going through that

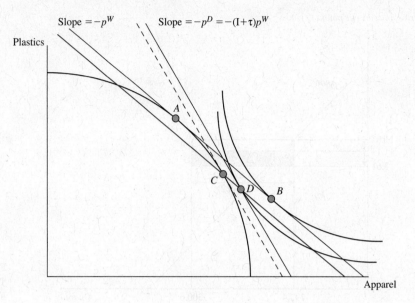

FIGURE 7.15
The Effect of a Tariff
in a Small Open
Economy: General
Equilibrium.

production point with slope equal to P^W. Consumption is at point B, where the budget line is tangent to the typical household's indifference curve. Note that for this economy, consumption of apparel exceeds production of apparel, so apparel is the imported good. Now, if the government places an *ad valorem* tariff τ on apparel imports, that will raise the domestic relative price of apparel to $(1 + \tau)P^W$, moving the production point to C. Suppose that the government distributes the revenue received from the tariff evenly to all households. Then the budget line no longer goes through the production point because each household will now receive some tariff revenue from the government. For each household, this tariff revenue is lump-sum income, which the household receives in addition to its income from selling labor in the labor market. Therefore, the budget line is not the broken line going through point C, but a parallel shift of that line, to the right.

In equilibrium, the value of this economy's consumption must equal the value of its production when evaluated at world prices, which means that the consumption point must lie somewhere along the blue line through point C. This can be called a balanced-trade condition since it implies that the value of the nation's imports of apparel at world prices is equal to the value of its exports of plastics at world prices, and the blue line can therefore be called a *balanced-trade line*. Note that since trade must balance *at world prices*, the blue line is parallel to the original black budget line going through point A. An example of how it may end up is with consumption at point D; of course, at the new consumption point, the new budget line (the steep black line passing through point D) must be tangent to an indifference curve. What is clear is that *since the blue balanced-trade line lies everywhere below the original budget line, welfare is lower with the tariff than without.* This is an illustration in general equilibrium of the point made earlier, that in a comparative-advantage model the optimal policy for a small open economy is free trade.

Figure 7.16 shows the same argument for a large economy. The diagram is marked exactly like Figure 7.15. The key difference is that the tariff changes the world relative price of apparel, pushing it down to $(P^W)' < P^W$, so the blue

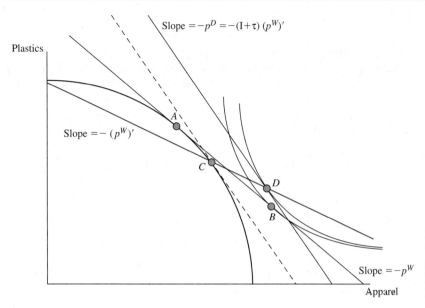

Plastics

$\text{Slope} = -p^D = -(1+\tau)(p^W)'$

$\text{Slope} = -(p^W)'$

A

C

D

B

$\text{Slope} = -p^W$

Apparel

FIGURE 7.16
The Effect of a Tariff in a *Large* Open Economy in General Equilibrium.

balanced-trade line is flatter than the original budget line and crosses it. As a result, it is possible (but not in general guaranteed) that the new consumption point will be superior to the old one, as D is superior to B.

Now relax the assumption that each country is composed of identical egalitarian families, with the same mix of skilled and unskilled workers in each. Suppose that each unskilled worker receives the unskilled wage and each skilled worker receives the skilled wage, so that incomes are unequal across workers. Now note that by raising the domestic relative price of apparel in an apparel-importing country, the tariff will raise the real wage for unskilled workers and lower the real wage for skilled workers, by the logic of the Stolper-Samuelson theorem studied in Chapter 6. Thus, in that country, the tariff will lower income inequality. In an economy that imports plastics, a tariff will have the opposite effects, thereby *increasing* income inequality. Thus, these general-equilibrium effects can provide a redistributive motive either for or against protection, depending on the country.

7.4.7 The Effective Rate of Protection

An industry is affected in general not merely by the trade protection applied to its own products, but also by any trade protection applied to any inputs that it might import. This fact gives rise to a distinction between an industry's *nominal rate of protection*, or the protection received by the industry's own output, and its *effective rate of protection* (ERP) which is a measure of the net effect of trade policy on the industry, taking into account effects on the domestic price of the industry's output and on the prices of its inputs. A common measure of the ERP is the ratio of the industry's value-added per unit at domestic prices to value-added per unit at world prices, minus one.

For example, suppose for simplicity that the production of sugar requires no intermediate inputs, so that all revenue from sale of sugar is value added. Then with a 100% *ad valorem* tariff on sugar imports the domestic price of sugar will be double the world price, so value-added per unit at domestic prices will be double value-added per unit at world prices, and the ERP will be simply $(2/1) - 1$, or 100%. In general, if there are no intermediate inputs, the nominal rate of protection is equal to the effective rate of protection.

Now, assume that production of candy requires labor and sugar, and imports of candy are subject to a 10% *ad valorem* tariff. In equilibrium, production of one case of candy requires $50 worth of labor and $50 worth of sugar. Suppose that the world price of the case of candy is $100, so with the tariff, the case of candy sells domestically for $110. Value-added per case of candy at domestic prices is $110 minus $50 for the sugar, or $60. Value-added per case at world prices is $100 minus $25 for the sugar, or $75. (Recall from the previous paragraph that in this example half of the domestic price of sugar is due to the tariff.) The ERP for the candy industry is then $(60/75) - 1$, or -20%, a *negative* number. Despite the fact that the sugar industry receives a nominal rate of protection equal to 10%, on balance domestic production of candy is discouraged by trade policy. In general, if there are traded intermediate inputs whose prices are affected by trade policy, nominal and effective rates of protection are different.

MAIN POINTS

1. In a perfectly competitive setting in which trade is driven by comparative advantage, a large country can improve its social welfare by restricting imports, either by an import tax (in other words, a tariff) or by quantitative restrictions (in other words, a quota).

2. This welfare improvement comes from a terms-of-trade improvement, meaning that the trade restriction pushes the price of the imported good down on world markets.

3. However, the trade restriction also distorts domestic production and consumption decisions in the importing country, creating an efficiency cost that must be weighed against the terms-of-trade benefit. If the tariff is too high or the quota is too restrictive, the importing country's social welfare will be lower than under free trade. This appears to be the case in the U.S. sugar policy, which is highly restrictive and appears to be driven by interest group politics rather than a terms-of-trade motive.

4. In any case, the terms-of-trade benefit for the importing country is equal to a terms-of-trade loss that it imposes on the rest of the world. As a result, social welfare of the world as a whole is reduced by the trade restriction.

5. An optimal tariff for a large economy is inversely proportional to the elasticity of export supply from the rest of the world. The optimal tariff for a small economy is zero.

6. A voluntary export restraint is a quota in which the exporter gets to keep the quota rent. This allows for the possibility that the export country benefits from the restriction, while social welfare in the importing country is guaranteed to fall.

7. An export subsidy never improves social welfare for the exporting country in a comparative-advantage world.

QUESTIONS AND PROBLEMS

1. Consider the following two-country model of the market for spinach. All producers and consumers take the price of spinach as given. Home's supply curve for spinach is given by

$$S^H = 5 + P,$$

where S^H is the quantity supplied by Home producers in millions of tons and P is the price in dollars per ton. Home's demand curve is given by:

$$D^H = 100 - P,$$

where D^H is the quantity demanded in Home. Foreign's supply and demand curve are given by:

$$S^F = 2P$$

and

$$D^F = 100 - P,$$

respectively.

(a) Derive the Home import demand curve and the Foreign export supply curve for spinach, and use them to find the free-trade equilibrium, including the world price of spinach and the quantity traded. Draw a diagram that shows this equilibrium.

(b) Now, assume that Home imposes a $5 per ton import tariff. Show diagrammatically how this shifts the import demand curve and changes the equilibrium. Compute the new world price and domestic price for spinach in Home.

(c) Does the tariff raise or lower Home's welfare? Show your calculations.

2. For the previous question, find a quota that would have equivalent effects to the $5 tariff. Show the effects, numerically and diagrammatically, on Home and Foreign welfare (a) under the assumption that Home traders capture the quota rents; (b) under the assumption that Foreign traders capture the quota rents.

3. Again for the same model, suppose that Home does not impose any trade policy, but Foreign provides a $5 per ton export subsidy.

(a) Analyze the effects on the equilibrium, showing how the Foreign export supply curve is shifted and how prices, trade quantities, and welfare are affected.

(b) Show the terms-of-trade effect in the Foreign welfare diagram. For which country is this a benefit? For which country is it a loss?

4. Draw the figure showing the marginal effect on the *importing*-country welfare of a small increase in tariff as in Figure 7.12, starting with a tariff of zero. Can you be sure whether or not the tariff improves importing-country welfare, or do you need more information?

5. U.S. policy makers must consider the elasticity of export supply from the rest of the world in formulating sugar policy. Suppose that in the rest of the world there are 1,000,000 consumers of sugar, each with the demand curve $Q^D = a - bP$, and 1,000,000 producers, each with the supply curve $Q^S = c + dP$, where Q^D and Q^S are the quantities demanded and supplied, respectively,

P is the price, and $a, b, c,$ and d are positive constants. Construct a diagram like Figure 7.2, showing how the rest-of-world export supply curve is constructed from the rest-of-world supply and demand. Now, double the number of foreign consumers and producers, and, on the same diagram as you have just constructed, draw the new rest-of-world supply, demand, and export supply curves for sugar. Next, double the numbers again, and draw the new curves, still on the same diagram, and finally draw what the export supply curve will look like eventually as the number of foreign producers and consumers becomes very large. What happens to the elasticity of export supply as the number of foreigners becomes large? What happens to the optimal U.S. sugar tariff? *BONUS*: To what value will the equilibrium world price converge with the U.S. optimal tariff in place, as the number of foreigners becomes large? You of course cannot come up with numbers, but you can come up with an algebraic expression.

Use the spreadsheet "optimal tariff.xls" for the *following questions.* The spreadsheet allows you to plot how welfare changes with a change in tariffs for an importing country under a range of assumptions. The first few columns show the parameters for demand and supply for a commodity produced by two countries, Home and Foreign, as well as welfare weights for producer and consumer surplus and tariff revenue and some additional policies. You can change these settings. Column K gives a range of possible values for Home's tariff, and the following columns give the equilibrium outcomes for various variables for each value of the tariff, conditional on the parameter settings in the first few columns of the spreadsheet. In particular, column R shows Home unweighted welfare, and column S shows Home weighted welfare, based on the weights given by cells F13–15.

6. Using the parameters for the U.S.-ROW sugar model detailed in Section 7.2, create a figure that plots U.S. social welfare on the vertical axis against the tariff level on the horizontal axis. Using this visual aid, find (to a reasonable approximation) the optimal tariff, and compare it to the tariff level of 12.38 cents per pound that is a good approximation for the actual policy. What can you learn from this comparison?

7. Examine how the "optimal" tariff might change with different priorities of the political decision makers as follows. Again, use the parameters for the U.S.-ROW sugar model.

(a) Plot unweighted welfare as a function of the tariff level. In the same figure, plot weighted welfare with $A^{cons} = A^{tax} = 1$ and $A^{prod} = 1.5$, and then with $A^{cons} = A^{prod} = 0$ and $A^{tax} = 1$.

(b) What is the optimal tariff in the case of a social-welfare-maximizing government? A government biased toward the sugar producers? A government that cares only about raising tariff revenue?

(c) Discuss the differences, and try to analyze why the optimal tariffs in the three cases are different in the way that they are.

8. Consider a country that is a net importer of oranges, in a partial-equilibrium comparative-advantage model of the same type as the U.S.-ROW sugar model in the text. This is a country that does produce some oranges, but it is a small country in the world orange market.

(a) What is the optimal tariff for this country, assuming that the political decision makers wish to maximize unweighted social welfare?

(b) Suppose that domestic orange growers argue that they should have tariff protection because foreign orange growers benefit from subsidies from their own governments, and as a result, the world price of oranges is artificially (and unfairly) low. Does this observation change your conclusion about the optimal tariff on orange imports for this country? Explain your reasoning very clearly.

REFERENCES

Belsie, Laurent (2002). "Bitter Reality: Candy Less Likely to Be 'Made in US." *Christian Science Monitor* (April 8), p. 1.

Bhagwati, Jagdish (1965). "On the Equivalence of Tariffs and Quotas," in R. E. Baldwin (ed.), *Trade, Growth and the Balance of Payments—Essays in Honor of Gottfried Haberler*, Chicago: Rand McNally, pp. 53–67.

Bovard, James (1995). "Archer Daniels Midland: A Case Study in Corporate Welfare." Cato Policy Analysis No. 241.

Business Week (1976). "When Competition Against Sugar Turned Sour." November 15, p. 136.

Elobeid, Amani, and John Beghin (2006). "Multilateral Trade and Agricultural Policy Reforms in Sugar Markets." *Journal of Agricultural Economics* 57:1, pp. 23–48.

General Accounting Office (GAO) (2000). *SUGAR PROGRAM: Supporting Sugar Prices Has Increased Users' Costs While Benefitting Producers.* Washington, DC: GAO/RCED-00-126.

Gökçekuş, Ömer, Justin Knowles, and Edward Tower (2003). "Sweetening the Pot: How American Sugar Buys Protection," in Devashish Mitra and Arvind Panagariya (eds.), *The Political Economy of Trade, Aid and Foreign Investment: Essays in Honor of Edward Tower.* Amsterdam: Elsevier, pp. 177–196.

Grossman, Gene M., and Helpman, Elhanan (1994). "Protection for Sale." *American Economic Review* 84:4, pp. 833–850.

Jusko, Jill (2002). "Bitter Goodbye; Confectionery Manufacturers Say U.S. Government Subsidies Boost Domestic Sugar Prices Unfairly, Making Moving Offshore an Appealing Prospect for Some." *Industry Week* (July), p. 23.

Krueger, Anne. O. (1974). "The Political Economy of the Rent-Seeking Society." *American Economic Review* 64:3 (June), pp. 291–303.

USA Today (2002). "Sugar Lobby's Clout Threatens Economic Decay." August 19, p. 14A.

USITC (2001). *Industry Summary: Sugar.* Washington, DC: USITC Publication 3405 (March).

Who Are the WTO, and What Do They Have Against Dolphins?

8

Flip Nicklin/NG Image Collection

The source of the problem. Photographed from below, a floating log at the surface of the ocean off of Costa Rica attracts a ball of small fish, which in turn attracts both tuna and dolphins. Since they often hunt in the same place, dolphins are often caught in nets intended for the tuna.

8.1 The Dolphin Fiasco and Other Stories

For many commentators who regard globalization as a problem, the dolphin fiasco is Exhibit A.

Dolphins tend to loiter under schools of tuna, as the two groups hunt for the same types of prey. As a result, industrial methods of catching tuna by dragging a gigantic net through the ocean to entrap tuna schools—encirclement nets, which became widespread in the 1950s—tend to kill large numbers of dolphins. During the 1960s and 1970s, public concern grew about the millions of dolphins killed in this way. In 1972, the U.S. Congress passed the Marine Mammal Protection Act, which banned the encirclement nets and further banned imports from countries that allowed them. The act was not enforced until the late 1980s, when a suit by an environmentalist group forced the government to take action. As a result, the

United States banned imports of tuna from Mexico, Venezuela, and Vanuatu, as countries harvesting tuna in dolphin-unsafe ways. A "secondary ban" was also imposed on imports from Costa Rica, Italy, Japan, Spain, France, the Netherlands Antilles, and the United Kingdom because those countries permitted imports of dolphin-unsafe tuna. (See Keleman, 2001, for a detailed account.)

Mexico filed a complaint with a panel of the General Agreement on Tariffs and Trade (GATT) (about which we will hear much more later) complaining that this ban was a discriminatory move, inconsistent with the United States' commitments under international agreements. The GATT panel ruled in favor of the Mexican government and struck down the U.S. import ban. To many citizens who wanted their government to be doing more to protect our environment, this signaled that institutions created ostensibly to foster free trade were an obstacle, standing in the way of good public policy and the democratic process itself (see, for example, the commentary by U.S. Senator Sherrod Brown in Brown, 2004, pp. 62−64, who concludes that the trade rules "simply would not let the United States do the right thing for the environment").

There have been several other prominent cases in which a similar outcome has occurred; a number of them are documented in Keleman (2001) and Brown (2004, Chapter 3). For example, in 1997, the World Trade Organization (WTO), which was created in the mid-1990s to govern the GATT, ruled against the United States in favor of shrimp-exporting countries whose exports had been banned because they did not require devices to protect sea turtles. These turtles are endangered species, and sometimes the turtles get caught in shrimp traps and drown. In these cases and in others, observers concerned with the environment have complained *that the institutions of international trade have gotten in the way of protecting the environment.*

On the other hand, there have been a good number of cases in which a regulation drafted ostensibly for health or environmental reasons appears to have recklessly interfered with international trade. One striking example is the case of Chilean grapes. Chile is a major supplier of grapes to the United States. In March 1989, anonymous calls to the U.S. embassy in Santiago warned of cyanide-contaminated grapes on their way to the United States from Chile. In response, U.S. officials quietly conducted inspections of 10% of all grape shipments from Chile, a substantial undertaking given imports of 600,000 boxes per day. On March 12, 1989, two grapes were found with what looked like puncture marks, and tests of those two grapes showed nonlethal traces of cyanide. The next day the U.S. government banned all Chilean grape imports. This occurred at the peak of the export season: 45% of the crop had already left Chile. The ban was devastating for Chile; over its 4-day lifespan, it is estimated to have caused $400 million of harm to the Chilean economy. Later, evidence emerged (partly through an investigation by the *Wall Street Journal*) that the grapes may have been contaminated not in Chile but in the United States. This fueled repeated, but unsuccessful, claims for compensation from the Chilean government. (See Engel, 2000, for a detailed account.)

In the grape case, the Chilean government complained that a flimsy and in fact erroneous claim of a health hazard led to an unwarranted disruption of trade that caused significant hardship to a trade partner. In a similar vein, the United States has complained that Russia's health standards imposed on frozen chicken from the United States, on one occasion banning imports of U.S. chicken altogether, are not motivated by genuine health concerns but rather by protection for domestic producers (White et al., 2004). Additional examples abound. In these cases, plaintiffs have argued *that a weak claim of a health or environmental issue has been used in a reckless and unwarranted way to disrupt international trade.*

How did these tensions arise, and in particular, how did the WTO wind up in the middle of such disputes? To understand these questions, it is essential to understand the arguments for the necessity of multilateral cooperation on trade policy that gave rise to the WTO in the first place. These arguments flow naturally from the analysis of trade policy discussed in the previous chapter, and that is what will be discussed here. The point is that any country's trade policy confers a *terms-of-trade externality* on other countries. In the analysis of a tariff in Chapter 7, for example, this took the form of a terms-of-trade loss imposed on trade partners equal in size to the terms-of-trade benefit enjoyed by the tariff-using country. Because of these terms-of-trade externalities, if each country sets its own tariffs independently of all others, the resulting outcome will be inefficient, and so there is good reason for countries to try to coordinate trade policies through negotiation. This gives rise to the GATT and the WTO.[1] However, as episodes such as the grape incident above illustrate, terms-of-trade externalities arise not only from trade policy, but from environmental and health policy as well as many others. As a result, the same forces that make governments try to coordinate *trade* policies also provide a motive to coordinate those other policies, or at least create rules to minimize the resulting inefficiencies. This, then, explains why the WTO gets involved in so many environmental disputes, giving rise to episodes such as the dolphin–tuna conflict.

In the next section, we will look at the argument for international cooperation in trade policy, due to the terms-of-trade externality conferred on other countries by any country's trade policy. In the following section, we will see how that argument implies a case for cooperation in other areas as well, because even a country's health or environmental policies also tend to confer a terms-of-trade externality. This helps explain why multilateral trade institutions tend to get caught up in environmental disputes. The next section shows how, further, environmental policy can be used as a proxy for trade policy. The final section of the chapter provides a brief summary of how international institutions have evolved to handle these tensions.

8.2 The Trade War Problem and the Need for Coordination in Trade Policy

Every government can set its own trade policy, which is part and parcel of controlling its own borders. However, since the end of the Second World War, governments the world over have put a tremendous amount of effort into coordinating their trade policies with each other. The main argument for doing so has to do with neutralizing terms-of-trade externalities. To see this, we will employ a simple, stylized partial-equilibrium model of the same type as we used in Chapter 7.

---

[1] The idea of the WTO as a response to the problem of terms-of-trade externalities has been articulated with great care by Bagwell and Staiger (2002), which is an excellent source of further reading on this subject for advanced students. The reasoning explored throughout this chapter draws heavily from that book, although it is presented in a different form. The analysis in Staiger and Sykes (2011) is also very closely related.

For the sake of argument, suppose that the world consists of two countries, the United States and Japan. We will focus on two goods, tuna and apples (because they happen to be good examples of environmental disputes that have popped up between the two countries).[2] Suppose that the demand curves for tuna in the United States and in Japan are identical and are given by:

$$D^T = 100 - P^T, \tag{8.1}$$

where D^T is the quantity of tuna demanded, in millions of pounds, and P^T is the price in dollars per pound. Suppose that the supply curve for tuna in the United States is given by:

$$S^{T,US} = P^T \tag{8.2}$$

and the supply curve in Japan is given by:

$$S^{T,J} = 2P^T, \tag{8.3}$$

where $S^{T,i}$ is the quantity of tuna supplied in country i. Thus, the supply curve in Japan is shifted to the right compared to the curve for the United States, implying (together with the identical demand curves) that Japan will be an exporter of tuna under free trade.

Assume that the market for apples is identical with the roles switched. That is, both countries will have a demand curve for apples given by (8.1), with D^A standing for the quantity of apples demanded, in millions of pounds, in place of D^T, and P^A standing for the price of apples in place of P^T, in dollars per pound; the U.S. supply of apples will be given by (8.3), with $S^{A,US}$ replacing $S^{T,J}$; and Japan's supply of apples will be given by (8.2), with $S^{A,J}$ replacing $S^{T,US}$. Thus, we have a simple, symmetric model, in which the United States has a comparative advantage in apples and Japan in tuna.

Suppose that each country's government sets its tariff optimally, independent of the other, and for now assume that each government maximizes its own country's social welfare. This implies that the United States will set an optimal tariff on Japanese tuna and the Japanese government will set an optimal tariff on American apples. It turns out that in this case the optimal tariff for each country is equal to $4.80 per pound. (This can be verified by using the "optimal tariffs.xls" spreadsheet, or by verifying that this value satisfies the inverse elasticity formula from Section 7.4.1—both of which are good exercises for additional practice.)

A term from game theory will be useful throughout this discussion. Recall from Chapter 4 that in any game, a *Nash equilibrium* is an outcome in which each player is maximizing his or her payoff, taking as given the action of the other player. If we think of the situation at hand as a game in which the players are the governments of the United States and Japan and the choice each one needs to make is the tariff on that country's imported good, then the tariff outcome just described (tariffs of $4.80 for each good imposed by its importing country) is actually a Nash equilibrium, since each government is

---

[2] Unlike previous examples, we will look at an illustrative numerical example to make the argument as clear as possible, rather than a model with parameters calibrated to the data.

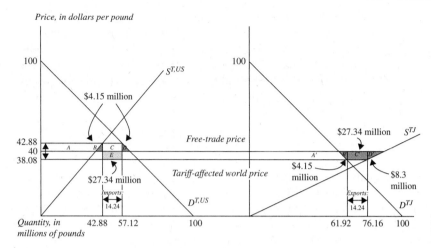

FIGURE 8.1
Tuna Protectionism.

choosing its tariff to maximize its own country's social welfare, taking the other country's tariff as given. Accordingly, we will refer to this outcome as Nash tariffs or noncooperative tariffs. It is also sometimes called a trade war.

Under Nash tariffs, we can calculate equilibrium outcomes just as with the sugar example in Chapter 7. The equilibrium is illustrated in Figure 8.1, with the U.S. market for tuna in the left panel and the Japanese market for tuna in the right panel. The welfare effects of the tariff are marked using the same color and notation as in Figures 7.7 and 7.8. The diagram for apples would be identical in every respect with the two countries' roles reversed, and so it is omitted. The equilibrium world price of tuna is equal to $40 under free trade and $38.08 under the Nash tariffs of $4.80 per pound. The domestic U.S. price of tuna is equal to $40 under free trade and $42.88 under Nash tariffs. The equilibrium quantity of tuna exported is 20 million pounds under free trade and 14.24 million pounds under Nash tariffs. For the crucial welfare outcomes, the U.S. consumption distortion amounts to $4.15 million, the production distortion also amounts to $4.15 million, and the terms-of-trade benefit equals the change in the world price of tuna, $(40 − 38.08) per pound, times the quantity imported, 14.24 million pounds, or $27.34 million. These are all shown in the left-hand panel of the figure. Clearly, the terms-of-trade benefit exceeds the sum of the two distortions, so the United States benefits from its tuna tariff.

Note from the right-hand panel of the figure, however, that the $27.34 million terms-of-trade benefit for the United States is also a $27.34 million terms-of-trade *loss* for Japan (recall that area E from Figure 7.7 is equal to area C' of Figure 7.8; the same principle applies here). This is the terms-of-trade externality: The U.S. tariff benefits the United States by improving its own terms of trade, which implies *worsening* its trade partner's terms of trade. Put in common language, the United States benefits from making Japanese tuna cheap, while the Japanese emphatically do not.

The same logic works in the opposite direction for apples: Japan receives a $27.34 million terms-of-trade *benefit* from its apple tariff, which amounts to a $27.34 million terms-of-trade *loss* to the United States. Therefore, in adding up the net effect on U.S. welfare of both countries' tariffs together, the terms-of-trade effects cancel out. All that is left is the sum of consumption and production distortions—thus an unambiguously negative effect. The analysis for Japan is identical: *Both* countries are hurt by the combination of the two tariffs. In game theory, this type of situation is often called a *Prisoner's Dilemma* problem, meaning a Nash equilibrium that is a Pareto-inferior outcome. Note that the Nash tariff outcome is worse for both countries despite the fact that, by definition, in a Nash equilibrium each player is being completely rational and behaving optimally. (Recall that we encountered a Prisoner's Dilemma in Chapter 4, Section 4.6.)

To summarize, *because of the terms-of-trade externality, world social welfare is higher under free trade than it is under the Nash tariffs, and both countries can be made better off by negotiating to free trade.*

Essentially, this explains the motivation for the General Agreement on Tariffs and Trade (GATT), which was signed by a broad coalition of governments in 1948 precisely to negotiate lower trade restrictions. The interwar years had been marked by a sharp rise in U.S. tariffs, notably the Smoot-Hawley tariff bill of 1930, and a subsequent rise in European tariffs. (Recall that we have seen a picture of the Smoot-Hawley tariffs, in the form of the giant mountain peak of Figure 1.3.) The resulting situation, interpreted by many as a trade war, was blamed by many for exacerbating the Great Depression.[3] Following World War II, governments around the world were eager to find ways to foster international cooperation, and as they created the United Nations to avoid future military conflicts, the World Bank to help with reconstruction following the devastation of the war, and the International Monetary Fund to coordinate monetary policies and provide stability to international financial markets, they also drafted the GATT, in the same spirit, to avoid future trade wars and move as close as possible to free trade.

There have been eight renegotiations of the original GATT agreement, called GATT Rounds, each lowering trade barriers a bit further than the one before. The result has been a steady drop in tariffs worldwide, such as the downward trend in U.S. tariffs since World War II illustrated with Figure 1.3, resulting in average tariffs at the end of the twentieth century that were about one-third of their level at midcentury. Inasmuch as the original function of the GATT was the reduction of trade barriers, a glance at Figure 1.3 (or the corresponding figure for any of the other major signatory countries) shows that it has been a resounding success. As we noted in Chapter 1, this was part of the process that produced the second great wave of globalization.

The latest GATT Round to be completed (1994) is the Uruguay Round, named for the location in which negotiations began. This round not only reduced trade barriers further, but also replaced the loose organization that had sprung up as part of the original GATT process with a new, much better formalized organization, the World Trade Organization (WTO). The WTO organizes the negotiation of new rounds of tariff-reduction and ancillary agreements, and adjudicates disputes between members (see Hoekman and Kostecki, 2001, for an overview of the GATT and WTO). The agreements have become much more far-reaching than the original rounds, which were focused on manufacturing tariffs. The WTO now treats issues of trade in

---

[3] Irwin (1998) reviews available research on this issue and provides some new estimates. He argues that the Smoot-Hawley tariffs probably reduced U.S. trade by something like 4% and lowered real GDP by less than 1%. It is quite possible that world leaders in the postwar period overestimated the role of Smoot-Hawley in exacerbating the Great Depression.

services and in agricultural products, rules of conduct for treatment of foreign direct investment, intellectual property, and—as we shall see—the handling of a wide range of issues in health, safety, and environmental regulation.

A current round, begun in Doha, Qatar, in 2001, is still in progress and appears to be bogged down in stalemate. This was to have been the development round, meaning that the organizers had hoped that developing countries would participate much more fully, reducing their own trade barriers (which tend to be much higher than those of rich countries) in return for rich-country concessions. To summarize a long story, a number of agricultural-commodity-exporting countries have insisted on a reduction in rich-country agricultural producer subsidies; developing countries want a reduction in rich-country use of antidumping and countervailing duties; and rich countries want more access to the developing-country markets. After 10 years, the failure of participants to come to agreement on any of these issues has led to widespread frustration with the multilateral process. It has also increased interest in trade agreements between small groups of countries, "regional," or "preferential" trade agreements, such as those studied in Chapter 15, as a substitute for the broader liberalization that had been hoped for from the WTO process.

The original GATT is a complex treaty, and subsequent revisions have increased its complexity, but a handful of principles underpin the whole enterprise. A key GATT principle is known deceptively as the *most-favored-nation principle* (MFN—Article I of the original GATT agreement). This is simply a nondiscrimination principle. The MFN rule requires that any trade policy concession, such as a lowered tariff, that any country offers to *any* country (whether a WTO member or not) must also be offered to *all* WTO members. (In other words, all members are most favored nations. But what it really means is that no member is favored. It is not clear whether the original negotiators deliberately chose the most confusing language possible or whether it just turned out that way.)

A second important GATT principle is *national treatment* (Article III of the GATT text), which requires each member government to treat any product produced in any member country no less favorably than a similar product produced domestically, once it is inside the country's borders. For example, Switzerland may place a tariff on imported brake pads, but it may not impose safety regulations on French brake pads that are more stringent than the regulations it imposes on Swiss brake pads.

Both of these principles are subject to a large number of exemptions. A few of the more important ones are as follows:

1. Article XXIV allows two or more GATT signatories to sign a preferential trade agreement (PTA), which allows them to remove mutual trade barriers without removing them for other members. For example, along with 25 other countries, Spain and France are part of the European Union, which provides for free trade among all of its members, so French brake pads are imported into Spain duty free and Spanish brake pads are imported into France duty free, but importers must pay a tariff to import Canadian brake pads into either country. These PTAs are permitted provided they satisfy some requirements stipulated in Article XXIV; they will be discussed in Chapter 15.

2. Article VI allows for antidumping policies and countervailing duties. *Dumping* means exporting a product at a price below "fair market value," a legal term infuriating to economists that can mean either the price at which the product is sold in the exporter's home market or the production cost plus a mark-up for "reasonable" profit. The GATT allows for an importing country that finds a product to have been dumped into its market to impose a temporary tariff, an *antidumping duty*, on the dumping exporter. Similarly, if an importing country finds that an exporting country has been subsidizing its exports, that importing country can impose a *countervailing duty* no greater than the amount of the subsidy. It is difficult to rationalize this particular set of provisions on the basis of economic reasoning, but they may be explained as serving a political function.

Both antidumping and countervailing duties have been extremely important and contentious forms of trade policy in practice, and their importance has grown as their practice has spread to more and more member governments over time. The use of antidumping duties first surged in the 1970s as the United States and a few other industrial countries issued changes to antidumping law that made it easier for a domestic firm to file a claim against a foreign competitor and receive a duty in response. From 1921 to 1967, about 15 antidumping cases were filed per year by U.S. firms, but by the 1980s this had jumped to 40 per year. At that time, antidumping cases worldwide were dominated by the United States, the European Union, Canada, and Australia. However, over the 1990s, as regular tariff levels fell, more and more countries such as India, South Africa, and Argentina began to use these duties regularly, and by 2000, "new users" amounted to 44% of the total antidumping cases worldwide (Lindsey and Ikenson, 2001). Bown (2005) has assembled a comprehensive international antidumping database and found that 15 countries account for 87% of antidumping actions worldwide, including such relative newcomers as Peru, Turkey and Mexico.

Countervailing duties have also been used heavily by some WTO members. Between 1980 and 2004, the U.S. government imposed countervailing duties on foreign firms 1,070 times.[4] A recent example is the decision made by the U.S. International Trade Commission in December 2009 to approve duties on U.S. imports of Chinese-made steel pipes for use in petroleum extraction, in order to counterbalance alleged Chinese government subsidies on the production of those pipes.[5] This is one of many similar actions taken against Chinese manufactures in recent years as Chinese exports to the United States have grown, but it may be abruptly ending as a U.S. judge has recently ruled that China is a nonmarket economy and U.S. countervailing duties may be applied only to market economies.[6]

---

[4] This can be calculated from the extensive data on the antidumping and countervailing duties data web page maintained by Prof. Bruce Blonigen of the University of Oregon at: http://pages.uoregon.edu/bruceb/adpage.html.

[5] "U.S. Duties on Pipes from China Approved," *New York Times*, December 31, 2009, p B4.

[6] Eric Martin and Susan Decker, "Tax Duties Against China Tire Subsidies Ruled Illegal." Bloomberg News, December 20, 2011.

In general, most economists regard the Article VI exemptions to be disruptive substitutes to normal tariff protection that have grown in importance as regular tariffs have fallen, which is perhaps unavoidable politically but hard to justify economically.

3. Article XIX, the escape clause, allows a country to suspend its tariff concession temporarily for a particular industry if it has suffered "material injury" due to a surge in imports.

   A famous example of the escape clause in practice was the aggressive set of tariffs raised against a variety of types of steel imports by U.S. President George W. Bush in March 2002. A WTO panel later ruled that these tariffs were inadmissible because they were not truly imposed during an import surge, and so the tariffs were quickly rescinded. A later example is the Obama administration's imposition of tariffs against Chinese tires in September 2009 (under a special safeguards arrangement to which the Chinese government had agreed as part of its process of joining the WTO in 2001, constructed broadly under principles of the original GATT escape clause).

4. Article XX allows for exceptions for the protection of life, health, or natural resources, and for similar motives.

   These exemptions and the other GATT articles form the basis of international trade law. The desirability of each of these articles is the subject of debate; the provisions for antidumping in particular are very unpopular with economists. The international trade law that this structure has created has become complicated, but the main point remains that the GATT and the WTO have been created to overcome the trade war problem and to facilitate coordination of trade policies to the advantage of every country.

8.3 Problem: In an Interconnected World, *All* Policies Are Trade Policies

The foregoing shows why the WTO serves a useful function in facilitating multilateral cooperation on trade policy, but it does not explain why the organization would get involved in environmental or consumer protection policies. This involvement becomes easier to understand, however, when it is pointed out that anything a government does domestically tends to change world prices to some extent, thus affecting trade partners indirectly. (Exceptions are small countries, and even then, if many small countries pursue the same type of policy at the same time, they will also affect world prices.) For example, if the United States taxes domestic consumption of tuna, no matter where the tuna is from, it will shift the U.S. tuna demand curve to the left, shifting the U.S. import demand curve to the left, lowering the world price of tuna, and lowering Japanese welfare. This is not to say that it should not be done, but merely to observe that a portion of the cost is borne by non-Americans, who might have an interest in negotiating with the Americans over the tuna tax. From the point of view of terms-of-trade externalities, one can say that *all* policies are trade policies.

Now, returning to the U.S.-Japan tuna–apples example, suppose that the two countries have successfully achieved free trade through negotiation, making both countries better off, but each learns of an environmental problem that arises from its trade with the other. Suppose, specifically, that each country perceives an environmental harm that could result from importing the other country's good and that this harm is valued at H dollars.[7] (For simplicity, the amount of the harm does not depend on the amount imported.) In the case of the United States, the harm is a disutility from knowing that dolphins are being harmed by the fishing methods of the Japanese tuna harvesters, and in the case of Japan, the harm is the damage to Japanese apple growers from insects transported with American apples.[8] Suppose that the only way of mitigating or avoiding this harm is by banning the imports altogether, as the United States did at one point with Japanese tuna (as described at the beginning of this chapter) and the Japanese did for many years with American apples (see Egan, 1993; the ban was lifted on January 10, 1995). This means that the cost to the United States, for example, of mitigating the harm of the dolphin—unsafe tunas is to give up the gains from trade in tuna with Japan. Let us assume at first that each government acts unilaterally to maximize its own citizens' social welfare, taking environmental costs into account.

The economic cost of banning the tuna imports is shown in the left panel of Figure 8.2. The free-trade price of tuna is $40, while the U.S. autarky price is $50. Banning the imports lowers U.S. tuna consumer surplus by $F + G$ and raises U.S. tuna producer surplus by F, resulting in a net welfare loss of G.

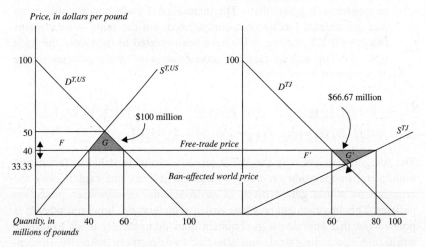

FIGURE 8.2
Economic Effects of a
Tuna Import Ban.

---

[7] It may seem odd to place an economic value on environmental harm, but it is unavoidable in environmental policy making. Some environmental damage is actually economic, as the Japanese government claimed was the case with the apples, which they argued could spread infestations that would lower the income of Japanese apple growers. More generally, the question is how much economic sacrifice voters would be willing to make for the benefit of the improved environment; there is always a limit to how much of their lifestyle voters would be willing to sacrifice for a given environmental aim. Of course, the measurement of these valuations is extremely difficult—and controversial. "How much of a reduction in salary would you be willing to contemplate in order to save the dolphins?" is a very difficult question for most people to answer.

[8] Strictly speaking, if insects infest the Japanese apple orchards, that should be expected to raise the marginal cost of producing apples in Japan and shift the Japanese apple supply curve. However, this is a complication that is immaterial to the point being made, and so we will assume that the supply curve is not affected.

This is the gains from trade in tuna for the United States. Since it is a triangle with a base of 20 million pounds and a height of $10 per pound, it amounts to a loss of $100 million. The right panel of the figure shows the loss to Japan of a U.S. ban on Japanese tuna. The price of tuna in Japan falls from the free-trade price of $40 to the Japanese autarky price of $33.33. Japanese tuna consumer surplus rises by F' and Japanese tuna producer surplus falls by $F' + G'$, for a net social welfare loss of G'. This amounts to a loss of $66.67 million. Of course, the diagram for an apple ban would be identical with the countries' roles reversed, yielding a loss to Japan of $100 million and a loss to the United States of $66.67 million.

As a result, if H is less than $100 million, neither government will ban the others' exports, and the environmental harm will be tolerated for the sake of economic exchange. If H is greater than $100 million, though, each government will ban the other country's exports, and there will be no trade in either good.

Suppose that H takes a value of $140 million. In that case, the Nash equilibrium environmental policy outcome is for each country to ban the other's exports. Each government's action makes sense because the gains from trade for each importing country are exceeded by the avoided environmental harm. However, note that *each country also imposes a trade cost on the other country*. Specifically, the United States imposes a $66.67 million economic loss on Japan by banning tuna imports, and Japan imposes a $66.67 million economic loss on the United States by banning apple imports. As a result, compared to free trade, each country's net welfare effect is equal to ($140 − $100 − $66.67) million, or −$26.67 million. The net effect, in this example, is *negative* (and it will be so for any value of H between $100 million and $166.67 million). Again we have a Prisoner's Dilemma: Both governments act rationally, but without coordinating their actions—and both wind up worse off.

Anti-WTO protesters, Seattle 1999.

The point is the same one made above about trade policy: Because environmental policy imposes a terms-of-trade externality, unilateral environmental-policy setting will generally be inefficient, and there are international gains from cooperation in this field.

8.4 The Sham Problem

Police clash with protesters against the WTO, Seattle 1999.

In the discussion so far, we have assumed that the governments are sincerely attempting to correct a legitimate environmental problem. However, part of the problem in practice is that governments often accuse each other of using a *fictitious* environmental problem to justify protection for domestic political purposes. Under this interpretation, an environmental measure is essentially used as disguised protectionism. This is sometimes called the sham problem; see Baldwin, 2001 for a detailed discussion.

For example, U.S. apple growers used to complain that the true purpose of Japanese regulations on imported apples—ostensibly imposed to protect the Japanese growers from insect infestations—was just to protect those growers from foreign competition. In 1993, U.S. growers in Washington State had produced a crop of apples to exacting standards, following Japanese government regulations to the letter, in order to tap into the Japanese market, growing apples headed for Japan separately from other apples, and even wrapping individual apples in paper while on the tree to ensure that they would be free of the pests. At the last minute the Japanese government found new pest threats that had not been previously raised and excluded U.S.-grown apples once again. U.S. growers complained bitterly that the Japanese government now had instituted a "bug-of-the-month club," meaning that it would always conjure up a new insect threat to keep U.S. apples out. One grower complained: "[W]e get this close and the Japanese move the goal posts again. We can't win." (Egan, 1993).

Similarly, as described above, Chilean authorities argued that the cyanide grape scare of 1989 was a sham (Engel, 2000). For another example, U.S. authorities have complained about Russian restrictions on U.S. frozen chickens, described in detailed reporting by White et al. (2004). The Russian government imposes an exceptionally tough food safety regime for frozen chicken imports, requiring every U.S. plant that ships to Russia to be visited by Russian inspectors, including veterinarians. Regulations cover "everything from where the walls should be located to the state of garbage-can lids. Factory grounds had to be clear of mud and workers were to wear special boots that could only be used inside plants." (White et al., 2004, p. A1). At one point in 2002, Russian authorities banned all imports of frozen chicken from the United States for three weeks, citing bacteria concerns. Things got so tense over chicken that in a presidential summit in 2003 at Camp David, Presidents George W. Bush and Vladimir Putin took time out of negotiating nuclear nonproliferation and terrorism to work out chicken issues—including what boots workers could wear at the plants. In all this, the Russian government has claimed that the issue is safety, but U.S. chicken producers believe that it is an attempt to help domestic chicken producers avoid competition with imports. Their case was helped when a Russian deputy minister of agriculture at one point quipped that "the only tool of trade policy the Agriculture Ministry has left are our veterinarians."

For an economic analysis of the sham problem, return to our tuna-and-apples model. Suppose that the current governments of the United States and Japan are both constrained by prior GATT commitments, perhaps made under previous governments, not to use tariffs in the market for tuna or apples, but both of those governments face political pressures to do something to help their respective import-competing producers. In the notation of Chapter 7, Section 7.3, suppose that $A^{cons} = A^{tax} = 1$ but $A^{prod} > 1$ in each country, where A^{prod} is the weight the government puts on producer surplus in tuna and apples. Suppose that in fact there is no environmental harm from Japanese tuna or U.S.-grown apples, so that in the notation of the previous section $H = 0$. Then if, for example, the U.S. government disingenuously claims environmental harm from Japanese tuna and bans it from the U.S. market, then the domestic price of tuna in the United States will rise from $40 to $50, which will raise U.S. tuna producer surplus and lower U.S. tuna consumer surplus more. If A^{prod} is high enough, the U.S. government will consider this trade-off worthwhile and will impose the ban. Similarly, with the same high value for A^{prod}, the Japanese government will ban the U.S. apples. Given its own political priorities, each government is acting optimally, and so banning the imports is a Nash equilibrium.

However, *once again* there is a terms-of-trade externality to consider. The Japanese ban on U.S. grown apples lowers the price received by U.S. growers from $40 to $33.33, decreasing their producer surplus by $F' + G'$ from Figure 8.2, or $489 million. This must be weighed against the gain to U.S. tuna producers accruing from the rise in the domestic U.S. tuna price from $40 to $50, a rise in producer surplus of F from Figure 8.2, or $450 million. Overall producer surplus in the United States, from tuna and apples combined, therefore falls by \$39 million. Compared to free trade, *both* consumer *and* producer surplus are lower in the Nash equilibrium. As a result, no matter how high A^{prod} is, the U.S. government would prefer free trade to the Nash equilibrium. So would the Japanese government, by parallel reasoning.

To summarize, *because of the terms-of-trade externality, even if the environmental measures are purely for domestic political motives, both governments may prefer coordination on environmental policies to noncooperative environmental policy setting.*

8.5 The WTO's Wobbly Tightrope Walk

This simple tuna-and-apples model has served to demonstrate that terms-of-trade externalities can go a long way in explaining why international coordination of trade and environmental policies is desirable and why an institution like the WTO has a role to play in both types of policy. In practice, the WTO has tried to play this role not by including environmental policies in the multilateral bargaining together with tariffs, but by devising a code of conduct for governments in forming environmental policy, as well as a dispute-resolution mechanism. In effect, in doing so, the WTO has attempted a kind of balancing act, trying to provide enough space for governments to realize environmental goals while at the same time imposing rules to prevent excessive disruptions of trade (as seen in Section 8.3) or disguised protectionism (as seen in Section 8.4). Many critics have argued that at various times the multilateral system has gotten the balance quite wrong. Pressure from activists to reform the WTO to allow for more protection of the environment culminated in a famous series of high-profile protests at the WTO meetings in Seattle, Washington, in 1999. Accounts of the evolution of WTO policy in this area include Keleman (2001), Hoekman and Kostecki (2001, pp. 185−201, pp. 441−448), Baldwin (2001), and Brown (2004, Chapter 3). The WTO website itself (www.wto.org) has a wealth of information on the organization's evolution on these issues.

In 1991, the code of conduct for this type of question was not very well developed, and the panel that ruled against the United States in the dolphin−tuna case cited two principles that it interpreted as implicit in the GATT agreement itself. The first is that although Article XX of the GATT allowed for interruptions of trade for health and environmental reasons, the panel interpreted that as applying only to *product regulations*, or rules regarding which products can be imported, not *process regulations*, or rules strictly regulating only the way in which a product is produced. Since dolphin−safe tuna and dolphin unsafe tuna are identical products, and differ only in the fishing techniques used to produce them, the panel ruled that Article XX could not justify the U.S. ban. Second, the panel ruled that Article XX could be used to protect only the health of consumers or the environment in the country imposing the regulation, whereas the U.S. ban was designed to protect dolphin populations throughout the world. In other words, in the language that has evolved to discuss this decision, the panel rejected *extraterritoriality* in trade-based environmental regulations.

The widespread outrage that followed this decision helped fuel a reexamination of the rules as part of the ongoing negotiations for the Uruguay Round. In 1994, along with the revision of the GATT and the formation of the WTO, two new agreements meant to clarify rules for this type of situation were agreed on. One was called the Technical Barriers to Trade Agreement (meaning an agreement on regulations that are not explicitly trade barriers but can act as one, such as requiring proof of dolphin-safe fishing techniques for all tuna sold). The other was the Sanitary and Phytosanitary Measures Agreement, which covers measures such as the rules to protect the domestic apple crop in Japan from contamination by foreign pests. These agreements essentially required that regulations be based in science and that they be nondiscriminatory and not unnecessarily disruptive of trade.

Another high-profile test came up in 1997, with the shrimp–turtle case. Shrimp harvesting often entangles sea turtles, which get caught in the net and drown. Nets can be fitted with Turtle Excluder Devices (TEDs), which U.S. law requires for shrimp harvesting in sensitive areas. In 1989, the United States banned imports of shrimp from any country that did not require TEDs. Banned countries included India, Malaysia, Thailand, and Pakistan, which filed a complaint with the WTO in 1997. The WTO panel ruled for the complainants—just as it did in the dolphin–tuna case. However, the reason is instructive. The panel ruled against the U.S. policy on the basis that it was discriminatory—the U.S. policy provided aid to some nearby countries to help comply with U.S. requirements, but left out other countries. The panel made it clear that it was not rejecting the policy because it was a process restriction or because of extraterritoriality; in the new legal regime, those were not obstacles to regulation. Indeed, following the decisions, the United States revised its policy to treat all affected exporters equally and was later ruled to be in compliance.

It is easy to argue that the multilateral process initially was biased toward excessive worry about disruption of trade (trying too hard to avoid a "poison-grapes problem" or "frozen-chicken problem," but in the process creating a "dolphin problem"), but that over time, with the help of a swift kick from public opinion, it has gotten the balance better over time.

MAIN IDEAS

1. Any trade policy imposes a terms-of-trade externality on other countries.

2. For this reason, the Nash equilibrium in trade policy tends to be inefficient.

3. An immediate corollary is that governments have an incentive to coordinate over trade policy, giving rise to institutions such as the GATT and WTO. Specifically, governments have an incentive to try to agree to lower trade barriers. A coordinated, mutual reduction of trade barriers has the potential to make every country better off.

4. The GATT dates from 1948 and is the primary multilateral agreement for lowering trade barriers.

5. The WTO dates from 1994 and is the organization that coordinates refinements of the GATT and dispute settlement.

6. In addition to trade policy, any environmental or heath and safety regulation (as well as almost any domestic regulation of anything) confers a terms-of-trade externality in an interconnected world. As a result, the Nash equilibrium in environmental policies tends to be inefficient.

7. This gives a motive for multilateral coordination of environmental, health, and safety regulations as well as trade policies. This has been done by adding a kind of code of conduct for such policies to the WTO. The multilateral system needs to balance the need for countries to set environmental regulation against the need to protect trade from unwarranted disruption. The record of success on that balancing act is mixed.

QUESTIONS AND PROBLEMS

1. In February 1996, President Bill Clinton signed the Telecommunications Act, which (among many other things) required all TV sets sold in the United States to be equipped with a V-chip, which allows parents to filter out sexual or violent content. The United States is a net importer of TVs. Suppose that the market for TVs can be represented by a partial-equilibrium model, much as the model of the market for tuna in the text, with TV exports supplied by Japan. If producing a TV with a V-chip increases the marginal cost of TV production by $10, how does the V-chip law affect producers, consumers, and social welfare in Japan? Explain diagrammatically (use no algebra).

2. Consider a model with two countries, Home and Foreign, and two goods, X and Y. The demand curve for each good in each country is given by:

$$D = 50 - P,$$

where D is the quantity supplied and P is the price. The supply curve for Y in Home and for X in Foreign is given by:

$$Q^S = P,$$

while the supply curve for X in Home and for Y in Foreign is given by:

$$Q^S = 4 + P,$$

where in each case Q^S stands for the quantity supplied.

(a) Use the spreadsheet "optimal tariffs.xls" to find the Nash equilibrium tariffs for each country for this model.

(b) Calculate the change in social welfare in each country if we move from Nash equilibrium tariffs to free trade. Illustrate with a diagram.

(c) Given your results, would Home and Foreign prefer to negotiate trade policy, or would they prefer to maintain their sovereignty and discretion by leaving each country to set its trade policy on its own?

3. In the previous problem, suppose that we increase the size of Foreign by multiplying the Foreign demand and supply curves all by the same *large* number.

(a) Recalling the discussion of tariffs and small countries in Chapter 7 (Sections 7.4.1 and 7.4.2), what will the Nash equilibrium look like now? (Answer qualitatively; describe the characteristics of the Nash equilibrium, not the exact value of the tariffs. No new computation is necessary.)

(b) If we move from the Nash equilibrium to free trade, will social welfare in both countries rise? Why or why not?

(c) Given your answers above, are small countries or large countries likely to be more interested in pursuing negotiated free trade?

4. Returning to Problem 2, suppose that good X is a consumption good with a negative consumption externality (for example, automobiles, which create local air pollution), so the Foreign government imposes a tax of $4 per unit consumed in Foreign. (Recall from basic microeconomics that an optimal response to a negative externality is a tax equal to the social cost of the externality, the standard economist's prescription for dealing with externalities. This is often called a Pigouvian tax, after A. C. Pigou, who first proposed it.)

(a) Show diagrammatically how this affects the Foreign import demand curve for good X and changes the world equilibrium, and compute the new world price of good X. (Assume that neither country is using any tariff or other explicit trade policy.)

(b) What effect does Foreign's domestic environmental policy have on producers of X, consumers of X, and social welfare in Home? Would the government of Home be interested in negotiating with Foreign over this policy?

(c) Now suppose that instead of Foreign imposing a domestic consumption tax on good X, it was Home that became worried about the externalities from consuming X, and therefore imposed its own tax of $4 per unit consumed. How would the effect on Foreign compare with the effect of Foreign's tax on Home? (Thre is no need to compute the new equilibrium.)

5. In the model of the sham problem in Section 8.4, would there be any role for multilateral cooperation on environmental policy if $A^{prod} = 1$? Explain in detail why or why not.

REFERENCES

Bagwell, Kyle, and Robert W. Staiger (2002). *The Economics of the World Trading System*. Cambridge, MA: The MIT Press.

Baldwin, Richard E. (2001). "Regulatory Protectionism, Developing Nations, and a Two-Tier World Trading System." *Brookings Trade Forum 2000*, pp. 237–280.

Bown, Chad P. (2005). "Global Antidumping Database Version 1.0." World Bank Policy Research Working Paper 3737, October.

Brown, Sherrod (2004). *Myths of Free Trade: Why American Trade Policy Has Failed*. New York: The New Press.

Egan, Timothy (1993). "Angered by Japan's Barriers, U.S. Apple Growers Retaliate." *New York Times*, August 17 .

Engel, Eduardo M.R.A. (2000). "Poisoned Grapes, Mad Cows and Protectionism." *Journal of Economic Policy Reform* 4:2, pp. 91–111

Hoekman, Bernard M. and Michel M. Kostecki (2001). *The Political Economy of the World Trading System: The WTO and Beyond* (2nd edition). New York: Oxford University Press.

Irwin, Douglas A. (1998). "The Smoot-Hawley Tariff: A Quantitative Assessment." *The Review of Economics and Statistics* 80:2 (May), pp. 326–334.

Keleman, R. Daniel (2001). "The Limits of Judicial Power: Trade-Environment Disputes in the GATT/WTO." *Comparative Political Studies* 34:6 (August), pp. 622–650.

Lindsey, Brink, and Dan Ikenson (2001). "Coming Home to Roost: Proliferating Antidumping Laws and the Growing Threat to U.S. Exports." Cato Institute Trade Policy Analysis No. 14, July 30.

Staiger, Robert W., and Alan O. Sykes (2011). "International Trade, National Treatment, and Domestic Regulation." *The Journal of Legal Studies* 40:1 (January), pp. 149–203.

White, Gregory L., Scott Kilman, and Roger Thurow (2004). "The Farms Race—Chicken Fight: In Global Food-Trade Skirmish, Safety Is the Weapon of Choice—As Tariffs Carry Less Weight, Standards Play Bigger Role; Russia Sends 'Napoleon'—Chipping Away at 'Bush's Legs.'" *The Wall Street Journal, December* 15, p. A1.

9

Should Developing-Country Governments Use Tariffs to Jump-start Growth?

Workers in a 20th-century American rayon plant. In its early days, the U.S. textile industry was incubated behind a high tariff wall, as were many industries in today's affluent economies during their early industrial growth. Was this protectionism a help or hindrance? And should today's developing economies follow the same strategy?

9.1 A Silver Bullet?

Recently, the columnist George Monbiot of the British newspaper, *The Guardian*, wrote a column entitled "One thing is clear from the history of trade: protectionism makes you rich." It succinctly summarized a particular theory of economic development:

> Neoliberal economists claim rich countries got that way by removing their barriers to trade. Nothing could be further from the truth. As Ha-Joon Chang shows in his book *Kicking Away the Ladder*, Britain discovered its enthusiasm for free trade only after it had achieved economic dominance. The industrial revolution

was built on protectionism. . . . Between 1864 and 1913 [the United States] was the most heavily protected nation on earth, and the fastest-growing. It wasn't until after the second world war, when it had already become top dog, that it dropped most of its tariffs. The same strategy was followed by Japan, South Korea, Taiwan and almost every other country that is rich today. . . . Protectionism, which can be easily exploited by corrupt elites, does not always deliver wealth; but development is much harder without it. (Monbiot, 2008)

The argument is that *temporary* import tariffs can be an effective way of starting economic growth. This is an extremely common—and extremely contentious—view among watchers of economic development and is indeed common enough to have its own name: the *infant-industry argument* for protection. Whether or not this argument holds water is an extremely important question, since it implies that pressure by rich-country governments to convince the low-income countries to open up their markets to trade could in fact condemn millions of people to a future of unrelenting poverty, while judicious use of tariffs could be the silver bullet that would break the curse of poverty.

We will look at the infant-industry argument, in history and in theory. First, some background may help.

9.2 The Infant-Industry Argument: Background

The most straightforward definition of infant-industry protection is *temporary protection of an industry in which a country does not currently have a comparative advantage, in the hopes that it will thereby gain a comparative advantage in it over time.* The standard form is a tariff to protect a nascent industry, which the government intends to remove once the industry is on its feet. Infant-industry protection is a commonly used strategy in countries whose governments are trying to promote industrialization. It is a key component of *import-substituting industrialization* (ISI), a strategy of aggressive import restrictions designed to jump-start industrial growth by replacing imported manufactures with domestically produced manufactures.

These strategies became very popular in middle- and lower-income countries after the Second World War (see Hirschman, 1968, for a description of the trend in Latin America). They have always been controversial, and many governments moved away from them in waves of trade liberalization in the 1980s and 1990s as frustration over the growth performance of ISI economies grew. The emerging majority view among economists was formulated by Anne Krueger (1981) as a call for "export-led growth," with unrestricted imports and exports encouraged or even subsidized, in contrast to growth based on import substitution (see Krueger, 1997, for a narrative account of mainstream development economists' thinking on these issues and how they changed over the years).

Argentina provides a clear example. Under Juan Peron in the 1940s, Argentina was a pioneer in ISI techniques, and the government imposed steep tariffs on a wide range of manufactures in order to support domestic industry.

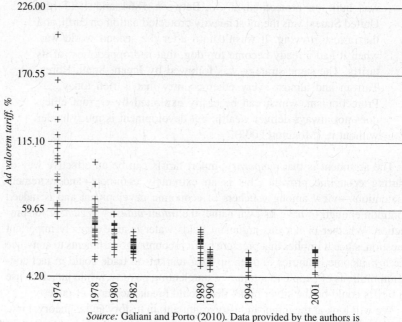

FIGURE 9.1
Tariffs in Argentina,
1974–2001.

Source: Galiani and Porto (2010). Data provided by the authors is gratefully acknowledged.
Each + represents the employment-weighted median tariff for one industry.

In recent years the government has switched to a much more open trade regime. This is illustrated by Figure 9.1, which summarizes the history of Argentinian manufacturing tariffs from 1974 to 2001. For this figure, Argentinian manufacturing has been aggregated into approximately 1,000 industries according to the 3-digit Standard Industrial Classification system. Each point in the figure marked as a blue cross shows the employment-weighted median tariff[1] for one of those industries for one year of the data. In the 1970s, not only were manufacturing tariffs high overall (with a median around 80%), but tariffs varied greatly, with favored, targeted industries receiving protection above 200%, while the least favored received a tariff close to 50%. This is a hallmark of an ISI policy: Tariffs were used aggressively to promote particular targeted industries to which the government gave a high priority. Since the 1970s, tariff policy in Argentina has changed dramatically, with the median, highest, and lowest tariffs all dropping, and the range of tariffs becoming much more compressed. Now, all industries have tariffs well under 50%. Note that there is *no overlap* between the 1974 tariffs and the 2001 tariffs; that is how enormous the policy shift has been. This pattern is similar to the tariff history of a great many Latin American countries.

A contrasting example is provided by Singapore and Hong Kong, two East Asian island economies with similar trajectories but very different policy

---

[1] This is simply a measure of the "typical" tariff in the data for that industry. Precisely, if we rank all product categories within one Argentinian industry in increasing order of their tariff levels, the employment-weighted median tariff is the value of the tariff such that the total number of workers employed in production of all product categories with tariffs higher than that value is equal to the total number of workers employed in production of all product categories with tariffs lower than that value.

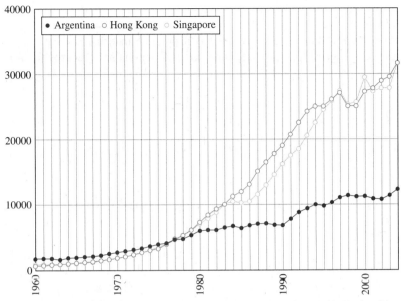

FIGURE 9.2
Real GDP Per Capita in
Three Countries,
1960–2004.

Source: Alan Heston, Robert Summers and Bettina Aten, Penn World Table Version 6.2, Center for International Comparisons of Production, Income and Prices at the University of Pennsylvania, September 2006 (data available at http://pwt.econ.upenn.edu)

histories (see Young, 1992). As of the end of the Second World War, both economies were very poor, but over the following three decades, both experienced spectacular, unimaginable growth, as shown in Figure 9.2: From 1960 to 1980, real per capita GDP grew by a factor of 11 in Hong Kong and 8 in Singapore. This growth transformed both countries into prosperous economic powerhouses in a single generation.

Although both are exceptionally open economies (and both are often used as examples of export-led growth), Singapore used a strategy of infant-industry protection as a central part of its strategy during the 1960s, 1970s, and 1980s. The government would identify an industry for targeting and then provide that industry with huge assistance in the form of a high tariff wall, tax breaks, and subsidized credit, all temporary. After a few years, a different set of industries would be identified as targets, and incentives and protection would move on to those new industries. The policy differed from an ISI policy such as was used in Argentina because each manufacturing industry was expected to export, and because protection for each industry was not only truly temporary, but short-lived; but infant-industry protection was still a central piece of the strategy. By contrast, Hong Kong, governed during this period by the British colonial governor, followed a policy of almost unalloyed free trade with no government intervention to favor one industry over another. Young (1992) describes the Hong Kong development approach as "minimalist" and the Singaporean approach as "maximalist." The difference can be seen in the rate of industrial transformation in the two economies: The shares of the economy accounted for by different industries changed in Singapore at a dramatically more rapid rate compared with Hong Kong.

We thus have three different economies with very different experiences: one (Argentina) that used infant-industry protection in an ISI strategy with modest growth results; another (Singapore) that used infant-industry protection in an export-promoting strategy with breathtaking results; and a third (Hong Kong) that followed free trade with spectacular success. The question arises: Is infant-industry protection ever a good idea? Is it possible that that is what led to Singapore's success? Is it possible that it led to Argentina's slower growth? We will look at the main theoretical arguments, first at the most common argument for infant-industry protection (learning by doing), which we will see is not a convincing argument on its own, and then at arguments based on market failures (credit-market failures and learning spillovers), which can be sufficient but come with qualifications and caveats. In doing so, we will fill out the last branch in our family tree of trade models. Finally, we will look briefly at the evidence.

9.3 Learning by Doing: An Insufficient Argument

The most commonly cited reason for infant-industry protection is *learning by doing*, which in general is an increase in productivity in a given economic activity that results from performing that activity over time. For example, Irwin and Klenow (1994) document the case of Dynamic Random-Access Memory (DRAM) chips for computers; production of these chips requires a great deal of learned skill on the part of the workers, and in practice the failure rate of produced chips is high. Over the lifetime of each model of chip, within each plant, the failure rate falls, as workers learn from their mistakes in previous batches. This suggests an argument for a tariff that has been made many times: *Our country does not now have a comparative advantage in (say) DRAM chips, but could have one in the future if only our workers and managers acquired experience in that industry; why not use a tariff to help fledgling DRAM chip makers survive, until they have become productive enough to withstand international competition?*

We can examine the logic of this idea with a simple model. Consider a worker in a hypothetical small economy who has two choices for how to make an income. She can stitch together blue jeans, with a productivity of 1,000 pairs per month, for which she will receive a piece rate of 10¢ per pair, or $100 per month. Alternatively, she can get a job in the new transistor radio manufacturing industry. In that job, she will earn $2.50 per radio she successfully assembles, but it is easy to make an error and produce a defective radio. Suppose that both of these piece rates are determined on world markets; manufacturers seek out the country in which blue jeans can be stitched together for the smallest price per 1,000 pairs, and the country in which radios can be assembled at the lower cost per unit. As a result, $0.10 is the world price of the task of stitching a pair of blue jeans, and $2.50 is the world price of the task of assembling a radio.

New workers produce quite a lot of defective radios, but they tend to get better over time. Suppose that the long-run goal for a radio assembly worker is 50 working radios per month, for an income of $2.50 × 50, or $125 per month. However, for a worker with t months of experience, the fraction of radios that are defective is:

$$\left(\frac{1}{1+g}\right)^t,$$

where g is a positive constant representing the growth rate of a worker's expertise. This expression, of course, takes a value of 1 when $t = 0$ and converges to 0 as t gets large. Thus, new workers (with $t = 0$) mess up all of their radios, while very experienced workers (with large t) have a negligible failure rate. As a result, in month t, the worker will make

$$50\left(1 - \left(\frac{1}{1+g}\right)^t\right)$$

usable radios.

Which job should this worker take? If she stitches blue jeans, she can receive a steady income of \$100 per month, with no prospect for increase. On the other hand, if she tries her hand at radios, she will make no money the first month, but enjoy gradually increasing income until finally she will be making \$125 per month. The first job is better in the short run, and the second is better in the long run. Which is better overall?

If the worker has access to a market for loans at a constant interest rate r, then it is optimal for her to choose the job with the highest present discounted value (PDV) of income. Using a beloved formula from high school algebra:

$$\sum_{t=0}^{\infty} \left(\frac{1}{\alpha}\right)^t = \frac{1}{(1-\alpha)},$$

for any number between 0 and 1, we obtain the PDV of income from the blue-jeans job:

$$\sum_{t=0}^{\infty} \left(\frac{\$100}{1+r}\right)^t = \$100 \frac{1+r}{r},$$

and the PDV of income from the radio job:

$$\sum_{t=0}^{\infty} (\$2.50)(50)\left(1 - \left(\frac{1}{1+g}\right)^t\right)\left(\frac{1}{1+r}\right)^t = \frac{\$125}{r} \frac{1+r}{\left(1+r+\frac{r}{g}\right)}.$$

Clearly, the PDV of income from the radio job is an increasing function of the growth rate of expertise, g. It takes its lowest value, 0, in the case in which $g = 0$, which would imply that usable output starts at zero and never gets better; and it takes its highest value, \$125/r, in the case in which g is very large, which would imply that the worker earns zero in the first month and \$125 per month permanently thereafter. Combining the expressions for the PDVs of the two jobs, the radio job has a higher PDV if:

$$1 + r + \frac{r}{g} \leq 1.25, \tag{9.1}$$

and otherwise the blue-jeans job does. Thus, for a given value of r, the worker is more likely to choose the radio job, the higher is g—in other words, the faster is learning by doing. This makes sense because learning by doing is the advantage of the radio job over the blue-jeans job. On the other hand, for a given value of g, the worker is more likely to choose the radio job the lower is r. This makes sense, since the radio job offers lower incomes early on but higher incomes later, so the more heavily the future is discounted, the more attractive the blue-jeans job will be.

The point is that, although the learning-by-doing job offers higher long-run income, that is not enough to conclude that it is the job that the worker will choose, or should choose, because the long-run benefit needs to be weighed against the up-front losses from the initial low productivity. Thus, two logical errors that creep into discussions of infant-industry policies can be cleared up quickly: First, even if an economy has a potential long-run comparative advantage in an industry because of learning by doing, it is not necessarily desirable to exploit that. If the future is sufficiently discounted or the learning is sufficiently slow, it will not be desirable to do so. Second, even if an economy has a current static comparative disadvantage in the learning-by-doing sector (as here, with the marginal product of labor in radios actually equal to zero at the start), there is no reason to assume that workers and entrepreneurs will not enter the sector and begin to acquire experience. Economic agents can take into account their future payoff from acquiring experience in their decision making, and enter an industry with short-term losses but long-term gains. Learning by doing does not imply that workers and firms will not be able to make the right decision; it merely implies a dynamic model, and it requires dynamic thinking.

Now, let us discuss infant-industry protection. Suppose that r is high enough and g is low enough that the worker chooses to take the blue-jeans job. With all workers facing the same choice, no one would choose to make radios, and the radio industry would not come into being in this country. Now, suppose that the government imposes an import tariff on radios, say, for five years, and explains as it does so that this is just until the radio industry gets on its feet. Such a tariff would raise the domestic price of radios as long as it is in effect, thus raising the local piece rate on radios. A high enough increase in this piece rate would then raise the PDV of income in the radio job above that of the blue-jeans job, causing the worker to switch to the radio industry, along with all other workers in similar situations.

Infant-industry protection would indeed "work," given that its purpose was to get a nascent radio industry going and keep it going until it can stand up to international competition.[2] However, is it beneficial? Note that the fact that the PDV of the worker's income was higher with the blue-jeans job than with the radio job implies that *the PDV of this country's GDP, evaluated at world prices*, is also higher with the blue-jeans job than with the radio job. Since the PDV of a country's consumption must be equal to the PDV of its production because of consumers' intertemporal budget constraints, we conclude that the tariff reduces the PDV of national consumption. It also creates a consumption distortion, as in Chapter 7, because consumers face distorted domestic prices when making their consumption decisions. Therefore, although infant-industry protection is successful on its own terms because it gets the new radio industry off the ground, it is harmful to national welfare.

---

[2] What does it mean to be "able to stand up to international competition" in this case? It means that the local radio workers have progressed far enough along their learning curve that they are willing to stick with the job even at the original tariff-free piece rate of $2.50 per radio. Clearly, if they have been at the job long enough before the tariff is removed, their usable output will be close to 50, and at the free-trade prices they will want to keep on making radios rather than stitching blue jeans.

The bottom line is that learning by doing is not, in and of itself, an argument for infant-industry protection (or any government intervention). It simply means that there is a dynamic element to costs, so economic agents need to make dynamic decisions, focusing on the PDV of costs and benefits rather than current static costs and benefits. There is nothing unrealistic about assuming that workers and firms can make plans for the future with learning by doing in mind. After all, firms do make long-term investments and suffer losses for several years in order to make profits later (such as development of new drugs, which take many years and have an uncertain outcome), and workers do make long-term career decisions that trade long-term benefits against short-run costs (attending graduate school, accepting apprenticeships, and so on). In order to make a case for infant-industry protection, *one needs to introduce a market failure*—a point forcefully argued in an influential paper by Baldwin (1969). We will now introduce the two most important of these market failures for infant-industry arguments: credit-market failures and learning spillovers.

9.4 Market-Failure Arguments for Infant-Industry Protection

9.4.1 Credit-Market Failures

If the worker in the above example wants to take the radio job because it would give her a higher PDV of income, she might need to take out a loan to smooth out her consumption due to the low income she will be receiving during the early stages of the job. Similarly, an entrepreneur wishing to enter a new industry may need to take out a loan to cover a few years of losses as learning by doing proceeds.

In both cases, if the loan is not available, we may have labor and capital stuck in the less remunerative sector. This is a consequence of credit-market failures and provides a possible rationale for infant-industry policies. If a tariff raises the domestic price of radios during the learning-by-doing period, that may alleviate the need for a loan, thus leading entrepreneurs and workers to enter the industry and profit from it. This creates a consumer distortion by distorting the prices consumers face, but since it corrects a production inefficiency, it may be worth it.

Credit markets can fail for many reasons. One important one is often called *financial repression*—regulations that keep interest rates for bank lending below market-clearing levels, and that keep banks' reserve requirements high, which have in the past been practiced by the governments of many medium- and low-income countries (see McKinnon, 1973, for a classic account). Financial repression, naturally, can lead to the rationing of loans (analogously to the rationing of apartments in a standard rent-control model), and thus to a failure of the economy to develop learning-by-doing industries to an optimal degree. As a result, it can lead to a case for infant-industry protection. However, it must be emphasized that this is a second-best policy: If the credit market is malfunctioning because of financial repression policies, the first-best strategy is to remove those policies rather than introduce a new distortion by imposing a tariff.

A second reason credit markets may fail is asymmetric information (the argument pioneered by Stiglitz and Weiss, 1981). *Asymmetric information* describes a situation in which one party to a transaction has information relevant to the transaction that the other party does not have. It is extremely common in lending: A lender always wants to know that the borrower is able to pay back the loan, but the borrower always knows more about his or her creditworthiness, and the riskiness of the project financed by the loan, than the lender does. Given this, a lender may worry that a high interest rate will discourage more high-quality borrowers than low-quality borrowers (since if a borrower knows that he or she is unlikely to pay back the loan anyway, then he or she will not be bothered by a high interest rate). As a result, it is possible that there can be a ceiling for the interest rate above which a lender will be unwilling to lend; if this ceiling is not very high, it can result in an equilibrium with credit rationing quite similar to the outcome with financial repression. Therefore, asymmetric information in the credit market can lead to a coherent case for infant-industry protection.

This argument contains an important pitfall, however. Infant-industry protection is, by definition, temporary assistance to the industry. As a result, the entrepreneurs for whom it will make the most difference are those who do not expect to be around very long. It is possible that the policy can therefore make things worse by encouraging the entry of fly-by-night operators and thereby worsening the asymmetric information problem.[3]

In sum, credit-market failures can provide a rationale for infant-industry protection, but the argument is far from ironclad.

9.4.2 Learning Spillovers

From here on in, we set aside the possibility of credit-market imperfections to discuss the other major market failure that is used to rationalize infant-industry protection: learning spillovers.

Now, suppose that the worker has accepted the radio job and proceeds down the learning curve month by month as described above, learning from her mistakes as she goes along. In addition, however, suppose that at lunch, during work breaks, and after hours, she also describes her experiences to her coworkers, who thereby also learn from her mistakes. Similarly, she learns from the experiences of her coworkers, not only at her own firm, but through informal interactions with workers from radio assembly operations in the area.

In this case, each radio worker confers a positive externality on the others: A portion of the learning achieved by each worker benefits other workers in the same industry. This phenomenon is called *learning spillovers* and is an important argument for infant-industry protection in its own right.

In the context of our model, we can stipulate that g is now a variable and is dependent on how many workers there are in the local radio manufacturing industry. The more local radio workers there are, the more abundant are the learning spillover opportunities and the higher is g.

This actually gives rise to a form of increasing returns to scale. Consider what happens if we double the number of radio workers in this location (along with other inputs, such as components, tools, and so on). For a fixed value of g, we would simply double the number of radios that can be assembled at each date, but given that g also increases, we will now *more* than double the output of radios at

---

[3] This argument was made formally by Grossman and Horn (1988), strictly speaking not in the context of a credit-market model, but the reasoning applies to credit markets. These adverse-selection effects are, unfortunately, difficult to test empirically.

each date (after the initial month). Doubling the input and more than doubling the output implies increasing returns to scale. Recalling Chapter 3, Section 3.2, as long as a portion of the learning spillovers is captured by workers in other firms, then this is a case of external increasing returns to scale. If the learning stays within the country, the increasing returns are external and national; if they spill out to other countries as well, the increasing returns are external and international.

This is an example of an important class of externalities called *agglomeration externalities*, or positive externalities from locating a particular economic activity close to other firms or workers undertaking the same activity. Agglomeration externalities can take a number of forms. For example, the productivity of a manufacturer can be enhanced by the local presence of a wide range of other manufacturers. The reason is that with transport costs unnecessary, the local manufacturing sector provides a wide range of intermediate inputs available at a low price and at short notice. This type of agglomeration externality is emphasized by Krugman and Venables (1995), who show that with this type of agglomeration externality, trade can lead to a sharp rise in international income inequality, as manufacturing concentrates in clusters. Agglomeration can also make it possible for firms to become more specialized, facilitated by a large local market for industrial inputs that makes specialized local input producers viable (Holmes, 1999) and by thicker markets that alleviate various contracting costs (McLaren, 2000).

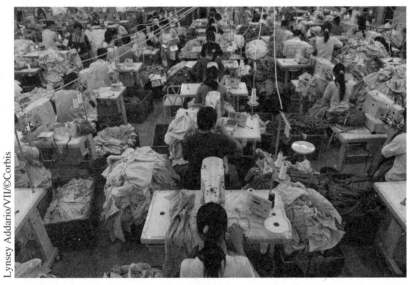

Lynsey Addario/VII/©Corbis

Workers sew shirts in a factory in China that makes apparel for Abercrombie and Fitch, J. Crew, and other leading American retailers.

Whatever their source, agglomeration externalities do appear to be important in practice, given the presence of industrial clusters in many areas, such as the famous Silicon Valley of California. Fallows (2007) describes the productivity benefits of a huge concentration of manufacturers in Shenzhen, China, the largest manufacturing center in the Pearl River Delta, which has become "the world's manufacturing center" (p. 50). Electronic inputs of every imaginable variety are available at a moment's notice, for example, at "the SEG

Electronics Market, a seven-story downtown structure whose every inch is crammed with the sales booths of hundreds of mom-and-pop electronics dealers" (p. 60). An entrepreneur explains:

> Anyplace else, you'd have to import different raw materials and components. . . . Here, you've got nine different suppliers within a mile, and they can bring a sample over that afternoon. People think China is cheap, but really, it's fast. (p. 62)

Agglomeration externalities, including learning spillovers, have significant ramifications for trade and trade policy. To focus on these, we will examine a simplified *static* model of trade with agglomeration externalities, a version of a model first explored in a groundbreaking paper by Ethier (1982). It captures the key features of the problem without the complications of the present-discounted-value calculations.

9.4.3 Agglomeration Externalities and Trade

Suppose that there are two countries, Home and Foreign. Suppose for simplicity that blue jeans and radios are the only two goods. Any worker can produce 1,000 pairs of blue jeans per month. Any worker can also produce:

$$\frac{50 L_R}{1,000} \tag{9.2}$$

radios per month, where L_R denotes the number of workers making radios in the same country. In other words, the productivity of each radio assembler depends on how many other radio workers there are in the same economy, due to the learning spillovers, and so the radio sector exhibits external national increasing returns. Note that if there were no increasing returns in the radio sector, so that the productivity of each radio worker took a constant value, this would be a Ricardian economy, just as the model we studied for Nigeria in Chapter 2.

Suppose that Home has L workers and Foreign has L^* workers. For the sake of concreteness, for now let $L = 1,200$. If there are B units of blue jeans being produced, then there are $B/1,000$ workers producing blue jeans, and so there are $(1,200 - B/1,000)$ workers left to make radios, each with productivity $50(1,200 - B/1,000)/1,000$ and consequently $50(1,200 - B/1,000)^2/1,000$ radios produced. This allows us to draw the economy's production possibilities frontier as in Figure 9.3. Note the unfamiliar, convex shape: This is a consequence of the increasing returns to scale in the radio industry.

Now, consider this economy in autarky. A full analysis of the equilibrium requires assuming a relative demand curve (as in the Ricardian model) and is more complicated than the models we have been investigating (see Ethier, 1982, for details). We will therefore not compute an equilibrium but rather will assume that we have one and deduce some points about trade from it. Suppose that under autarky, 800 of Home's workers make radios, implying production at point A. From (9.2), the productivity of each of those workers is $50 \times 800/1,000 = 40$ radios per month, and so if the price of a radio is P^R, the income of a radio worker will be equal to $40P^R$. The income of a blue-jeans maker will be equal to $1,000P^B$, where P^B is the price of a pair of blue jeans. Given that some Home workers choose to enter one industry and some choose the other industry, it must be the case that $40P^R = 1,000P^B$, so $P^R/P^B = 25$.

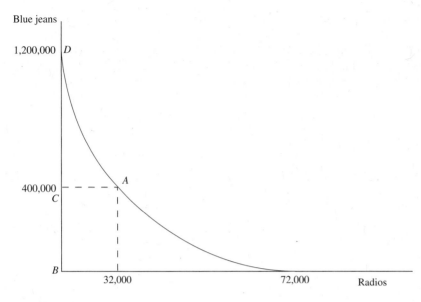

FIGURE 9.3
The Production Possibilities Frontier With External Increasing Returns.

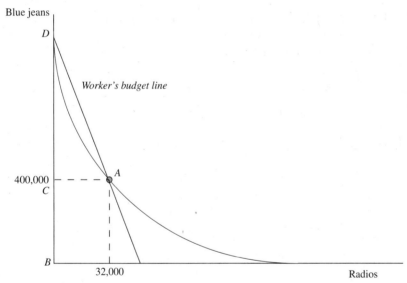

FIGURE 9.4
The Worker's Budget Line With External Increasing Returns.

The relative price is equal to the ratio of productivities in the two industries, $1,000/40 = 25$.

This logic can be illustrated graphically in Figure 9.4. The distance AC represents the number of radios produced, which of course is equal to the number of workers making radios times their productivity per worker. The distance CD represents the number of workers who make radios, times their *opportunity cost* productivity of 1,000 blue jeans per worker, since BD is the maximum number of pairs of blue jeans that would be produced, if all workers produced blue jeans, while BC is the number of pairs of blue jeans actually produced in equilibrium. Therefore, the ratio CD/AC is equal to the ratio of the productivity of a worker in the blue-jeans industry to the productivity of a worker in the radio industry. Just as in the Ricardian model of Chapter 2, for a worker to be willing to work in either industry, it must be the case that the relative price of the two goods must be equal to the ratio of the productivities, so the relative price of radios P^R/P^B must be equal to the ratio

CD/AC of a worker's productivity in the blue-jeans industry to the worker's productivity in the radio industry.

This observation can help us draw the typical Home worker's budget line. The budget line must pass through the production point A, since it is always feasible to consume what one produces, and it must have a slope equal to the relative price P^R/P^B, which we have just seen is equal to the ratio CD/AC. These facts together tell us that the budget line can be constructed quite simply as *the straight line connecting point A with point D*, or the production point with the upper limit of the production possibilities frontier. Further, following the chain of logic that has led to this conclusion, the same point can be made for *any* equilibrium in which some of both goods are produced: The budget line must take the form of a straight line from the highest point on the production possibilities frontier to the actual production point.

Notice that this indicates something different from what one sees in models without externalities: The budget line is not tangent to the production possibilities frontier. It actually cuts through it. This is because the social opportunity cost of producing radios is less than the private opportunity cost, given that a worker moving into that industry takes into account the income she will receive but not the social benefit of the learning spillover to which she will contribute.

Under autarky, the production point must be equal to the consumption point, so in Figure 9.5, an indifference curve for the typical Home worker has been added, tangent to the budget line at point A. Clearly, due to the failure of tangency just noted, the equilibrium does not maximize the utility of the typical Home worker, conditional on the economy's production possibilities. There is a range of points along the production possibilities frontier to the right of point A that are on a higher indifference curve than the equilibrium indifference curve. Put differently, the economy does not produce enough radios. This is a direct consequence of the learning spillover: There is a positive externality from production of radios, and so the economy on its own does not produce enough of them. We can call this the spillover distortion, and it calls, ideally, for a government subsidy to radio production, or some other policy to encourage more workers to produce radios.

Now, consider what happens when we open up Home to trade. Suppose that Foreign is somewhat larger than Home ($L^* > L$), so that under autarky Foreign has more workers producing radios, and therefore more productive radio

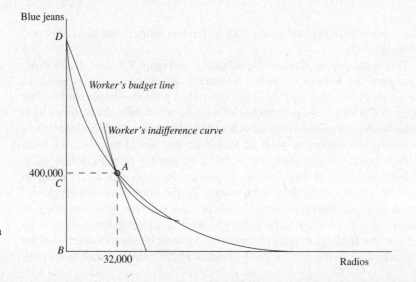

FIGURE 9.5
Autarky Equilibrium
With External
Increasing Returns.

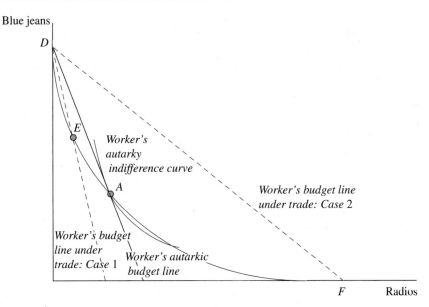

FIGURE 9.6
The Welfare Effects
of Trade With
External Increasing
Returns.

workers and a lower relative price for radios. Then, when the two countries are able to trade with each other, before the labor allocations in the two countries have had a chance to adjust, the relative price of radios in Home will fall below its autarkic value of 25, and Home workers will be able to earn a higher income producing blue jeans than they can producing radios. As a result, the radio sector in Home will shrink; Home radio workers will become less productive; and Home will move upward and to the left along its production possibilities frontier. There are two possible outcomes:

Case 1. *The Home radio sector survives, but on a smaller scale than it had under autarky.* This will happen if Foreign is not quite large enough to absorb the entire world radio industry on its own, and is represented by point *E* in Figure 9.6. Notice that, since once again the budget line is the straight line connecting point *D* with the new production point, the new budget line in this case is the broken blue straight line *DE*, which lies entirely below the original budget line *DA*. In this case, every worker in Home is hurt by trade. This result, strikingly different from all other trade models we have seen, results from the spillover distortion. The original autarkic allocation of labor was inefficient, because it had a suboptimal number of workers making radios; trade with a larger economy exacerbates this inefficiency.

This outcome is likely if the radio sector takes up more than half of the workforce under autarky (as it does in this example). If Foreign is not too much larger than Home; these two conditions make it possible that Foreign will not be able to satisfy all of world demand for radios on its own.[4]

Case 2. *The Home radio sector is wiped out by competition with the radio sector in Foreign.* In this case, the Home production point is at *D*. We

---

[4] Note that, paradoxically, after labor has reached its new allocation in both economies, the relative price of radios is higher in this trading equilibrium than in Home's autarky equilibrium. However, no Home worker can increase her income by switching from blue jeans to radios, because with a small number of other Home workers making radios, her radio making productivity would be low.

cannot know without more information exactly where the budget line will lie, but we do know that it will begin at D and have a slope equal to the new relative price of radios. If Foreign is sufficiently larger than Home, the new relative price of radios will be lower than the autarkic price in Home, and the new budget line will look like the broken blue line DF in Figure 9.6, ensuring that Home workers will all benefit from trade. Here, the spillover distortion is exacerbated by trade, but the terms-of-trade benefit of the cheap radios that Home citizens can enjoy as consumers is more than enough to compensate. Picture a tiny island economy that always produced its own radios under autarky, at very high unit cost because it was on a small scale; but with trade it can import them cheaply from large countries that make them on a huge scale.

Thus, the outcome is that Home benefits from trade either if it is the large country or if it is much smaller than its trade partner. If it is just a little bit smaller than its trade partner, it is possible that it loses from trade because trade exacerbates the spillover distortion without providing a large terms-of-trade benefit to compensate.

The implication is that there is some scope for trade restrictions to improve Home's welfare by preventing deindustrialization, but only in the event that the Home economy is in the middle range of sizes consistent with Case 1 above that produces a budget line like DE. If Home is quite small, then it has a serious natural disadvantage in the industry with increasing returns, and its best strategy is to welcome deindustrialization and benefit from low prices abroad.[5]

Of course, in a static model such as this one, a dynamic concept like infant-industry protection has no meaning, but the learning spillovers could be built into a richer dynamic model with learning by doing such as has been sketched. The basic point would carry over: There would be a role for a temporary tariff until the learning by doing is complete, provided that Home is small (or inexperienced in radio production) compared to its trade partners, but not *too* small or *too* inexperienced.

It should be emphasized that where protection is called for, it must be given *only* to the industry with the learning-by-doing spillovers, and the problem is muddied considerably if there are multiple such industries. In this simple model, if we assumed that the blue-jeans industry also offered such spillovers, there would be no presumption that the market produces too few radios and no presumption in favor of a radio tariff. In practice, learning-by-doing spillovers could show up anywhere, in agriculture or in manufacturing, and in any manufacturing industry. Knowing where those spillovers are is a very serious informational constraint on the use of infant-industry policy.

9.5 What Has Actually Happened?

To sum up so far, a case can be made *in principle* for trade protection as a strategy of industrial development, but it needs to be made carefully and it depends on special conditions—particular forms of market failure, particular values of parameters, and so on—that may or may not be satisfied in practice.

---

[5] Of course, that implies that this type of model has trouble rationalizing the success of small industrial powerhouses such as Hong Kong and Singapore, but this is a problem common in the theory of economic growth.

We cannot say as a matter of theory whether or not this use of trade policy will help spur growth. It is an empirical question, which has been investigated in many ways and been the subject of a rich and vigorous debate.

One way this has been approached is through case studies. As George Monbiot noted in the column quoted at the beginning of the chapter, the United States government used infant-industry protection aggressively in the nineteenth century. Head (1994) studied the use of this strategy in the steel rail industry. Steel rails were crucial to the expansion of railroads, and the U.S. steel rail industry had a disadvantage against the more experienced British industry. The U.S. government employed high and temporary tariffs to get U.S. industry up to speed, and for the last quarter of the nineteenth century U.S. steel-rail tariffs were well above 50%, even approaching 100% for a time. After the turn of the twentieth century, with the U.S. industry well established, the tariffs fell and eventually were eliminated. Head formulates a partial-equilibrium model of learning-by-doing spillovers in the production of steel rails and fits it to the data to estimate rates of learning by doing as well as the supply and demand relationships. He found that, taking the consumer distortions into account, the tariff had a positive but very small effect on U.S. welfare. Interestingly, Head biases his study in favor of infant-industry protection by assuming that *all* of the learning by doing is external—that it is a pure spillover—and yet the estimated benefit from the program is minimal. Irwin (2000) uses similar techniques to evaluate late-nineteenth century U.S. infant-industry protection for the tinplate industry and finds a small negative effect on welfare. Thus, although George Monbiot is unquestionably right that infant-industry protection was a central part of U.S. trade policy in the nineteenth century, these studies do not provide evidence that such policies actually helped the country much.

Another way of investigating this question is to collect data on growth rates across countries over time together with data on each country's trade restrictions to see whether a positive correlation exists between trade restrictions and growth, which would provide some ammunition for infant-industry proponents, or a negative correlation, which would bolster the export-led growth proponents.

Such an investigation is fraught with difficulties in practice. First, a country's degree of trade restrictiveness is difficult to measure. One can measure average tariffs (by adding up tariffs across industries and dividing by the number of industries), but it does not make much sense to add up with equal weight a tariff that applies to $1 billion worth of imports and a tariff that applies to $1 million worth of imports, so most researchers use *weighted* average tariffs with weights given by import shares (so the $1 billion import commodity will have 1,000 times the weight given to the $1 million import commodity). However, import shares themselves respond to tariffs; if the tariff on sugar increases to $1,000 per pound, sugar will no longer be imported and its share of imports will go to zero. Thus, the tariff on sugar will not have any more effect on the weighted average tariff than if it were $0 per pound. Furthermore, for many countries quantitative barriers (such as quotas) are more important than tariffs, but it is much more difficult to measure their restrictiveness than it is for a tariff. Researchers have spent many hours working through these conundrums.

A very widely read and influential survey that reviews and synthesizes a great deal of research on the relationship between trade policy and growth, taking these measurement issues into account, is Rodriguez and Rodrik (2000).

Essentially, Rodriguez and Rodrik conclude that the data do not provide a strong case for *either* interpretation, that trade restrictions are robustly correlated with growth negatively *or* positively, once the various measurement problems have been taken into account. This is a matter of ongoing debate, but it should be pointed out that Figure 9.2 itself suggested the possibility that the data would not show a very clear message about the relationship between growth and trade restrictiveness. When two of the most successful economies in the world are found to have pursued almost opposite policy strategies, and two different economies that used targeted protection (in very different ways) are found to have extremely different success rates, it should not be surprising that the data do *not* provide a simple story about one policy as a recipe for success and the other as a path to failure.

Some authors have argued that whether or not infant-industry protection can help, it is at best a small benefit that is a distraction from the large issues that really make a difference in growth outcomes. For example, a number of authors have argued that the quality of political and legal institutions is central to long-run growth, and Acemoglu et al. (2001) provide empirical support for the claim. Rodrik et al. (2004) build on that study to show that once these institutional quality measures are controlled for, there is no relationship in the data between openness to trade and growth, even though there appeared to be one before controlling for institutional quality. They argue that this implies that the most important thing a country can do to pave the way for long-run growth is to develop high-quality political and economic institutions; trade policy is far less important. In a similar vein, Rodrik (1998) shows that measures of macroeconomic policy are much more strongly correlated with good growth performance in sub-Saharan Africa than are measures of trade openness.

The message is that no trade strategy—not infant industry protection, not free trade, not export promotion—appears to be either a silver bullet that solves the growth problem or an insurmountable obstacle to growth.

MAIN IDEAS

1. Infant-industry protection is the temporary protection of an industry from import competition, in the hopes that it will develop and become more productive under protection and subsequently be able to survive foreign competition without protection. It has been used extensively by now-rich economies in their early growth and by many middle- and low-income countries more recently.

2. The existence of learning by doing is often cited as a reason for infant-industry protection, but on its own it does not justify any protection at all, permanent or temporary.

3. A market failure is needed to make a case for infant-industry protection. Two of the most important sources of market failure for infant-industry arguments are credit-market failures and learning spillovers.

4. An argument for infant-industry protection based on credit-market failures is difficult to make, once the reasons for the credit-market failures have been taken into account. If the credit-market failure comes from a policy distortion in the credit market, any trade policy response is a second-best policy. If it comes from an asymmetric-information problem, one needs to be concerned that an infant-industry tariff could make that asymmetric-information problem worse.

5. Learning spillovers that generate external increasing returns in an industry lead to market failure, so that the industry with the spillovers is smaller than it should be. Opening up to trade with a net exporter of that industry's good can worsen this inefficiency by causing that industry to shrink, in which case trade protection for that sector can be welfare-enhancing.

However, if the country is small enough, trade will eliminate the industry and provide the country's consumers with cheap imports of the good with spillovers, enhancing welfare. In this case, trade protection is not desirable.

6. The evidence on the effectiveness of trade openness as a growth strategy is mixed. It may be that the importance of trade policy lies in areas other than growth, such as its effects on domestic income distribution.

WHERE WE ARE

We have added trade with external increasing returns to the increasing-returns branch, and have thus completed the family tree of trade models.

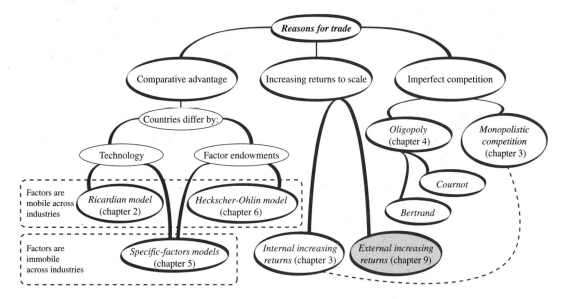

QUESTIONS AND PROBLEMS

1. Recall the "trade data spreadsheet.xls" used in the problems for Chapter 1. For each country, compute GDP per capita, and then find the rate of growth of GDP per capita from 1971 to 2001. (These are *nominal* rates of growth, since GDP is measured in current U.S. dollars. Therefore, they are not useful for evaluating how successful any one country's growth performance was, but they *are* useful for comparing growth rates across countries.)

   (a) Identify the five countries with the highest 1971–2001 per capita GDP growth rates, and the countries with the lowest. Compare the openness to trade of these two groups (use 1971 figures).

   (b) Identify the five most and the five least open economies in 1971, and compare their per capita GDP growth rates.

   (c) Can you conclude anything about whether or not openness is good for growth? Suggest at least one reason why you might *not* be able to conclude anything about this question from these calculations.

2. *Infant-industry protection without spillovers.* Consider a country, called Home, that is thinking about starting up a semiconductor chip industry. There are already many producers of the chips in other countries, and there are initially no producers in Home. Suppose that to produce semiconductor chips one must first construct a plant, at a cost of $150. The capacity of such a plant is 10 units per period. Suppose that there are two periods. In period 1, a new producer can set up a plant and begin production. The marginal cost for a new producer is $10 per unit. If a new producer produces up to capacity in period 1, then he or

she becomes an experienced producer, and his or her marginal cost will drop to 0 in period 2. However, even for experienced producers, the capacity constraint of 10 units still holds. (*Note*: There are no spillovers.)

Home country consumers demand semiconductor chips according to the demand curve:

$$Q = 36 - P,$$

where Q is the quantity they consume in a given period and P is the price they face in that period. Home is small in the world market for chips, so it takes the world price as given. That price is $12 in both periods.

Finally, assume for simplicity that the interest rate is zero, so the present value of a firm's profits (producer surplus) is just the profits (net of fixed cost, if any) in period 1 (PS_1) plus the profits in period 2 (PS_2). We will write $PS_{TOT} = PS_1 + PS_2$. Similarly, we calculate total consumer surplus by adding together consumer surplus in each of the two periods: $CS_{TOT} = CS_1 + CS_2$, and similarly with government revenue when there is any: $GR_{TOT} = GR_1 + GR_2$.

(a) Will any Home firm invest in chip production under free trade?

(b) Calculate PS_{TOT}, CS_{TOT}, and social welfare under free trade. (*Note*: For simplicity, assume that there is at most only one firm in Home. It will, of course, be a price-taker on world markets.)

(c) Now suppose the government follows a policy of infant-industry protection. Specifically, suppose that it imposes a tariff of $2 per unit on imported chips in period 1 and then returns to free trade in period 2. This policy is made public at the beginning of period 1 and is intended to give Home chip makers a chance to become competitive on world markets. Now answer (a) again.

(d) Under the policy described in (c), repeat the calculation in (b). Be sure to include the surplus to the government in the calculation of social welfare.

(e) Is the policy of infant-industry protection successful? Is it beneficial? Explain.

3. *Infant-industry protection with spillovers.* Now, consider the model of the previous problem with the following small changes. There are initially no semiconductor chip producers in Home, but two firms in Home would be willing to invest in

chip production if they thought it would be profitable. The cost of building a plant is negligible, but since this industry is new to the country, a foreign consultant will need to be hired to train plant managers. The consultant's fee is $150. It is impossible to set up shop in this industry without acquiring the knowledge of the consultant. The important thing about the consultant is that once he or she has trained the managers in one firm, the other firm can pick up on that advice for free just by observing the actions of the first firm. Thus, if only one firm pays the $150 fee, the entire domestic industry can get started. (Assume that the two domestic firms do not trust each other, so that a joint venture is impractical.)

Suppose that there are two periods. In period 1, a new producer can set up a plant and begin production. The marginal cost for a new producer is $10 per unit. If a new producer produces up to capacity in period 1, then he or she becomes an experienced producer, and his or her marginal cost will drop to 0 in period 2. However, even for experienced producers, the capacity constraint of 10 units still holds.

(a) Assume free trade. Show that if one firm hires the consultant and sets up shop, then it will be profitable for the other firm to set up shop.

(b) Continue assuming free trade. Now show that the firm that actually hires the consultant will lose money.

(c) Summarizing (a) and (b), what will be the outcome under free trade?

(d) Calculate PS_{TOT} (for both firms), CS_{TOT}, and social welfare under free trade.

(e) Now suppose the government follows a policy of infant industry-protection. Specifically, suppose that it imposes a tariff of $2 per unit on imported chips in period 1 and then returns to free trade in period 2. Now repeat (a), (b), and (c).

(f) Under the policy described in (e), repeat the calculation in (d).

(g) Is the policy of infant-industry protection successful? Is it beneficial? Explain. Compare this outcome with the version of this model in Question 2.

4. Recall the model of learning by doing in Section 9.3. Draw a box with g measured on the horizontal axis and r measured on the vertical axis.

Show the part of the box where the blue-jeans job would be better and the part where the radio job would be better. (You can use algebra, or you can use a spreadsheet to compute the threshold value of r for a number of values of g, and then connect the dots.)

5. *Agglomeration externalities and trade.* Consider a world with two goods, corn and electronics, and two identical countries, Home and Foreign. There is only one factor of production, labor, and there are 1,500 workers in each country, each of whom takes all prices as given. Corn is produced with constant returns to scale, and in both countries, one unit of labor is required to produce one unit of corn. However, electronics are produced with increasing returns to scale that are national and external. Thus, the productivity of any one electronics worker depends on how many other workers in the same country are producing electronics. Specifically, if L_E is the number of workers producing electronics in a given country, then the productivity of any one electronics worker in that country is equal to $L_E/300$.

   (a) Suppose that under autarky 40% of each country's labor force is devoted to electronics. What must be the autarchy relative price of electronics?

   (b) From this, deduce the budget line of a typical worker in autarchy.

   (c) Now, suppose that the two economies are opened up to trade. Suppose that in the free-trade equilibrium we still have the same total number of workers producing electronics worldwide, but that they are all located in Foreign. Compare the equilibrium worldwide quantity of electronics and corn produced under autarchy and free trade. Which outcome is more efficient? (*Note:* The relevant

concept of efficiency here is productive efficiency. Recall that an allocation of resources is productively inefficient if more of one good can be produced without reducing production of the other good.)

   (d) Under the assumption in (c), is the equilibrium relative price of electronics higher or lower under free trade than it is under autarky?

   (e) Have Home workers suffered as a result of losing their electronics industry? Explain using the budget set of a typical Home worker.

   (f) Has the *percentage change* in real income been higher in Foreign than in Home? Put differently, did Foreign *disproportionately* gain from trade, in virtue of having captured the high tech sector?

6. In the model of Question 5, suppose that under autarky there are 900 workers making electronics in Home. Foreign is slightly larger, and after trade is opened up between the two countries, only 600 workers make electronics in Home. Draw the Home production possibilities frontier and the budget line of a typical Home worker before and after trade is opened. In this case, does Home benefit from trade? Why or why not?

7. (*More of a challenge—perhaps a group project*) Choose a country that has used an ISI strategy in the past and abandoned it in favor of more open trade. (Your instructor can help you find examples if you are stuck.) Gather what data you can to show how the country's trade barriers fell over time, and describe what has happened to (a) the size of that country's trade flows, and (b) that country's growth performance, before and after the end of ISI. How has the economy responded to the change in policy?

REFERENCES

Acemoglu, Daron, James A. Robinson, and Simon Johnson (2001). "The Colonial Origins of Comparative Development: An Empirical Investigation." *American Economic Review*, 91 (December), pp. 1369–1401.

Baldwin, Robert E. (1969). "The Case Against Infant Industry Protection." *Journal of Political Economy* 77, pp. 295–305.

Ethier, Wilfred J (1982). "Decreasing Costs in International Trade and Frank Graham's Argument for Protection." *Econometrica* 50:5 (September), pp. 1243–1268.

Fallows, James (2007). "China Makes, the World Takes." *The Atlantic* 300:1 (July/August), pp. 49–72.

Galiani, Sebastian, and Guido G. Porto (2010). "Trends in Tariff Reform and Trends in the Structure of Wages." *Review of Economics and Statistics* 92:3 (August), pp. 482–494.

Grossman, Gene M., and Henrik Horn (1988). "Infant-Industry Protection Reconsidered: The Case of Informational Barriers to Entry." *Quarterly Journal of Economics* 103:4 (November), pp. 767–787.

Head, Keith (1994). "Infant Industry Protection in the Steel Rail Industry." *Journal of International Economics* 37, pp. 141–165.

Hirschman, Albert (1968). "The Political Economy of Import-Substituting Industrialization in Latin America." *Quarterly Journal of Economics* 82.1, pp. 1–32.

Holmes, Thomas J. (1999). "Localization of Industry and Vertical Disintegration." *Review of Economics and Statistics* 81:2 (May), pp. 314–325.

Irwin, Douglas A. (2000). "Did Late Nineteenth Century U.S. Tariffs Promote Infant Industries? Evidence from the Tinplate Industry." *The Journal of Economic History*, 60:2 (June), pp. 335–360.

Irwin, Douglas A., and Peter J. Klenow (1994). "Learning-by-Doing Spillovers in the Semiconductor Industry." *Journal of Political Economy* 102 (December), pp. 1200–1227.

Krueger, Anne O. (1974). "The Political Economy of the Rent-Seeking Society." *American Economic Review* 64:3, pp. 290–303.

_____ (1981). "Export-Led Industrial Growth Reconsidered," in W. Hong and L. Krause (eds.), *Trade and Growth of the Advanced Developing Countries in the Pacific Basin*. Seoul: Korea Development Institute.

_____ (1997). "Trade Policy and Economic Development: How We Learn." *The American Economic Review* 87:1 (March), pp. 1–22.

_____, and Baran Tuncer (1982). "An Empirical Test of the Infant Industry Argument." *American Economic Review* 72:5, pp. 1142–1152.

Krugman, Paul R., and Anthony J. Venables (1995). "Globalization and the Inequality of Nations." *Quarterly Journal of Economics* 110:4 (November), pp. 857–880.

McLaren, John (2000). " 'Globalization' and Vertical Structure." *American Economic Review* 90:5 (December), pp. 1239–1254.

McKinnon, Ronald I. (1973). *Money and Capital in Economic Development*. Washington, DC: Brookings Institution.

Monbiot, George (2008). "One Thing Is Clear from the History of Trade: Protectionism Makes You Rich." The Guardian, Tuesday, September 9, Comment & Debate section, p. 31.

Rodriguez, Francisco, and Dani Rodrik (2000). "Trade Policy and Economic Growth: A Skeptic's Guide to the Cross-National Literature." *NBER Macroeconomics Annual 2000*.

_____ (1998). "Trade Policy and Economic Performance in Sub-Saharan Africa." National Bureau of Economic Research Working Paper 6562.

Rodrik, Dani, Arvind Subramanian, and Francesco Trebbi (2004). "Institutions Rule: The Primacy of Institutions over Geography and Integration in Economic Development." *Journal of Economic Growth* 9(2) (June), pp. 131–165.

Stiglitz, Joseph E., and Andrew Weiss (1981). "Credit Rationing in Markets with Imperfect Information." *The American Economic Review* 71:3 (June), pp. 393–410.

Young, Alwyn (1992). "A Tale of Two Cities: Factor Accumulation and Technical Change in Hong Kong and Singapore," in Olivier-Jean Blanchard and Stanley Fisher (eds.), *NBER Macroeconomics Annual 1992*. Cambridge, MA: The MIT Press, pp. 13–54.

Was Ronald Reagan Punked by Japanese Automakers?

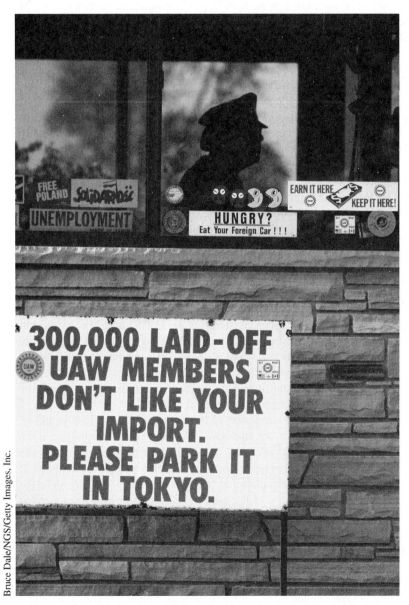

Tensions over auto imports: Signs in a United Auto Workers parking lot, 1982.
Photo copyright Bruce Dale, National Geographic.

10.1 A Paradox of Aggressive Trade Policy

The 1970s were brutal for the U.S. auto industry, partly because of sharp increases in gasoline prices and macroeconomic factors that reduced demand for autos, but also because of surging supply from Japanese automakers. In the second half of the 1970s, the Japanese share of the U.S. market had more than doubled, to a quarter, and in 1980, the Big Three U.S. automakers suffered losses of $4 billion and laid off 120,000 workers (Denzau, 1988). As a result, there was powerful pressure on the U.S. government to do something to help the industry recover.

The newly installed administration of President Ronald Reagan obliged. On May 1, 1981, it concluded an agreement with the Japanese government under which the Japanese Ministry of International Trade and Industry (MITI) would limit U.S. exports of Japanese-made automobiles to 1.68 million per year, about a 7% reduction from the previous year. Similar restrictions were to be in place until 1985 (Tharp, 1981). Recalling language from Chapter 7, this is a classic example of a voluntary export restraint (VER).

It may seem surprising that Reagan, who had campaigned on a platform of free-market ideology, should, as almost his first official act, implement a protectionist measure, but it turns out that his administration had a fairly protectionist bent (see Richman, 1988, for a critical account from a committed free trader). At any rate, by that time Congress was beginning to explore protectionist measures of its own if the administration did not act to crack down on the Japanese producers.

However, something odd happened. When the agreement restricting Japanese auto exports was announced, Japanese automaker stocks jumped *up* in value. This is documented by Denzau (1988) and also by Ries (1993), who estimates that the market value of Japanese automaker stocks rose by $2.2 billion as a result of the announcement of the VER. This suggests that traders in financial markets may have anticipated that the VER was going to increase the profits of Japanese automakers. Some studies of the way the VER subsequently worked out, such as Berry et al. (1999) and Mannering and Winston (1987), also concluded that the VER raised the profits of Japanese automakers at least in some years. The restraints were popular enough in Japan that after the agreement with the U.S. government expired and the Reagan administration indicated that it had no interest in continuing the VER, the Japanese government unilaterally extended it.

How could it be that the consensus of businesspeople at the time would be that Japanese firms would make more money by being partially shut out of the American market? We will look at this question by seeing whether or not it is a plausible outcome under the various trade models we have at our disposal. It turns out that it is extremely plausible that in an international oligopoly the firms that are the "victim" of a VER can be made better off by the restrictions— but only in the right sort of oligopoly.

10.2 A First Attempt: A Competitive Model

Recall the perfectly competitive model of Chapter 7. We could in principle use that model to analyze the market for automobiles. Scratching out "sugar" and substituting "cars," and writing "Japan" in place of the "rest of the world," we note that in that model the VER necessarily reduces Japanese producer surplus in cars by pushing down the world price. However, it could raise Japanese social welfare by creating quota rents large enough to compensate. Indeed, if the Japanese automakers themselves are allowed to capture the quota rents because they are given the licenses—which is roughly the way the U.S.-Japanese auto VER was administered—then it is quite possible that the overall profits of Japanese automakers (producer surplus plus quota rents) would increase as a result of the VER.

This is not the right model, however. First, it assumes that each automaker is a price-taker. This assumption is untenable in the highly oligopolistic automobile industry. Toyota does *not* take the price of the Camry as given. Rather, Toyota management chooses this price after long internal deliberations, and there is nothing forcing the price of a Camry to be the same as, say, a Chevrolet Impala. This consideration is important, because price-taking behavior is central to how a VER can help the exporting country in a competitive model: In effect, it helps the exporting country act a little bit like a monopolist, even if every producer is a price-taker. Recall the sugar model of Chapter 7: Without the VER, sugar suppliers in the rest of the world price at marginal cost, but with the VER, exporting countries sell in the United States at a price above the marginal production cost. That is how sugar exporting countries could be made better off by a sugar VER, but that logic does not apply in the auto industry, since each auto firm already prices above marginal cost.

Furthermore, Mannering and Winston (1987) make a striking claim: that the U.S. automakers produced fewer cars during the VER than would have been predicted without it, correcting for such factors as GDP and interest rates.[1] In other words, they interpreted the data as saying that the VER *reduced* the output of U.S. automakers. This finding would be completely incompatible with a competitive model. Recall that in the sugar model, U.S. production of sugar unambiguously rises due to the quota because the domestic price rises and U.S. sugar producers move along their supply curves.

We conclude that a model with perfect competition is not adequate to understand the 1980s automotive VER. Next, we will turn to models of trade with oligopoly to see if they do any better.

10.3 Does a Cournot Interpretation Work?

Now, suppose that the industry is structured as a Cournot oligopoly, as in Sections 4.3 to 4.6 of Chapter 4. To simplify matters, let us collapse the Japanese auto industry into one firm, Toyota, and the American industry into General Motors (GM), and let us assume that the two firms produce cars that are interchangeable from the point of view of consumers. These are not realistic assumptions and would be poor assumptions to make for many purposes, but the main argument developed here will not depend on these simplifications.

In equilibrium, Toyota and GM each chooses a quantity to sell in order to maximize profits, understanding how price will respond, and taking as given what the other firm will choose. Figure 10.1 shows what equilibrium looks like in the U.S. market, as the intersection of the two firms' reaction functions. Assume that transport costs are zero and that both firms have the same marginal

---

[1] This is by no means a unanimous conclusion in the literature. For example, Berry, Levinsohn, and Pakes (1999) come to the opposite conclusion, through a very different method.

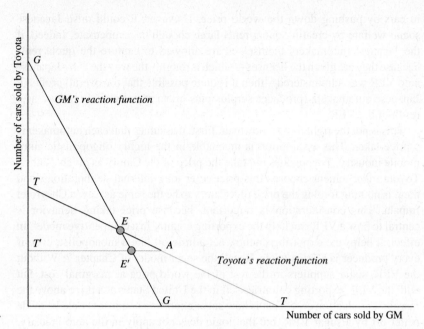

FIGURE 10.1
A VER with Cournot
Oligopoly: U.S. Market.

cost, so that the two firms split the market evenly. In the figure, the free-trade
equilibrium is shown as point *E*, with GM's and Toyota's free-trade reaction
functions shown by solid black lines and denoted *GG* and *TT*, respectively.
Now, suppose that the two governments work out a VER agreement that
restricts Toyota's sales in the United States to a quantity below Toyota's free-
trade exports. This truncates Toyota's reaction function, resulting in a new
reaction function for Toyota given by *TAT'* and marked in blue. As a result, the
equilibrium moves down and to the right along GM's reaction function to
the new equilibrium at point *E'*, implying that GM will definitely increase its
U.S. sales above the amount it would have sold under free trade.

From Toyota's point of view, this agreement is disastrous. Not only is it not
permitted to choose its quantity to maximize its profit taking as given what
GM does, but *now GM also floods the market with a higher volume of sales
than it would have chosen without the VER*, lowering the price that Toyota can
expect to receive for any quantity it picks. On both grounds, Toyota's profit
must be lower with the VER than it was under free trade.

It is clear that we cannot explain what actually happened with a Cournot
model. Next, we see if we can have better luck with a Bertrand model.

10.4 Trying on a Bertrand Model

Now, suppose that the auto industry is structured as a Bertrand model, as
described in Section 4.7 of Chapter 4. Thus, Toyota and GM each chooses a
price to maximize profit, taking the other firm's price as given. Once again, to
see the argument as simply as possible, assume that the two firms' cars are
interchangeable to consumers, that transport costs are zero, and that both firms
have the same marginal costs. For concreteness, suppose that the demand for
cars in the United States is given by:

$$Q = 20,000,000 - 2,000P, \tag{10.1}$$

where Q denotes the number of vehicles sold per year and P denotes the price (in 1981 dollars). Suppose that the marginal production cost for both firms is $5,000 per vehicle. Then, following the logic of Chapter 4, in equilibrium under free trade, both firms will price their cars at $5,000. (If Toyota priced at $6,000, say, it would be optimal for GM to price at $5,999 and capture the whole market, reaping a large profit. But if GM were to price at $5,999, it would be optimal for Toyota to price at $5,998 for the same reason. The only choice of price that is not vulnerable to such undercutting is marginal-cost pricing.)[2] With both firms charging the same price, we will assume that they split the market evenly, implying sales of 5 million vehicles for each firm. Note that neither firm is making economic profits in this situation, nor is it able to do so; if GM raised its price above its unit cost, for example, it would simply lose all of its customers. (Of course, the two firms are earning zero economic profits; they may be earning substantial accounting profits, since the marginal cost includes the opportunity cost of the firm's capital and managerial skill.)

Now, consider the effects of a VER. To take a simple example and to make a point, suppose that the VER prohibits Toyota from selling any more than 5 million cars in the United States. At first glance, it would seem that this will have no effect, since Toyota is not selling any more than that even under free trade. However, a crucially important change now takes place: Now, if GM decides to charge more than $5,000 per unit, *it will not lose all of its customers because Toyota cannot increase the number of U.S. customers it serves.* As a result, GM will gladly charge more than $5,000 and earn a strictly positive profit. But then the fact that GM will charge more than $5,000 will be good news for Toyota because that will allow Toyota to increase its own price somewhat above $5,000 as well and still sell 5 million units. Thus, *by weakening competition between the oligopolists, it is possible that the VER can make both firms better off.* In effect, the VER can allow the automakers to act somewhat closer to the way a cartel would act, since if the firms formed a cartel they would both agree to raise prices in order to maximize joint profits; in the wording of Krishna (1989) in her pioneering paper on this question, the VER acts as a 'facilitating device.'

To be more precise about the new equilibrium, we need to assume something about how the VER changes the game played by the firms. One possibility is that both firms still choose their prices simultaneously, just as they do under free trade, the only difference being that if the resulting prices result in more than 5 million units of demand for Toyotas, then Toyota's sales are stuck at 5 million units. We can call this the "simultaneous moves" interpretation of a VER. This is the approach of Krishna (1989), who shows—perhaps surprisingly—that in that sort of situation generally there is no Nash equilibrium that does not involve *randomization of prices*.[3] In equilibrium, each firm

[2] Strictly speaking, it is also an equilibrium for one firm to charge $5,000 and the other to charge $5,001, thereby ceding the whole market to the other firm. Since each firm makes zero profits anyway, either firm would be willing to do this. We will ignore this, however, and stick with the equal-division equilibrium. We should point out that this simple undercutting story obviously disappears if we allow for the fact that Toyota's cars are not actually interchangeable with GM's, so that if Toyota raises its price a bit it will lose some but not all of its U.S. customers. In that case, analyzing the equilibrium is much more complicated, but the basic point being made here about the effects of VERs still stands.

[3] Krishna's model is based on the much more realistic assumption that the two firms' cars are not perfect substitutes, so if one firm charges a higher price there are still some consumers who will choose to buy from it. The model is much more complex than the simple one presented here, but the basic point about the effects of the VER is the same.

will have to guess what the other firm will charge, but, unlike in the basic Bertrand model, it will not know exactly what price to expect because each firm will choose randomly from a range of prices. To see the reason for this somewhat vexing result, note that no equilibrium with nonrandom prices above $5,000 will work because of undercutting logic similar to the logic of Section 4.7. At the same time, a price of exactly $5,000 will not work either for the reasons just given in the previous paragraph: If Toyota is expected to price exactly at $5,000, then GM will price above $5,000 to make a positive profit, but if GM is expected to price above $5,000, Toyota will also charge above $5,000, slightly undercutting GM; but that contradicts Toyota's assumed price of $5,000. (Think of rock-paper-scissors as a good model for this kind of reasoning; if either player is predictable, the other will take advantage of that.) The result is that each firm randomizes its prices in the range from $5,000 to the monopoly price, but the important point for us is that the prices finally observed in the marketplace would almost surely be higher than $5,000, and the expected profits of both firms in the statistical sense would be above zero.

On the other hand, one could assume, as in Harris (1985), that under the VER Toyota is forced to wait for its own price decision until GM has announced its price, thereby picking a price that will generate sales demand for Toyotas that does not exceed 5 million units. We can call this the "Stackelberg leader" interpretation of a VER. (That is the name given to the form of oligopoly in which one firm moves before all others.) Under this interpretation, whatever price GM charges, Toyota will want to charge one dollar less and sell its full 5 million units.[4] From GM's point of view, then, for each price it might consider charging, it can sell the market demand at that price minus the 5 million units sold by Toyota. Its residual demand is therefore just the market demand curve shifted to the left by 5 million units, as shown by the broken blue line in Figure 10.2, and this can be treated algebraically by subtracting 5 million from the demand curve (10.1):

$$Q^{GM} = 15,000,000 - 2,000P,$$

where Q^{GM} denotes GM's residual demand. Based on this residual demand curve, GM can compute its marginal revenue MR^{GM}:

$$MR^{GM} = 7,500 - Q^{GM}/1,000,$$

and set it equal to the marginal cost of $5,000 to find its optimal quantity and price, as in Figure 10.3. The result is that GM sells 2,500,000 cars at a price of $6,250 per car, well above the $5,000 that the automakers charged under free trade—and recall that the VER quota in this example is set at exactly the level that Toyota sold under free trade. Further, GM clearly makes positive monopoly profit, and Toyota charges $6,249, thus clearly making positive profit with the VER, which it was unable to do under free trade.

Finally, notice that with the higher price, fewer cars are sold in the United States under the VER than were sold under free trade. Since the same number,

---

[4] Strictly speaking, if GM set a price above $7,500, Toyota would not undercut by a dollar because for such high prices it would not be able to sell its full quota of 5 million cars. For such a high GM price, Toyota would ignore GM and engage in monopoly pricing instead. We do not need to worry about this complication, though, because GM will never want to set a price that high.

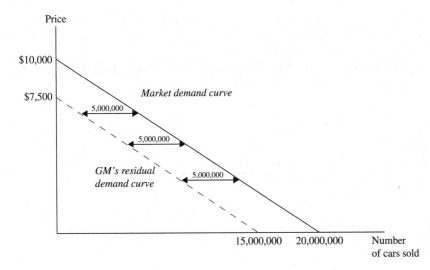

FIGURE 10.2
GM's Residual Demand
Under the VER.

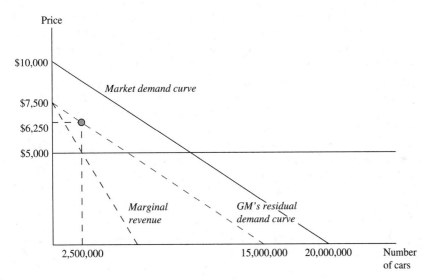

FIGURE 10.3
The Effect of the VER.

5 million, are sold by the foreign supplier with or without the VER, we conclude that *fewer cars are sold by GM* under the VER than under free trade.[5]
This is a striking finding, and the reason is important. The VER does not
merely allow GM to sell a given volume of cars at a higher price than it could
under free trade; it also gives GM a certain measure of monopoly power by
increasing GM's control over its price. Without the VER, GM effectively faces
a flat residual demand curve: if GM increased its price above Toyota's price at
all, it would lose all of its customers. By contrast, under the VER it faces a
downward-sloping residual demand curve, and so it has an incentive to restrict

---

[5] To make a point, we have focused on a VER that restricts Toyota to the same level of U.S. sales as it
had under free trade. Of course, the actual VER restricted Japanese sales to a point *below* their free-
trade level. It is easy to confirm that a more restrictive quota can result in either an increase or a
decrease in GM's U.S. sales, depending on how restrictive it is.

output to some extent in order to keep its price high, just as a monopolist does. This increase in monopoly power conferred to the protected firm is a key feature of VERs under oligopoly.

Thus, both of the paradoxes of the 1980s case—that Japanese firms appear to have profited from the VER and that U.S. auto production may have been reduced by it—are explained in a Bertrand model, but not in the other models we have examined.

To sum up the bottom line, the Reagan administration was not, of course, *literally* tricked by Japanese automakers into pursuing this policy; it was under considerable domestic political pressure to help the Detroit automakers. However, given the results the policy produced, it almost amounts to the same thing.

10.5 A Closer Look: Trade Policy with Cournot Oligopoly

The story of the 1980s U.S.-Japanese automotive VER illustrates a fairly general point: The effects of trade policy in the case of an oligopoly can be *very* different from its effects under perfect competition. We will illustrate this point further with a look at tariffs and export subsidies under Cournot and Bertrand oligopoly.

Consider a Toyota-GM Cournot duopoly as described in Section 10.3. Both firms have constant marginal costs of $5,000 per car, and to simplify matters assume that both companies sell in the U.S. market without transport costs. In each country, the demand curve is given by (10.1). If we denote the quantity sold by GM and Toyota in the U.S. market by q_{GM} and q_T, respectively, then, following the logic of Chapter 4, GM's marginal revenue is given by:

$$MR^{GM} = 10,000 - \frac{q_T}{2,000} - \frac{q_{GM}}{1,000},$$

and equating this with the marginal cost of $5,000 per car yields GM's reaction function:

$$q_{GM} = 5,000,000 - \frac{1}{2}q_T.$$

Recalling that under free trade with no transport costs Toyota faces the same costs in the U.S. market, its reaction function is similar:

$$q_T = 5,000,000 - \frac{1}{2}q_{GM}.$$

This results in Nash equilibrium quantities of 3.33 million cars sold in the U.S. market for each firm. This is shown in Figure 10.4 as point E, the intersection of the two firm's free-trade reaction functions, which are drawn as solid lines. Plugging the combined quantity into the demand curve (10.1) results in a market price of $6,667 per car. Of course, the same analysis would apply to the Japanese market as well.

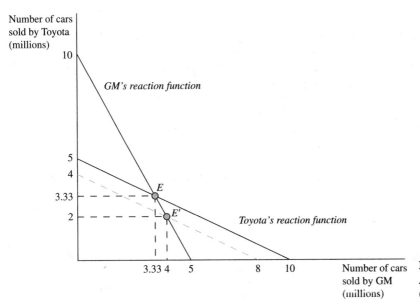

FIGURE 10.4
A Tariff with Cournot
Oligopoly: U.S. Market.

Now, consider a tariff on imported cars, in the amount of $1,000 per car. This raises the marginal cost of servicing the U.S. market to $6,000 for Toyota, changing its reaction function to:

$$q_T = 4,000,000 - \frac{1}{2}q_{GM},$$

while leaving GM's reaction function unchanged (and leaving both reaction functions in the Japanese market unchanged). This can be seen in Figure 10.4, where Toyota's tariff-affected reaction function is shown as a broken blue line and the new equilibrium is at point E'. As a result of the tariff, Toyota's U.S. sales fall to 2 million cars, and GM's rise to 4 million. Plugging the total sales of 6 million into the demand curve, this results in a price of $7,000 per car. Toyota's sales in the U.S. market have fallen, and GM's sales have increased by a smaller amount, resulting in a smaller quantity sold and a higher price for U.S. consumers.

It is clear that GM's profits have increased as a result of the tariff. Profits per unit are given by price minus unit cost, which takes a value of $(6,667 − 5,000) before the tariff and $(7,000 − 5,000) with the tariff. Multiplying this by GM's U.S. sales of 3.33 million before the tariff and 4 million with the tariff yields a profit of $5.55 billion before the tariff and $8 billion with the tariff. The important point to note is that GM's profits go up because the tariff induces Toyota to withdraw partially from the U.S. market. The reduction in Toyota's sales from 3.33 million to 2 million units leaves more of the market to GM, shifting its residual demand curve to the right and allowing it both to expand its sales and to raise its price. This is called *rent shifting*—the process by which trade policy can shift some oligopolistic profits from a foreign firm to its domestic firms.

Clearly, this rent shifting occurs at the expense of U.S. consumers, who now face higher auto prices. This, in addition to the benefit of tariff revenue (equal to the tariff rate of $1,000 per car, times Toyota's U.S. sales of 2 million cars) must be taken into account in reckoning the effect of the tariff on U.S. welfare (measuring U.S. welfare as GM profits plus consumer surplus plus tariff revenue). It is easy to check that in this case U.S. welfare does rise because of the tariff, showing that it is entirely possible for a country to be made better off by a tariff that shifts oligopolistic profits from a foreign firm to a domestic one.

Now, for a trickier question: Is it possible to use an *export subsidy* to improve national welfare? Recall from Chapter 7 that with perfect competition this is not possible, because an export subsidy creates a production and consumption distortion plus a terms-of-trade *loss* for the country that uses it. (See Section 7.4.5.)

In this case, a U.S.-government subsidy of automobile exports amounting to $1,000 per car would not have any effect on the U.S. market, but it would affect the market in Japan by lowering GM's marginal cost of servicing the Japanese market from $5,000 to $4,000. This would shift GM's reaction function in Japan to the right, as shown by the broken blue line in Figure 10.5, increasing GM's sales in Japan from 3.33 million to 4.67 million, and lowering Toyota's sales in Japan from 3.33 million to 2.67 million. Once again, GM's profits rise, as its price-cost margin and quantity sold both rise. Once again, this is due partly to the shrinking output of Toyota, which understands that GM will produce more due to the subsidy and so optimally cuts back on its sales plans. Once again, the export subsidy shifts oligopolistic rents from Toyota to GM.

U.S. welfare in this case can be computed as GM's Japanese profits minus the fiscal cost of the subsidy to U.S. taxpayers (the amount of the subsidy per car, $1,000, times the number of cars that GM sells in Japan). U.S. consumer surplus and profits from GM's U.S. sales can be ignored here because they will

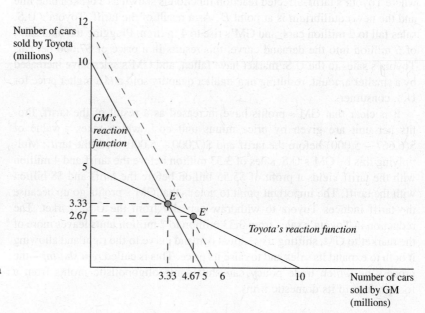

FIGURE 10.5
An Export Subsidy with Cournot Oligopoly: Japanese Market.

not be affected by the subsidy. It can be verified quickly that in this example as well, U.S. social welfare rises with the subsidy.

Note an important paradox: The subsidy pushes the prices of cars in the Japanese market *down*, since the total quantity sold in Japan under the subsidy is greater than the quantity sold under free trade. This means that, just as in the competitive model of Chapter 7, the export subsidy does worsen the terms of trade of the country that uses it. However, in this example it still raises U.S. welfare. The reason is the rent-shifting effect, which appears only in the presence of imperfect competition. In equilibrium, price is above marginal cost, so any consumer switched from Toyota to GM increases GM's profit. If the subsidy is not too high, this effect will make the subsidy worth it.

The idea that in an oligopolistic market export subsidies could be welfare-improving for the country that used them was first explored by Brander and Spencer (1985). The term *strategic trade policy* is often used to denote trade policy used for rent shifting as in this example, which Brander and Spencer pointed out was an important motivation for trade policy in some cases and was completely distinct from the terms-of-trade motive that we studied in Chapter 7.

10.6 Trade Policy with Bertrand Oligopoly

Now, suppose that the oligopoly has a Bertrand structure, so that GM and Toyota each chooses a price for each market rather than a quantity. Consider a tariff of $1,000 imposed by the U.S. government on imported automobiles. Again, the tariff raises Toyota's marginal cost of servicing the U.S. market to $6,000. Recall from the analysis of Chapter 4, Section 4.7, that in an oligopoly of this sort, with price competition and a higher marginal cost for one firm than the other, the lower-cost firm will capture the whole market but charge a price equal to the marginal cost of the higher-cost firm (to within a dollar). In this case, that means that although both firms continue to split the Japanese market, GM will capture the entire U.S. market and charge a price of $6,000 per car. Figure 10.6 shows the welfare effect in the United States. Social welfare in the

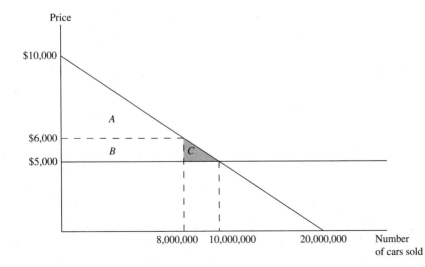

FIGURE 10.6
A Tariff with a
Bertrand Oligopoly.

United States accruing from the U.S. market is equal to areas $A + B + C$ under free trade (because that is consumer surplus given a price of $5,000; note that there is no profit in equilibrium). With the tariff, U.S. social welfare is given by areas $A + B$, of which A is the new, lower consumer surplus with the price of $6,000 and B is GM's U.S. profit. The difference is a deadweight loss of area C, which is similar to the deadweight loss that would be caused by monopoly and that the tariff creates simply because it allows GM to price above marginal cost. In this case, there is no rent shifting because the fierceness of the competition under free trade burns off any oligopolistic profit to begin with—so Toyota does not have any profits to grab.[6] The only effect of the tariff is to introduce a monopoly distortion, so that it can only hurt U.S. social welfare.

Finally, consider an export subsidy. If the U.S. government pays GM a $1,000 per car export subsidy, GM's marginal cost of serving the Japanese market will drop to $4,000. Following the above logic, GM will capture the entire Japanese market and charge a price of $5,000. Using the demand curve (10.1), this implies sales of 10 million cars for GM in Japan, with a profit of $5,000 − $4,000 = $1,000 per car. We need to subtract the fiscal cost of the subsidy to find the effect on U.S. social welfare, and the subsidy costs U.S. taxpayers $1,000 per car sold by GM in Japan. As a result, the benefit to GM exactly cancels out the cost to the U.S. taxpayer, and the net effect of the export subsidy on U.S. welfare is zero.[7]

The conclusion is that tariffs and export subsidies can be attractive in a Cournot oligopoly, but not in a Bertrand one.[8] This has emerged as a pitfall in the use of strategic trade policies in practice: The desirability of strategic trade policy, and the type of strategic trade policy that is optimal, depend on fine details of market structure such as the Cournot-Bertrand distinction, which are the kinds of information that a policy maker is unlikely to have. This problem was explored in detail by Eaton and Grossman (1986).

MAIN POINTS

1. Trade policy can have very different effects in the presence of oligopoly compared to perfect competition.

2. The best way of interpreting the U.S.-Japanese automotive VER is probably in the context of a Bertrand price-setting oligopoly. This explains how the VER could act as a facilitating device, meaning that it moved the oligopoly's behavior closer to cartel pricing. This also helps explain why the VER appears to have been good for Japanese automakers' profits and stock prices, and why the Japanese government chose to maintain the VER even after the U.S. government lost interest in it.

3. More generally, oligopoly allows for the possibility that trade policy can be used to shift oligopoly profits from foreign firms to domestic firms—the rent-shifting motive, which gives rise

---

[6] This conclusion would not hold if we took account of the differences in the cars sold by the two companies, which is the focus of sophisticated analyses such as Krishna (1989) and Berry, Levinsohn, and Pakes (1999). The reason is that if the two firms' cars are imperfect substitutes, a $1 tariff can result in less than a $1 increase in consumer price, so the tariff revenue is larger than the reduction in consumer surplus. Looked at slightly differently, in the imperfect-substitutes case, both firms receive some oligopolistic profits in equilibrium, so there is once again a rent-shifting motive for a tariff.

[7] If we allow for differences between U.S. and Japanese cars, the effect of an export subsidy on the exporting country's welfare in a Bertrand model is generally strictly negative. See Eaton and Grossman (1986).

[8] Recall that this needs to be amended in the case of a tariff if the two firms' cars are imperfect substitutes.

to so-called strategic trade policy. With Cournot oligopoly, both tariffs and export subsidies can fill this role. The latter is a striking contrast with the case of perfect competition, under which export subsidies are never welfare-promoting for the exporting country.

4. However, both types of strategic trade policy are less likely to be attractive under Bertrand competition. The dependence of strategic trade policy on the type of oligopoly is a serious limitation of its usefulness in practice.

QUESTIONS AND PROBLEMS

1. Write down three industries in which you suspect that strategic trade policy is a tool that governments could potentially use, and three in which you suspect that it is not. Explain your reasoning in plain English (no need for extensive research or data work). (*Note*: Remember that oligopoly is key to the whole logic of strategic trade policy.)

2. A key argument made by policy makers for trade protection is the preservation of jobs in the affected industry. Going through the different examples in this chapter, what are the cases in which domestic employment in the affected industry will be increased by the trade policy in question, and what are the cases in which it will be reduced?

3. Consider the market for transistors, which are produced in Home by firm H and in Foreign by firm F. These are only two countries in the world. In either country, the demand curve for transistors is:

$$Q = 10 - P,$$

where Q is the number of transistors sold and P is the price consumers face. Both firm H and firm F produce at a constant marginal cost of $4 per transistor, and they compete as Cournot competitors.

(a) Compute the equilibrium under free trade and show it on a diagram with H's sales in the Home market on the horizontal axis and F's sales in the Home market on the vertical axis.

(b) Now, suppose that the Home country government imposes a $1 per transistor import tariff. Compute the new equilibrium, and show it on the same diagram as you have drawn for part (a).

(c) Analyze the welfare effect of the tariff in a diagram that shows the effect on Home consumer surplus, profit, and tariff revenue. Does it raise Home welfare? Does it successfully shift profits from the F firm to the H firm?

4. For the model of Question 3, suppose that the Home government convinces the Foreign government to impose a VER on the F firm.

(a) Suppose that the VER restricts F's exports to be no more than its free-trade exports. Does this change the equilibrium? Explain. If necessary, compute the new equilibrium and diagram it on a reaction-function diagram.

(b) Now, suppose that the VER restricts F's exports to be no more than *half* of its free-trade exports. Does this change the equilibrium? Compute the new equilibrium quantities and price, and show the equilibrium on a reaction-function diagram.

5. Again for the model of Question 3, suppose that the Home government provides a $1 per transistor export subsidy to the H firm.

(a) Show how this changes the equilibrium, computing the new equilibrium prices and quantities and showing the new equilibrium in the reaction-function diagram for the Foreign market.

(b) Show the welfare effects of the export subsidy in a diagram that shows the H firm's profit and the Home taxpayer's burden. Does Home benefit from the subsidy?

(c) Does Foreign benefit from Home's export subsidy? Explain.

6. Now consider the model of Question 3, with the important modification that the industry is now a price-setting Bertrand oligopoly. Analyze the effect of a $1 per transistor import tariff imposed by the Home government.

(a) What are the effects on each firm's sales and profits in each country, as well as consumer surplus and tariff revenue?

(b) Does it raise Home welfare?

(c) How do its effects compare with the effects of the same policy in the event of Cournot competition (as in Question 3)? What is the reason for the differences?

7. Again with the Bertrand oligopoly of Question 6, consider a VER in which Foreign limits the F firm's exports to be no greater than they were under free trade. Use the Stackelberg leader interpretation of how a VER works in this case.

   (a) Analyze the effect on both firms' sales and profits, as well as consumer surplus.

   (b) Is this a policy that the F firm would like? Would the Foreign government like to continue this policy even if the Home government was not demanding it? Explain.

8. Again with the Bertrand oligopoly of Question 6, suppose that Home provides the H firm with a $1 per transistor export subsidy.

   (a) Analyze the effect on both firms' sales and profits, as well as consumer surplus.

   (b) Does this subsidy improve Home welfare? If the answer is different from the answer in the Cournot case (Question 5), explain why.

   (c) Now, add transport costs to the model. Suppose that each firm needs to pay a 50¢ per transistor transport cost to sell in the other country's market. How does this change the analysis of the $1 export subsidy? In particular, what is the effect of the subsidy on Home welfare?

9. *Oligopoly, Increasing Returns, Tariffs and FDI.* Recall from Chapter 3 that one motivation for setting up a branch plant in a foreign country is to avoid transport costs and tariffs, but this has to be weighed against increasing returns, which argues for concentrating production in one location. Here, we can put those ideas together with oligopoly. Consider the model of the auto industry from Section 10.5, using the demand curve and production costs introduced in Section 10.4

but maintaining a Cournot assumption, and introduce transport costs, so that now either automaker must pay a cost of $1,000 per car sold in the other country. Suppose that in addition to the marginal production cost of $5,000 per car, each firm must incur a fixed cost per plant, and under free trade this fixed cost is enough that GM chooses to maintain just its U.S. plant, exporting to Japan, and Toyota maintains just its Japanese plant, exporting to the United States. However, if the U.S. tariff is high enough, Toyota will choose to set up a U.S. plant, from which it can supply the U.S. market without paying transport costs or tariffs. This is called *tariff-jumping FDI*.

   (a) Compute the equilibrium in the U.S. market under free trade, taking the transport costs into account.

   (b) Now, do the same under the assumption that the U.S. government imposes a tariff high enough to induce Toyota to set up a U.S. plant.

   (c) Taking into account consumer surplus, GM profit, and tariff revenue, what is the effect of the tariff described in part (b) on U.S. welfare?

   (d) Usually, a tariff on an imported product raises the domestic price of that product, lowering consumer surplus. Is that true of this tariff? Explain.

   (e) Usually, a tariff on an imported product raises the income of domestic producers of that product. Is that true of this tariff? Explain.

   (f) Does this example suggest that a tariff to encourage FDI is an attractive strategy? Explain.

REFERENCES

Berry, Steven, James Levinsohn, and Ariel Pakes (1999). "Voluntary Export Restraints on Automobiles: Evaluating a Trade Policy." *The American Economic Review* **89**:3 (June), pp. 400–430.

Brander, James A., and Barbara J. Spencer (1985). "Export Subsidies and International Market Share Rivalry." *Journal of International Economics* **18**, pp. 83–100.

Denzau, Arthur T. (1988). "The Japanese Automobile Cartel: Made in the USA." *Regulation* **12**:1, pp. 11–16.

Eaton, Jonathan, and Gene M. Grossman (1986). "Optimal Trade and Industrial Policy under Oligopoly." *The Quarterly Journal of Economics* **101**:2 (May), pp. 383–406.

Harris, Richard (1985). "Why Voluntary Export Restraints Are 'Voluntary'." *The Canadian Journal of Economics* **18**:4, pp. 799–809.

Krishna, Kala (1989). "Trade Restraints as Facilitating Devices," *Journal of International Economics* **26**, pp. 251–270.

Mannering, Fred, and Winston, Clifford (1987). "Economic Effects of Voluntary Export Restrictions," in Winston, Clifford (ed.), *Blind Intersection: Policy and the Automobile Industry*. Washington, DC: Brookings Institution, pp. 61–67.

Richman, Sheldon L. (1988). "The Reagan Record on Trade: Rhetoric vs. Reality. *Cato Policy Analysis No.* 107 (May 30).

Ries, John C. (1993). "Windfall Profits and Vertical Relationships: Who Gained in the Japanese Auto Industry from VERs?" *The Journal of Industrial Economics* **41**:3 (September), pp. 259–276.

Tharp, Mike (1981). "U.S. and Japan Agree on Ceilings for Car Shipments." *The New York Times*, May 1, 1981, p. A1.

11 Should the iPod Be Made in the United States?

The Video iPod. Photograph copyright Herman Yung.

11.1 Made All Over

American manufacturing has had a lot of trouble in recent years keeping up with foreign competitors, losing market share in one product category after another. In this landscape, the iPod is a striking success story: An American product that, following its introduction in 2001 by the Apple Corporation of Cupertino, California, took the world by storm and revolutionized the way people listen to music.

But is the iPod really an American product? A team of academics at the University of California analyzed the production of the 30-gigabyte Video iPod (without the help of the Apple Corporation) to see where each stage of production is located and what share of the income is captured by each country involved (Linden, Kraemer, and Dedrick, 2007). They found that the unit contains more than 400 components, most of which are of undetermined origin. All of the major components do have identifiable origins and were obtained from manufacturers who produced the components in Japan, China, Taiwan, Singapore, or Korea. In addition, the iPods are assembled in China, under contract by companies such as the Taiwanese-based Foxconn. Many of these companies are located in a sprawling complex in Longhua, near Hong Kong, that employs and houses 200,000 workers (see the report by the British Newspaper, *The Mail on Sunday* (2006)).

So the iPod is assembled outside of the United States, from components made almost entirely outside the United States and yet it is the product of an American company. This is an example of a trend that has been accelerating over the last decade. This trend is often called the *globalization of production* (or sometimes the *fragmentation* of production), whereby corporations procure inputs from several countries and allocate the tasks of production across several countries in order to minimize costs. If a corporation hires workers in another country to perform business services that would otherwise be done at home, such as computer programming, data entry, accounting, or call-center work, it is engaging in *services offshoring*. If a corporation hires workers in another country to perform a manufacturing task, such as sewing or assembly, instead of workers in the corporation's own country, we will say that it is *offshoring production*.[1]

This can be almost indistinguishable from importing intermediate inputs that would otherwise have been produced domestically. All of these forms of globalization of a firm's operations are closely related and can have similar economic effects.

The degree to which the iPod production process has been globalized is striking. For example, as reported in *Mail on Sunday* (2006), a central component for the iPod Nano is the PortalPlayer microchip, made with "technology . . . licensed from British firm ARM, then modified by PortalPlayer's programmers in California, Washington state and Hyderabad, India. The finished chip will carry about one million lines of code." The chip is then made by a firm in Taiwan, processed further by another firm in Taiwan and yet another

---

[1] There is a lot of variation in the terms used to describe these phenomena. For example, what will be called offshoring here is sometimes called international outsourcing, and in the popular press is usually called simply outsourcing. These terms can be confusing because sometimes outsourcing means hiring a *separate firm* to do the task, whether the firm is domestic or foreign. Offshoring simply means moving the task to another country, regardless of whether it is performed by an outside firm. That is our focus in this chapter.

in Korea, shipped to Hong Kong to be stored in a warehouse until needed, and finally sent to mainland China for inclusion in the iPod. This is all for a *single part*—one of the 400.

The iPod example may take the complexity of globalization of production to extremes, but in important respects it is not at all unusual. Hummels, Ishii, and Yi (2001) document the rise in vertical specialization, or imports of inputs for use in creating goods for export, which they show is growing rapidly worldwide and accounts for a third of the growth in world trade. Offshoring has been on the rise throughout the U.S. economy: Stories of the offshoring of call centers and information technology services to India have been common, and U.S. corporations have expanded their offshoring of tasks to the Mexican assembly plants known as maquiladoras since passage of the North American Free Trade Agreement (NAFTA) in 1994 (see Hummels, Rapoport, and Yi, 1998). Offshoring of business services by U.S. manufacturers grew by 6.3% per annum in the 1990s (Amiti and Wei, 2006; see also Bhagwati, Panagariya, and Srinivasan, 2004). Many commentators see this as a threat.[2] A number of questions arise: Is this a problem? Is it bad for the economy? Is it bad for blue-collar workers in industrial countries? Bluntly, should the iPod be made in the United States?

We will look at a handful of the more influential approaches to these questions by international economists and see if they bring us closer to answers. Along the way, we will need to pick up theories of offshoring that are much more general than the iPod question, and can help shed light on services offshoring and related practices as well.

11.2 Offshoring and Inequality: The Feenstra-Hanson Theory

Perhaps the best-known theory of the effects of offshoring is provided by Feenstra and Hanson (1996), who construct a formal model of the allocation of tasks across countries. In their model, offshoring allows producers in skill-abundant countries to move their least skill-intensive tasks to skill-scarce economies. Although these tasks are the least skill-intensive tasks in the skill-abundant economy, they are *more* skill-intensive than the tasks already performed in the skill-*scarce* economy. As a result, the skill intensity of work in both economies rises, raising the relative demand for skilled workers and raising the relative wages for skilled workers, in both countries. Thus, the Feenstra and Hanson theory predicts that offshoring will tend to raise income inequality everywhere.

To see how the theory works, consider an extremely stylized and simplified version of the story (the original model is richer and more complicated than what is presented here and differs in many details, but the germ of the argument is the same). Suppose that there are two countries, called the United States and Mexico, in which a single product is produced by a large number of price-taking firms (all headquartered in the United States) using skilled and

---

[2] In a 2004 opinion poll, "global economic competition and the outsourcing of American jobs" beat out terrorism among issues Americans were worried about; 63% of respondents were "very concerned" or "extremely concerned" about the issue, and 46% called it the most important or second most important issue concerning them (p. 5). See Greenberg Quinlan Rosner Research (2004).

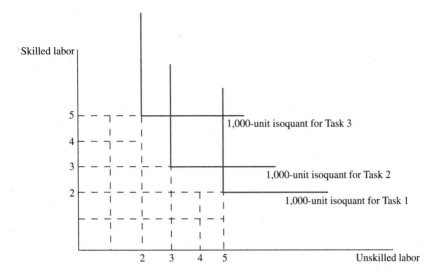

FIGURE 11.1
The Technology of
Production.

unskilled labor. Suppose, for concreteness, that the product is a transistor radio and fix the price of a radio at $1. Three tasks are required in order to produce each radio. Task 1 is component assembly, in which the interior electronic components are put together. Task 2 is exterior assembly, in which the outer case and consumer-controlled knobs and switches are applied. Task 3 is testing to make sure the product works as required. Each radio must go through all three stages to be ready for sale.

Suppose that each task requires both kinds of labor, which combine in fixed proportions. To perform Task 1 for 1,000 radios requires 5 units of unskilled labor and 2 units of skilled labor. To perform Task 2 for 1,000 radios requires 3 units of each kind of labor. To perform Task 3 for 1,000 radios requires 2 units of unskilled labor and 5 units of skilled labor. These production functions are the same for both countries and are illustrated in Figure 11.1, with the isoquants for each task drawn for production of 1,000 radios, and the two kinds of labor measured on the two axes. Clearly, Task 3 is skilled-labor intensive relative to Task 2, and Task 2 is skilled-labor intensive relative to Task 1.

Suppose that workers cannot move from one country to another, but each worker can choose how much to work. Therefore, in each country there is an upward-sloping supply curve for skilled labor as a function of the skilled wage and an upward-sloping supply curve for unskilled labor as a function of the unskilled wage. (The labor supply curves depend on the *real* wage, but note that with the price of radios fixed at $1, there is no difference between nominal wages and real wages.) To make things simple, suppose that the elasticity of labor supply for both types of labor in both countries is constant at a value $\varepsilon > 0$, so that the ratio of skilled to unskilled labor supplied in each country is an increasing function of the relative skilled wage w^S/w^U. Assume that the United States is skilled-labor abundant relative to Mexico, in the following way: Suppose that for any value of the relative skilled wage, the U.S. ratio of skilled to unskilled workers is three times the ratio in Mexico. This difference in labor supplies is the only difference between the two countries. In a model such as this, the implication is that in equilibrium the relative wage for skilled workers w^S/w^U must be lower in the United States than in Mexico.

Wages must adjust so that producers choose to locate some productive tasks in the United States and some in Mexico. Note that this implies that the more

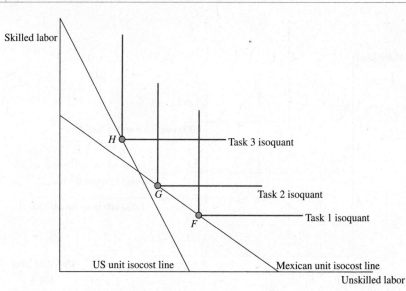

Skilled labor

H

Task 3 isoquant

G

Task 2 isoquant

F

Task 1 isoquant

US unit isocost line   Mexican unit isocost line

Unskilled labor

FIGURE 11.2
Sorting Tasks Across
Countries.

skilled-labor-intensive tasks will be done in the United States, while the least skilled-labor-intensive tasks will be done in Mexico. This is illustrated in Figure 11.2, which shows a unit isocost line for the United States (meaning the combination of all bundles of skilled and unskilled labor that cost $1 to hire), and a unit isocost line for Mexico. The line for Mexico is flatter because the slope is equal to the relative unskilled wage w^U/w^S, which takes a lower value in Mexico than in the United States. Each radio producer locates Task 1 in the country where it can get the most units of Task 1 done for each dollar spent, so it will find the maximum amount of Task 1 that can be done along each country's unit isocost line and pick the country where that quantity is larger. The largest amount of Task 1 that can be done for $1 of expenditure in Mexico is given by point F in Figure 11.2. As drawn, that $1 expenditure purchases a larger quantity of Task 1 in Mexico than it can buy in the United States, because the U.S. unit isocost line does not reach the isoquant for point F. Therefore, Task 1 can be done more cheaply in Mexico, and that is where firms will choose to do it. By similar reasoning, the largest quantity of Task 3 that a firm can get done in the United States for $1 is given by point H. This is more than can be done in Mexico for the same expenditure because the Mexican unit isocost line does not reach point H. Therefore, Task 3 is done in the United States.

Note that the way the figure is drawn, Task 2 can be done most cheaply in Mexico (at point G). Suppose that although radio manufacturers would all *like* to do Task 2 in Mexico, they are initially prevented from doing so. This can be either because of difficulties in coordinating that task across borders with the other tasks, or because of prohibitively high tariffs that would need to be paid to ship the unfinished goods back and forth across the border. Perhaps Task 2 requires a lot of supervision, and it is difficult for managers in the United States to keep in close enough communication with a plant in Mexico to provide that level of supervision. In that case, the production of radios requires Task 2 and Task 3 to be done in the United States, while Task 1 is done in Mexico. Production of 1,000 radios per month requires enough U.S. skilled labor to do 1,000 units of Task 2, plus enough skilled labor to do 1,000 units of Task 3.

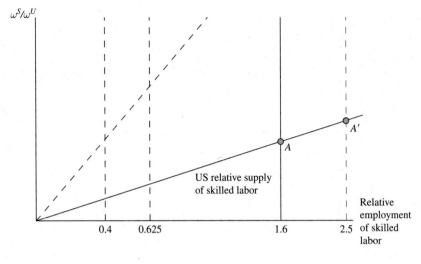

FIGURE 11.3
The Labor Market in
the U.S.

Therefore, to find the total U.S. skilled labor required we add 3 units of skilled labor for Task 2 to 5 units of skilled labor for Task 3 to obtain 8 units of skilled labor. Production of 1,000 radios per month also requires enough U.S. unskilled labor to do 1,000 units of Task 2, plus enough unskilled labor to do 1,000 units of Task 3, so we add 3 units of unskilled labor for Task 2 to 2 units of unskilled labor for Task 3 to obtain 5 units of unskilled labor. This implies a relative demand for skilled labor in the United States equal to 8/5, or 1.6. Similarly, in Mexico, the relative demand for skilled labor is equal to the 2 units of skilled labor required for 1,000 units of Task 1 divided by the 5 units of unskilled labor that correspond to it, or 0.4.

Equilibrium relative wages are determined by the requirement that the relative supply of skilled labor in each country equal the relative demand. For the United States, this is represented in Figure 11.3, with the relative skilled wage w^S/w^U on the vertical axis and the relative employment of skilled workers on the horizontal axis. The vertical black line shows relative skilled-labor demand, and an upward-sloping curve represents relative skilled-labor supply. The equilibrium is shown as point A. Figure 11.4 shows the same information for the Mexican labor market, with equilibrium at point B.[3]

Now, suppose that it becomes feasible to offshore Task 2. This may be because a breakthrough in communications technology has now made it possible to perform Task 2 in Mexico, coordinating the task with the other tasks effectively, or because tariffs that made it too costly to ship unfinished goods back and forth across the border have been removed. If Task 2 is moved to Mexico, relative labor demand in the United States will need to be derived from the Task 3 labor requirements, or 5 units of skilled labor divided by 2 units of

---

[3] Working out the full equilibrium is more complicated. There are five endogenous variables: the four wages and the number of radios produced, which we can denote R. There are four labor-market clearing equations, one for skilled labor in each country and one for unskilled labor in each country. For example, the demand for unskilled labor in the United States is equal to 2 units per radio produced for Task 3 plus 3 units per radio produced for Task 2, or $(3 + 2)R$; this must equal U.S. unskilled labor supply, which is a function of the unskilled wage. There is also a zero-profit condition, which is simply that the total cost of all three tasks per radio adds up to $1. This together gives us five equations and five unknowns. We need not concern ourselves with these details to get at our main point, however.

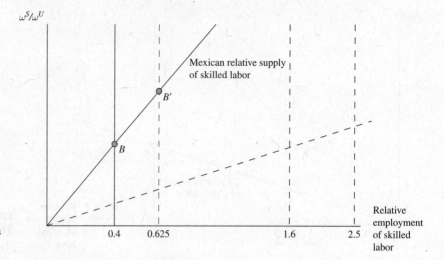

FIGURE 11.4
The Labor Market in Mexico.

unskilled labor, for a ratio of 2.5.[4] This is shown by the broken blue vertical line in Figure 11.3. Since this implies a rise in the relative demand for skilled labor, the relative skilled wage in the United States must rise, as shown at the new equilibrium point A'. In Mexico, the relative labor demand before offshoring had been given by the labor requirements for Task 1, but with offshoring it will be given by the combined Task-1-and-Task-2 requirements, or 2 units of skilled labor for Task 1 plus 3 units of skilled labor for Task 2, divided by 5 units of unskilled labor for Task 1 plus 3 units of unskilled labor for Task 2, yielding a value of 5/8, or 0.625. This is indicated by the broken blue vertical line in Figure 11.4. Again, this is a rise in the skilled-labor intensity of labor demand, so that the relative wage in Mexico must rise, as shown by the new equilibrium at point B'. This gives the main result: Offshoring increases wage inequality and increases the relative supply of skilled labor, in *both economies*.

The point is that the task that is moved from the skill-abundant country to the skill-scarce country, Task 2, is the *least* skill-intensive task in the skill-abundant country, but it becomes the *most* skill-intensive task in the skill-scarce country. Here is an important note about this theory: It can help explain the conundrums of the labor-market experience that we discussed in Chapter 6, namely, that as globalization has proceeded, in countries at many different per capita income levels and in many industries within each country there has been a simultaneous increase in the relative wages of skilled workers together with their relative employment levels. The Feenstra-Hanson theory suggests that this can be a consequence of the globalization of production, which can be thought of as trade in tasks or intermediate inputs, while it is difficult to explain it as a consequence of trade in final goods.

Note that it does not matter for our purposes here whether the offshoring of Task 2 to Mexico is done by outsourcing the task to a Mexican firm or by a U.S. multinational hiring Mexican workers directly. The ABC Radio Corporation of Sheboygan, Michigan, could offshore Task 2 by contracting with a local

---

[4] A full analysis of the equilibrium would take account of the possibility that Task 2 would be done partly in the United States and partly in Mexico. We are omitting that discussion for simplicity.

company in Mexico, which would own and run the production facility and hire the workers. This is sometimes called outsourcing, or arm's length trade. On the other hand, the ABC company could set up its own affiliate in Mexico, run its own production facility, and hire workers directly through that affiliate. This would, of course, be vertical FDI. Either of these would constitute offshoring of Task 2 and would have exactly the same effects on the equilibrium.[5]

A final point about the Feenstra-Hanson theory is that it is consistent both with the possibility that offshoring raises U.S. unskilled wages and the possibility that it lowers them. If Mexican wages do not rise too much as a result of the off-shoring, then U.S. national income goes up, but at the same time unskilled workers' share of that income falls: U.S. unskilled workers get a smaller share of a larger pie. Depending on which effect dominates, unskilled wages in the United States could rise or fall. On the other hand, with the rise in the demand for Mexican labor, Mexican wages could rise by enough that U.S. national income actually *falls*, in which case U.S. unskilled wages are a shrinking share of a *smaller* pie and so they definitely fall. This is essentially a case in which the U.S. terms of trade is worsened because this is a model in which the United States imports Mexican labor. Consequently, any rise in Mexican wages is good for Mexican living standards but bad for the U.S. terms of trade.

We can summarize by noting that the model has a clear prediction that offshoring raises *wage inequality* (in both countries), but no clear prediction about the effect on the *absolute level* of U.S. wages.

11.3 Offshoring and Productivity: An Alternative Model

A related interpretation of offshoring with quite different conclusions is presented in a paper by Grossman and Rossi-Hansberg (2008). They argue that the opportunity to offshore some of the tasks previously performed by unskilled labor can in effect raise the productivity of unskilled labor, resulting in higher unskilled wages.

To see this argument in its simplest form, consider a small open economy called Home that produces radios and apparel. To produce one radio, 3 units of skilled labor are required to perform management functions, and in addition, some unskilled labor is required to do the physical production. This unskilled labor takes the form of 1 unit of labor for Task 1 (component assembly, say) and 1 additional unit for Task 2 (final assembly, say). To produce 1 unit of apparel, 2 units of skilled labor are required to perform management functions, and in addition some unskilled labor is required to do the physical production. This unskilled labor takes the form of 2 units of labor for Task 1 (cutting fabric according to a precise template for trousers, say), plus 2 more units of labor for Task 2 (sewing the pieces into a finished pair of trousers, say). The price of a radio and the price of a unit of apparel are both equal to $1, which will not change, since this is a small open economy. Note that in this story, one *good* (radios) is skilled-labor-intensive relative to the other good, but, unlike in the Feenstra and Hanson story, all *tasks* are equally unskilled-labor intensive.

---

[5] The decision whether to outsource the task to another firm or keep it within the firm is the subject of a rich literature in the industrial organization field. It can matter quite a bit for some aspects of economic efficiency, but it is not central to the income-distribution questions that we are examining here.

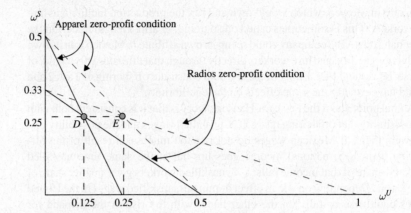

FIGURE 11.5
Offshoring in the
Grossman/
Rossi-Hansberg
Model.

Initially, both tasks for both goods must be performed in Home. The wages for both kinds of labor are determined by the zero-profit conditions:

$$(1+1)w^U + 3w^S = 1 \quad \text{and}$$
$$(2+2)w^U + 2w^S = 1,$$

where w^U denotes the unskilled wage and w^S denotes the skilled wage. The first equation is the zero-profit condition for radios, and the second is for apparel. Solving these together for the wages, we find $w^U = 0.125$ and $w^S = 0.25$, shown as point D in Figure 11.5, where the two zero-profit conditions are drawn as black lines.

Now, suppose that Home is able to offshore both the Task 1 for radio production and the Task 1 for apparel production to another country where labor is very cheap. For the sake of argument, suppose that labor costs in the foreign country in question are negligible, so that to a close approximation the tasks are now being done by foreign workers for free. Unskilled workers in Home are concerned that now producers are considering eliminating some of the unskilled workers' jobs and replacing them with extremely low-wage workers abroad.

What is the effect of the offshoring on wages in Home? Since now Task 1 in each industry is done essentially for free, the zero-profit conditions become:

$$w^U + 3w^S = 1 \quad \text{and}$$
$$2w^U + 2w^S = 1.$$

Solving these for the wages, we obtain $w^U = 0.25$ and $w^S = 0.25$, shown as point E in Figure 11.5, where the new zero-profit conditions are drawn as broken blue lines. The wage for skilled workers is unchanged, but the wage for unskilled workers is now *doubled*.

It may be surprising that unskilled workers in Home are better off as a result of the offshoring, since they are, in effect, being replaced by very low-wage workers. The point, however, is that the offshoring works in the same way as a doubling of the Home unskilled workers' productivity: A Home employer who hires a Home worker now gets twice as much work out of the hire as the employer would have without offshoring. In this perfectly competitive model, that increase in productivity is passed on in wages. Geometrically, the two zero-profit lines in Figure 11.5 shift to the right by a factor of two, so doubling the equilibrium unskilled wage without touching the skilled wage restores equilibrium.

We can summarize by noting that the model predicts a reduction in *wage inequality* (in at least the offshoring country), in addition to a rise in the *absolute level* of U.S. unskilled wages.[6]

11.4 How Do These Theories Stand Up to the Data?

The two models of offshoring presented in this and the previous section suggest extremely different interpretations of the phenomenon. How do they stand up to the data?

In a nutshell, the Feenstra-Hanson hypothesis of rising wage differentials has been supported by a number of different studies, starting with empirical work in the original 1996 paper. Using data on 450 U.S. industries, the authors measured the degree of offshoring for an industry by its imports of intermediate inputs. (This is not exactly the same thing as a measure of "tasks" offshored, but it is quite close, since buying, say, a hard drive from a foreign producer instead of buying it locally is almost the same thing as hiring foreign workers to build a hard drive instead of hiring workers to build it locally.)

Feenstra and Hanson then showed that the change over time in an industry's degree of offshoring was positively correlated with the change in skilled labor's share of domestic wages paid for that industry. This is as predicted by the theory. Further, on the Mexican side of the border, they showed that the wages of non-production workers rose relative to the wages of production workers, and that the employment of nonproduction workers rose relative to the employment of nonproduction workers, over a period of rising offshoring to Mexico (the 1980s). This is significant and is consistent with the theory because nonproduction workers tend to be in managerial and technical fields such as engineering and accounting and hence are highly skilled. Therefore, the nonproduction worker/production worker split is a reasonably good proxy for the skilled worker/non-worker split. Further, the two models examined the rapid growth of the maquiladora sector—that sector of plants near the U.S. border that do assembly work for export and that are largely used by U.S. multinationals for offshoring purposes. The rise in relative wages and employment for nonproduction workers was sharpest for the states containing large numbers of maquiladora plants, which suggests that offshoring may be the driving force, as in the Feenstra-Hanson model. Considerable subsequent work has backed up the Feenstra-Hanson predictions; see their later survey (Feenstra and Hanson, 2002), and Sitchinava, 2008), who provides an exhaustive review with updated and refined estimation.

The much more recent Grossman/Rossi-Hansberg hypothesis has not been subjected to the same amount of empirical testing. Taken literally, the finding that U.S. unskilled wages rise with offshoring, while skilled wages do not, does not fit the data. Note that this implies that offshoring lowers wage inequality, but the available evidence discussed above suggests that it *raises* wage inequality. However, the best way of interpreting the model is as a way of highlighting the productivity effect of offshoring in a particularly clear way. There have not been many studies of that link. One example is Sethupathy (2009), who provides

---

[6] We have presented here the most basic version of their model. The original paper (Grossman and Rossi-Hansberg, 2008) shows how these results can be overturned in a richer version.

evidence that firms offshoring to Mexico have realized a productivity effect, part of which they pass on to their domestic workers in higher wages.

It is worth underlining that one thing the Feenstra and Hanson theory does not do is to make it clear whether unskilled workers in the high-skilled country will see a rise or a fall in their real incomes as a result of offshoring. Their share of their country's GDP falls, but because of the added productivity from being able to source tasks in their lowest-cost locations, GDP has increased. As a result, in that theory, the real incomes of U.S. workers could rise or fall with offshoring, which is easy to forget because the reduction in the *relative* unskilled wage receives the most focus. The Grossman/Rossi-Hansberg model makes this productivity effect, and the attendant possibility of a rise in unskilled real wages, as clear as could be.

11.5 Another Approach: Evidence from Aggregate Employment

Another way of evaluating the effects of offshoring on workers is to look at trends in aggregate employment. To understand this approach, think of a simple trade model such as the mixed specific-factors model (also called the Ricardo-Viner model) presented in Section 5.5. Suppose that there are two industries, one that produces output through multinational firms that have facilities at home and also in other countries, and another that produces output solely through domestic firms, whose production facilities are all in the home country. For simplicity, assume that the multinational sector produces a single good and that the nonmultinational sector also produces a single good (this is not essential for the point we will be making), and that the prices of both goods are fixed on world markets and will not change (this is more substantive; see Bhagwati, Panagariya, and Srinivasan, 2004, for an analysis of terms-of-trade effects in offshoring). In addition, assume that all labor is homogeneous; we will not focus here on the difference between skilled and unskilled labor. Initially, suppose that offshoring is not possible; the multinationals produce abroad for the foreign market, but they are not able to use foreign workers to help in producing for the domestic market. The equilibrium is as shown in Figure 11.6. The vertical axis measures the wage. The demand for labor due to the multinational sector is the blue downward-sloping curve from the left axis, with domestic employment by multinationals, L^M, measured rightward from the left axis. The demand for labor due to the nonmultinational sector is the blue upward-sloping curve sloping up to the right-hand axis, with employment by nonmultinational firms, L^N, measured leftward from the right axis. The initial equilibrium wage is represented as ω^*.

Now, suppose that because of a change either in technology or in policy, it becomes possible for multinationals to use some portion of their overseas facilities to help in their production for the domestic market. There are two possibilities. Either the tasks that the foreign workers do as part of this globalization of production will be a *substitute* for the use of home labor, or they will be a *complement* to home labor. An example of the former case would be a production process that has only one task in it, which foreign workers can perform just as well as domestic workers, but are willing to do at a wage below w^*. An example of the latter would be the replacement of some

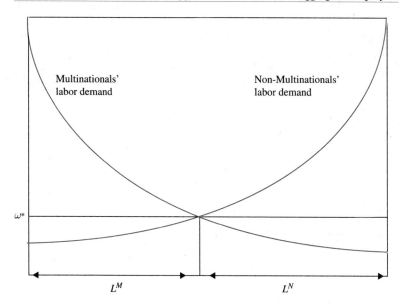

FIGURE 11.6
Equilibrium with a
Multinational Sector.

tasks by foreign workers who have an advantage in those tasks, allowing domestic workers to become more productive by focusing on the tasks in which they have an advantage.[7] For example, perhaps the globalization of production allows home workers to focus on design, finishing touches, and marketing, while foreign workers do assembly and testing. For this discussion, we will simply assume that the effect is either pure substitutability or pure complementarity.

To be more precise, there are two possibilities. Within this model, the availability of foreign workers in the production process can either *decrease* the marginal product of domestic workers in the multinational sector, shifting the multinational demand for labor curve in Figure 11.6 down, or *increase* the marginal product of domestic workers in the multinational sector, shifting the multinational demand for labor curve up. If the former case occurs, we will say that foreign labor and domestic labor are substitutes, and if the latter case occurs, we will say that they are complements.

Suppose first that foreign labor is substitutable for domestic labor. What that means in this simple model is that multinationals now have available to them for domestic production some supply, say L^F, of foreign workers, at a wage w^F, where the F stands for foreign. Then the equilibrium shifts as in Figure 11.7. The box is now longer by the amount of the additional labor L^F, and the new labor demand curve for the multinational sector, drawn as a broken blue curve, is the same as the old one but is shifted to the left by the amount of the additional labor. From the point of view of domestic workers, the result is as if the multinationals' demand curve for labor has been shifted down by the offshoring. As a result, the new equilibrium wage, w^{**}, is lower than the original wage. Clearly, in this case offshoring hurts domestic workers (even though it raises national income, so the gain to owners of specific factors

---

[7] The model of Section 11.3 is an example of the latter type: The foreign workers are complementary to domestic workers. The model of Section 11.2 combines some elements of both substitutability and complementarity.

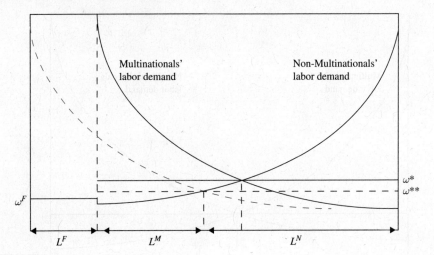

FIGURE 11.7
Offshoring When
Foreign Labor
Substitutes for
Domestic Labor.

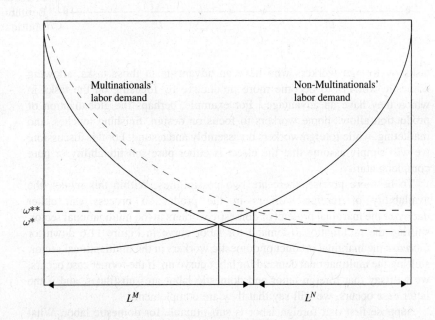

FIGURE 11.8
Offshoring When
Foreign Labor
Complements
Domestic Labor.

exceeds the loss to workers). In addition, the multinational sector will reduce its domestic labor force, as is indicated by the fact that the new equilibrium is to the left of the old one (put differently, L^M is smaller in Figure 11.7 than it was in Figure 11.6). As a result, in the data, we should see that the multinational sector's share of domestic employment will fall. In addition, the multinationals' foreign labor force will grow as its domestic labor force shrinks (the rise in L^F causes a drop in L^M). These observations can function as telltale signs for the substitutability hypothesis.

Now, suppose that foreign labor is complementary to domestic labor. In this case, the equilibrium shifts as in Figure 11.8. The new demand curve for labor in the multinational sector is given by the broken blue curve, and the new wage, again denoted by w^{**}, is higher than the original wage. Clearly, here offshoring *benefits* domestic workers. In addition, the multinational sector will *increase* its domestic labor force, and in the data, we should see that the multinational sector's share of domestic employment will rise. In addition, multinationals' foreign labor force will move in the same direction as its domestic labor force — they will both grow. These observations can function as telltale signs for the complementarity hypothesis.

Slaughter (2004) attempted to test these two hypotheses against each other, using publicly available data from the Bureau of Economic Analysis (BEA) on employment by multinational firms from 1991 to 2001. First, to clarify terms, each multinational firm consists of a "parent," meaning the operations of the firm in its home country (here, the United States), plus one or more "affiliates," meaning the multinational firm's operations in other countries. In some cases the affiliate will be a production or distribution facility wholly owned by the multinational, but in other cases it will be a foreign firm in which the multinational has part ownership. The 1990s were a period of rapidly growing offshoring possibilities, as the maquiladora sector in Mexico grew very quickly and China and India became much more integrated with the world economy. During this period, Slaughter notes that foreign affiliate employment by U.S. multinationals grew very rapidly, from 6.9 million in 1991 to 9.8 million in 2001, for a rise of 42%. However, employment by the American parent firms also grew, from 18 million in 1991 to 23.5 million, for a rise of 30.6%. Furthermore, the rise in U.S. parent employment, 5.5 million, greatly exceeded the rise in affiliate employment, 2.9 million, leading Slaughter to conclude (p. 1) that "for every one job that U.S. multinationals created abroad in their affiliates they created nearly two U.S. jobs in their parents." In addition, the share of U.S. multinational parent employment in total U.S. employment grew from 16.6 to 17.8%, indicating that multinational domestic employment grew faster than domestic nonmultinational employment. Overall, these data fit the telltale signs indicated for the complementarity model of Figure 11.8. Together with evidence compiled by Slaughter that the parents and affiliates tend to perform different kinds of work (such as manufacturing versus wholesale trade, for example), they seem to provide strong evidence for the complementarity hypotheses over the period 1991–2001.

We can update Slaughter's test with more recent BEA data, as reported in Figure 11.9, based on data from 1988 to 2006. (A vastly more sophisticated updated analysis with far more rigorous methods and broadly similar results is found in Desai, Foley, and Hines, 2009.) The black curve on Panel (a) shows U.S. parent employment by U.S. multinationals, or employment by multinationals within the United States, while the blue curve shows affiliate employment by the multinationals, meaning employment by the multinationals in other countries. (The data here are restricted to majority-owned foreign affiliates, which is a slight difference from Slaughter's report, due to data availability.) Panel (b) shows the change in the same two variables since 1988 (in other words, the current value minus the 1988 value), to make it clearer how these two variables have moved together. The figure shows a steady increase in parent employment up to the year 2000, with a sharp drop after that; at the same time, affiliate employment is much smaller but shows a slow, steady increase. As a result, if one looks at the period up to and including 2000, one finds parent employment and affiliate employment moving in the same direction. This is what Slaughter found, and what led him to conclude that the foreign and domestic labor were complements to each other. If one looks at the data following the year 2000, one sees a sharp drop in parent employment but a small

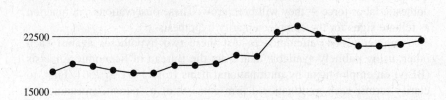
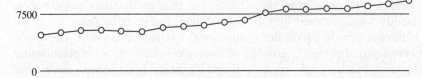
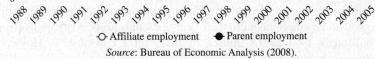

FIGURE 11.9a
US Multinationals'
Parent and Affiliate
Employment,
1988–2006.
(Thousands of
Workers).

-○- Affiliate employment   -●- Parent employment

Source: Bureau of Economic Analysis (2008).

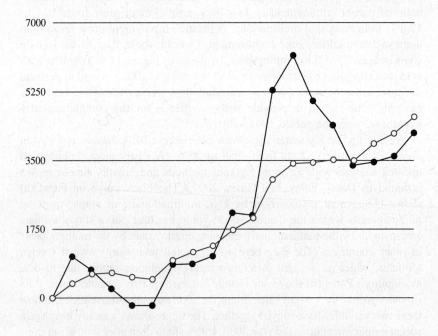
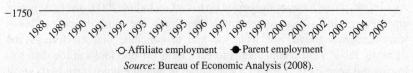

FIGURE 11.9b
Change Since 1988
(Thousands of
Workers).

-○- Affiliate employment   -●- Parent employment

Source: Bureau of Economic Analysis (2008).

increase in affiliate employment, which in and of itself looks like a case of substitutable workers. Overall, however, parent and affiliate employment tend to move in the same direction much more than in opposite directions.[8]

Taken over the whole period, parent employment grew from 17.7 million to 21.9 million for an increase of 4.2 million, and affiliate employment grew from 4.7 million to 9.4 million, for an increase of 4.7 million. Slaughter's dramatic observation that multinationals created two U.S. jobs for each foreign job is an artifact of the late-1990s surge in domestic hiring by U.S. multinationals; over the longer horizon, the ratio is much closer to 1:1. However, the important point is the sign: Over a period of dramatic increases in globalization of production, U.S. multinationals have increased their domestic workforce just as much as their foreign workforce, behaving much more like the complementarity model of Figure 11.8, rather than the substitutability model of Figure 11.7.

In addition to the co-movement of parent and affiliate employment, the finding of a rising multinationals' share of U.S. employment also must be tempered by more recent experience, as is shown in Figure 11.10, which shows multinationals parents' share of domestic U.S. employment over the same

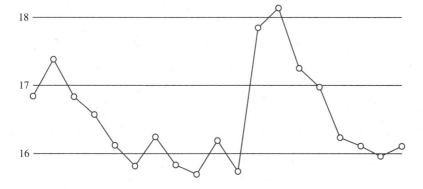

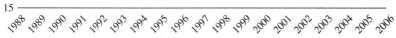

Source: Bureau of Economic Analysis (2008) and The Economic Report of the President, Table B-46.

FIGURE 11.10
Multinational Parents'
Share of Domestic U.S.
Employment (%).

---

[8] A more formal way to evaluate this is as follows. Compute the year-to-year change in parent employment (or the "first difference" in parent employment), or in other words $PE_t - PE_{t-1}$, where PE_t denotes parent employment in year t. Then do the same for affiliate employment, and find the correlation between these two first-differenced variables. The correlation works out to 90%, a very high number, indicating that parent employment tends to move in the same direction as affiliate employment the great majority of the time.

period. Multinationals' share of employment had been around 16% for most of the 1990s before surging to 18% at the end of the decade, which is the rise noted by Slaughter. Since then it has dropped back to around 16%, indicating that domestic multinational employment has grown more slowly than domestic nonmultinational employment. On its face, the period since 2000 could look like the model of Figure 11.7, with globalization of production allowing multinationals to replace domestic workers with foreign workers. Over the long haul, however, both the rapid rise in the multinational share in the late 1990s and its rapid drop after that appear to be atypical. Overall, multinational employment just seems to keep up with national employment, maintaining a long-run share of around 16%.

An important qualification to these conclusions is provided by Harrison and McMillan (2006), who studied detailed firm-level BEA data on U.S. multinationals from 1982 to 1999. They show that, over that period, although the average multinational expanded both its parent labor force and its foreign affiliate workforce, the subset of multinationals with affiliates in low-income countries *reduced* their parent workforce and expanded the foreign, low-wage workforce. Thus, the overall picture appears to be one in which high-wage foreign workers are complements to U.S. workers, but low-wage foreign workers are substitutes to U.S. workers. One possibility is that this could be because U.S. FDI in high-wage countries is mainly horizontal FDI, aimed at serving the foreign market, while U.S. FDI in low-wage countries is mainly vertical.

Overall, it looks as if the expansion of foreign affiliates of U.S. multinationals is more likely to have increased the demand for U.S. workers rather than decreased it. But that observation is qualified by the fact that affiliates in low-income countries appear more likely to have had the opposite effect, and also by the fact that the period since 2000 has looked somewhat different than the years before.

Some Caveats. Two important limitations to this approach should be mentioned. First, it does not separate the various functions a foreign affiliate may have. In this chapter our focus is on vertical FDI, whose purpose is to locate part of the production process in another country, while in Chapter 3, Section 3.3, we examined a case of horizontal FDI, whose purpose is to serve the market in another country. The BEA data in question here do not separate affiliates resulting from horizontal FDI from those resulting from vertical FDI (nor is there any guarantee that it is really possible to do so). Therefore, the employees in foreign affiliates are not by any means all involved in offshoring, and so the analysis here could be overstating offshoring.

Second, much globalization of production is not conducted through affiliates at all, but from a manufacturer contracting with, or purchasing inputs from, a separate firm in the other country—so-called arm's length trade. The iPod case fits this category, since the foreign firms that do the assembly, such as Foxconn, are not part of the Apple Corporation. Workers hired to offshore production through such arm's length trade will not show up in the BEA foreign-affiliate data at all. For that reason, the analysis here could be *understating* offshoring. There is no easy correction for these data problems, so no conclusions made from these data can be really ironclad. Nonetheless, the data do strongly suggest a number of tentative conclusions as discussed earlier.

11.6 A Bottom Line, Open Questions, and the Obama Critique

The expansion of a multinational's activities abroad can have very different implications for home-country workers, depending on the type of expansion. If the multinational is creating a foreign affiliate to generate sales abroad for domestically produced output, that will tend to raise demand for domestic labor. If the multinational is hiring abroad (either in foreign affiliates or at arm's length) to take over some productive tasks from domestic workers, that can raise or lower demand for domestic labor, depending on whether what the foreign labor is doing is substitutable (as seen in Figure 11.7) or complementary (as seen in Section 11.3 and the model of Figure 11.8) to domestic labor.

The iPod seems to be a case that belongs firmly in that last category: Hiring foreign workers whose efforts are complementary to those of domestic workers. The tasks done abroad include the entire assembly, testing, and packaging portions of the supply chain, as well as the production of almost all of the inputs. U.S. workers are involved in design, marketing, and sales—a completely separate set of functions requiring a completely separate set of skills. Further, U.S. workers have been capturing a substantial amount of income from their ends of the value chain. At the time of Linden et al.'s (2007) calculations, a 30GB Video iPod had a wholesale price of $224, of which $80 was estimated to be gross profit to Apple and $144 was estimated to be the cost of all inputs including assembly labor. The $80 includes marketing, research and development, and administration. as well as net profit. In addition, $75 is estimated to be spent on distribution and retail after the iPod is sold by Apple (pushing the retail price to $299). This implies $80 plus $75, or $155, out of the purchase price of every iPod sold in the United States that is paid to Americans, a large fraction of which will be in the form of wages and salaries (although the study is not able to break out exactly what that fraction is).

The low labor costs of the assembly process in Chinese factories are well documented. For example, the *Mail on Sunday* (2006) interviewed iPod assembly workers who work 15-hour days in the factory for 27 (about $40) per month. Given that this represents a small fraction of U.S. wage rates, manufacture of the iPod and its components in the United States would likely increase the $144 cost of inputs and assembly several-fold and price the $299 item out of the market. Thus, without a very substantial amount of offshoring, the product likely would not exist, and the $155 per iPod captured by Americans likely would be forfeited. This appears to be a case in which U.S. workers clearly benefit from offshoring. (We will return in Chapter 14 to the question of the effect on foreign workers.)

However, that is not necessarily true of all offshoring. Feenstra and Hanson have shown that the offshoring of intermediate inputs in U.S. manufacturing is strongly correlated with a rise in an industry's skilled-wage premium, consistent with their theory that such offshoring raises the relative demand for skilled labor. That theory raises the possibility that blue-collar workers in skill-abundant countries can be hurt by a rise in offshoring. Feenstra and Hanson indeed argue that this process can help explain some of the lackluster U.S. labor-market performance discussed in Chapter 6. Harrison and McMillan's finding, that when U.S. multinational firms hire in low-income countries, on average they reduce their domestic workforce, is also suggestive of that possibility. However, the question has not been settled definitively. The tendency for offshoring of intermediate inputs to raise *wage inequality* (by raising skilled wages relative to unskilled wages) is fairly well established, but the harder question of whether it raises or lowers the *absolute level* of blue-collar workers' real income is not.

One final point involves policy. Since offshoring is a form of importing, specifically the import of a task, the same sort of reasoning that applies to the analysis of trade policy regarding trade in final goods applies here as well, although the question of optimal policy toward offshoring has not attracted a great deal of research attention. For example, a tax on offshoring could improve welfare in exactly the same way as an import tariff can in a model of final-goods trade, by improving the offshoring country's terms of trade. In this case, that means lowering wages in the country to which the tasks have been outsourced. On the other hand, a subsidy to offshoring is likely to have the opposite effect and to be unattractive for that reason. These questions are currently on the policy agenda of the U.S. government because of features of the U.S. tax code that allow corporations to delay taxes on income from foreign affiliates until the corporation repatriates that income, which simply means bringing it back to the United States. Because of this flexibility, corporations can time their taxes on affiliate income in ways they cannot for parent income, and so a dollar of affiliate income will result in a smaller present discounted value of U.S. income tax than a dollar of parent income will. This feature of the tax code acts as a hidden subsidy to offshoring. President Barack Obama has declared his intention to eliminate this hidden subsidy. For example, in his speech to Congress on February 24, 2009, he declared that "we will restore a sense of fairness and balance to our tax code by finally ending the tax breaks for corporations that ship our jobs overseas"—meaning, apparently, exactly this provision. More research devoted to measuring the effects of this type of policy on U.S. and foreign wages would be most welcome.

MAIN IDEAS

1. Offshoring, often called outsourcing in the popular press, is the practice of dividing up a production process into multiple pieces spread across two or more countries in order to lower costs.

2. The Feenstra and Hanson model of offshoring focuses on differences in the skilled-labor intensity of different productive tasks. In that theory, an increase in offshoring moves the least-skilled-intensive task away from the skill-abundant country, moving it to a skill-scarce country where it will be the most skill-intensive task. In this way, the relative demand for skilled labor, as well as the relative wage for skilled labor, rises in both countries. This can help explain some of the labor-market puzzles discussed in Chapter 6, which trade in final goods cannot, such as how wage inequality has increased simultaneously in countries at every level of income.

3. The Grossman/Rossi-Hansberg model of offshoring ignores differences in the skill intensity

of tasks to focus on an important effect of offshoring: Getting tasks done abroad more cheaply than they can be done domestically can raise domestic unskilled wages by effectively raising the productivity of unskilled domestic workers.

4. A key distinction in understanding offshoring is the substitutability or complementarity of foreign labor for domestic labor. Simple models suggest that if foreign labor is a substitute for domestic labor, a rise in offshoring should lower the domestic employment by multinational firms while it raises the foreign employment by the same firms, and at the same time lower domestic wages. If they are complements, a rise in offshoring should *raise* domestic employment by multinational firms while it raises foreign employment by the same firms; raise the multinational share in domestic employment; and raise domestic wages. Overall, it appears that the

effects more closely resemble the first case for expansion of multinationals in low-income countries and the second case for expansion of multinationals in high-income countries.

5. It should be emphasized that these questions are primarily about distributional issues: In most

models of offshoring (certainly the models of Sections 11.3 and 11.4), offshoring increases national income in the country that does the offshoring, even though it may raise or lower the income of unskilled workers in that country.

QUESTIONS AND PROBLEMS

1. Think of a domestic corporation that produces some product that you know, and create a list of some of the tasks that are required to create the product and bring it to domestic consumers. Divide the list up into groups: one group of tasks that would seem to be plausibly offshored, and another set of tasks that would seem to be necessarily performed domestically. Explain why you put each task in each category.

2. Re-create Figure 11.6.

   (a) Shade in the area of the diagram indicating total national income (without offshoring), distinguishing income to multinational firms, nonmultinational firms, and workers.

   (b) Now, modify the diagram as in Figure 11.7 to show the effects of offshoring with substitutable labor. Again, shade in the diagram to show total national income, distinguishing between income to multinational firms net of payments to domestic and foreign workers, income to non-multinational firms net of payments to domestic workers, and income to domestic workers.

   (c) Can you tell from these diagrams whether national income has gone up or down as a result of offshoring? Show the change in national income in the diagram.

3. For this question, use the spreadsheet "multinational employment.xls."

   (a) Recall that Slaughter made a point that over the course of his data, "for every one job that U.S. multinationals created abroad in their affiliates they created nearly two U.S. jobs in their parents." Let us see how well that pattern holds up in the data. Focus on the period 1988–2001, and calculate the ratio of U.S. jobs created by multinationals to foreign jobs created by multinationals. (For this exercise, "U.S. jobs created as of 2000" will be measured by the U.S. jobs as of 2000 minus the U.S. jobs as of 1988, and so on.) Could this ratio be used as an argument that the

activities of foreign affiliates of U.S. multinationals are good for U.S. workers? Or could it be used by an antiglobalization advocate as an argument that those activities hurt U.S. workers? Whichever you choose, show how this might be done, but write a sentence or two that might use the statistic for this purpose.

   (b) Now, focus on the period 2001–2006, and do the same thing. (Once again, for this exercise "U.S. jobs created as of 2004" will be measured by the U.S. jobs as of 2004 minus US jobs as of 2001.)

   (c) Now, show how U.S. multinationals' share of U.S. employment changed from 1998 to 2001, and how it changed from 2001 to 2006, and explain how those findings can be interpreted as evidence for or against a positive effect of offshoring on U.S. workers.

   (d) Is the lesson one obtains from these data sensitive to the time period one uses? Explain.

4. Consider the following simple offshoring model of the type described in Section 11.2. The United States and Mexico both produce radios, using skilled and unskilled labor. Each radio requires three tasks to complete. Task 1 requires 4 units of unskilled and 2 units of skilled labor per radio; Task 2 requires 3 units of unskilled and 3 units of skilled labor per radio; and Task 3 requires 2 units of unskilled and 4 units of skilled labor per radio. In the United States, the supply curve for unskilled labor is given by $L^U = 100w^U$, where L^U is the quantity of labor and w^U is the unskilled wage; similarly, the supply curve for skilled labor is given by $L^S = 100w^S$. In Mexico, the supply curve for unskilled labor is given by $L^{U*} = 300w^{U*}$, where L^{U*} is the quantity of unskilled labor supplied in Mexico and w^U is the Mexican unskilled wage; and the supply for skilled labor is given by $L^{S*} = 100w^{S*}$. The price of radios is fixed at $1, and in both countries this is the only industry. Suppose that we know which

tasks are done in the United States and which are done in Mexico (and that no task is done in both countries). If R radios are produced, we can then find the demand for skilled and unskilled labor in each country by multiplying R by the unit labor requirements given above and equate that to the supply as a function of the wage using the supply curves as given above; call these the labor-market clearing conditions. We can then put those equations together with the zero-profit condition, which requires the total cost of both kinds of labor in both countries for all three tasks to add up to $1. This gives us five equations in five unknowns, the four wages and R. (In what follows, we will give part of the answer by revealing the equilibrium value of R, to save students from having to invert the 5×5 matrix.)

(a) Suppose that we know that Task 2 is done only in the United States because logistical problems or tariffs make it infeasible to do it in Mexico. Then Tasks 2 and 3 are done in the United States, while Task 1 is done in Mexico. Suppose we know that $R = 1.2$. Use the labor-market clearing conditions for Mexico to find the Mexican wages, then use the labor-market clearing conditions for the United States to find the U.S. wages. Show that the wages you have computed satisfy the zero-profit condition (to a reasonable approximation), so you have indeed computed a full equilibrium.

(b) For the equilibrium you have just completed, verify that it would be cheaper to conduct Task 2 in Mexico rather than the United States, so if radio manufacturers were able to offshore it, they would do so.

(c) Now, suppose that it becomes feasible to do Task 2 in Mexico. Then Task 3 is done in the United States, while Tasks 1 and 2 are done in Mexico. Suppose we know that $R = 1.63$. Use the labor-market clearing conditions for the

United States to find the U.S. wages, then use the labor-market clearing conditions for Mexico to find the U.S. wages. Show that the wages you have computed satisfy the zero-profit condition (to a reasonable approximation), so you have indeed computed a full equilibrium.

(d) What is the effect of the offshoring of Task 2 on wage inequality in the two countries? What is the effect on the skilled-unskilled employment ratio?

(e) Who benefits from the offshoring of Task 2? Who is hurt by it? Why? Analyze in detail.

5. (The Grossman/Rossi-Hansberg offshoring model) Suppose that a small open economy produces Good X and Good Y using skilled and unskilled labor. Each unit of Good X requires 1 unit of skilled labor and 4 units of unskilled labor, of which 1 unit of unskilled labor is used for each of 4 tasks. Each unit of Good Y requires 2 units of skilled labor and 4 units of unskilled labor, of which 1 unit of unskilled labor is used for each of 4 tasks. Initially, all of these unskilled-labor tasks were performed domestically, but now for both good X and good Y it becomes possible for one of these tasks to be performed in another country, where labor is so much cheaper that to a good approximation we can treat that task as being done for free. The price of both Good X is fixed on world markets as $24, and the price of Good Y is fixed on world markets at $36.

(a) Find the skilled and unskilled wages before offshoring occurs. Draw the zero-profit diagram that shows these wages as the equilibrium.

(b) Find the skilled and unskilled wages with offshoring. Show how the zero-profit diagram changes, adding the shifted curves to the diagram you just drew.

(c) Who gains from offshoring in this example? Explain why.

REFERENCES

Amiti, Mary, and Shang-Jin Wei (2005). "Fear of Service Outsourcing: Is It Justified?" *Economic Policy* 20:42 (April), pp. 308–347.

——— (2006). "Service Offshoring and Productivity: Evidence from the United States." NBER Working Paper No. 11926 (January).

Bhagwati, Jagdish, Arvind Panagariya, and T. N. Srinivasan (2004). "The Muddles over Outsourcing." *Journal of Economic Perspectives* 18:4 (Fall), pp. 93–114.

Bureau of Economic Analysis (BEA) (2008). "Summary Estimates for Multinational Companies: Employment,

Sales, and Capital Expenditures for 2006." Bureau of Economic Analysis News Release BEA-08-15, April 17, 2008.

Desai, Mihir, C. F. Foley, and J. R. Hines Jr. (2009). "Domestic Effects of the Foreign Activities of U.S. Multinationals," *American Economic Journal: Economic Policy* 1:1 (February), pp. 181–203.

Feenstra, Robert C., and Gordon H. Hanson (1996). "Foreign Investment, Outsourcing and Relative Wages." In R. C. Feenstra, G. M. Grossman, and D. A. Irwin (eds.), *The Political Economy of Trade Policy: Papers in Honor of Jagdish Bhagwati*, pp. 89–127. Cambridge, MA: MIT Press.

(2002). "Global Production Sharing and Rising Inequality: A Survey of Trade and Wages." In E. Kwan Choi and James Harrigan (ed.), *Handbook of International Trade*, pp. 146–185. Blackwell Publishing.

Greenberg Quinlan Rosner Research (2004). "National Public Radio Frequency Questionnaire: March 12 14."

Grossman, Gene M., and Esteban Rossi-Hansberg (2008). "Trading Tasks: A Simple Theory of Offshoring." *American Economic Review* 98(5), pp. 1978–1997.

Harrison, Ann, and Margaret McMilllan (2006). "Dispelling Some Myths about Offshore Outsourcing." *Academy of Management Perspectives* 20:4, pp. 6–22.

Hummels David, Jun Ishii, and Kei-Mu Yi (2001). "The Nature and Growth of Vertical Specialization in World Trade." *Journal of International Economics* 54, pp. 75–96.

Hummels, David, Dana Rapoport, and Kei- Mu Yi (1998). "Vertical Specialization and the Changing Nature of World Trade." *Federal Reserve Bank of New York Economic Policy Review* (June), pp. 79–99.

Linden, Greg, Kenneth L. Kraemer, and Jason Dedrick (2007). "Who Captures Value in a Global Innovation System? The Case of Apple's iPod." Personal Computing Industry Center (PCIC) Working Paper, Paul Merage School of Business, University of California at Irvine.

Mail on Sunday (2006). "The Stark Reality of iPod's Chinese Factories." August 18, 2006 (available at www.mailonsunday.co.uk).

Sethupathy, Guru (2009). "Offshoring, Wages, and Employment: Theory and Evidence." Working Paper, Johns Hopkins University.

Sitchinava, Nino (2008). "Trade, Technology, and Wage Inequality: Evidence from U.S. Manufacturing, 1989–2004." University of Oregon Economics Department Working Paper.

Slaughter, Matthew J. (2004). "Globalization and Employment by U.S. Multinationals: A Framework and Facts." Discussion paper, Dartmouth College.

12 Should We Build a Border Fence?

Pro-immigration protestors, Los Angeles, May 1, 2006.

LUCAS JACKSON/REUTERS/NewsCom

12.1 Calls for a Crackdown, and Calls for Compassion

On March 25, 2006, a lively crowd variously estimated at anywhere from 400,000 to 1,000,000 filled the streets of Los Angeles for what may be the largest demonstration in the history of the city. The rally was for the most part peaceful and festive, but it was organized as a protest by pro-immigration groups—followed up by May Day rallies in several U.S. cities and a "day without immigrants" workplace boycott—to protest moves by the U.S. government to crack down on illegal immigration (for journalists' accounts see Watanabe and Becerra, 2006, Archibold, 2006, and Gorman et al., 2006). One such move was a bill, HR 4437, in the House of Representatives that would have made it a felony to enter the country illegally (when previously it had been a misdemeanor); it also would have made it a felony to give any assistance to anyone in the country illegally. Another was a proposal to build a tall fence running the length of the border between the United States and Mexico to keep out illegal immigrants.

The debate on immigration into the United States, in other words, had become a major political conflict.

The last four decades have seen a sharp acceleration of immigration into the United States, almost tripling the foreign-born share of the labor force (recall Figure 1.5) (a trend that has to some degree reversed itself with the recession of 2008). In recent years, the share of the immigrant population that is in the country illegally (or "undocumented") has also surged.[1] Some voters became angry at these trends, and politicians such as Representative James Sensenbrenner (Republican of Wisconsin) responded with aggressive anti-illegal immigrant measures in Congress. Sensenbrenner was one of the authors of HR 4437 in December 2005, one of the toughest ever proposed. It would have had wide-ranging consequences; for example, some religious leaders were afraid that their charitable activities such as running a soup kitchen could be criminalized if some illegal immigrants benefited (*New York Times*, 2006). The bill passed in the House but died in the Senate. That previous January Representative Sensenbrenner also had introduced legislation to fund the fence at the southern border, an expense of billions for a wall almost 2,000 miles in length, which was signed into law in May 2005.

The burst of anger and political assertiveness from immigrants and their supporters expressed in the March 25 and May Day marches of 2006 was largely a response to these moves and partly an attempt to generate momentum for legislation that would be friendlier to immigrants already here and more open to new ones. The most important proposal along these lines was compromise legislation introduced in the Senate by Senator Larry Craig in 2005 and Senators John McCain and Edward Kennedy in 2006. These measures would have dealt with the flow of illegals by creating a system of guest workers who could enter the country temporarily, and it would have created a path to citizenship for workers in the United States illegally. They failed, however, due to the resistance of conservative Republicans in the House (see Klein, 2007 (a, b), for a journalistic account).

---

[1] Passel and Cohn (2011) estimate the number of immigrants in the United States illegally at 8.4 million in 2000, increasing every year to a peak of 12.0 million in 2007, followed by a reduction to 11.6 in 2008 and small reductions after that.

The upshot is a kind of paralysis, and approximately 11 million workers living in the country illegally (Passel and Cohn, 2011), working, producing goods and services, paying a number of taxes, and raising families but living in terror of deportation.

The one clear change in immigration policy in recent years is an increased aggressiveness against undocumented workers.[2] This is not without its costs. The federal government has increased the frequency of its immigration raids, such as the May 2008 raid on a meatpacking plant in Postville, Iowa. Federal authorities had information that the plant was largely staffed by undocumented workers, many of whom had purchased forged documents with Social Security numbers to present themselves as legal immigrants. Federal agents arrested 389 workers and bussed them to a makeshift mass court 75 miles away, charging them with document fraud and identity theft (ironically, because their use of Social Security numbers that did not belong to them meant that they were paying payroll taxes into the pension system from which they could not benefit). In proceedings widely criticized by human-rights activists as a travesty of due process against bewildered, illiterate, and unilingual workers (Preston, 2008), 262 were sentenced to short prison terms, to be deported afterward. The disruption to the town was enormous; with 10% of the population in custody, attendance at the local school after the raid was half the normal rate, and local businesses suffered as well, leading the school's superintendent to characterize the event as "like a natural disaster—only this one is manmade" (Hsu, 2008). Ongoing arrests of suspected undocumented workers have led to the construction of a detention facility for holding entire families while their cases are under review, leading critics to question the effect on children held in a prison-like setting (Blumenthal, 2007). The border fence itself, which was canceled in January 2011 after many delays and cost overruns, has been in places quite disruptive of ordinary life near the border— at one point projected to run right through a municipal golf course and at other places bisecting nature preserves harboring endangered species (Hylton, 2009). Of course, there is also the direct fiscal cost of interdiction, with $13 billion budgeted for border security as of 2008 (see Hanson, 2007, p. 25).

One might ask: *Is this worth it?* Are there costs to immigration that justify the fiscal, ecological, and humanitarian costs of restricting it? In particular, are there costs to *illegal* immigration that justify the costs of *interdiction*? This book will not settle this lively and passionate debate, but we will look at the key issues in theory and see what the evidence is.

12.2 Three Theories, and One Thing They Agree On

The main point of economic debate regarding immigration is the same as the main point in debates over offshoring, as seen in Chapter 11: the question of whether foreign workers are substitutes for, or complements to, domestic workers.

---

[2] For example, Immigration and Customs Enforcement (ICE), the agency of the U.S. government that handles these matters, boasts an increase in the number of persons it has deported in every year since 2007, from a value of 245,601 deportations in 2007 to 319,077 in 2011 (www.ice.gov/removal-statistics).

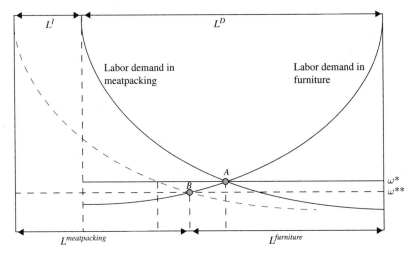

FIGURE 12.1
Immigration, Assuming Foreign Labor *Substitutes* for Domestic Labor.

Consider Figure 12.1. This figure shows how equilibrium in the domestic labor market is changed if we allow immigrants to enter in a mixed specific-factors model (otherwise known as a Ricardo-Viner model) as in Section 5.5, under the assumption that immigrants are indistinguishable from domestic workers. For concreteness, we assume that the economy can be summarized as having two industries, meatpacking (the industry of the Postville immigrants) and furniture, whose prices are fixed on world markets and can be taken as given. The domestic labor force is L^D, and this is the length of the box without immigration (marked on the upper boundary of the box). The equilibrium without immigration is at point A, the intersection of the two black labor-demand curves, with a wage of w^*. Now, allow some immigrants to enter this economy, and to examine the simplest case of substitutability assume that they are identical to domestic workers in every way. In the figure, L^I immigrants enter the economy. This stretches the box to a length of $L^D + L^I$ and moves the demand curve for labor in meatpacking to the position indicated by the broken blue curve (a parallel shift to the left). Being identical to domestic workers, they will receive the same wage as domestic workers, and the increase in labor supply pushes the domestic wage down to w^{**}, shown at the new equilibrium, point B. Clearly, here, domestic workers are *hurt* by immigration: Immigration raises the domestic supply of labor, pushing wages down.

Now, consider the case of complementarity in labor. Suppose that immigrants have a completely different set of skills compared to domestic workers, due to different levels of education, different types of education, different cultures, different language skills, or different work experiences. As a result, employers hire immigrants to do different tasks than domestic workers do. In this case, the equilibrium with immigrants will look more like Figure 12.2. Here, the horizontal dimension of the box measures only domestic labor; immigrant labor is a different factor of production, like land or capital, and there is no reason to expect it to be paid the same wage as domestic labor. In this case, the presence of immigrants raises the marginal product of domestic labor in one or both industries. In this example, it shifts up the demand for domestic labor in meatpacking, perhaps because of skills the immigrants bring

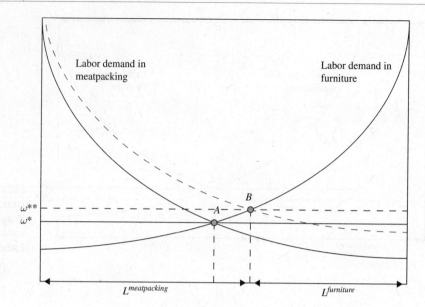

FIGURE 12.2
Immigration,
Assuming Foreign
Labor *Complements*
Domestic Labor.

with them from ranching or butchering traditions at home. These skills allow them to specialize in particular tasks they do well and permit native-born workers to become more productive by specializing in others. The new demand curve for domestic labor in meatpacking is given by the broken blue curve. The equilibrium without immigrants is once again marked as point *A*, and the equilibrium with immigrants is at point *B*, which has a *higher* wage. Clearly, in this case domestic workers *benefit* from immigration: Immigration raises the demand for domestic labor, pushing wages up.

Now, consider one last model, this one focusing on the effects of immigration on consumer demand. As one scholar of immigration puts it:

> Population growth creates jobs because people consume as well as produce: they buy things, they go to movies, they send their children to school, they build houses, they fill their cars with gasoline, they go to the dentist, they buy food at stores and restaurants. When the population declines, stores, schools, and hospitals close, and jobs are lost. This pattern has been seen over and over again in the United States: growing communities mean more jobs. (Chomsky, 2007, p. 8)

In other words, because they add to local demand, immigrants can provide for a wider variety of goods and services available locally, making for a livelier local economy. One way to interpret this is through the monopolistic competition model of Section 3.4. (A rich mathematical treatment of this sort of model, with immigration added, is Krugman, 1991.) Suppose that there are two countries, each of which has identical workers and no other factors of production. A worker in either country can produce corn, producing one unit of corn output per unit of labor input; or the worker can start a business to produce some distinctive product, hiring other workers to produce the output through an increasing-returns-to-scale production function, which is the same

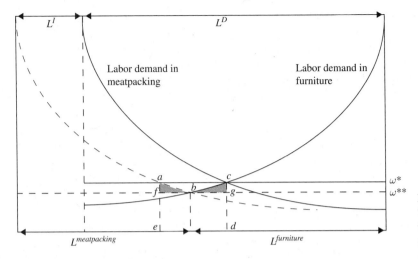

FIGURE 12.3
The Rise in Income to
the Native-born
Population.

for all producers. There is free entry, so this market for differentiated goods is monopolistically competitive. Suppose that there is no trade (to make the point as clearly as possible; this is not an essential assumption). One could think of the monopolistically competitive sector as providing local services, such as hair salons or restaurant meals.

Suppose that we are initially in equilibrium, as in Figure 3.2. Each monopolistically competitive producer is maximizing profit by setting marginal cost equal to marginal revenue from the demand curve for its unique product or service; the number of monopolistically competitive producers adjusts through free entry until each producer makes zero profits. Now, allow a few million people to immigrate from one country to the other. In the immigration-receiving country, each firm's demand curve will now shift to the right, due to the additional demand from the arrival of the new consumers (who, at the very least, can make some income producing corn). As a result, each firm will now be making positive profits, causing entry of new firms, which will shift each firm's demand curve back to the left until a zero-profit equilibrium is restored. The upshot is that the immigrant-receiving country will have more firms offering a wider variety of products and services than it did before. Consequently, all workers in the immigrant-receiving country will benefit—as *consumers*, who now have more consumption options—and by the same logic all workers in the immigrant-sending country will be worse off. Immigration benefits domestic workers by generating a wider variety of goods and services available locally. We can call these effects *demand externalities*.

These three models are clearly very different, but one element that they all have in common is that they predict a rise in aggregate real income to the native-born population of the immigrant-receiving country as a result of immigration. For the substitutability model of Figure 12.1, the logic is traced out in Figure 12.3. GDP is the area under the two marginal-product-of-labor curves. This area is the same after immigration as it is before immigration, except that the figure has been split in two at point A of Figure 12.1, with the two pieces pulled apart, and a new area, *abcde*, added between them. Therefore, GDP has gone up with immigration by *abcde*. From this we need to subtract wage payments to immigrants in order to find net income to the native-born population. Wage payments to immigrants are equal to the new equilibrium wage, or a height of *ef*, times the number of immigrants, or the distance *ed* (which is equal to L^1). Consequently, wage payments to immigrants are equal to *fgde*, and so the additional income to the native-born population as a result of immigration is equal to the shaded area *abf* plus *bcg*, which is always positive.

In the complementarity model of Figure 12.2, GDP is again equal to the area under the two marginal-product-of-labor curves, which is higher when those curves take the form of the blue broken curves under immigration than the solid black curves before immigration. This is the increase in GDP due to the addition of the immigrants. To get the net effect on the income of the native-born population, we again need to subtract the wage payments made to immigrants. However, as long as immigrant workers are paid their marginal value product, and as long as their marginal value product is a decreasing function of the number of immigrant workers, these wage payments will be less than the increase in GDP the immigrants create. (In other words, all immigrants are paid the marginal product of the last immigrant to be hired, so all but the last one hired have a marginal product greater than the wage.) This implies once again that the net income to the native-born population has gone up.

In the monopolistic-competition model, the change is more subtle, but the rise in the variety of products and services available, together with a reduction in the price of each item due to a rise in competition, provide a reduction in the consumer price index that raises *real* incomes.[3]

All three models, therefore, predict a rise in the real incomes of people who already live in the country as a result of the arrival of immigrants. If that was the only consideration, the optimal policy would be to let as many immigrants in as want to come. There are two principal reasons that the optimum might be less than that in practice. The first is that in the substitutability model of Figure 12.1, although the income of the native-born population rises in the aggregate, the income of native workers *falls*, while the income of native capital and land-owners rises. In other words, there are distributional issues. As with trade policy, the first-best solution would be to deal with this by taxes and transfers, but if that is not possible, a limit on immigration may be called for. The second has to do with the existing system of taxes and government services. All immigrants—even illegal ones—pay taxes, at the very least sales taxes. Many pay income taxes, and in the United States, many illegal immigrants use a Social Security number that does not belong to them to pay payroll taxes into the Social Security system, from which they cannot later benefit (which is what attracted the attention of federal authorities to the Pottsville workers). At the same time, they receive some benefits from government services, such as access to public schools and free treatment from emergency rooms. In principle, the net payment to illegal immigrants from all of these features together could be positive or negative. In the event that these net payments are positive, the country may wish to limit immigration to some finite optimal level.

Clearly, there is no theoretical presumption about whether immigration is good or bad for domestic labor. We need to look at the evidence to see what the effect is in practice.

---

[3] Note, for example, that if previously there were no Afghan restaurants in town, when one finally opens, the local price of a meal in an Afghan restaurant drops from infinity to a finite number. Consequently, a rise in product diversity can be interpreted as a drop in consumer prices.

12.3 Three Key Pieces of Evidence

The research literature on the economic effects of immigration is vast; see Lowenstein (2006) for a readable overview. Here, we will highlight three findings that have been particularly influential.

1. *The Mariel Boatlift.* On April 20, 1980, Cuban President Fidel Castro declared, as a culmination of a series of political disputes, that any citizen who wished to leave Cuba could do so through the port of Mariel for a short interval of time. From May to September of that year, thousands of Cubans climbed aboard an improvised ragtag flotilla and sailed for Miami. Approximately 125,000 arrived during those five months, amounting to an increase of 7% in the local labor force overnight.

   This is a particularly stark example of a natural experiment in immigration, and in a famous paper, Card (1990) studied the effects of the boatlift on wages and unemployment rates for Hispanic workers, Cuban workers, black workers, white workers, and high-skilled and low-skilled workers in Miami compared to comparable workers in other cities. The result is that across the board, it is difficult to find *any* effect of the boatlift on wages or unemployment rates for *any* class of workers in Miami.

   This can be seen from Figure 12.4, which shows the average hourly wage for each of a number of demographic groups, whites, blacks, and Hispanics, covering a period beginning just before the boatlift in 1979 and ending in 1985. (The wages are reported in 1980 U.S. dollars.) The average wages are computed separately for workers in Miami and for workers in a sample of other cities similar in most respects to Miami, to act as a control group; those wages in the control group are indicated in the figure as "Other Whites," and so on. For the Miami sample only, Card is able to separate out a subgroup of the Hispanic sample who are identified as Cuban in origin. From the substitutability model of Figure 12.1, we would have expected reductions in wages among Miami workers in 1980, or at least in 1981, as a result of the 1980 boatlift, compared to workers in

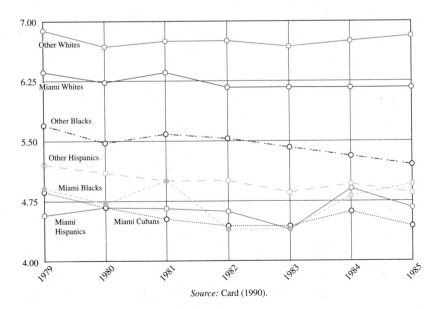

Source: Card (1990).

FIGURE 12.4
Wages in Miami and Comparison Cities.

other cities, but it is evident from Figure 12.4 that there is no such effect in the data. The only large movement is a significant *improvement* in wages for black workers in Miami in 1981, followed by a large drop in 1982. Since 1982 was the trough of a severe nationwide recession, that drop is much more plausibly attributed to macroeconomic events than to the 1980 boatlift. The data do show a drop in the average wage of *Cuban* workers in Miami, but Card shows that this is consistent with low-wage Mariel workers joining the labor force alongside previously arrived higher-wage Cuban workers, and bringing the average wage down without lowering any worker's wage. A similar story emerges from data on unemployment rates. Card concludes that local labor-intensive manufacturing industries such as textiles and apparel, which were abundant in Miami, were able to absorb the new workers quickly and easily.

The Mariel case study is striking because it was a huge, sudden shock to the local labor supply and yet had no observable effect on the local labor market. It suggests that smaller, more common local immigration shocks might also have a small effect on the local labor market.

2. *The National Labor Market Approach.* Borjas (2003) suggested that the local approach might be misleading because labor can reallocate itself across locations within the same country. If 100,000 immigrants enter the labor force in one town, perhaps that will lead a similar number of native workers who were going to move there to reconsider that decision, or convince some local workers already there to move out. In this way, local immigration shocks can be smoothed out, as wages are equalized across locations within the same country. If this is correct, then the addition of 100,000 new workers to one town, swelling its labor supply by 7%, will have no effect on wages, but the addition of enough workers *nationally* to increase the national labor supply by 7% *will* have an effect on wages.

Borjas therefore suggested looking for immigration effects at the national level. Now, this is not straightforward. One can, for example, look at the average worker's wage at each date and the number of immigrants at each date and see how they are correlated over time. No one would be particularly persuaded that this correlation would tell us anything about the effect of immigration on wages, however, because at the macroeconomic level so much else is going on that affects wages through many different channels. To isolate the effect of immigration, Borjas broke up the national labor market into 32 categories based on each worker's experience and education. Thus, we can consider the market for high school dropouts with 1−5 years' job experience; the market for high school graduates with 1 to 5 years' experience; and similarly for workers with some college and workers with a college degree. Then, we can consider the market for high school dropouts with 6−10 years' experience, high school graduates with 6−10 years' experience, and so on. Arguing that these different categories of worker are not close substitutes for each other, Borjas looked for a relationship between wages for each category of worker and the national supply of that category of immigrants, over time, with U.S. data, controlling for macroeconomic fluctuations that affect all categories at the same time. He found a strong negative relationship, suggesting that an increase in immigrants that raises the national supply of labor within a category by 10% will lower the average wage within that category by approximately 4%

(the exact number varies with different techniques that Borjas tries, but they all are in that neighborhood). This appears to restore the credibility of the substitutability model of Figure 12.1.

3. *The Elasticity-of-Substitution Approach.* The story does not end there. The Borjas approach described above looks, for example, at the negative effect of 1 million new high school-educated immigrant workers with 6−10 years of work experience on the wages of U.S.-born high school educated workers with 6−10 years of work experience (and similarly with the 31 other worker categories). But it does not allow for any effect that those new workers might have on the wages of, say, U.S. workers with some college and 11−15 years of experience, who might be able to *hire* those new immigrants and raise their own productivity and income accordingly. In other words, Borjas estimated an *own-wage effect* of immigration for each of the 32 categories of worker, but ignored possible *cross-wage effects*. If each category of labor has a positive effect on the marginal product of other categories of labor, then estimating the effect of immigration by each labor/experience category on that own type's wage alone will give an excessively pessimistic picture of the effect of overall immigration on overall wages. In fact, in principle it could be the case that 1 million new high school-educated immigrants with 6−10 years of work experience would lower the wages of native high school-educated workers with 6−10 years of experience. And yet 1 million workers *evenly spread across all 32 categories* would *raise* the wages of all native workers.

Looking for these cross-wage effects is even harder than looking for the own-wage effects that Borjas was looking for, and is the task undertaken in a paper by Ottaviano and Peri (2008). The heart of their approach was to estimate an elasticity of substitution between native-born and immigrant labor within each labor category. The *elasticity of substitution* between any two factors of production is a measure of how similar, how interchangeable, the two factors are, from the point of view of potential employers. Formally, it is calculated as the proportional change in the relative demand for the two factors caused by a change in one or the other of their prices, divided by the proportional change in the relative factor price. For example, if the elasticity of substitution between native-born workers and foreign-born workers within a worker category is 5, then if the wage paid to foreign-born workers goes up by 10% without anything else changing, the ratio of foreign-born workers to native-born workers employed will fall by $5(0.1) = 0.5$, or 50%. If native-born and foreign-born workers are viewed as identical by employers, the elasticity will be infinite (since they will not want any native-born workers at all if they are even slightly more expensive than foreign-born ones). If native-born and foreign-born workers are employed in fixed proportions, the elasticity of substitution will be zero. The substitutability model of Figure 12.1 requires the elasticity of substitution to be infinite, while the complementarity model of Figure 12.2 requires it to be low. Borjas implicitly assumed it to be infinite.

Ottaviano and Peri argue that estimation of this elasticity of substitution is central to understanding the impact of immigration:

> Whether it is because immigrants tend to choose a different set of
> occupations, because they are a selected group, or because they

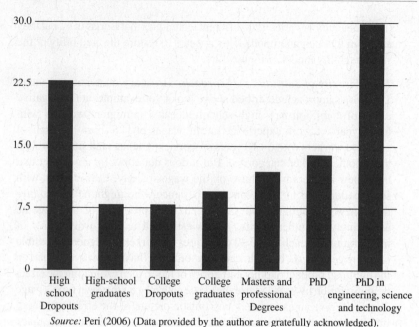

Source: Peri (2006) (Data provided by the author are gratefully acknowledged).

FIGURE 12.5
Foreign-born Share of
U.S. Labor Force, by
Education Level,
2003.

have some culture-specific skills, it seems reasonable to allow them
to be imperfect substitutes for natives even within an education-
experience-gender group and to let the data estimate the corresponding elasticities of substitution. (Ottaviano and Peri, 2006, p. 3)

The elasticity is crucial to assessing the effect of immigration on domestic
wages because it controls how much the relative wage paid to native-born and
immigrant workers will change when additional immigrant workers are added to
the labor force (the mathematics of how the wage effects are computed from
the elasticities are somewhat complicated, and are omitted here). Using U.S.
Census data, the authors estimate the elasticity as around 20. This is fairly high—
higher than the elasticity of substitution between workers with a college education and those without, for example—but it is certainly not infinite. (By
contrast, the elasticity of substitution between male and female workers *is*
estimated to be infinite.) This implies that employers do not see a domestic and a
foreign-born worker as identical, even if they both have the same level of
education and work experience. Using this together with all of the other information available, Ottaviano and Peri come to a striking conclusion: That
immigration into the United States has only very slightly decreased wages of
average workers in the short run, and it has *increased* the wage of the average
U.S. worker in the *long* run. In their interpretation, the workers whose wages are
depressed by new immigrants are not native-born workers, but previously
arrived immigrants.

This result can be interpreted as coming from three factors. The first is the
size of the elasticity of substitution between native-born and foreign-born
workers for a given level of education and experience, as discussed above.

Second, immigrants to the United States have a very different *mix* of education and experience than native-born workers. This can be illustrated with
Figure 12.5, which is a re-creation of Figure 2 from Peri (2006) and is constructed using data from the 2003 American Community Survey of the U.S.

Bureau of the Census (data provided by the author is gratefully acknowledged). Each bar in the figure represents an educational category, arranged from High School Dropouts up to PhDs, with an extra bar for PhDs in engineering, science, and technology. The height of each bar represents the fraction of the U.S. labor force in that category that is comprised of foreign-born workers. For example, 8% of workers in the United States with a high school diploma and no college (the category of high school graduates in the figure) were born outside the United States. Clearly, the highest bars in the figure—by far—are the first and the last. Foreign-born workers comprise 23% of high school dropouts and 30% of workers with a PhD in science, while making up only 11% of the overall workforce. The foreign-born share of the middle categories ranges from 8% for high school graduates to 14% for PhDs. In other words, compared to the native-born population, immigrants are disproportionally found in the two extremes of no high school diploma on the one hand and a PhD in engineering and science, on the other. Most American workers do not fall into either category; for example, in these data 59% of U.S. workers have a high school diploma but no college degree. This is an additional reason to think of immigrants as complements rather than substitutes for the majority of U.S. workers.

The third factor is the adjustment of capital. Ottaviano and Peri point out that the domestic supply of capital will not likely remain unchanged in response to the increase in the domestic supply of labor caused by immigration, and they include a predicted response of capital in their analysis. As a result, the short-run estimated response of U.S.-born workers' wages to a sudden surge of immigrants, before capital has had a chance to respond, is modestly negative, but the long-run response is slightly positive.

Overall, Ottaviano and Peri argue that, taking long-run adjustment into account, the data are closer to the complementarity model of Figure 12.2 than to the substitutability model of Figure 12.1.

One additional note about the evidence is that the last model mentioned in Section 12.2, with expanded product and service variety due to the effects of demand externalities with a monopolistically competitive sector, is difficult to test formally. Thus, whether or not it fits the data is an open question. However, it shows up frequently in anecdotal and newspaper accounts of the after-effects of immigration crackdowns, as journalists report local shops and restaurants closing down following the crackdown (for example, Walker, 2007, Wucker, 2007, and Hsu, 2008). It would be of great interest to learn if such effects could be found in the data through formal methods.

12.4 The Upshot

We can now return to the question posed at the outset: Should the United States forge ahead with policies such as the border fence to eliminate illegal immigrants from the economy?

To answer this question, Hanson (2007, pp. 19–26) reviews the existing evidence on the increase in GDP due to illegal immigration net of wage payments to immigrants, which he calls the "illegal immigration surplus." Noting that plenty of uncertainty surrounds this figure, he adopts a middle-ground estimate of 0.03% of GDP. Then he reviews available studies of the net fiscal effect of illegal immigrants to the United States, taking account of the tax payments illegal immigrants make and the cost of providing public services to them. He adopts an estimate of 0.1% of GDP as the net transfer to illegal immigrants. The net effect of these two is therefore a loss to native-born Americans from illegal immigration amounting to 0.07% of GDP. Hanson points out that given the uncertainty surrounding both estimates, this should be considered indistinguishable from zero. At the same time, budgeting expenditures for interdiction and apprehension of illegal immigrants at the time amounted to 0.1% of GDP, which was larger than the estimated loss from the illegal immigration in the first place. In addition, those expenditures were still not expected to eliminate more than a fraction of the flow of undocumented workers. Thus, eliminating that flow (not to mention apprehending and removing the existing population of undocumented workers) would require a much larger expenditure.

Now, consider that the economic studies that Hanson cited on the illegal immigration surplus do not take into account Ottaviano and Peri's findings on complementarity (2008) (or the as yet untested potential benefits of product and service variety through demand externalities), so that those estimates of the immigration surplus should be thought of as underestimates. Furthermore, the costs considered in Hanson's accounting are purely fiscal costs and do not include, for example, the environmental effects of the border fence. All told, it seems difficult to rationalize the interdiction approach, including the border fence, on economic grounds.

A protestor for immigrant rights, Los Angeles, April 10, 2006.

Of course, even if one agrees with this conclusion (and not everyone will), the question of what optimal policy should be remains. Note that one conclusion that Borjas and Ottaviano and Peri agree on is that immigration into the United States has lowered the wages of native high school dropouts,[4] who are a

---

[4] This is an oversimplification. To be precise, Ottaviano and Peri (2008) find that all native workers in the United States suffered small wage losses in the short run and small wage gains in the long run due to immigration. For low education workers the short-run losses were larger and the long-run gains were smaller than for more educated workers. Of course, low-income workers have fewer tools to smooth consumption, and so the long-run gain is less likely to make up for the short-run loss than is the case with high-income workers.

small minority of the workforce (13% of the 2003 ACS sample) but obviously the lowest-income workers. Therefore, any decline in income is obviously a serious concern for them. This suggests a rationale for coupling immigration reform with redistributive policy to assist low-wage workers. Moreover, the status quo is clearly inefficient and inequitable, with thousands of workers undertaking dangerous illegal border crossings per year and millions living and working in a country in which they are constantly hiding from the government. Whether the ideal policy is a simple open door (perhaps with an entrance fee), a guest worker program such as the Kennedy-McCain proposal or some other scheme remains the subject of lively debate.

MAIN IDEAS

1. The effects of immigration on the economy and on the distribution of income among the native-born population depend on the nature of the interaction between immigrant and native-born labor. The more substitutable native-born and immigrant labor are, the more likely it is that domestic wages will be pushed down by immigration. The more complementary they are, the more likely it is that domestic wages will be pulled up by immigration.

2. However, in both of these cases standard models predict that GDP net of wage payments to immigrants will be *increased* by immigration, so that in the absence of fiscal transfers to immigrants (such as access to free public schools), aggregate income of the native born will be increased by immigration. In fact, in standard models, if there are no fiscal transfers, the more immigration there is, the larger the income of natives will be.

3. However, in practice many immigrants do receive fiscal transfers in the form of public services, while they also contribute to tax revenues. In the event that net fiscal transfers to immigrants are positive, the optimal level of immigration from the point of view of the native-born population will generally be positive but finite.

4. Empirical studies of *local* effects of immigration generally find small effects, or none at all. By contrast, studies based on the idea of a *national* labor market for each category of worker have found evidence of negative effects of immigration of a given category on wages *of that category*, but positive effects on wages of other categories. Native-born and immigrant labor appear to be imperfectly substitutable, allowing for the possibility that immigrants raise not only aggregate income net of immigrant wages, but also native-born wages.

5. However, the possibility that, in the case of the United States, the wages of high school dropouts are reduced by immigration raises important distributional issues that might be dealt with through redistributive policy.

6. One effect of immigration that might be important but has received little scholarly attention is the creation of a greater variety of local goods and services due to demand externalities. This effect arises naturally in a monopolistic competition model with nontraded or imperfectly traded products, and though it features in journalistic accounts, it has not been subjected to formal empirical scrutiny.

QUESTIONS AND PROBLEMS

1. Consider the model of trade between the United States and China presented in Chapter 6. Suppose that we alter that model by assuming that 6 million unskilled workers move from China to the United States.

    (a) How will the supply of plastics and apparel change in China as a result of the immigration? (Provide exact numbers.)

    (b) How will the supply of the two goods change in the United States?

    (c) Compute the new world relative supply of plastics.

    (d) What will the new equilibrium relative price of plastics be?

    (e) How will the budget sets for skilled and unskilled workers in both countries change as a result of the immigration? In particular, are unskilled workers in the United States harmed by the immigration of these unskilled workers?

(f) Economist Robert Mundell has argued that (in a Heckscher-Ohlin world) trade and international factor movements are substitutes—that they have the same economic effects. Does this example illustrate that point or refute it?

2. Recall Figure 12.3, showing the effect of immigrants on the net income of the native-born population, and redraw it with a larger number of immigrants than is already depicted in the figure. Show how the equilibrium changes as a result of the increased immigration, and shade in the area that indicates the increase in income net of wage payments to immigrants (compared to the equilibrium in Figure 12.3, with the lower initial number of immigrants).

3. Consider a model of immigration with labor complementarity presented in Figure 12.2. Suppose that the demand for domestic labor in meatpacking is perfectly inelastic (because there are only so many machines, and each machine requires a fixed number of workers to work with it), and suppose that the arrival of immigrants from some country with well-developed woodworking traditions doubles the marginal product of domestic labor in the furniture industry for each level of employment. Assume that the opportunity cost to immigrant workers is very low, so that the cost of hiring them is a negligible portion of the production costs in the furniture industry.

(a) Draw Figure 12.2 for this case, showing how the diagram and the equilibrium are affected by equilibrium.

(b) Do domestic employers benefit from immigration? Why or why not?

4. *General-equilibrium effects with labor complementarity.* Consider an economy comprised of 100 cities. Each city initially contains 1 million each of high school dropouts, high school graduates, workers with some college, and college graduates. There is free mobility across cities, so that no matter what happens, wages for each category of worker are equalized across cities. Suppose that the equilibrium in the labor market works in such a way that the response of wages for high school dropouts to immigration flows is given by: $(\Delta w^{HSD})/w^{HSD} = -3(\Delta I^{HSD})/L^{HSD} + (\Delta I^{HSG})/L^{HSG} + (\Delta I^{SC})/L^{SC} + (\Delta I^{CG})/L^{CG}$, where w^{HSD} is the wage for high school dropouts and Δ indicates a change; I^{HSD} is the number of high school dropouts in the national immigrant pool, and L^{HSD} is the number of high school dropouts in the existing national labor force, so $(\Delta I^{HSD})/L^{HSD}$ represents the proportional immigrant supply shock for high school dropouts. Similarly, the other three terms measure the immigrant supply shock for high school graduates (*HSG*), workers with some college (*SC*), and for college graduates (*CG*), respectively. Suppose that the wage response of the other groups is symmetric, so that for high school graduates the response is given by $(\Delta w^{HSG})/w^{HSG} = -3(\Delta I^{HSG})/L^{HSG} + (\Delta I^{HSD})/L^{HSD} + (\Delta I^{SC})/L^{SC} + (\Delta I^{CG})/L^{CG}$, the response for workers with some college by $(\Delta w^{SC})/w^{SC} = -3(\Delta I^{SC})/L^{SC} + (\Delta I^{HSD})/L^{HSD} + (\Delta I^{HSG})/L^{HSG} + (\Delta I^{CG})/L^{CG}$, and the response for college graduates by $(\Delta w^{CG})/w^{CG} = -3(\Delta I^{CG})/L^{CG} + (\Delta I^{HSD})/L^{HSD} + (\Delta I^{HSG})/L^{HSG} + (\Delta I^{SC})/L^{SC}$. In other words, for each category of worker, the "own effect" of that immigration is three times the size of, and opposite in sign to, the "cross effect."

(a) Suppose that 100,000 high school dropouts immigrate, landing in city number 12 (for example), thereby raising the number of high school dropouts in city 12 by 10%. What will be the effect on the wages of high school dropouts in city 12? In the rest of the country? Now, compare this with the effect of 100,000 new high school dropouts immigrating into every city at the same time. Can this contrast help explain the contrast between the findings of the local-impact studies and the national labor-market studies in Section 12.3?

(b) Now, suppose that 100,000 workers of *each* category immigrate to each city, adding 10% to the total labor force. What happens to all wages? Can a comparison of this result with the result of part (a) help explain the tension between the results of Borjas and Ottaviano and Peri in Section 12.3?

(c) Now, try a different thought experiment. Suppose that immigrants are distributed randomly across cities. For example, suppose that the country receives 10 million high school dropouts as immigrants (and no others) and that those 10 million are scattered across the 100 cities, with some cities receiving a few and some cities receiving a lot. Draw a scatterplot with the local immigration supply shock measured on the horizontal axis and the proportional change in the local high school dropout wage on the vertical axis, and where each dot in the scatterplot represents the value of those two variables for one of the 100 cities. Show what the scatterplot would look like, and explain how it could be misinterpreted as a demonstration that immigration has no effect on wages.

REFERENCES

Archibold, Randal C. (2006). "Immigrants Take to U.S. Streets in Show of Strength." *The New York Times*, May 2.

Blumenthal, Ralph (2007). "U.S. Gives Tour of Family Detention Center That Critics Liken to a Prison." *The New York Times,* February 10, p.A9.

Borjas, George J. (2003). "The Labor Demand Curve Is Downward Sloping: Reexamining the Impact of Immigration on the Labor Market." *The Quarterly Journal of Economics* 118:4 (November), pp. 1335–1374.

Card, David (1990). "The Impact of the Mariel Boatlift on the Miami Labor Market." *Industrial and Labor Relations Review* 43:2 (January), pp. 245–257.

Chomsky, Aviva (2007). *"They Take Our Jobs!" And 20 Other Myths about Immigration*. Boston: Beacon Press.

Gorman, Anna, Marjorie Miller, and Mitchell Landsberg (2006). "Marchers Fill L.A.'s Streets." *The Los Angeles Times*, May 2.

"The Gospel vs. H.R. 4437" [editorial] (2006). *The New York Times*, March 3.

Hanson, Gordon H. (2007). "The Economic Logic of Illegal Immigration." Council Special Report No. 26 (March), Council on Foreign Relations.

Hsu, Spencer S. (2008). "Immigration Raid Jars a Small Town." *The Washington Post*, May 18, p. A1.

Hylton, Hilary (2009). "Opponents of the Border Fence Look to Obama." *Time*, January 21.

Klein, Rick (2007a). "Kennedy, McCain Try Again on Immigration." *Boston Globe*, February 28.

(2007b). "Kennedy-McCain Partnership Falters." *Boston Globe*, March 22.

Krugman, Paul (1991). "Increasing Returns and Economic Geography." *Journal of Political Economy* 99:3 (June), pp. 483–499.

Lowenstein, Roger (2006). "The Immigration Equation." *The New York Times*, July 9, p. 36 (Section 6).

Ottaviano, Gianmarco I.P., and Giovanni Peri (2006). "Rethinking the Effects of Immigration on Wages." *NBER Working Paper No.* 12497 (August).

Ottaviano, Gianmarco I.P., and Giovanni Peri (2008). "Immigration and National Wages: Clarifying the Theory and the Empirics." *NBER Working Paper No.* 14188 (July).

Passel, Jeffrey S., and D'Vera, Cohn (2011). *Unauthorized Immigrant Population: National and State Trends, 2010*. Washington, DC: Pew Research Center, Feburary 1.

Peri, Giovanni (2006). "Immigrants, Skills, and Wages: Measuring the Economic Gains from Immigration." Immigration Policy in Focus 5:3 (March), Immigration Policy Center.

Preston, Julia (2008). "An Interpreter Speaking up for Migrants." *The New York Times*, July 11, p. A1.

Walker, Devona (2007). "Immigration Crackdown Called Devastating to Economy." *The Oklahoman*, September 18, p. 1A.

Watanabe, Teresa, and Hector Becerra (2006). "The State; 500,000 Pack Streets to Protest Immigration Bills; The rally, part of a massive mobilization of immigrants and their supporters, may be the largest L.A. has seen." *The Los Angeles Times*, March 26, p. A1.

Wucker, Michele (2007). "A Safe Haven in New Haven." *The New York Times*, April 15, p. 14LI.

13 Trade and the Environment: Is Globalization Green?

DAVID EVANS/NG Image Collection

A factory near the Wu River branch of the Yangtze River.

13.1 A Disaster on a Global Scale?

The Philippines has a large-scale copper smelting operation, the PASAR Corporation, that turns copper ore sourced from multiple counties into copper cathodes. The cathodes are almost entirely exported and are used in the manufacture of electrical equipment. The operation is an example of a fear that some observers have about the consequences of globalization. Globalization critic David C. Korten (1995, p. 31) points out that the PASAR operation was originally funded partly by a Japanese consortium, and that it has caused significant environmental repercussions, contaminating local water supplies with boron, arsenic, and other toxins, reducing fish yields, and increasing the incidence of respiratory problems. His interpretation is that globalization has allowed the smelting operation to be much more damaging to the environment than it otherwise would be because it allows the operation to be located in a low-income country with lax environmental standards rather than in a high-income country like Japan with strict environmental standards.

> The company has prospered. The local economy has grown. The Japanese people have a supply of copper at no environmental cost to themselves. The local poor—the project's professed beneficiaries—have lost their means of livelihood and suffered impaired health. The Philippine government is repaying the foreign aid loan from Japan that financed the construction of supporting infrastructure for the plant. And the Japanese are congratulating themselves for the cleanliness of their domestic environment and their generous assistance to the poor of the Philippines. (Korten, 1995, p. 32)

Korten's conclusion is that globalization allows damaging production processes to be shipped to impoverished populations worldwide, with devastating consequences for the environment and for human health. This is a common concern and is a charge of such gravity that it could overwhelm all of the other issues we have discussed related to globalization. In this chapter we will briefly look into some of the research that has been directed at this question, and try to determine whether or not globalization is on balance violent to the environment.

13.2 Two Theories (but One Model)

Researchers have looked at the relationship between globalization and the environment from many angles (see Copeland and Taylor, 2003, for a comprehensive survey), but we will focus on what seem to be the two most influential theories.

The first hypothesis is the *Pollution Haven Hypothesis*. This hypothesis is explored theoretically in great detail in Copeland and Taylor (2003, Chapter 5) and can be summarized as follows. (i) Rich countries have tougher environmental standards than poorer countries. (ii) As a result, industries that generate a lot of pollution face relatively higher costs in rich countries, so that in effect poorer countries have a comparative advantage in "dirty" industries. (iii) This means that when trade is opened up, "dirty" industries contract in rich countries and expand in poor countries. (iv) Because this constitutes a transfer of production of dirty industries from countries where they face strict pollution regulation to countries where they face relatively lax pollution regulation, total world pollution goes up as a result. Consequently, under the Pollution Haven Hypothesis *trade increases world pollution.*[1]

A contrasting hypothesis, promoted, for example, by Antweiler, Copeland, and Taylor (2001) (also studied in Copeland and Taylor, 2003, Chapter 6), suggests that trade can have a beneficial effect on world pollution through Heckscher-Ohlin effects. This theory can be summarized as follows. (i) Rich countries have tougher environmental standards than poorer countries. (ii) But rich countries are rich because they have a lot of capital, and this gives them a comparative advantage in capital-intensive industries. (iii) Consequently, when trade is opened, capital-intensive industries expand in rich countries and contract in poor countries. (iv) But capital-intensive industries are also the polluting industries, so this constitutes a transfer of production of dirty industries from countries where they face lax pollution regulation to countries where they face relatively strict pollution regulation. Total world pollution goes *down* as a result.

This second theory does not appear to have a recognized name in the literature,[2] but we can name it the Antweiler-Copeland-Taylor-Heckscher-Ohlin theory, with the acronym ACTHO. Given the acronym, we might as well refer to it as the *Sneeze Hypothesis*. (After all, a sneeze is a healthful response to airborne particulates, just as is the equilibrium trade response in the ACTHO theory.) Under the Sneeze Hypothesis, *trade lowers world pollution.*

Although they are clearly in sharp conflict with each other, both of these hypotheses can be derived from a general-equilibrium model of trade. Consider the Heckscher-Ohlin model of trade with substitutable factors, as presented in Section 6.5. For concreteness, let the two countries be once again the United States and China, but now let us assume that the two factors of production are labor (L) and capital (K). The two goods are apparel, with price denoted P^A, and chemicals, with price denoted P^C. Apparel is relatively labor-intensive and low in pollution emissions, while the chemicals industry is capital-intensive and relatively highly polluting (see Kahn and Yoshino, 2004, Table 1, p. 12). The United States is relatively capital-abundant, and China is labor-abundant.

Suppose for simplicity that apparel production produces no pollution, but chemicals production normally produces a fixed amount of pollution per unit of output. This can be avoided by incurring abatement costs, in other words, changing the technique of production, installing costly scrubbers in the smokestack, and so on. Suppose that pollution by any firm in the chemicals sector can be eliminated entirely by using abatement techniques, but that results in a loss of a fraction θ of that firm's output. Because this cost is borne entirely by the individual firm, and the benefits of lower pollution are spread

---

[1] This term is used in different ways by different authors. Many authors use the term *pollution haven hypothesis* to mean the hypothesis that a country's production pattern will shift away from dirtier industries when its emissions regulations become more strict, which is related to, but different from, the definition presented here. When reading anything in this literature that uses the term, the reader should always be clear about which definition the author is using.

[2] Antweiler, Copeland, and Taylor (2001) call it the Factor-Endowments Hypothesis, but we will stay away from that term to avoid confusion with the predictions of the basic Heckscher-Ohlin model (recall Chapter 6).

across all members of society, no firm will want to use pollution abatement techniques unless it is compelled to do so by government.

Suppose that each consumer in both countries has the same utility function, which can be written as:

$$U(A, C) - d(E),$$

where A is consumption of apparel, C is the consumer's use of chemicals, E is total emissions of pollutant, U is a strictly increasing utility function, and d is a strictly increasing *dis*utility function that shows how much each consumer dislikes pollution. The function U is assumed to have the property that the marginal rate of substitution is unchanged if we multiply A and C by a common factor (this is called homotheticity), which allows us to use the relative-demand curves used in Chapter 6. However, we allow U to be strictly concave so that the marginal utility of income is lower at high incomes than at low ones. This approach helps rationalize stricter environmental policies in high-income countries than in low-income ones. There are two contrasting assumptions for E: It could represent aggregate emissions within the consumer's own country only, in which case this is a model of *local pollution effects*; or it could represent total world emissions, in which case this is a model of *cross-border pollution*.

To make the point as simply as possible, suppose that the U.S. government requires all chemicals producers within its borders to use abatement techniques, bringing chemicals-industry pollution down to zero in the United States. However, the Chinese government does not require any abatement. Obviously, in the real world environmental policy differences are not this stark, but the higher income-per-capita countries do tend to have tougher environmental laws and enforcement.

Consider first the case in which θ is equal to zero. In that case, we would have a standard Heckscher-Ohlin model. The relative supply curves of the two countries would be as depicted in Figure 13.1 as a function of the relative price of apparel, P^A/P^C. As noted in the discussion between Figures 6.11 and 6.12, with substitutable factors, the relative supply curve slopes upward. Furthermore, since the United States is capital-rich, the Rybczynski effect implies that

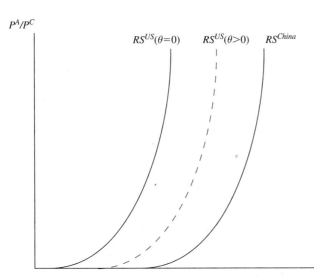

FIGURE 13.1
Relative Supply with
Pollution Abatement
Costs.

the Chinese relative supply curve will lie to the right of the U.S. curve. The capital-rich U.S. economy would export chemicals, and the labor-rich Chinese economy would export apparel. The autarky relative price of apparel in China, P^{China}, would be below both the autarky relative price in the United States and the free-trade price, P^{FT}.

Now, increase θ above zero. Holding the relative price of apparel constant, there are two effects on the U.S. relative supply of apparel. First, for a given allocation of labor and capital, the output of chemicals will fall, since the direct effect of the abatement cost θ is to lower output. Second, holding output prices constant, the zero-profit locus for chemicals will shift to the left (recalling Figure 6.11 for the analogous case in Chapter 6). As a result, following the logic used to derive the Stolper-Samuelson theorem as in Figure 6.11, the U.S. wage will rise and the U.S. price of capital services will fall, leading both industries to choose a larger amount of capital per unit output and a smaller amount of labor per unit output. Thus more capital and labor will have to be allocated to apparel and less to chemicals (again, following the logic of Section 6.5 that shows why the relative supply curve slopes upward). Both because of the direct effect that lowers chemicals output for a given allocation of factors, and because of the indirect effect that allocates more factors to apparel and fewer to chemicals, a rise in θ therefore raises the U.S. relative supply of apparel for a given relative apparel price. Consequently, the U.S. relative supply curve shifts to the right, as shown in Figure 13.1.

Since by assumption there is no emissions abatement required in China, the Chinese relative supply curve will be unchanged. In addition, the world relative supply curve (not shown) will lie in between the two national ones and will be shifted to the right by θ somewhat because of the shift in the U.S. relative supply curve. If θ becomes large enough, the U.S. relative supply curve will shift far enough to the right that the pattern of trade will be reversed, and the United States will begin exporting apparel and importing chemicals. The critical value of θ above which the pattern of trade is reversed can be called θ^*. If $\theta < \theta^*$, the autarky relative price of apparel in China will be below the U.S. autarky price and the free-trade price, while if $\theta > \theta^*$, the reverse is true.

Putting all this together with the other elements of the world economy produces Figures 13.2 and 13.3, which show the world relative supply curve

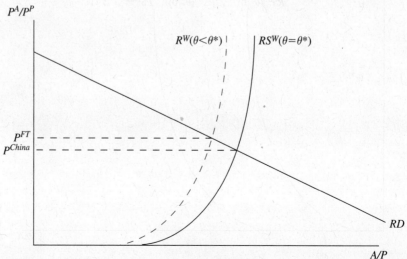

FIGURE 13.2
The Sneeze
Hypothesis.

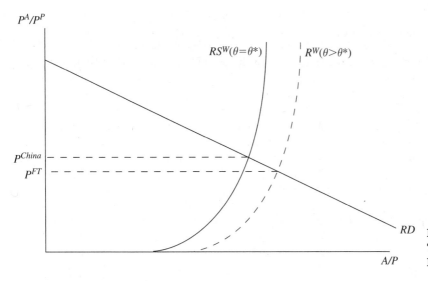

FIGURE 13.3
The Pollution Haven
Hypothesis.

and the relative demand curve (we will again assume that the relative demand curve is the same for both countries). Figure 13.2 shows the equilibrium if θ is small enough that the abatement costs are not sufficient to reverse the pattern of comparative advantage (that is, $\theta < \theta^*$). The world relative supply curve with θ in this range is the blue broken curve; for comparison, the black curve is what the relative supply curve would be with $\theta = \theta^*$. Since the United States is capital-rich, with $\theta < \theta^*$ the U.S. exports chemicals and China exports apparel. Further, trade raises the relative price of apparel in China (from the autarky relative price of P^{China} to the free-trade price, P^{FT}). This implies that when trade is opened up, the Chinese economy moves along its production possibilities frontier, producing more apparel and less chemicals output than it did under autarky. Since the amount of pollution is proportional to the quantity of chemicals output in China, this means that *trade has reduced pollution*, both pollution in China and total pollution worldwide. (Recall that, by assumption, chemicals production in the United States is required to be emissions-free.) This is an example of the Sneeze Hypothesis detailed earlier. Note that the shift in China away from the dirty industry has accompanied a shift in the U.S. economy *toward* the dirty industry. This phenomenon occurs because trade lowers the relative price of apparel in the United States from the high U.S. autarky price to P^{FT}, causing a movement along the U.S. production possibilities frontier toward chemicals and away from apparel.

Figure 13.3, on the other hand, shows what happens if θ is big enough to reverse the pattern of comparative advantage (that is, $\theta > \theta^*$). In that case, as in Figure 13.3, in a free-trade equilibrium the United States exports apparel and China exports chemicals. The free-trade price P^{FT} is now below the Chinese autarky price P^{China}, so free trade makes apparel cheaper in China than it was under autarky. Consequently, trade causes the Chinese economy to move along its production possibilities frontier, producing less apparel and more chemicals than it did under autarky. Since pollution is proportional to the quantity of chemicals produced in China, *trade increases pollution*, both pollution in China and the total quantity of pollution worldwide. This is an example of the Pollution Haven Hypothesis at work. Notice that while the Chinese economy shifts toward the dirtier industry as a result of trade, the U.S. economy shifts toward the cleaner industry.

The point is that both hypotheses make theoretical sense as part of an economic equilibrium, but for different values of the underlying parameters. Precisely, as shown in Figures 13.2 and 13.3, it depends on whether $\theta < \theta^*$ or $\theta > \theta^*$. If $\theta < \theta^*$, the Sneeze Hypothesis holds, but if $\theta > \theta^*$, the Pollution Haven Hypothesis holds. The capital-rich country has a natural comparative advantage in the capital-intensive industry, which is also the dirty industry. Therefore, if on one hand the abatement costs are not large enough to overwhelm that comparative advantage, trade will move that industry toward that country and total pollution will fall. On the other hand, if abatement costs in the capital-rich country are high enough, the pattern of comparative advantage will be driven by abatement costs instead of factor abundance, and trade will drive the dirty capital-intensive industries toward the capital-poor country, increasing total pollution.

Note that the welfare effects of trade are more complicated than they are in a model without pollution. Suppose that θ is large enough that the Pollution Haven Hypothesis holds. Then if pollution is local—meaning, China's pollution causes disutility to Chinese citizens but does not affect Americans—then the United States unambiguously gains from trade, since the reasoning of Chapter 6 applies to the United States without amendment. At the same time, the Chinese nation receives the usual gains from trade, which is a benefit, but it also suffers from increased pollution, which is a cost. It could well be that the rise in local pollution caused by trade overwhelms the standard gains from trade, and China would have been better off under autarky. In this case, the Chinese government may consider restrictions on trade or even a ban on trade as a substitute for effective environmental regulation. Clearly, however, its incentive to institute serious environmental protections is strengthened by the effects of globalization.

Conversely, if pollution is not local—if pollution in one country affects citizens of another, as in the case of greenhouse gases that cause global warming—then the United States itself can be made worse off by trade under the Pollution Haven Hypothesis because of its effects on the global environment.

Both of these hypotheses, the Pollution Haven and the Sneeze Hypotheses, are coherent possibilities as a matter of theory. The next question is whether or not they stand up to the data.

13.3 The Evidence

An exhaustive literature has examined trade data to test the Pollution Haven Hypothesis. As summarized in Kahn and Yoshino (2004) and Levinson and Taylor (2008), it has mostly found very weak pollution haven effects or none at all. Notably, as mentioned earlier, Antweiler, Copeland, and Taylor (2001) show that overall in world trade data, it is the high-per-capita income, capital-rich countries rather than the low-per-capita income, capital-poor countries that tend to be net exporters of industries that produce a lot of emissions—the opposite of the Pollution Haven Hypothesis prediction. This conclusion is reinforced by recent findings that China's imports are significantly more pollution-intensive than its exports.[3]

As shown in recent work, however, existing studies may have missed pollution haven effects that are really there. An example is Levinson and Taylor

---

[3] See Dean and Lovely (2010), who apply an innovative method to Chinese data, as discussed later in this section.

(2008), who point out two important features of earlier work. First, many existing studies look at the average costs incurred by firms in an industry for pollution abatement as a fraction of total industry value added; we can call this measured abatement costs. (Here, *abatement* indicates any costs a firm incurs to prevent pollution or to clean it up after it has occurred.) This variable is then used as a measure of how stringent environmental regulation is in that industry. Authors look for a correlation between it and import penetration rates, meaning imports of an industry's products as a fraction of total domestic consumption (or production, or shipments) of those products. In these studies, a positive correlation between industries' measured abatement costs and their import penetration rates would be taken as evidence of a pollution haven effect. This would be evidence that tighter environmental regulation in an industry discourages domestic production of that industry and encourages imports from countries whose environmental regulation is not as stringent. Generally, these studies find a weak or zero correlation between measured abatement costs and import penetration rates, suggesting that there is no pollution haven effect.

Levinson and Taylor (2008), however, point out some problems with this approach; in particular they refer to a problem of measurement. Each industry in the data is always inevitably an aggregation of firms producing a whole range of products. Some of them will be fairly high-pollution firms and some will be less-polluting firms. If pollution regulations are tightened for the industry as a whole, then this is likely to raise abatement costs for each firm, which will tend to raise the measured abatement cost for the industry as a whole. We can call this the *direct effect*. However, the tightening of the regulation may also drive some of the more polluting firms to move their operations to a country with laxer standards, which will leave behind a less-polluting mix of firms and as a result *lower* measured abatement costs for the industry. We might call this second effect the *industry-composition effect*. When we combine the direct effect and the industry-composition effect, it is therefore conceivable that a tightening of pollution regulations for an industry will not produce any increase in measured abatement costs at all. In this case, then, measured abatement costs are obviously a poor measure of policy.

Levinson and Taylor correct for this problem with econometric techniques[4] and find clear evidence of a positive correlation, indicating that when U.S. pollution regulations for a given industry become tighter, the U.S. economy tends to import more of that industry's products, rather than producing them at home. However, the effect is modest: The authors' calculations suggest that tightening U.S. environmental regulations may be responsible for about 4% of the growth in imports from Mexico and 9% of the growth of imports from Canada.

It is not difficult to reconcile the findings of these different studies. The Antweiler-Taylor-Copeland study seems to imply that θ is small enough that when trade is opened, the United States becomes a net exporter of chemicals.

---

[4] The details need not concern us here. A simple summary would be as follows: The authors note that environmental regulations are likely to be more stringent in U.S. states that have a large pollution problem than in states that do not, so the overall stringency of pollution regulations that an industry faces is likely to be correlated with a measure of how concentrated an industry is in states with a big pollution problem. Call this the *geography variable*. Following a standard technique in econometrics called the instrumental-variables approach, Levinson and Taylor use the portion of measured abatement that is predicted by the geography variable to purge measured abatement of the industry-composition effect.

The Levinson-Taylor study, on the other hand, implies that if θ is increased slightly, the United States will produce a slightly smaller quantity of chemicals and import slightly more of its chemicals from China. The Antweiler-Taylor-Copeland finding is on the *overall* effect of pollution regulation, while the Levinson-Taylor finding is on the *marginal* effect. The two results are perfectly consistent. However, putting the two together, the conclusion remains that opening up trade on balance appears more likely to have lowered world pollution than to have increased it.

An alternative way of looking at trade data and pollution is explored in a recent study by Levinson (2009). Levinson uses estimates employed by the Environmental Protection Agency (EPA) of the average pollution generated by each U.S. manufacturing industry per dollar of output to analyze trends in pollution and its relationship with trade.

To elaborate, an important feature of the model examined in Section 13.2 is that under the Pollution Haven Hypothesis (or, in other words, in the case with $\theta > \theta^*$), as trade is opened up, the *composition of output* in the rich country becomes "cleaner," with a decline in the share of highly polluting industries, while in the low-income country the composition of output becomes "dirtier." This feature can be tested, as follows. Suppose that for each industry i we have a measure z_i of pollution intensity, meaning the amount of pollution produced by that industry per dollar of output. Suppose that the value of industry i's output at date t is $v_{i,t}$, and that the total value of manufacturing output is $\sum_i v_{i,t}$. Then a good measure of how dirty the composition of output is for a given country can be computed as:

$$D_t^{output} \equiv \frac{\sum_i z_i v_{i,t}}{\sum_i v_{i,t}}.$$

This measure is the average pollution intensity, weighted by each industry's share of total output. In computing D_t^{output} the pollution intensities z_i are held constant over time, in order to isolate the effect of the composition of output on pollution, separate from effects of changes in technique or regulation over time. This is useful for our purposes because changes in the composition of output are the mechanism through which both the Pollution Haven and Sneeze Hypotheses work. For U.S. manufacturing from 1987 to 2001, the values of D_t^{output} are plotted in Figure 13.4, where the pollution intensities Z_t are the sulphur dioxide (SO_2) emissions per dollar of output.[5] The figures are normalized to take a value of 100 in 1987. Sulphur dioxide is an air pollutant notorious for causing the acid rain that can kill lakes; the results for other pollutants are similar. As can be seen clearly from the figure, the composition of U.S. manufacturing output has moved sharply in the direction of cleaner industries, with the average pollution intensity dropping by about 9% over a period of rapid globalization (after an initial slight movement in the other direction). This finding is exactly consistent with what would be predicted in the PollutionHaven Hypothesis in the model of Section 13.2.

A second feature of the Pollution Haven Hypothesis is the prediction that the production of the lower-income country shifts toward dirtier production, even as

[5] These data are compiled by the World Bank from 1987 U.S. data from the U.S. Environmental Protection Agency. The values in Figure 13.4 correspond to the ratio of line (3) to line (1) in Figure 1 of Levinson (2009). Data from Levinson (2009) provided by the author are gratefully acknowledged.

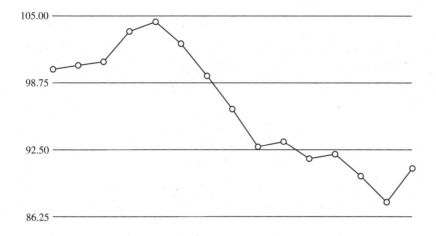

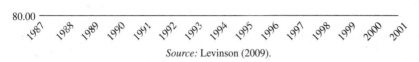

Source: Levinson (2009).

FIGURE 13.4
Composition Effect on
Pollution Intensity:
U.S. Manufacturing,
1987–2001.

its consumption shifts toward cleaner goods. (Recall that in Figure 13.3 the relative price of apparel falls in China when trade is opened, resulting in an increase in the chemical industry's share of output but a reduction in its share of consumption). Under this model, as globalization proceeds, viewed from the U.S. perspective, the composition of imports from the rest of the world should shift progressively toward dirtier goods. The Levinson data can be used to assess that implication as well. Define the average pollution intensity of net imports as:

$$D_t^{imports} \equiv \frac{\sum_i z_i m_{i,t}}{\sum_i m_{i,t}},$$

where $m_{i,t}$ denotes net imports of industry i's products by the United States at date t. The value of $D_t^{imports}$ from 1987 to 2001 is plotted in Figure 13.5,[6] where again the pollutant in question is SO_2 and again the figures are normalized so that the 1987 value is 100. In this case, the movement is even more striking than it was in Figure 13.4: The industry composition of imports has moved sharply in the direction of cleaner industries, as the average pollution intensity by the end of the data is 20% lower than it was at the beginning.[7] This, then, is the opposite of what the Pollution Haven Hypothesis would predict. The finding is reinforced by Dean and Lovely (2010), who have shown that the industry composition of China's exports has shifted toward cleaner industries over time as the country's exports have exhibited explosive growth.

---

[6] The values in Figure 13.5 correspond to the ratio of the Direct Coefficients values to the All Imports values in Figure 2 of Levinson (2009).
[7] Levinson shows that this conclusion holds even after correcting for the pollution generated by intermediate inputs required to produce each product imported from abroad.

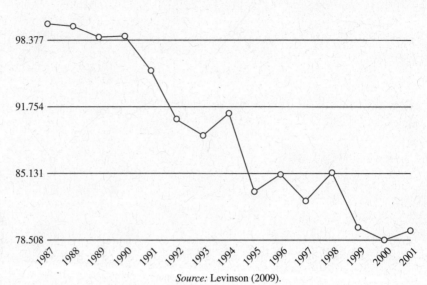

FIGURE 13.5
Composition Effect on
Pollution Intensity:
U.S. Imports,
1987–2001.

Source: Levinson (2009).

Consequently, the data on composition of industry do not really fit either hypothesis of Section 13.2. Either due to greater awareness of environmental issues or to political pressure on governments to tighten regulations, as globalization has proceeded, both world industry and world consumption seem to be shifting toward cleaner industries. In fact, Levinson's paper actually shows that a much larger effect is in play as well, aside from the composition-of-output effects we have focused on here. Pollution per dollar of output in each industry has fallen a great deal over the period, probably as a result of tightening regulations combined with improved technology and resulting in a substantial drop in U.S. manufacturing pollution despite a large increase in manufacturing output. The main point for our purposes, however, is that the broad picture does not seem to be one in which trade harms the environment.

MAIN IDEAS

1. High-income countries tend to have much more stringent environmental regulations than low-income countries. This could well lead lower-income countries to have a comparative advantage in dirtier industries, so that opening up trade reallocates dirtier industries to lower-income countries, raising world pollution: the Pollution Haven Hypothesis.

2. It is also possible, however, that trade will *lower* world pollution by reallocating dirty industries to high-income countries because they are capital-intensive and the capital-abundant high-income

countries have a comparative advantage in capital-intensive industries. We have labeled this the Sneeze Hypothesis.

3. Both of these hypotheses are consistent with a general-equilibrium theory of trade; in fact, they are both special cases of the *same* general-equilibrium theory of trade. The Sneeze Hypothesis emerges from a Heckscher-Ohlin model with pollution from the capital-intensive industry and pollution abatement costs added, if the abatement costs in the capital-abundant country are not so high as to overwhelm that country's natural

comparative advantage in capital-abundant goods. The Pollution Haven Hypothesis emerges if the abatement costs in the capital-abundant country are high enough to reverse the natural pattern of comparative advantage.

4. Empirically, it appears that there is a modest pollution haven effect at the margin, meaning that when a country tightens environmental regulations affecting a given industry, it does drive some of that industry abroad. However, the overall pattern of trade looks much more like the Sneeze Hypothesis, with rich countries exporting the output of dirtier industries and poorer countries exporting the output of cleaner industries, than like the Pollution Haven Hypothesis, which carries the opposite prediction. Furthermore, as globalization has advanced, the composition of U.S. imports from the rest of the world has shifted sharply in the direction of cleaner industries (and this shift is faster than the similar shift in U.S. manufacturing). Overall, it looks rather more as if trade is good for the environment rather than harmful.

QUESTIONS AND PROBLEMS

1. *Post-hoc logic* is a logical fallacy in which the inferrer concludes that because A happened after B, B must have caused A. Consider the two following examples.

   (a) In the years since the second wave of globalization took off in the 1970s, environmental regulations worldwide have become much tougher, and in industrial countries each category of manufacturing has become much less polluting (see Levinson, 2009, for U.S. evidence). Can we conclude from this that globalization *caused* environmentally friendly regulation? Or are there plausible alternative explanations?

   (b) In the years since the Chinese economy opened to international trade in the 1980s, Chinese air pollution has become disastrously out of control (although the situation seems to be improving—see Dean and Lovely, 2010). From this can we conclude that globalization *caused* the Chinese pollution problem? Or are there plausible alternative explanations?

2. Can you provide a reason globalization might give a government an incentive to use tougher-than-optimal environmental regulation? (Chapter 8 might provide some useful examples.) Can you provide a reason globalization might give a government an incentive to use *weaker*-than-optimal environmental regulation?

3. Consider the model of Section 13.2. Suppose that θ is initially positive but increases due to tightening emissions regulation (choose either the case $\theta < \theta^*$ or $\theta > \theta^*$ and stick to it). Trace through the changes in diagrams to show how the equilibrium changes. In particular:

   (a) How does the factor market equilibrium in the United States (as represented by zero-profit conditions) change for given output prices?

   (b) How does the U.S. production possibilities frontier change?

   (c) How does the U.S. relative-supply curve change?

   (d) How does the world relative-supply and relative-demand diagram change? Show the original world equilibrium and the new equilibrium on the same diagram.

   (e) Given the change in equilibrium world prices, how does the production point on both countries' production possibilities frontiers change?

4. Given your analysis of the previous question, what is the effect of the increase in θ on *world* pollution?

5. Now, suppose that U.S. policymakers do not actually care about pollution, but merely about real purchasing power of U.S. incomes. What is the effect of an increase in θ on the terms of trade, and on U.S. and Chinese welfare? Does your answer depend on other assumptions not specified in the question (and if so, how)? Would the U.S. government ever have an incentive to increase θ (say, by increasing the amount of paperwork and time used up in complying with the pollution standard)? Explain clearly.

REFERENCES

Antweiler, Werner, Brian R. Copeland, and M. Scott Taylor (2001). "Is Free Trade Good for the Environment?" *American Economic Review* 94:1, pp. 877–908.

Copeland, Brian R., and M. Scott Taylor (2003). *Trade and the Environment*. Princeton, NJ: Princeton University Press.

Dean, Judith M., and Mary E. Lovely (2010). "Trade Growth, Production Fragmentation, and China's Environment," in Robert C. Feenstra and Shang-Jin Wei (eds.), *China's Growing Role in World Trade*, Chapter 11. Chicago: University of Chicago Press.

Kahn, Matthew E., and Yutaka Yoshino (2004). "Testing for Pollution Havens Inside and Outside of Regional Trading Blocs." *Advances in Economic Analysis & Policy* 4:2, Article 4.

Korten, David C. (1995). *When Corporations Rule the World*. Sterling, VA: Kumarian Press.

Levinson, Arik (2009). "Technology, International Trade, and Pollution from U.S. Manufacturing." *American Economic Review* 99:5 (December), pp. 2177–2192.

Levinson, Arik, and Scott Taylor (2008). "Unmasking the Pollution Haven Effect." *International Economic Review* 49:1 (February), pp. 223–258.

Sweatshops and Child Labor: Globalization and Human Rights

Two boys working to irrigate a rice paddy, Vietnam.

14.1 Globalization and Child Labor

14.1.1 Did a Child Slave Pick the Cocoa for My Chocolate Bar?

If you eat chocolate, there is a good chance that you have eaten something picked by someone like Malick Doumbia. He is a young Malian man who, at age 14, working on his family farm, decided to try and escape the grinding poverty of his village by heading south to the Ivory Coast, where it was rumored there was money to be made. He went with a recruiter for cocoa pickers who promised him a good job, but instead he was sold to a cocoa farmer who kept him in bondage for several years.

> *He was never paid and rarely fed, living on a diet of green bananas and yams, which the boys would grill for themselves on a fire. At night, he was locked up with the others. The children and teenagers became ill; some of them died. After many months, Malick asked to be paid, and he was beaten. He never asked again. (Off, 2006, p. 126)*

Eventually, Malick escaped and made his way home with the help of a courageous Malian consular official, but it was clear that this atrocity was an example of everyday practice in the cocoa industry in the Ivory Coast, with well-organized traffickers and new child slaves arriving every day.

Child labor has always been with us, but, thankfully, is in a declining trend worldwide (see Basu, 1999, for a survey). Malick's case is in the category of the "worst forms of child labor," namely, coercive work that can be dangerous and is conducted far from the protections offered by family. But child labor takes many forms, and even at its most benign it raises concerns about the lost educational opportunities for children who spend a large fraction of each week at income-generating work.

An issue arises naturally from noting that all of the cocoa Malick tended and picked was being raised for export. Similarly, in Ecuador bananas for export to the United States are often tended by child laborers (Forero, 2002); in India, large numbers of carpets for export are produced by child labor in distressing conditions (Seidman, 2007); and in China, rings of con men have been discovered who trick impoverished families to hand over their children for slavery in factories for export goods (Barboza, 2008). In each of these cases and in many others, child labor has been used to produce products for export, leading to the natural question: *Does globalization cause child labor?* Are rich-country consumers causing misery and destroying children's futures by consuming these products? And if so, what ought to be done about it? In the following section, we will look at some of the research that has been done on this issue and try to clarify the relationship between these problems and globalization. In the subsequent sections we will look at a number of other ways in which the economics of globalization affect areas of human well-being of great concern to noneconomists—labor rights and sweatshop issues, democratic rights, and women's rights—that we can loosely bundle under the heading of human rights. Economic analysis can help us understand the (complicated and often ambiguous) role of globalization in those areas, as we will try to show.

14.1.2 Globalization and Child Labor—Some Theory

The most influential study of the relationship between globalization and child labor is a pioneering paper by Edmonds and Pavcnik (2005). A simplified version of their model can help illustrate the type of causal connections to look for in the data. The model is essentially a version of the specific-factors model of Chapter 5, with enough richness added to allow us to discuss child labor. Consider an economy that can produce two goods, rice and manufactures. There are households in the countryside that can produce rice but not manufactures, and there are urban households that can produce manufactures but not rice. In other words, each household's labor is specific to one industry. A rural household can produce one unit of rice with each unit of labor, and an urban household can produce one unit of manufactures with each unit of labor. (If the marginal product of labor in either industry was different from 1, we could always redefine the unit of measurement to make it so without changing anything of importance.) For simplicity, we will ignore the role of land and capital in production, as these are immaterial to the main points at issue. We will assume that this is a rice-exporting economy, so that globalization raises the domestic price of rice relative to manufactures.

Suppose that each household consists of a number of adults and a number of children, all of whom consume rice and manufactures, and all of whom have time available for work and for leisure. The term *leisure* includes any use of time other than for earning a wage or production of commodities, and it can include rest, play, social interaction, domestic chores, and, in the case of children, attendance at school. In the absence of a convenient term that accurately encompasses all such activities, we will fall back on the inadequate but traditional term *leisure*.

We will assume that a benevolent household head makes economic choices for the whole family and has a well-defined utility function defined over the consumption of all household members. For simplicity, assume that rice and manufactures are always consumed in equal proportions, so that we can summarize goods consumption for any household by:

$$G = \min\{R, M\},$$

where G stands for goods consumption, and R and M stand for rice and manufactures consumption, respectively. (Again, nothing essential depends on this particular consumption pattern, which is used here for convenience.) Given this assumption, if P^R is the price of rice and P^M is the price of manufactures, then the price of a unit of goods consumption is $P^G = P^R + P^M$.

Suppose that each household has $\bar{L}$ hours of time each week to spend on work or leisure, including the time belonging to each member of the household, adult and child. (This could be, for example, 24 hours per day minus 8 hours for sleep for each household member.) Suppose that $\bar{L}^C$ of these hours belong to children in the household and the rest, $\bar{L}^A$, belong to the adults (so that $\bar{L}^C + \bar{L}^A = \bar{L}$). We will make the assumption that the household prefers to use up all adult hours for work before using any children's hours for work—the household prefers to protect children from child labor, other things being equal. This implies that if the household enjoys a total number of leisure hours equal to L, then if $L > \bar{L}^C$, only adults are working, but if $L < \bar{L}^C$, adults are working for $\overline{L}^A$ hours per week while children are working for $\overline{L} - L - \overline{L}^A = \overline{L}^C - L$ hours per week.

Figure 14.1 shows the budget line for a representative rural household. The downward-sloping line shows the amount of goods consumption, G, that can be consumed for any level of leisure, L. For example, a household that takes no leisure can consume at point A, working $\overline{L}$ hours per week, producing $\overline{L}$ units of rice per week, selling that rice to earn income of $P^R\overline{L}$ per week, and purchasing $\frac{P^R\overline{L}}{(P^R + P^M)}$ units of goods. In this case, the children do $\overline{L}^C$ hours of work per week. At the opposite extreme, a household that does no work at all will take $\overline{L}$ units of leisure and have no goods to consume, as represented by point D. In this case, child labor is obviously zero. The intermediate case B is one in which adults take no leisure, and children take $L < \overline{L}^C$ units of leisure and therefore do $\overline{L}^C - L$ units of work, while case C is where adults do some work and take some leisure, while children do no work.

Given this budget line, whether there will be any child labor, and if so, how much, will depend on preferences. Figure 14.2 shows one possibility. The downward-sloping curves are the household head's indifference curves. Consider what happens when globalization raises the domestic price of rice relative to manufactures. The vertical intercept $\frac{P^R\overline{L}}{(P^R + P^M)}$ of the budget line can

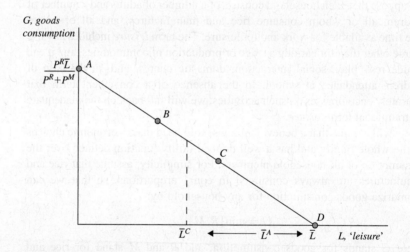

FIGURE 14.1
The Household's
Budget Line.

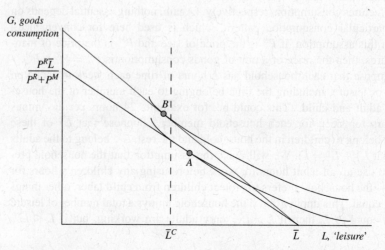

FIGURE 14.2
A Case in Which
Globabilization
Causes Child Labor.

be written as $\frac{\bar{L}}{1+P^M/P^R}$, so the change in relative prices pivots the budget line up. In the example illustrated, globalization shifts the budget line up from the black line to the blue one. This moves the household from point A, with no child labor, to point B, with positive child labor, so globalization does indeed cause child labor in the rural household. The interpretation is that globalization raises the marginal value product of time spent on the farm working, and the household head takes advantage of that by making everyone work more— including children.

Globalization could also have the opposite effect. In particular, Basu and Van (1998) have suggested that for the majority of households the most realistic assumption is that they direct their children to work only when it is an economic necessity to do so in order to allow the household to attain a minimum subsistence level of consumption—what Basu and Van call the luxury axiom (because it implies that for very low-income households children's leisure is a luxury good). For example, we could specify that there is a minimum level of goods consumption, $\bar{G}$, such that if the household can attain that level of consumption without child labor, it will do so. For example, the household head's utility function could look like:

$$U(G,L) = min\left\{G - \bar{G}, L - \bar{L}^C\right\}. \tag{14.1}$$

Indifference curves for this utility function are depicted in Figure 14.3. Note that with these indifference curves, a household would never resort to child labor (or in other words, choose $L < \bar{L}^C$) if it was possible to attain the basic-needs consumption level $\bar{G}$ without it. Now, again, consider the effect of globalization that raises the domestic relative price of rice, pivoting the household's budget line up from the black line to the blue one. In this case, the outcome could move from a point like A in Figure 14.3, in which child labor is used, to a point like B, in which child labor is not used. In this case, globalization has ended child labor in the rural household. The interpretation is that globalization has made it possible for the household to ensure its basic needs without resorting to child labor, and since that is what the household wants, that is what it chooses to do.

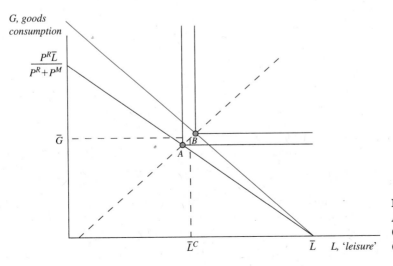

FIGURE 14.3
A Case in Which
Globalization Eliminates
Child Labor.

Clearly, both possibilities are consistent with economic theory. The big difference between the two is the relative strength of income and substitution effects. When the relative prices change and the budget line pivots up, the opportunity cost of an hour of leisure increases, providing an incentive to substitute away from leisure (including children's leisure) and toward goods production and consumption. This is the substitution effect, and it is dominant in Figure 14.2. On the other hand, the household's income also goes up, providing an increased demand for leisure (including children's leisure) since leisure is a normal good. This is the income effect, and it is dominant in Figure 14.3. Which of these two effects will dominate in the real world is an empirical question.

An additional point needs to be made here as a matter of theory. We have commented so far on rural households, but the same mechanisms work in the opposite direction for urban households. The vertical-axis intercept for an urban household's budget line is $\frac{P^M \bar{L}}{(P^R + P^M)}$, which can be written as $\frac{\bar{L}}{P^R/P^M + 1}$, so the rise in the relative price of rice that is expected with globalization will pivot the urban household's budget line *down*. As a result, if the substitution effect is dominant, as in Figure 14.2, globalization will reduce urban households' use of child labor, while if the income effect is dominant as in Figure 14.3, globalization will increase it. More generally, the model predicts that globalization will have different effects on child labor in different sectors of the economy: If the substitution effect is dominant, child labor will be increased in export sectors and reduced in import-competing sectors, while if the income effect is dominant, the effect will be the reverse.

This simple model provides a natural framework for looking at the data, to which we will turn next.

14.1.3 Evidence and Implications for Policy

The Edmonds and Pavcnik (2005) study focuses on the case of Vietnam. The Vietnamese economy has a strong comparative advantage in rice as well as in labor-intensive manufactures. During the 1990s, the country went through a rapid period of globalization and a rapid reduction in child labor, and the question is whether or not the two are related. The form of globalization that is the focus of the Edmonds-Pavcnik study concerns rice exports. In the early 1990s, the government restricted exports of rice through a system of quotas to keep prices low for consumers. In the mid-to-late 1990s, the government eliminated these quotas, allowing the domestic price of rice to rise. However, rice prices did not rise to the same degree in every part of the country; regions more integrated with the world market saw a more rapid rise in rice prices than more remote regions. As a result, the effects of this globalization episode can be measured cleanly.

Edmonds and Pavcnik used data from the Vietnam Living Standards Survey recorded in 1992–1993 and in 1997–1998 at each of 115 different randomly selected rural "communes," or local administrative units. During that period, as the rice export quotas were relaxed, domestic rice prices rose rapidly, but with a great deal of local variation. This can be seen in Figure 14.4, which reproduces Figure 1 from Edmonds and Pavcnik (2005) and shows the percentage change in rice price observed in each commune over this period on the horizontal axis, plotted against the fall in child labor in that commune (data received from the authors is gratefully acknowledged). Rice prices more than

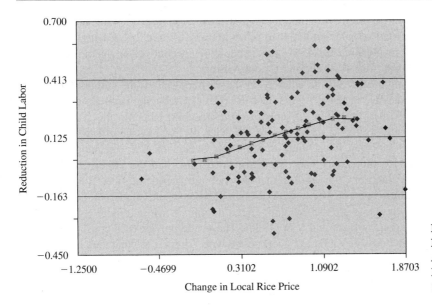

FIGURE 14.4
Drop in Child Labor
Against Change in
Rice Price, Vietnam,
1992−98.

doubled in many communes, while in many others the price increase was much more modest, and the rice price even fell in a few communes, even by as much as a half. This variation is very useful to the researcher, as it allows a comparison between the effect of a large price increase and the effect of a small one, which makes it possible to isolate the effect of the price rise itself (and therefore the effect of globalization).

The degree of child labor in each commune was defined as the fraction of 6- to 15-year-olds who either did more than 7 hours per week of household labor, who worked in agriculture or a family business enterprise, or who did any work for wages. Over the whole sample between these two dates, there was a significant decline in child labor overall, from 60 to 48%. The vertical axis of Figure 14.4 records this drop in each commune as a percentage-point difference, so, for example, if child labor in a given commune was at 60% in 1992−1993 and 48% in 1997−1998, the height of the point in Figure 14.4 representing that commune would be 60−48, or 12. Each blue point shows the rice price change and drop in child labor for one of the communes. The figure indicates a positive correlation between the change in price and the improvement in child labor, which is confirmed by the upward slope of the best-fit curve running through the scatter cloud. The same conclusion emerges from detailed statistical analysis, controlling for a large number of other factors: On average, a rural commune with a 10-percentage-point higher increase in rice price experienced a 3-percentage-point larger decline in child labor.

Given that the average rise in rice prices was approximately 30% after correcting for inflation, Edmonds and Pavcnik estimate that eliminating the export quotas was responsible for approximately a 9-percentage-point reduction in rural child labor. Recall that overall rural child labor in this sample declined from 60 to 48%, or 12 percentage points, over this period. If 9 percentage points of that change are due to increases in rice prices, and if the change in rice prices is due to globalization, then that implies that two-thirds of the overall improvement in child labor was due to globalization. An earlier version of the study (Edmonds and Pavcnik, 2002) used the same method on an extended sample that included urban households and found that globalization was responsible for 45% of the reduction in child labor overall. By either measure, this is an enormous contribution.

Some other details emerge. In the earlier version, the authors found that an increase in the rice price had the effect of reducing rural child labor, but it also had the effect of *increasing urban* child labor. In the 2005 version, the authors found that a rise in the price of rice had the effect of reducing child labor in households that are net sellers of rice (meaning that they produce more rice than they sell), but it also had the effect of increasing child labor in households that are net purchasers of rice. Both of these findings are consistent with the simple household model of the previous subsection, with the income effect dominant, as in Figure 14.3, and as assumed by Basu and Van (1998). These findings are also consistent with a great body of empirical work elsewhere, suggesting that the main determinant of child labor is simply poverty. Households that are below the poverty line tend to require their children to work, and households above the poverty line generally do not.

The same basic story emerges from Indian data in a paper by Edmonds, Pavcnik, and Topalova (2010). They examine household data before and after the trade liberalization of 1991, in which average Indian tariffs fell from 83 to 30%. The tariffs did not affect each part of the country equally; some locations were heavily dependent for jobs on industries whose tariffs were cut sharply, while other locations were not. The authors use employment-weighted average tariffs for each geographic district, which we can call local average tariff, as a measure of how much tariff protection each local labor market has.[1] Over the period in question, child labor rates fell sharply and school enrollment rates rose sharply across India. The authors find that districts that saw a large drop in the local average tariff tended to have significantly more modest drops in child labor and more modest increases in school enrollment compared to districts with a smaller drop in local average tariff, both in the countryside (Edmonds, Pavcnik, and Topalova, 2010) and in the cities (Edmonds, Pavcnik, and Topalova, 2009). This finding is again consistent with a model in which income effects dominate. If a district depends on one heavily protected industry for most of its jobs, and that industry loses its tariff, then (provided it is difficult for workers to move to another part of the country or for capital to move into the district), it makes sense to expect a drop in wages in that district, and therefore a rise in both local poverty and in the number of households that need to use their children's labor to survive. At the same time, districts whose industries are not hit with tariff reductions (such as export industries) will see higher real wages due to the lower consumer prices on imported goods whose tariffs are being cut. As a result, those districts will see falling poverty rates and reduced use of child labor.

---

[1] For example, if 90% of the workers in district A work in the textile sector, which has a 30% tariff, and 10% work in the software sector, which has a zero tariff, the local average tariff for district A is $(0.9)(0.3) + (0.1)(0.0) = 27\%$. If 90% of the workers in district B work in software, while 10% work in textiles, the local average tariff for district B is $(0.1)(0.3) + (0.9)(0.0) = 0.03$. Clearly, in the event that all tariffs are eliminated, workers in A are more likely to suffer than workers in B, and workers in B are more likely to benefit.

14.1.4 Bottom Line on the Child Labor Question

In summary, what all this says about globalization and child labor is that, empirically, globalization seems to affect the prevalence of child labor primarily through its effect on household income. Those households whose incomes rise—because they own factors specific to exporting, for example—tend to reduce their use of child labor, even if globalization increases their opportunities to use child labor for profit; and those households whose income falls—because they own factors specific to import-competing sectors, for example—tend to increase their use of child labor. Thus, the question, "What effect does globalization have on child labor?" is not separate from the question, "What effect does it have on incomes?" This point is borne out not only in microeconomic data, but also in aggregates (Edmonds and Pavcnik, 2006). There is a strong negative correlation between trade openness and child labor across countries (the countries that have the highest trade-to-GDP ratios use child labor the least), but it appears to be driven entirely by the strong positive correlation between trade openness and incomes (familiar to students who did Problem 5 of Chapter 1). After controlling for income per capita, the correlation between trade openness and child labor across countries disappears.

14.2 Sweatshops and Multinationals

An issue related to the relationship between trade and child labor is the relationship between sweatshops and multinational firms. A *sweatshop* is a loose term denoting a factory in which very poorly paid workers labor for long hours under very poor conditions. The term is sometimes reserved for factories that coerce workers in one way or another or that violate local labor laws. A good example, representative of many others, is the Meitai Plastics & Electronics Factory in Dongguan City, Guangdong, China. A detailed examination of the factory can be found in a report issued by the Pittsburgh-based labor-rights watchdog group, the National Labor Committee (2009). A few highlights from the report are as follows. The factory produces thousands of computer keyboards every day. Workers at the factory, mostly young women, are required to work 12-hour shifts seven days a week with a single day off every other week, despite laws requiring a 40-hour work week with a worker's right to refuse overtime. One day per month an 18-hour shift is required. They are also required to live in company dormitories, for which they are charged; 10–12 workers sleep in each small room, facing a strict curfew and regulations with no real privacy, and four days out of the week are required to get company permission if they wish to leave the grounds for any reason. One worker characterized the situation with the remark: "I feel like I am serving a prison sentence" (p. 2). The workspace is often unbearably hot because of the equipment and lack of ventilation, and many workers develop rashes from excessive sweating. Any medical treatment this requires must be paid for by the worker (p. 51). The company supplies food, including a thin, watery rice gruel for breakfast. All of this provides a reward of 76 cents per hour, or $57.19 per week.

If you use a computer sold by Dell, Hewlett-Packard, Lenovo, or IBM, there is a good chance that the keyboard was made in this factory. It also makes keyboards for Microsoft.

The existence of the Meitai Plastics & Electronics Factory and many others like it raises natural questions about globalization. Since the work done in that factory and others like it is almost entirely for export, it is natural to ask if sweatshops are a pernicious consequence of globalization; if consumers should refuse to buy items made in them; if consumer activism can make life better for the workers in them. Economics can offer some perspective on these questions, as outlined in the following argument.

14.2.1 Sweatshops Arise from Poverty

First, it is difficult to tell a story in which the ability of rich-country firms to hire in low-wage countries lowers the wages in the low-wage country. It is much easier to understand how multinational firms seeking cheap labor in a low-wage country can raise the demand for labor there, thus *raising* wages. For example, consider a low-wage economy represented in Figure 14.5. Think of this economy as a (mixed) specific-factors economy, with labor perfectly mobile across sectors as in the model of Section 5.5. The length of the box is the total supply of labor in the economy. The downward-sloping curve shows the horizontal sum of the labor-demand curves for all domestic industries (agriculture, manufacturing, services, and so on). If foreign multi-nationals have not set up any production facilities in this economy, the total domestic demand for labor must equal the domestic supply, yielding an equilibrium at point A, with a wage of w^{NSS} (which stands for no sweatshops). Assume this equilibrium wage is well below the poverty line for U.S. households. If U.S. corporations enter the economy to hire some fraction of those workers for their own factories, paying them the low equilibrium wage in this economy, so that outside observers would call those factories sweatshops, then that will introduce a new source of demand for labor, as indicated by the upward-sloping curve in Figure 14.5. (Employment in sweatshops is measured from the right-hand axis leftward, just as in the model of Section 5.5.) This moves the equilibrium from point A to point B, raising the wage for all workers

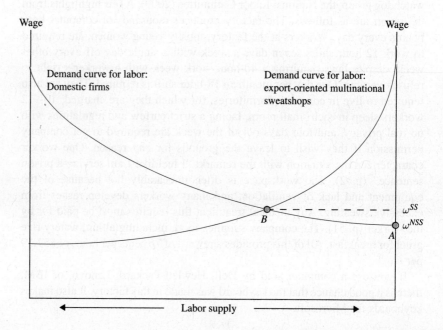

Wage   Wage

Demand curve for labor: Domestic firms

Demand curve for labor: export-oriented multinational sweatshops

B

w^{SS}
w^{NSS}

A

Labor supply

FIGURE 14.5
The Effect of
Sweatshops on
Wages.

in this economy from w^{NSS} to w^{SS} (which stands for sweatshops). Within this framework, workers in this economy are cheap for the multinationals to hire because they have a low opportunity cost. Since the available stock of capital for manufactures and the stock of quality land for agriculture are small relative to the labor supply, in the absence of the multinationals their wages would be even lower than they are with the sweatshops. Put differently, the poverty of the workers hired in the sweatshops is not caused by the sweatshops; rather, the sweatshops are caused by the poverty. The sweatshops also reduce domestic poverty somewhat by raising wages.

Note that this analysis is not fundamentally changed by extending it to include working conditions, on-the-job safety, health benefits, worker privacy, and so on, instead of merely focusing on wages. Employers offer a bundle of job attributes in order to attract workers, and the bundle must offer the worker a level of utility at least as high as her opportunity cost in order to be willing to accept the job (unless there is coercion or deception involved, which of course is an issue in some cases). If the demand for workers increases, we should expect to see employers offering a more attractive bundle, including an improvement across the board in wages, working conditions, and fringe benefits.

The point that wages and working conditions are poor in export-oriented factories in low-income countries because the workers have low opportunity costs is made forcefully by Timmerman (2009), an American author who traveled the world to find and interview the people who made his clothing. For example, he interviews a husband and wife who work in the urban factory in China where his flip-flops were made (the wife sews a tag and a strap on each pair, and the husband paints them), working more than 300 hours per month for a monthly pay of no more than $225 (Chapter 20). He then makes the 30-hour train trip to their home village in the countryside to interview the relatives to whom they hope someday to return and describes vividly the lack of economic opportunity there, and the lack of young and middle-aged adults, all of whom have gone to the city to make money (Chapter 22). Even with their meager wage, the couple he interviews have been able to improve their standard of living far beyond what would have been possible in the village, building a concrete house for themselves and paying for catastrophic health care for a parent. He concludes (p. 173):

> The people who make boots or sandals in China aren't free. They, like most of the people who make our apparel, are bound to their work because they don't have any other options.

The point comes out more forcefully still when Timmerman visits a trash dump in Phnom Penh, Cambodia, where two thousand scavengers search for recyclables and earn an average of $1 per day, often scrambling perilously among the heavy equipment to get the best pickings. Many of them are former farmers who "chose to leave their villages where the air is fresh, the space is vast, and the options nil" (p. 144) and who heard of the "opportunity" at the dump. Describing an 11-year-old girl who lives in the dump, he observes (p. 147):

> Being one of 85 people sewing blue jeans or giving them that cool look at the grindstone or sandblasting them, while working six-days a week, and getting paid

*$50 a month—half of which you have to send home so your family could eat—
doesn't sound like much of a life to me. But to this girl, it's a life she would be lucky
to have.*

14.2.2 Multinationals May Be Part of the Solution

If we agree that the deprivation associated with sweatshops is caused by the
lack of economic opportunity in the economies in question and the resulting
low opportunity income for workers, then it follows that the presence of
sweatshops may actually make the situation better. There are two ways this
improvement can occur. First, as pointed out above, a simple analysis of
supply and demand suggests that any increase in the local demand for
labor, including the appearance of export-driven sweatshops, will tend to
drive the market wage up as in Figure 14.5, improving the opportunity
income that is the source of the problem. However, these effects are difficult to confirm in the data. In an extensive survey of research on the
effects of FDI, Lipsey (2004) concludes that the evidence on these effects is
inconclusive.

Second, multinational firms tend to pay *more* than market wages in the
economy in which they are hiring, and unlike the effect on domestic employers' wages, this is perhaps the most robustly well-documented empirical
finding in international economics. Again, see Lipsey (2004). One of the best-
known studies (Lipsey and Sjöholm, 2006) examines multinationals in
Indonesia and finds that they pay about 50% higher wages than comparable
domestically owned firms. Controlling for location and industry cuts the gap in
half for blue-collar workers, and controlling for plant size cuts the gap some
more (since part of the reason multinationals pay higher wages is that they
have larger plants, which other things being equal tend to pay higher wages
than small plants). But the overall finding is that in Indonesia and everywhere
else, a worker receives a higher wage at a foreign-owned plant than at a
domestically owned one. The reasons for this multinational wage premium are
a subject of lively debate. It could be that the multinationals are able to screen
for the most able workers, or it could be that the multinationals have stronger
incentives to deter pilfering or quitting, and consequently pay an above-market
wage to make sure that employees do not do those things (often called an
efficiency wage).

So, the multinationals' hiring creates a possible effect of raising wages paid
by domestic firms, as well as a well-established effect of paying higher wages
than domestic firms. Averaging over these two groups, the data make it clear
that *the introduction of multinational firms to a labor market tends to increase
average wages* (see Section 3 of Lipsey, 2004).

14.2.3 But There May Still Be Good Reason to Keep the Pressure On

If we grant that the arrival of sweatshops is not the cause of poverty and that
they tend to improve matters by raising average wages, that does not mean that
the best solution is to let the market work without any tending or tinkering.
If rich-country consumers wish to improve the lives of the workers in low-
income countries who produce the products they buy, and are willing to pay a
bit more in product prices in order to share some more of the benefits of

globalization with those workers, then they can pressure the companies to improve pay and other conditions. Multinational firms have proven themselves highly susceptible to pressure in this vein.

Seidman (2007) provides a detailed history of activist campaigns to improve treatment of workers by multinational firms and Third World export manufacturers. For one example, shareholder activism during the apartheid era in South Africa prodded U.S. multinationals to agree to a code of conduct known as the Sullivan Principles, which required them to desegregate their South African workplaces, contribute to local institutions, and in other ways contribute to racial progress. More recently, consumer activism has induced the manufacturers of hand-stitched soccer balls to take aggressive measures to eliminate child labor from the production process (Seidman, 2007, pp. 99–100).

An intriguing case study of the effect of activism on the labor market is found in Harrison and Scorse (2010). They studied the textile, apparel, and footwear sector in Indonesia, a sector that attracted considerable media and activist attention over the 1990s for the use of sweatshops and child labor in production of goods for consumers in high-income countries. In particular, anti-sweatshop activists put intense pressure on Nike, Adidas, and Reebok to improve the treatment of workers in their Indonesian operations, using a network of in-country observers together with a well-thought-out media campaign aimed at the companies' rich-country consumers.

Harrison and Scorse have data on employment and wages in Indonesian manufacturing plants over this period, and although they do not have information to identify which plants were doing work for Nike, Adidas, and Reebok, they do have information on which plants were located in districts that were the focus of anti-sweatshop activism.[2] What they have found is that from 1990 to 1996, plants in the footwear, textiles, and apparel industry that were either foreign-owned or export-oriented—the group most subject to the activists' scrutiny—increased their wages for unskilled workers 10 to 12% more than other plants. Further, within the footwear, textiles, and apparel industry, large plants that were either foreign-owned or export-oriented and located in the districts focused on by activists increased their wages by *a full* 52% more than other plants. These results hold up after controlling for a large number of additional variables, and provide strong circumstantial evidence that the activists were successful in increasing the wages of workers in their targeted plants. In addition, those plants showed no sign of eliminating workers or hiring fewer workers over this period than other firms. The authors take this information to be strong evidence that anti-sweatshop activism successfully induced multinationals to provide higher incomes for their workers, without sacrificing jobs. In contrast, the Indonesian government doubled its minimum wage over the same period, and the evidence suggests that this substantially increased wages for employed workers but also reduced aggregate job growth. In this respect,

---

[2] This requires some explanation. The authors use Indonesian Census of Manufactures data, which indicates the district in which each plant in their data was located, but not the identity of the firm, and in particular whether or not each plant did work for Nike, Adidas, or Reebok. However, the three multinationals themselves publicize information on the district in which each plant producing for Nike, Adidas, or Reebok is located, so the authors can at least identify which of the plants in the data are in the same district as one or more of those plants that were the target of activist attention.

anti-sweatshop activism appears to have avoided a major disadvantage of the minimum-wage strategy for increasing the incomes of low-wage workers.

A similar analysis applies to the issue of sweatshops and college merchandise, such as t-shirts and coffee mugs with university logos. During the 1990s, a number of organizations sprang up as part of an anti-sweatshop movement whose purpose was to monitor manufacturers of college-licensed merchandise and certify them as sweatshop- and child-labor free. A university could join the Workers Rights Consortium, the Fair Labor Association, or the Council on Economic Priorities Accreditation Agency, paying a membership fee to cover the cost of its work. The organization would then monitor the university's merchandise suppliers and alert the university if any violations were discovered. A coalition of economists called the Academic Consortium on International Trade (ACIT) circulated a letter[3] on July 29, 2000, arguing that this anti-sweatshop movement may be backfiring:

> Both of these groups, however, seem to ignore the well-established fact that multinational corporations (MNCs) commonly pay their workers more on average in comparison to the prevailing market wage for similar workers employed elsewhere in the economy. . . . We are concerned therefore that if MNCs are persuaded to pay even more to their apparel workers in response to what the ongoing studies by the anti-sweatshop organizations may conclude are appropriate wage levels, the net result would be shifts in employment that will worsen the collective welfare of the very workers in poor countries who are supposed to be helped.

This argument can be represented by Figure 14.6, which is an elaboration of Figure 14.5 to account for the effect of anti-sweatshop activism. The

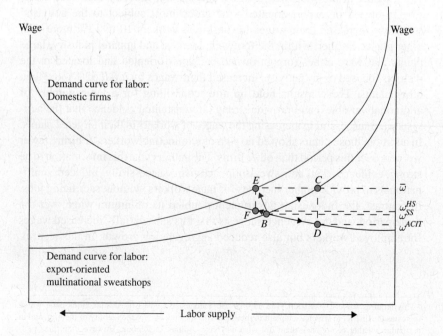

FIGURE 14.6 The Effect of Anti-sweatshop Activism.

[3] The letter can be found at the ACIT web page, at www.spp.umich.edu/rsie/acit.

equilibrium wage with sweatshops but without anti-sweatshop activism is, as before, marked as w^{SS}, with the equilibrium allocation of labor at point B (ignore the blue curve for the moment). In this model, if the multinational sector is forced to pay a high wage such as $\overline{w}$ under threat of boycott by activists, then it will reduce its hiring, moving along its labor demand curve from point B to point C. This will leave the workers it sheds to be absorbed by the domestic employers, and so the market wage must fall in order to induce them to hire the extra workers. The domestic employers will move along their labor-demand curve from B to D, with their wage falling from w^{SS} to w^{ACIT} (so labeled to represent the concerns expressed in the ACIT letter). This lower wage is now received by *all* workers not employed by multinationals. As a result, in this interpretation, sweatshop activism has helped the lucky few who still have jobs with the multinationals but has harmed everyone else. Clearly, if $\overline{w}$ is high enough, workers in this economy as a whole will be hurt by the anti-sweatshop activism.

In practice, we do not have much evidence on the wage effects of anti-sweatshop activism, but the one formal case study conducted by Harrison and Scorse (2010) suggests that this pessimistic case has not occurred. Indeed, its *opposite* may have occurred, at least in Indonesian footwear manufacturing: Foreign-owned and exporting plants in the affected areas may have actually *increased* their hiring modestly in response to the activism.[4] The reason for this is not clear. It may be, for example, that the activists had, in effect, convinced consumers that they could purchase the shoes in good conscience now that monitoring was in place, thus increasing demand. In Figure 14.6, if this allows the multinationals to sell their sneakers at a higher price than before, that shifts the marginal-value-product of labor curve in Figure 14.6 upward, as shown by the blue curve. In this case, the sweatshops increase their hiring as they increase their wage, jumping from point B to point E. For this outcome to be possible, domestic employers now need to be induced to *give up* some of their workers, so the domestic wage must increase, and the domestic employers move along their labor-demand curve from B to F. The new domestic wage is marked w^{HS} (in honor of Harrison and Scorse). The point is that if this indeed occurred, it implies that Indonesian workers across the board likely benefited from the activism, and not merely those in the footwear plants. However, any conclusions about this issue must be regarded as tentative; we need a great deal more evidence on these questions before we can be confident that these results are typical.

Thus, one way of looking at the sweatshop problem from an economist's point of view is as follows: (i) Sweatshops are a symptom of poverty rather than a cause of it. (ii) They may actually be a part of the solution, in that any increase in demand for workers in a low-wage labor market will tend to push wages up somewhat. However, (iii) pressure on multinationals from consumers who are concerned about the plight of the worker who make their iPods and flip-flops can improve matters even more.

---

[4] The estimated increase in hiring varies depending on the statistical technique employed. In general, the authors cannot rule out a zero increase, but the highest estimate is 16%. See Table 6B of their paper.

14.3 Globalization and Human Rights More Generally

We have reviewed the effect of globalization on child labor and on sweatshops, two economic topics that often are treated as human rights issues. It is worth pointing out that the economic force of globalization can have significant impacts on other human rights issues that fall outside of economics. We will comment on how it can affect democratic rights and also how it can at times even trigger civil war, before mentioning its relationship with women's rights.

14.3.1 The Effect on Democracy: The Political Influence of Multinational Firms

The presence of multinational firms can have a wide variety of effects on the evolution of democratic rights in a country. Examples of perverse effects abound, but there are a number of positive ones as well. A well-known case is that of mineral-extraction multinationals allegedly colluding with host governments to silence dissent in order to smooth mining or oil extraction operations. For example, many critics have accused oil companies of propping up the military dictatorship in Nigeria in the 1990s and helping it violently crush dissent. Chevron allegedly lent a helicopter to the regime to attack protesters in 1998 (see, for example, Renner, 2002, pp. 46–47), and Shell recently settled a lawsuit accusing it of helping the government repress ethnic Ogoni protests, supplying weapons, and encouraging police to kill protesters (Usborne, 2009). The lawsuit was filed by the son of Ken Saro-Wiwa, the author hanged by the government in 1995, and family members of other dissidents killed by the government, offenses for which the families involved hold Shell partly responsible. Another example is ExxonMobil, which is being sued by the International Labor Rights Fund for allegedly collaborating with the Indonesian army to murder and torture people living in the Aceh province who protested the company's natural-gas operations there.[5] Another category is technology firms, which are increasingly accused of helping political repression in the countries in which they operate. Yahoo! has been accused of helping the People's Republic of China track down at least four dissidents, who are now in prison for online dissent. One of these dissidents has sued the company in U.S. courts as an accomplice in his torture (Blakely, 2007).

These are all examples of ways in which globalization, in the form of increased movements of capital and foreign operations of multinational firms, can impede the progress of democratic rights because of the way multinational firms and host governments interact. However, the influence can at times go in the other direction. John Kamm is a former regional vice president of Occidental Chemical Corporation, stationed in Hong Kong, and a former president of Hong Kong's American Chamber of Commerce. Kamm became so concerned about the Chinese government's treatment of its dissidents that he turned his back on his business career and became a full-time human rights activist, using the connections and credibility he had earned with the

---

[5] See news reports such as BBC Online, June 22, 2001: "Exxon 'Helped Torture in Indonesia,'" or Agence France-Presse, August 27, 2008: "ExxonMobil Case Said to Highlight Indonesia Rights Abuses."

government to campaign for the release of many political prisoners (Rosenberg, 2002). Some commentators argue that multinationals in South Africa under apartheid helped to foster more progressive attitudes that helped nudge the country toward political liberalization, at least after many U.S. multinationals adopted the voluntary code of conduct known as the Sullivan Principles.[6]

The general point is that foreign direct investment does not affect a host country simply by hiring workers and conducting productive activities there, but also, more subtly, by the effect that the foreign firms have on the conduct of government in the host country. This can occur through many channels, direct and indirect. There is some evidence that foreign firms are on average better able to persuade host governments to shape policy in ways beneficial to them than domestic firms (Desbordes and Vauday, 2007). Obviously, this can have positive or negative effects on democratic progress, depending on the intentions and political agenda of the foreign firms in question, as the examples here illustrate. It is another area in which pressure from shareholders and consumers of multinational firms can be decisive.

14.3.2 The Effect on Democracy: The Effect of Trade

Even in the absence of multinational firms, simply opening up international trade can have substantial effects on the development of democracy. Acemoğlu and Robinson (2005, Chapter 10) survey many ways in which opening trade can affect the likelihood that a country will move to democracy. One of these mechanisms, formalized by Rosendorff (2000), can be summarized as follows. Suppose that a country is ruled by an elite with dictatorial power and that its purpose in holding power is to protect its wealth. However, in order to maintain this dictatorial power, the elite must spend considerable resources in security forces, suppression of rebellions, surveillance of dissidents, and so forth, which is a cost to the elite that must be weighed against the benefit of protecting its own wealth. The alternative is to allow democracy, in which case the elite does not need to spend resources on repression, but it must suffer the rise of redistributive taxation when poor or middle-class voters take control of government. The elite understands that the poorer is the poorer half of the population compared to the elite, the more redistribution will result. Therefore, the larger the gap is between the rich and poor, the more fearful the elite is of democracy. Therefore, under this theory, *income inequality slows progress toward democracy, and any reduction in income inequality will speed it up.*

It is clear that trade can affect this process in a variety of ways because, as we know, trade can have powerful effects on income distribution. For example, in a Heckscher-Ohlin world such as is depicted in Chapter 6, countries that are abundant in unskilled labor will see a reduction in income inequality due to the opening of trade, while countries where unskilled labor is scarce will see an increase. Therefore, under this theory, in poor economies trade is a force for democracy, while in rich economies it works against democracy. Acemoğlu and Robinson (2005) point out that since most rich countries are already democratic, this theory establishes a presumption that

---

[6] This is the subject of lively debate; see Seideman (2007, pp. 63–67) for a review.

trade is on balance a force for democracy. This idea does have some empirical support. López-Córdova and Meissner (2008), for example, show that in a broad cross section of countries over a long historical time span, higher openness to trade is correlated with a greater propensity toward democracy. Eichengreen and Leblang (2008) find similar results, taking close account of the fact that democracy can affect globalization at the same time as globalization can affect democracy.

In individual cases, however, the interaction between trade and democratization can be very complex. Rosendorff (2000) argues that trade *embargoes* likely helped speed the path toward democratization in South African, not merely for the usual reason that they accentuated diplomatic pressure on the government, but also because they depressed the profits of the large mining companies and other multinationals more than unskilled wages, thus reducing income inequality. For another example, a recent free-trade agreement between Peru and the United States required the Peruvian government to enact decrees to open large swathes of jungle to development by logging and energy multinationals. To streamline the process, the decrees allowed development to proceed in areas inhabited by indigenous peoples without the consent of local indigenous authorities. This decision prompted an outraged response by various native groups, who in June 2009 seized a highway and some oil facilities. (See Romero, 2009.) A series of extremely violent confrontations ensued between the protesters and security forces, after which the government suspended the decrees. This illustrates the general principle that trade frequently brings domestic political conflict, as some Peruvians expected to gain from the agreement and some expected to be harmed. Distributional conflict can put a serious strain on democratic institutions.

14.3.3 Globalization and Civil War

War is the mother lode of human rights violations. If globalization can contribute to the outbreak of civil war, that could dwarf all of its other effects on human well-being. An argument that it might be doing so in a number of cases was advanced in a study by Collier and Hoeffler (1998), who showed a strong statistical relationship between a country's dependence on primary commodity exports and the probability that the country will become embroiled in a civil war. The authors' interpretation is that civil war in the modern age often is driven by a desire for plunder, with armed bands constituting themselves as rival armies competing for control of a valuable resource, such as a mineral deposit or other primary-commodity endowment.[7] In this interpretation, the violence is intimately tied to globalization because the resource in question is always an export commodity, which raises the question of whether war might not have occurred had the world price of the commodity been lower.

Examples of civil wars driven or worsened by exportable primary commodities are unfortunately common; Renner (2002) and Ross (2004) provide

---

[7] Specifically, the countries found to be least likely to have a civil war are countries with either very little or very great dependence on primary commodities; countries with intermediate dependence were found to have the highest rate of civil war. This cannot happen for countries that have little primary-commodity wealth, while for countries with a sufficiently abundant endowment the government is able to fund a strong defense with the wealth it generates, and so in either case there is no possibility of civil war. There is some debate about how clear the data are on these questions; see Fearon (2005) for a critique.

detailed reviews. One of the best known cases is the war in Sierra Leone, which ran from 1991 to 2002 and involved rival armies competing partly over control of diamond fields. The war featured exceptionally intense violence against civilians and much recruitment of child soldiers. In 2000 the Sierra Leonian ambassador to the United Nations went as far as to assert: "The root of the conflict is and remains diamonds, diamonds, and diamonds" (Renner, 2002, p. 22). The Biafran War in Nigeria in the 1970s had control of oil-rich territory at its heart. Current violence in the Democratic Republic of the Congo is largely centered on control of fields where the mineral called coltan is mined. The mineral is unfamiliar to most people, but it is an essential ingredient in the manufacture of electronics items such as mp3 players and cell phones. It has few sources of supply worldwide, but it can be easily harvested from surface deposits in the Democratic Republic of the Congo (see Renner, 2002, p. 51). The competition for access to coltan fields by armed groups, including some from neighboring countries, has been accompanied by a devastating rain of violence on local civilians, including what the United Nations calls an epidemic of rape involving tens of thousands and perhaps hundreds of thousands of victims (Gettleman, 2008). The violence against civilians appears to have had an economic purpose in intimidating civilians to stay out of the way of the militias' plundering, and also to compel labor (Dias, 2009), but it also appears to have taken on a life of its own as the war has dragged on.

The implications for trade policy are not clear. In the case of diamond-driven wars, one constructive response that has emerged is a series of international attempts to ban conflict diamonds from the world market. Renner (2002, pp. 54−64) summarizes various efforts of this sort for diamonds and other conflict commodities, pointing out the enormous practical difficulties involved in enforcement. Author Eve Ensler, who has spent considerable time with victims of violence in the Democratic Republic of the Congo, has suggested that there is a need for a labeling system to allow consumers to be sure that they are buying "rape-free" electronics products (Paczkowski, 2009).

At the same time, it has been argued that the *right kind* of globalization can reduce the propensity toward civil war. There is evidence that good overall performance in an economy reduces the probability that it will be embroiled in a civil war. For example, African evidence on this point is provided by Miguel, Satyanath, and Sergenti (2004), who interpret their results as showing that a robust economy creates jobs, raising the opportunity cost of workers who might be tempted to join a rebel army. Bradsher (2002) describes how a boom in employment due to tuna processing for export killed off several guerrilla movements in Mindanao in the Philippines. The implication is that controls on imports of the primary commodities that fuel the conflicts, together with open imports of labor-intensive exports from the conflict-prone countries, may help alleviate the problem of civil war.

14.3.4 A Note on Women's Rights

Globalization can have subtle effects on the status and rights of women. Here are a few examples.

First, in a number of low-income countries, labor-intensive manufacturing for export to rich countries is predominantly an employer of women, as well as a major force for generating economic opportunities and even a first entry into the labor force for women. Milner and Wright (1998) document this fact for the manufacturing-export boom in Mauritius of the 1980s, noting that the surge in manufacturing employment for export was driven almost entirely by women workers, many of whom had never before worked outside of the home. Timmerman (2009) and Chang (2009), based on interviews with workers, offer accounts of the phenomenon for a variety of countries. This is relevant for women's empowerment because women's bargaining power is enhanced whenever they generate their own income streams and possess their own savings. Evidence shows that as women's place in the workforce expands, gender gaps in social indicators such as life expectancy tend to diminish (Mammen and Paxson, 2000).

Second, there is some evidence that economic openness can reduce the scope for gender discrimination in wages. Black and Brainerd (2004) argue that import competition has been a powerful force against discrimination in the U.S. labor market. They show that while the earnings gap in the U.S. labor market between male and female workers has been shrinking, it has diminished the most during periods when trade has expanded the fastest. Furthermore, study of industry-year male/female wage gaps, after correcting for education and race, shows that the biggest reductions in the gaps have occurred in industries that are highly concentrated (meaning that a small number of firms dominate the market) and in years in which the industry has been hit by rapidly growing imports. Black and Brainerd's interpretation (following the work of labor economist Gary Becker) is that wage discrimination results from a lack of competition: Employers who have a prejudice against women workers and would prefer not to work with them sacrifice profitability of the firm by passing over female candidates in favor of male candidates, even when the male candidate is less qualified. In a concentrated industry with no import competition, this bias is possible because the firm does not face much competition, but if the firms need to compete with imports, the bigoted employers no longer have the luxury of indulging their prejudices and are forced to hire the most qualified available candidates regardless of gender in order to remain profitable enough to survive.

In general, globalization can have positive or negative effects on women's rights. It seems to have enhanced women's empowerment in a number of low-income countries by giving women employment, and to have reduced discrimination in the United States—but no-one would argue that the export demand for coltan has had a positive effect on women's rights in the Democratic Republic of the Congo.

14.4 Conclusion: Getting the Globalization You Want

An accurate but infuriating way of summarizing this discussion is that globalization has myriad indirect effects on human rights, in addition to its direct effects on economic variables such as prices and incomes; and that these indirect effects can either strengthen or weaken human rights, depending on the case. A rich-country consumer who merely wants to know whether his or her consumption habits help or hurt in these issues would be frustrated by this analysis. However, such a consumer can take the problem in a constructive direction: Identify the ways in which trade appears to be injurious to human rights, and use his or her power as a consumer to change it. The same applies to a rich-country investor. One can, in effect, strive to have the globalization that one wants.

Professor Kristen Branson of the University of California, San Diego, maintains a website entitled "Stop Chocolate Slavery,"[8] which provides a wide array of information on the issues discussed in Section 14.1.1, along with a consumer's guide to "slavery-free chocolate." Consumers can use that information to inform their own consumption choices, and then they can contact the corporations involved to let them know that they are voting with their wallets, and then get their friends to do the same. Consumer and investor pressure together with publicity can have enormous effects on corporate behavior. The effects on the high-profile footwear industry have already been noted. Timmerman (2009) describes improved working conditions in Cambodian plants for U.S. bluejeans resulting from consumer-country pressure. Activist pressure persuaded the diamond giant De Beers to stop buying from rebels in Angola, a practice that had helped prolong the civil war there, and the Belgian airline SABENA similarly stopped shipping coltan from civil-war-plagued Central Africa (Renner, 2002, p. 59) under pressure of publicity. If consumers and investors want products that support human rights rather than erode them, it is within their power to demand them.[9]

MAIN IDEAS

1. Globalization can, as a matter of theory, increase or decrease the use of child labor. For example, in export agriculture, if the price of the exportable commodity goes up, as can be expected as a result of globalization, it will tend to make farm families richer—an income effect that will reduce child labor. However, it will also raise the opportunity cost of an hour spent in "leisure"—a substitution effect that will tend to increase child labor.

2. In practice, the income effect seems to dominate, and child labor falls when poverty falls. Evidence suggests that in low-income countries, globalization tends to raise the use of child labor in import-competing sectors and to lower it in export sectors. In Vietnam open trade appears to have had the net effect of significant reductions in child labor.

3. "Sweatshops" are an imprecisely defined term indicating factories with very low wages and very poor working conditions. The root cause is not globalization but poverty, which implies a low opportunity cost for workers. There is good theoretical reason to expect that multinationals hiring in low-income labor markets will lower poverty by increasing the demand for labor, even if their factories are sweatshops. Empirical evidence suggests that multinationals improve average wages mostly due to the higher wages they pay.

4. However, even with this effect, low-wage workers still capture only a small share of the surplus generated by the exports of the goods they produce, and that share can be increased by activism in consumer countries.

5. Foreign direct investment has had strong effects on democratization, but the effect varies from case to case. There are numerous examples of multinationals helping host governments crack down on dissidents, but it is not unknown for multinationals to apply pressure in the opposite direction.

6. By one theory, trade openness helps ease progress toward democracy in low-income countries by reducing income inequality, making autocratic

[8] It can be found at http://vision.ucsd.edu/kbranson/stopchocolateslavery.
[9] Seidman (2007) extensively surveys the history of consumer activism toward multinationals, emphasizing the limits to such activism and arguing that government action is often needed to achieve the activists' aims.

elites less fearful of majority rule. There is empirical evidence for a pro-democracy effect of trade openness over a long time span.

7. Probably the most troubling interaction between globalization and human rights springs from civil wars over exportable primary commodities. International vigilance on import of conflict commodities together with promotion of labor-intensive manufactures—the "right kind" of globalization—offer some partial hope of alleviating this problem.

8. Globalization can have significant indirect effects on women's rights, by expanding women's role in the paid labor force, which tends to improve women's bargaining power and social outcomes; and by intensifying market competition, which appears to reduce the scope for labor-market discrimination.

QUESTIONS AND PROBLEMS

1. Suppose we can take as given an empirical finding that increased trade openness reduces child labor somewhat in the export sectors and increases it somewhat in import-competing sectors. Can you think of a hypothetical example in which it would increase child labor in every sector of the economy? Can you think of a hypothetical example in which it would reduce child labor in every sector of the economy?

2. Consider the household model of Section 14.1.2. Suppose that each household has $\overline{L}^A = 40$ hours of adult time and $\overline{L}^C = 60$ hours of children's time to allocate between labor and leisure. The price of manufactures is always equal to 1. Suppose that the household head's utility function is given by (14.1), with $\overline{G} = 24$.

   (a) Suppose that the price of rice is equal to 1. How much total labor is done by the household? How much child labor? Illustrate using a diagram with the household's budget line and indifference curve at the optimum.

   (b) Now, suppose that the price of rice has gone up to 1.5, because rice is an export good and the cost of shipping the rice abroad has fallen. Repeat the analysis part (a).

   (c) Now, repeat for a household that makes manufactures.

   (d) In this model, what effect does globalization have on child labor? Explain. (If you can interpret in terms of income and substitution effects, all the better.)

3. Now, repeat Question 2, but with the following different assumption on preferences. If we denote goods consumption by G and leisure by L, assume that the household's preferences are such that the marginal rate of substitution between labor and leisure (or the marginal utility of leisure divided by the marginal utility of goods consumption) is equal to G/L. (This is another way of saying that the utility function is Cobb-Douglas with equal weights on goods and leisure.)

   (a) Suppose that the price of rice is equal to 1. How much total labor is done by the household? How much child labor? Illustrate using a diagram with the household's budget line and indifference curve at the optimum.

   (b) Now, suppose that the price of rice is equal to 1.5, because rice is an export good and the cost of shipping the rice abroad has fallen. Repeat the analysis in part (a).

   (c) Now, repeat for a household that makes manufactures.

   (d) In this model, what effect does globalization have on child labor? Explain. (If you can interpret in terms of income and substitution effects, all the better.)

4. Consider the theory of democratization described in Section 14.3.2. In the world economy described in Question 2 of Chapter 6, with the United States, China, and Colombia, suppose that initially Colombia is ruled by an autocratic regime. What would then be the effect of opening up trade in Colombia on Colombian democratization (a) if China has not opened up to trade; and (b) if China has opened up to trade? Explain.

5. Think of the idea explored by some researchers, summarized in Section 14.3.4, that increased competition through trade can reduce employment discrimination. Specifically, assume that some employers are prejudiced against women and are willing to give up some profit in order to avoid hiring them, agreeing to hire a woman only if the wage is sufficiently lower than a man's wage. On the other hand, if a firm is barely breaking even, an employer places a higher priority on making a profit and less on indulging his prejudices, and will be willing to hire more women. Assume that the industry in question is

monopolistically competitive, and do the following two questions without math, following the economic logic of the models.

(a) Suppose that all employers are equally prejudiced, but as in the Melitz model discussed in Section 3.5, they differ in their productivity. Which firms do you think are going to be most willing to hire women in equilibrium? What will the equilibrium look like?

How will international trade affect the pattern of discrimination?

(b) Now, answer the same question under the assumption that different employers are all equally productive but differ in their degree of prejudice, and consequently in their willingness to hire women. Explain how your answers change from the previous assumption, and why.

REFERENCES

Acemoğlu, Daron, and James A. Robinson (2005). *Economic Origins of Dictatorship and Democracy.* Cambridge, UK: Cambridge University Press.

Barboza, David (2008). "Child Labor Rings Reach China's Distant Villages." *The New York Times*, May 10, p. A5.

Basu, Kaushik (1999). "Child Labor: Cause, Consequence, and Cure, with Remarks on International Labor Standards." *Journal of Economic Literature* 37:3 (September 1999), pp. 1083–1119.

Basu, Kaushik, and Pham Hoang Van (1998). "The Economics of Child Labor." *American Economic Review* 88:3, pp. 412–427.

Black, Sandra E., and Brainerd, Elizabeth (2004). "Importing Equality? The Impact of Globalization on Gender Discrimination." *Industrial and Labor Relations Review* 57:4 (July), pp. 540–559.

Blakely, Rhys (2007). "Yahoo! Sued Over Torture of Chinese Dissident." *Times Online*, April 19.

Bradsher, Keith (2002). "Drugs, Terror and Tuna: How Goals Clash." *The New York Times*, May 16, p. A1.

Chang, Leslie T. (2009). *Factory Girls: From Village to City in a Changing China.* New York: Random House.

Collier, Paul, and Anke Hoeffler (1998). "On Economic Causes of Civil War." *Oxford Economic Papers* 50, pp. 563–573.

Desbordes, Rodolphe, and Julien Vauday (2007). "The Political Influence of Foreign Firms in Developing Countries." *Economics and Politics* 19:3 (November), pp. 421–451.

Dias, Elizabeth (2009). "First Blood Diamonds, Now Blood Computers?" *TIME Magazine*, July 25.

Edmonds, Eric V., and Nina Pavcnik (2002). "Does Globalization Increase Child Labor? Evidence from Vietnam." NBER Working Paper W8760 (January).

———— (2005) "Does Globalization Increase Child Labor? Evidence from Vietnam." *Journal of International Economics* 65:2 (March), pp. 401–441.

———— (2006). "International Trade and Child Labor: Cross-Country Evidence." *Journal of International Economics* 68:1 (January), pp. 115–140.

Edmonds, Eric V., Nina Pavcnik, and Petia Topalova (2010). "Trade Adjustment and Human Capital Investment: Evidence from Indian Tariff Reform." *American Economic Journal: Applied Economics* 2:4 (October), pp. 42–75.

———— (2009). "Child Labor and Schooling in a Globalizing World: Some Evidence from Urban India." *Journal of the European Economic Association* 7:2–73 (April), pp. 498–507.

Eichengreen, Barry, and David Leblang (2008). "Democracy and Globalization." *Economics and Politics* 20:3, pp. 289–334.

Fearon, James D. (2005). "Primary Commodity Exports and Civil War." *Journal of Conflict Resolution* 49:4 (August), pp. 483–507.

Forero, Juan (2002). "In Ecuador's Banana Fields, Child Labor Is Key to Profits." *The New York Times*, July 13, p. A8.

Gettleman, Jeffrey (2008). "Rape Victims' Words Help Jolt Congo into Change." *The New York Times*, October 18, p. A1.

Harrison, Ann, and Jason Scorse (2010). "Multinationals and Anti-Sweatshop Activism." *American Economic Review* 100:1 (March), pp. 247–273.

Lipsey, Robert E. (2004). "Home and Host Country Effects of FDI," in Robert E. Baldwin and L. Alan Winters (eds.), *Challenges to Globalization*, pp. 333–379. Chicago: University of Chicago Press.

Lipsey, Robert E., and Fredrik Sjöholm (2006). "Foreign Firms and Indonesian Manufacturing Wages: An Analysis with Panel Data." *Economic Development and Cultural Change* 55:1 (October), pp. 201–221.

López-Córdova, J. Ernesto, and Meissner, Christopher M. (2008). "The Impact of International Trade on Democracy: A Long-Run Perspective". *World Politics* 60:4, pp. 539–575.

Mammen, Kristin, and Christina Paxson (2000). "Women's Work and Economic Development." *Journal of Economic Perspectives* 14:4 (Fall), pp. 141–164.

Miguel, Edward, Shanker Satyanath, and Ernest Sergenti (2004). "Economic Shocks and Civil Conflict: An Instrumental Variables Approach." *Journal of Political Economy* 112:4, pp. 725–753.

Milner, Chris, and Peter Wright (1998). "Modelling Labour Market Adjustment to Trade Liberalization in an Industrializing Economy." *Economic Journal* 108 (March), pp. 509–528.

National Labor Committee (2009). *High Tech Misery in China: The Dehumanization of Young Workers Producing Our Computer Keyboards. Dongguan Meitai Plastics & Electronics Factory.* Pittsburgh, PA: National Labor Committee.

Off, Carol (2006). *Bitter Chocolate: The Dark Side of the World Most Seductive Sweet.* New York: The New Press.

Paczkowski, John (2009). "Eve Ensler Calls for Rape-Free Cellphones." *All Things Digital website*, May 27, at http://allthingsd.com.

Pavcnik, Nina, and Eric Edmonds (2006). "International Trade and Child Labor: Cross Country Evidence." *Journal of International Economics* 68:1 (January), pp. 115–140.

Renner, Michael (2002). *The Anatomy of Resource Wars.* Worldwatch Paper 162 (October), Worldwatch Institute, Washington, DC.

Romero, Simon (2009). "Protesters Gird for Long Fight over Opening Peru's Amazon." *The New York Times*, June 11.

Rosenberg, Tina (2002). "John Kamm Third Way." *The New York Times Magazine* (March 3), p. 58.

Rosendorff, B.P. (2000). "Choosing Democracy." *Economics and Politics* 13:1 (October), pp. 1–29.

Ross, Michael (2004). "How Does Natural Resource Wealth Influence Civil Wars? Evidence from Thirteen Cases," *International Organization* 58 (Winter), pp. 35–67.

Seidman, Gay W. (2007). *Beyond the Boycott: Labor Rights, Human Rights, and Transnational Activism.* New York: Russell Sage Foundation.

Timmerman, Kelsey (2009). *Where Am I Wearing? A Global Tour to the Countries, Factories, and People that Make Our Clothes.* Hoboken, NJ: John Wiley and Sons.

Usborne, David (2009). "Shell Settles Nigerian Human Rights Abuses Lawsuit for $15.5m." *The Independent,* June 9, p. 24.

Is NAFTA a Betrayal of the Poor or a Path to Prosperity?

15

Workers at a factory in Irapuato, Mexico, put finishing touches on bluejeans to give them a rugged, worn look.

Jonathan Tobin/Flickr/Getty Images, Inc.

15.1 A Competition: Who Hates NAFTA the Most?

February 2008 offered a striking example of the politics of international trade policy. As the presidential election in the United States geared up, Senators Hillary Clinton and Barack Obama competed for the Democratic Party nomination, campaigning in Ohio in anticipation of that state's primary voting at the beginning of March. (The Republican nomination had already been wrapped up by Senator John McCain.) A central issue of the campaigning by both candidates was a piece of trade policy—the North American Free Trade Agreement (NAFTA), signed by the governments of the United States, Mexico, and Canada in 1993.

NAFTA was a move toward closer integration between the three North American economies, which had already become closely intertwined. The Canada-U.S. Auto Pact of 1965 that created free trade in autos and parts between those two countries has already been discussed in Chapter 3, and the

Canada-U.S. Free-Trade Agreement (CUFTA) of 1988 had provided for duty-free treatment for essentially all other trade between the two countries. At the same time, U.S. manufacturers had made heavy use of *maquiladoras* in Mexico, which were factories in designated areas where Mexican workers would do assembly work for export back to the United States.[1] At the time of the agreement, Canada was the largest source of imports to the United States and the largest buyer of exports from the United States, while on both counts Mexico was the third-largest (after Japan). Thus, by the time NAFTA was signed, North American economies were already highly integrated, and the agreement made them more so by eliminating tariffs between the three countries following a negotiated schedule. It does seem to have had an effect on trade patterns: From 1990 to 2000, the Mexican share of U.S. imports and exports doubled.[2]

Despite that fact that the agreement had been signed by a president of the same party (Bill Clinton—indeed, married to one of the candidates), and ratified by a Congress of the same party, both Democratic candidates competed to outdo each other in expressing disapproval of the agreement and a commitment to undoing its alleged damage. After noting that the agreement does not "put food on the table," candidate Obama declared that workers in Ohio had "watched job after job after job disappear because of bad trade deals like Nafta," and candidate Clinton claimed that she had tried but failed to convince her husband not to support the agreement when he was president and that she would renegotiate it as president (Leonhardt, 2008). A major political dust-up occurred when a rumor arose that a top Obama adviser had secretly assured the Canadian government that Obama would not abrogate the agreement as president (Austen, 2008).

This political theater reflected the fact that the agreement was extremely unpopular in Ohio, blamed by many voters for the loss of jobs the state had suffered in recent years. More generally, the agreement had been divisive from the beginning, generating intense populist opposition from those who believed it would reduce American employment and wages. This stance was exemplified by the presidential candidacy of Ross Perot, who in a presidential debate in Richmond, Virginia, in 1992, famously declared that the consequences for American workers would be dire:

> If you're paying $12, $13, $14 an hour for factory workers, and you can move your factory south of the border, pay $1 an hour for labor. . . . have no health care—that's the most expensive single element in making a car—have no environmental controls, no pollution controls and no retirement and you don't care about anything but making money, there will be a giant sucking sound going south. (Associated Press, October 15, 1992)

---

[1] Maquiladora plants had the right to import materials duty-free into Mexico provided they were used only for assembly for export. The finished goods shipped to the United States were charged tariffs only on the maquiladora value-added. See Hufbauer and Schott (2005, pp. 103–105), for example.

[2] Canada's share of U.S. imports and exports barely changed, however, likely because trade between those two countries was already duty free due to the CUFTA. From 1990 to 2000, Canada's share of U.S. imports went from 18.42 to 18.84%, and its share of U.S. exports went from 21.11 to 22.61%. Over the same period, Mexico's share of U.S. imports went from 6.08 to 11.17%, and its share of U.S. exports went from 7.22 to 14.32%. Figures are from www.usitc.gov.

Perot's formulation of the "giant sucking sound" became the catchphrase for years for opponents of the agreement. His subsequent opposition gained him many supporters as well as detractors, and it is striking that more than a decade after it went into effect, the agreement remains a potent political issue, and extremely divisive. This chapter will attempt to evaluate the agreement and others like it in the light of economic theory and the evidence that has been amassed since 1994.[3] First, it will be necessary to understand some points of basic theory, which will be addressed in the following section.

15.2 Preferential Trade Agreements: Background and Key Principles

NAFTA is an example of a preferential trade agreement (PTA), or an agreement that lowers trade barriers between signatories of the agreement but not between them and others. For example, NAFTA guarantees that an American importer can bring Mexican strawberries or Canadian lumber into the United States without paying import tariffs, but it does not provide for tariff-free import of Guatamalan strawberries or Brazilian lumber into the United States. The preferential—or, in blunter terms, discriminatory—nature of these agreements is crucial. These agreements are sometimes called regional trade agreements because most of them are signed between adjacent countries, but PTA is a more accurate term since there are plenty of such agreements signed between countries that are quite far apart from each other, such as the U.S.-Israel Free Trade Agreement (entered 1985) and the European Union-South Africa Free Trade Agreement (entered 2000).[4]

15.2.1 Types of Agreement

PTAs come in a variety of forms. The most important division is between free-trade agreements and customs unions. A *free-trade agreement* is an agreement that eliminates trade barriers on substantially all trade between two or more countries without coordinating their trade policies toward other countries. A *customs union* is a free-trade agreement that stipulates a *common external tariff* (CET), or a set of tariffs on imports from nonmember countries that is the same regardless of which member country is importing the product in question. For example, NAFTA is, as the name suggests, a free-trade agreement. It does not require that the three member countries impose the same tariffs on nonmember countries. Indeed, as discussed in Chapter 7, the United States persistently maintains much higher tariffs on sugar than Canada or Mexico does. The tariff schedules for the three member countries on non-NAFTA country goods remain very different, even though NAFTA has virtually eliminated tariffs between the NAFTA countries. Other important free-trade agreements are the ASEAN Free Trade Area, comprising Southeast Asian member countries; the Dominican Republic-United States-Central America Free Trade Agreement, known as CAFTA-DR, signed in 2004; and the New-Zealand-Australia Free Trade Agreement (NZAFTA) from 1965.

---

[3] Since Canada and the United States already had a free-trade agreement in place and Canada-Mexico trade is still fairly small, the agreement does not seem to have had much effect on Canada, and so most of our analysis will focus on the United States and Mexico. An exception is Section 15.5, on dispute mechanisms.
[4] See Freund and Orñelas (2010) for an exhaustive review of research on PTAs.

An important difference between free-trade agreements and customs unions is that free-trade agreements always come with a set of negotiated *rules of origin*. The idea of these rules is as follows: Suppose that Country A, with high tariffs on a particular good, signs a free-trade agreement with Country B, which has low tariffs on that good. An exporter of this good in Country C, which is not party to the free-trade agreement, will have an incentive to find some way to get his or her product considered to be made in Country B, because then it can be shipped to Country A duty-free. For example, a manufacturer of shoes might export shoes without laces to Country B, paying the low tariff; hire some workers in Country B to add laces to the shoes; and then stick a "Made in Country B" sticker on the boxes and ship them duty-free to Country A, to be sold to Country A consumers. This would defeat the purpose of Country A's high tariff. In effect, Country A's tariff would be the low, Country B tariff, except that the Country A government would derive no revenue from it. In order to prevent this outcome, negotiators for free-trade agreements negotiate rules on just how much Country B content must be present for a given product in order to be able to earn the Made in Country B sticker for the purposes of the agreement. These rules are what is referred to as *rules of origin*. Clearly, they do not have the same relevance in customs unions, since all countries in a customs union have the same tariff.

The most important customs union is the European Union (EU), formed initially with six countries by the Treaty of Rome in 1957, which maintains zero tariffs between its 27 member countries and a CET on imports from the rest of the world. For example, a raincoat produced in Thailand will be charged exactly the same tariff if it is imported into the United Kingdom, Spain, or Germany, all members of the EU. It can then be shipped tariff-free between those three countries. Another important customs union is the MERCOSUR (a Spanish-language acronym for the Common Market of the South), whose members are Brazil, Argentina, Uruguay, and Paraguay and which was formed in 1991 by the Treaty of Asunción. The oldest customs union is the Southern Africa Customs Union (SACU), formed in 1910, whose members are Botswana, Lesotho, Namibia, Swaziland, and South Africa. The Andean Pact, formed in 1992 between Bolivia, Colombia, Ecuador, and Peru, has moved steadily in the direction of a customs union.

Henceforth the term *PTA* will refer to free-trade agreements and customs unions. Additional degrees of integration are possible. A group of countries that shares a common currency and that therefore has a common monetary policy is called a *monetary union*, and a monetary union that is also a customs union and has a unified economic policy more broadly including free movement of factors between members is called an *economic union*. The most prominent example of a monetary union is the European Monetary Union, a subset of EU countries that share the euro; the EU itself is evolving in the direction of an economic union but has not made it all the way. Here we will restrict attention to the more modest forms of integration, as embodied by free-trade agreements and customs unions.

15.2.2 Article XXIV

As mentioned in Chapter 8, PTAs are permitted as an exception to the most-favored-nation (MFN) principle under Article XXIV of the GATT, provided that some requirements are met. The main requirements are as follows.

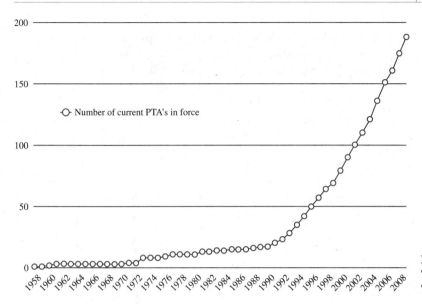

FIGURE 15.1
The Rise of Preferential
Trade Agreements.

1. The agreement should not raise trade barriers on countries that are not members of the PTA (Article XXIV, section 5(a)).

2. The agreement should eliminate trade barriers on all trade between members of the PTA within a specified time horizon (sections 7 and 8).

3. The PTA needs to be reported to GATT signatories and approved by them as consistent with the requirements of Article XXIV.

Because of the third requirement, the WTO has a list of essentially all PTAs in existence. Figure 15.1 shows how they have accumulated over time. For each year from 1958 to the present, one point in the plot shows how many of the PTAs were in force as of that date (of all of the PTAs in existence as of the end of 2009). Note the very sharp acceleration in recent years: Of the 188 PTAs currently in force, 119 have been signed since 2000, and there are many more on the way.[5] Clearly, preferential trade liberalization has surged as a very important force in international trade-policy setting, alongside the multilateral GATT/WTO process (indeed, some would say, eclipsing it).

15.3 The Classic Trade-off: Trade Creation and Trade Diversion

Is this surge in preferential trade liberalization a positive thing? Analyzing this question brings up all of the issues discussed in analyzing the effects of trade in previous chapters. Breaking down trade barriers can allow for national real income to increase due to: efficiency gains as countries specialize along the lines of comparative advantage and avoid the production and consumption

---

[5] The chronology of PTAs used here comes from the Regional Trade Agreements Database on the WTO's website, www.wto.org. Agreements listed as accessions have not been included, on grounds that those indicate expansion of an existing trade block, rather than creation of a new one. Annulled or disbanded PTAs are not included.

distortions of tariffs (Chapters 2 and 6); the rationalization benefits of concentrating the production of each product in one location to reap the benefits of increasing returns to scale (Chapter 3); the benefits of increased competition (Chapter 4), the winnowing-out of less productive firms (Chapter 3); and the increase in product diversity available to each consumer (Chapter 3). At the same time, reductions in trade barriers can have perverse efficiency effects in oligopolistic settings, creating incentives for rent-seeking behavior (Chapter 4), and in settings with learning spillovers, where an industry that is too small in autarky can shrink even further under trade (Chapter 9). Add to this list the distributional issues that trade can create, so that some groups may lose out even if their economy as a whole benefits (Chapters 5 and 6). All of these issues apply to the analysis of PTAs as well as to multilateral trade liberalization.

Because they are *preferential* liberalizations, PTAs also create new issues, pioneered most famously by Jacob Viner (1950). Viner pointed out that PTAs not only reduce trade barriers between member countries, but also introduce a discrepancy in the tariffs between member countries and nonmember countries. Therefore, they can result not only in *trade creation*, but also in *trade diversion*, as the discriminatory tariffs applied to nonmember countries prevent more efficient suppliers in nonmember countries from supplying members of the PTA, substituting less efficient suppliers from inside the PTA. Figure 15.2 shows how this mechanism can work.

Suppose that the United States consumes bluejeans but does not produce them. Suppose that all producers and consumers in this market take price as given and that the industry is small enough in GDP and in consumers' budget sets that we can use partial-equilibrium analysis. The downward-sloping curve in the figure shows the U.S. consumer demand curve for bluejeans. Assume that bluejeans can be produced in Mexico for a constant marginal cost of P^{MEX} and that they can also be bought on the world market for a price of $P^W < P^{MEX}$. Assume that both the United States and Mexico are small

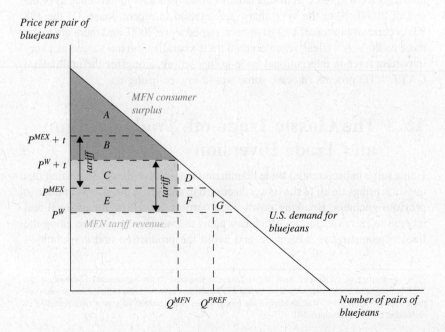

FIGURE 15.2
The Effect of a
Preferential Tariff
Reduction.

compared to the world market for bluejeans, so that P^W can be taken as given. Since the marginal cost of producing bluejeans in Mexico is determined only by factor prices in Mexico, which are not affected by the bluejeans market, we can also take P^{MEX} as given.

Suppose that initially the United States has a tariff of t dollars per unit on all imports of bluejeans—a most-favored-nation (MFN) tariff, which, as can be recalled from Chapter 8, simply means a tariff that applies equally to imports from all WTO members. Then, to import a pair of bluejeans from Mexico would require paying $P^{MEX} + t$, and importing it from the rest of the world would require paying $P^W + t$, which is less than $P^{MEX} + t$. Therefore, U.S. consumers will import bluejeans only from the rest of the world, and the cost of procuring them from Mexico will be irrelevant. American consumers import and consume Q^{MFN} pairs of bluejeans, realizing consumer surplus equal to area $A + B$. Tariff revenue is equal to the tariff per pair of jeans, t, times the quantity imported, Q^{MFN}, or area $C + E$.

Now, consider a preferential liberalization: Suppose that the United States eliminates its tariff on Mexican bluejeans, but not on bluejeans from any other country. Now, it will cost only P^{MEX} to import a pair of bluejeans from Mexico, while it still costs $P^W + t$ to import them from the rest of the world. If the prices are as shown in the figure (with the gap between P^W and P^{MEX} not too big), it will now be cheaper for an American consumer to import from Mexico. Now, American consumers import and consume Q^{PREF} pairs of bluejeans, enjoying consumer surplus equal to area $A + B + C + D$. The U.S. government now receives no tariff revenue, since all of the bluejeans are imported tariff-free from Mexico.

U.S. social welfare under MFN was equal to $A + B + C + E$, while with preferential liberalization it is equal to $A + B + C + D$. The change is $D − E$ and is shown in Figure 15.3. Area D is called the *gains from trade creation*. To understand this figure, note that under the MFN tariff, the United States suffered the welfare loss $D + F + G$, which, using the language of Chapter 7, is

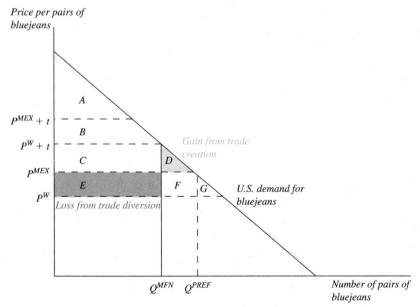

FIGURE 15.3
Trade Creation and
Trade Diversion.

the consumption distortion due to the bluejeans consumption discouraged by the tariff. (In this simple case there is no production distortion because by assumption there is no domestic production, and there is no terms-of-trade benefit because we are assuming that the United States takes the world price of bluejeans as given.) A portion of that consumption distortion is removed by the preferential liberalization, as consumption increases from Q^{MFN} to Q^{PREF}, and this benefit is exactly D. Area E, on the other hand, is called the *loss from trade diversion*. This is the effect that Viner brought to the attention of economists and that is found only in *preferential* liberalization: It is the increase in cost per unit due to switching from the low-cost rest-of-world supply to the high-cost Mexican supply (in other words, the difference between P^W and P^{MEX}), times the amount imported. In other words, the loss from trade diversion is the inefficiency resulting from the way the tariff now discriminates in favor of Mexican production, and thus encourages import from a high-cost source instead of a low-cost source. In this example, clearly $E > D$, so trade diversion is greater than trade creation, and the United States is worse off because of the tariff preference. In general, it could go either way, and so the welfare effect of a PTA is an empirical question.

Measuring the welfare effects of trade creation and diversion is tricky. One influential approach was developed by Krishna (2003). He analyzed a simple three-country model with perfect competition, in which each country produces a single good, and all three goods are consumed in each country. Krishna shows that a reduction in Country 1's tariff to Country 2, holding Country 1's tariff against Country 3 constant, will increase Country 1's welfare if and only if

$$t^{21}\Delta m^{21} + t^{31}\Delta m^{31} \tag{15.1}$$

is positive, where t^{ij} is the (initial) *ad valorem* tariff imposed by country j on goods from country i, m^{ij} is the value (at world prices) of goods that country j imports from country i, and Δm^{ij} is the change in that import value due to the preferential tariff reduction. Conversely, if the expression in (15.1) takes a negative value, the preferential tariff reduction will lower Country 1's welfare. Usually, $\Delta m^{21} > 0$, since the tariff reduction makes Country 2 goods cheaper for Country 1 consumers, but $\Delta m^{31} < 0$, since Country 1 consumers substitute away from Country 3 goods toward Country 2 goods as the latter become cheaper. Krishna's finding simply says that if the sum of a country's total imports, *as weighted by the appropriate initial tariffs*, goes up, then the effect of trade creation dominates the effect of trade diversion.

Krishna estimated the value of (15.1) for a wide range of U.S. trade partners to see with which countries the United States could benefit from preferential liberalization, and found that in the majority of cases, expression (15.1) was positive, indicating that trade creation dominates trade diversion. In addition, there was no tendency for nearer countries or countries with larger U.S. trade volumes to be the ones most beneficial to the United States, suggesting that in evaluating NAFTA the physical closeness of the three countries together with their high mutual trade shares noted in Section 15.1 do not make an argument in favor of the agreement.

The Krishna study is a look at big patterns in the welfare effects of PTAs, rather than a detailed study of NAFTA. To return to NAFTA, was *that* agreement primarily trade-creating, or did it also introduce distortions through trade diversion? Early reports on this question were encouraging. For example,

Gould (1998) showed that after the agreement went into force in 1994, U.S. trade with Mexico was substantially higher than would have been predicted on the basis of past trends (taking into account the severe Mexican recession of 1995). This trade creation is not surprising and would be predicted by any model of PTAs. However, he also showed that U.S. trade with *non*-NAFTA countries was *also* higher following 1994 than would have been predicted from past trends. This is the opposite of what would be expected if NAFTA were significantly trade-diverting. Thus, early trends were encouraging that NAFTA had little or no trade-diverting effects, and thus positive effects overall.

Subsequent work, such as Fukao et al. (2003) and Romalis (2007), has forced a revision of this view. Romalis (2007) points out that one reason U.S. trade with non-NAFTA countries may have grown is the expansion of exports from China and Southeast Asia over that period—which had nothing to do with NAFTA. To control for this effect, Romalis suggests using the EU, which had the same Asian import shock, as a point of comparison.[6] Using very detailed data on narrowly defined industries, Romalis shows that for industries for which the U.S. tariff on Mexican goods fell the most, Mexico's share of U.S. imports rose the most (relative to Mexico's share of EU imports of the same good). The correlation is very strong, indicating that the source of supply for U.S. imports is highly sensitive to the tariff preference that NAFTA gives to NAFTA countries. This suggests that trade diversion was substantial. Putting his estimates into a general-equilibrium model, Romalis concludes that the welfare effects of trade diversion and trade creation just about cancel each other out (or $D = E$ in Figure 15.3), so that the United States did not gain or lose significantly from the agreement. Mexico is estimated to have suffered a small welfare loss from NAFTA.

Thus, the net effects of the agreement on aggregate welfare are probably small, as it introduced distortions similar in size to the distortions it reduced.

15.4 Distributional Concerns

15.4.1 U.S. Workers

Aside from aggregate welfare, it is important to ask what the effect of the agreement is on workers, particularly blue-collar workers. This is a contentious area. There is no doubt that the greater integration with the Mexican economy has hurt some U.S. workers. For example, Youngstown Steel Door in Youngstown, Ohio, was, for much of the twentieth century, one of the largest manufacturers of doors for railway boxcars in the United States. In 2005, the factory closed down, and some of its capital was relocated to Mexico to begin production there. Although it is difficult to speculate on what would have happened to the plant without NAFTA, the existence of the agreement certainly is an encouragement to such moves, and residents of Youngstown do blame it for much of the city's decline and hardship in recent years.[7]

---

[6] The idea is similar to using a control group in a medical study. The treatment group receives the drug or therapy being tested, while the control group does not, and the difference in outcome for the two groups is used to measure the effect of the treatment on health. In the Romalis study, the "treatment" is NAFTA, the "treatment group" is made up of the North American economies, and the "control group" is made up of the European economies.

[7] See Leonhardt (2008), Canada NewsWire, March 11, 2004: "Global Railway to Acquire Manufacturing Assets of Ohio-Based Railway Supplier, YSD Industries, Inc.," and Canada NewsWire, December 6, 2005: "Global Railway Closes on Sale of YSD Subsidiary's Land and Building."

At the same time, some U.S. workers have enjoyed a great surge in opportunity due to NAFTA. For example, the border town of Laredo, Texas, saw a huge boom in employment following NAFTA, as the volume of cargo passing through the town to and from Mexico doubled in just a few years. Jobs grew rapidly in the transportation sector and in services such as motels and restaurants to support truckers and related personnel. Per capita income in the town doubled over the 1990s, along with problems related to noise and congestion (Duggan, 1999). Texas more generally has benefited greatly by exports to Mexico, particularly in electronics, chemicals, and transportation equipment (Kumar, 2006).

But individual examples do not tell what the effect of the agreement was on workers in the aggregate; data are required to make that evaluation. Here the evidence points in different directions. First, note that during the second half of the 1990s, as NAFTA came into effect and trade between Mexico and the United States grew very quickly, U.S. median and blue-collar wages grew quite robustly, more than they have for a quarter century (see Section 6.1). This does not prove anything about causation, but it does set up a hurdle for those who argue that NAFTA hurt U.S. blue-collar workers as a whole. It is difficult to estimate the effects of NAFTA on average wages or employment levels econometrically because of the difficulty in extracting the effect of NAFTA from other effects, but studies based on simulation of computer models predict small effects on average U.S. wages (see Burfisher et al., 2001).

The data are more revealing about the effect of NAFTA on wage *inequality*. In Chapter 11, we have already noted Feenstra and Hanson's (1996) findings that offshoring to Mexico raised wage inequality on both sides of the border by increasing the premium paid to skilled workers. Since offshoring to Mexico increased rapidly following NAFTA, this suggests that NAFTA probably promoted rising wage inequality. Once again, this example says nothing about whether the wages of low-skilled workers were increased or decreased by NAFTA in absolute terms. One optimistic piece of evidence on that question, emanating from data on individual firms, is supplied by Sethupathy (2009). He shows that over the period in which NAFTA came into force U.S. firms that already were offshoring to Mexico significantly increased their offshoring to Mexico; their operating profits per U.S. worker; and the wages they paid to their U.S workers—without, apparently, reducing their U.S. workforce. This seems to suggest that the offshoring promoted by NAFTA benefited U.S. workers, in a manner similar to the Grossman and Rossi-Hansberg (2008) model discussed in Chapter 11. Offshoring to Mexico seems to have conferred productivity benefits, some portion of which was captured by U.S. workers in the offshoring firms.

In contrast, Hakobyan and McLaren (2010) argue that a sizable minority of U.S. workers suffered substantial reductions in income from NAFTA. The study defines an industry as "vulnerable to NAFTA" if it initially had a substantial tariff against imports from Mexico and if Mexico was a net exporter of that industry's products. Looking at U.S. Census data from 1990 and 2000, the authors show that after controlling for a wide range of personal characteristics, workers without a college degree employed in industries that were particularly vulnerable to NAFTA had substantially lower wage growth than workers in other industries. For the most extreme cases, high school dropouts in the most vulnerable industry (footwear), wage growth over the 1990s is estimated to be 17 percentage points lower than for similar workers in an industry that was not vulnerable (such as a nontraded service industry). Such a decline would be devastating to a worker who is already managing on a low income, as high school dropouts generally are.

The conclusion is that it is hard to make a case that NAFTA injured U.S. workers on the whole, but there appear to have been important income distribution effects. The agreement likely increased the spread in incomes between highly educated and less educated U.S. workers, increased the incomes of employees of multinationals, and substantially lowered the incomes of blue-collar workers in the most NAFTA-vulnerable industries.

15.4.2 The Mexican Poor

Of course, NAFTA did not affect only Americans. It is also important to try to assess its effect on people in Mexico, and particularly on the Mexican poor. This subject is a source of passionate debate. Supporters of the agreement argued that it would reduce poverty in Mexico as well as illegal immigration to the United States by providing manufacturing jobs in Mexico. Opponents argued that it would flood Mexico with cheap U.S. corn, produced under generous subsidies that make it artificially cheap, and thus destroy the livelihoods of poor farmers who depend on corn as their primary crop. For example, Oxfam (2003) documents a dramatic surge in corn exports from the United States to Mexico in the years following NAFTA implementation, together with a 70% drop in prices for corn within Mexico. Anger at falling corn prices has triggered political activism among Mexican corn farmers, and one farmer told Oxfam: "While the price of corn has fallen, the cost of producing it has hit the roof. We no longer have enough for our family" (Oxfam, 2003, p. 5).

The claim that NAFTA has worsened poverty in Mexico through cheap corn has been challenged by some statistical studies, however. For example, McMillan et al. (2007) studied worker-level and household-level data and concluded that the vast majority of poor corn farmers in Mexico did not sell corn, implying either that they did not participate in the market (in which case the drop in corn prices would not affect them) or that they were net purchasers of corn (in which case the price drop would help them). Thus, McMillan et al.'s results suggest that poor corn farmers were at least as likely to benefit from NAFTA as to be hurt by it.[8]

A pair of studies by Prina (2009, a, b) also ask whether or not NAFTA did cause widespread hardship in the agricultural sector in Mexico. The studies focus on the role of the "border prices" for agricultural commodities in the Mexican economy—that is, the price received by a Mexican exporter or paid by a Mexican importer (inclusive of tariffs) if that importer or exporter is located right at the border with the United States. (This can be quite different from prices in the rest of the country because of transport costs within Mexico.) Prina (2009a) makes three points. First, the changes in tariffs that were specified in NAFTA are correlated with changes in the border prices for corn, fruits, and vegetables in exactly the way that a simple model would

[8] The full picture is more complex than this. The income of poor and middle-income corn farmers did fall over the 1990s, with the loss partly made up for by increased government transfers, while the income of high-income corn farmers rose (pp. 225–227). Whether these changes were caused by NAFTA or by other forces is not clear.

predict, such as the model of Chapter 7, Section 7.2.2. Specifically, it appears that the Mexican government's phase-out of its tariffs on U.S. corn significantly reduced the price Mexicans in the northern end of the country pay for corn, and the U.S. government's phase-out of tariffs on fruits and vegetables imported from Mexico significantly increased the price received by Mexican producers of those commodities, much as is shown in Figure 7.5: A tariff raises the price of the commodity in the importing country and lowers it in the exporting country. Second, a drop in the border price of corn is correlated with a drop in farm profits but a proportionally *larger* drop in the profits of *larger* farms, suggesting that the farms heavily invested in corn tend to be large. By contrast, a rise in the border price of fruits and vegetables is correlated with a rise in farm profits, but a proportionally *larger* rise in the profits of *smaller* farms. Thus, within the farming sector the distributional effects of NAFTA have been somewhat progressive: Cheap U.S. corn has disproportionately hurt large farmers, and opening the U.S. market to fruit and vegetable exports has disproportionately benefited small farmers. Finally, there is no evidence of any effect in the south of Mexico, suggesting that the transport costs required to ship commodities to and from the U.S. border are great enough that U.S. trade policy is roughly irrelevant to farms in that region. Recall that Oxfam singled out the poor farmers in the south as having been particularly hard hit by low corn prices; it may be that for them, NAFTA itself is not the culprit because the south is just not well integrated into the rest of the North American economy.

The other study, Prina (2009b), looks at wages and employment in rural Mexico following NAFTA. A worry for many observers has been that not only would farmers be hurt by cheap U.S. corn, but that landless laborers would see their wages fall, as demand for labor from hard-hit corn farms would fall. However, Prina finds no effect of border prices for agricultural commodities on rural wages, suggesting that perhaps labor is mobile enough that the response is found in movement of labor rather than a drop in the local wage.

Overall, these three studies paint a much more optimistic picture of the effects of NAFTA on rural Mexican poverty than many observers expected. They suggest that price changes driven by NAFTA hurt mainly large farmers, benefited small farmers, and had negligible effects on rural wages and no effect on the impoverished farmers of the south.

A very different approach to the question of NAFTA and Mexican poverty is presented in Hanson (2007), who looks at labor-income data from the Mexican general census of 1990 and 2000. Hanson divides up the country into states with low exposure to globalization and those with high exposure, based on three criteria: The importance of maquiladoras in the state economy; the stock of FDI in the state; and the size of imports relative to state GDP. Hanson finds that, over the decade that saw NAFTA come into being, the poverty rate rose in the "low globalization exposure" states relative to the "high globalization exposure" states. This evidence suggests that NAFTA had a favorable effect on Mexican poverty (although the globalization exposure variable is not limited to NAFTA).

Overall, the data seem to present a much more positive picture of the effect of NAFTA on Mexican poverty than critics had feared. The available evidence is more suggestive of the possibility that NAFTA has helped the poor in Mexico rather than hurt them.

15.5 The Notorious Chapter 11

Perhaps the most bitterly contested feature of NAFTA is only tangentially about trade, and instead—perhaps surprisingly—concerns dispute-settlement procedures. Most of the discussion in the agreement on dispute settlement is dry, lawyerly material on how any of the three governments in the agreement can raise a claim of noncompliance by one of the other two, and how such claims can be settled. Most of it is similar to what is found in other agreements of the type. However, Chapter 11 of NAFTA contains something unusual: provisions for a *corporation* to sue any of the NAFTA governments for violation of that government's commitments under the agreement. In particular, Article 1110 allows a corporation to sue if it believes that it has experienced either expropriation or government conduct "*tantamount* to nationalization or expropriation" (italics added). That latter phrase – "tantamount to expropriation"—is a key to the problem. Article 1110 not only offers corporations redress in case a government actually nationalizes its productive facilities—which is not unknown in the history of Latin America and so could be a worry for investors in Mexico—but it also allows the corporations to sue in the event that a government takes an action that could be interpreted as *similar* to expropriation. In the broadest possible interpretation, this could include any regulation or policy change that reduces the firm's profits. (See Hufbauer and Schott, 2005, pp. 201–207) for a detailed account.

The negotiators who wrote NAFTA apparently intended to encourage investment by allaying fears of opportunistic behavior by governments, particularly the Mexican government, which had been somewhat hostile to foreign direct investment in the past but had reduced barriers to multinationals in recent years. The provisions in Chapter 11 could go a long way toward convincing corporations not to fear a reversal of this new openness in the future. However, by writing 1110 with such broad language, the negotiators opened the door to aggressive attacks on a wide range of policies, particularly environmental policies, that would not otherwise be expected to be endangered by a trade agreement. (Of course, the true intentions of the negotiators is known only to them, and many critics of NAFTA question whether these effects were inadvertent or intentional.)

An early indication of what these provisions might do was the case of Metalclad Corporation.[9] Metalclad is an American waste-disposal corporation that had arranged to establish a hazardous-waste-disposal site in the state of San Luis Potosí, Mexico, in 1995. The Mexican government assured the company that it had approval for the project, and the company began work. The company later had to cancel the project when the *state* government declared the site to be an ecological preserve. The company sued under NAFTA article 1110, arguing that this action was tantamount to expropriation, and eventually the Mexican government paid $16 million to settle the suit. This created a stir similar to what followed the dolphin-tuna case under the WTO discussed in Chapter 8: An institution purportedly set up to protect trade was penalizing a country for taking a measure to protect its environment.

Part of what some observers found objectionable is that the panels set up by Chapter 11 had no obligation of transparency. They are not part of any court;

---

[9] See Kass and McCarroll (2008); Hufbauer and Schott (2005, p. 207); and "Eye on Investors, Mexico Pays U.S. Company," *The New York Times*, October 29, 2001.

instead they are set up as tribunals of experts providing binding arbitration, and they are modeled after panels designed to handle contract disputes between firms (see DePalma, 2001, or Kass and McCarroll, 2008). In such panels, the contesting parties can request confidentiality for the proceedings and the evidence. As a result, there is not in general any way the public can scrutinize the proceedings, even though with Chapter 11 panels, one of the contesting parties is a government and the issue in contention is a matter of public policy such as an environmental regulation.[10] In the view of the head of one watchdog group, "What we're talking about here is secret government. . . . This is not the way to do the public's business" (DePalma, 2001).

Another case that raised many of the same issues arose in 1997, when the Canadian government considered banning the gasoline additive MMT, produced by the Ethyl Corporation of Richmond, Virginia (Brown, 2004, pp. 166–168). The Canadian government had become concerned about the possible health effects of the additive, but when legislation was proposed to ban it, Ethyl sued under NAFTA Article 1110, citing lost profits from the inability to sell in Canada, plus damage to its reputation from the proposed ban. The Canadian government settled without waiting for the panel's decision, abandoning the ban and also paying Ethyl Corporation $13 million. Once again, a corporation had trumped an environmental policy through the Chapter 11 procedures. In this case, the victory was more striking than in the Metalclad case because the suit not only provided payment of compensation, but reversed the policy decision as well.

A third case, however, may indicate a changing tide. Methanex is a Canadian company that produces a gasoline additive called MTBE, which the government of California has decided to phase out because it is concerned about health effects. The additive has been found in the drinking water supply for Santa Monica, requiring the shutdown of several municipal wells. When the phase-out was announced, Methanex sued under Article 1110, asking for the eye-opening sum of $970 million in compensation. Once again, the argument was that phasing out MTBE was an act "tantamount to expropriation." This time, however, the tribunal ruled against the company, finding that the phase-out had a reasonable scientific basis and was executed under due process in a nondiscriminatory way (Kass and McCarroll, 2008). The California attorney general called the decision "a resounding victory for the rights of Californians to keep their drinking water safe and clean" (*Sacramento Bee*, August 10, 2005, p. D1). More generally, if the logic followed by the Methanex panel is applied more generally, it will be much more difficult for corporations to combat environmental regulations through Article 1110 actions because it will no longer be sufficient to demonstrate harm to the plaintiff from the environmental action.

The parallels with the WTO's struggles with environmental law, detailed in Chapter 8, are clear. The WTO has an interest in protecting trade from reckless environmental actions that impose a cost on trading partners out of proportion to the environmental benefit, and also from protectionism disguised as environmentalism. At the same time, governments need to be able to take action to protect the environment, even if that sometimes interferes with trade. In its

---

[10] A privately maintained website, www.naftaclaims.com, maintains an archive of documents from these panels, but it has no authority to compel any party to provide any documents.

early efforts to balance these two motives, the WTO tended to give little weight to the environment, but perhaps in response to public anger it adjusted the balance over the years. The NAFTA Chapter 11 process is similar, designed to protect foreign direct investment as well as trade per se, but the issues are the same. Early uses of the provisions have been hostile to environmental action, but the system seems to have been evolving in the direction of more balance, as well as becoming more transparent and more open to amicus briefs from nongovernmental organizations (Kass and McCarroll, 2008).

15.6 Some Issues That Affect PTAs More Broadly

Many issues arise in analyzing NAFTA that come up very frequently in discussions of PTAs more generally.

15.6.1 Counting Lost Jobs: A Popular Mismeasurement

Section 15.4 looked at a number of ways of gauging NAFTA's effects on workers. A brief note should be made on one way of measuring these effects that probably should *not* be used. First, a definition: A *trade deficit* is a country's imports minus its exports, and a *bilateral trade deficit* is a country's imports from one particular other country minus its exports to that country. Occasionally, one sees a study that computes the change in the U.S.-Mexico trade deficit following NAFTA, multiplies that by a number of "jobs per dollar of trade deficit," and uses that to produce a number of "U.S. jobs lost due to NAFTA" (if the United States has a trade deficit with Mexico) or "U.S. jobs created by NAFTA" (if the United States has a trade surplus with Mexico). Since in the years following NAFTA U.S. imports from Mexico increased much more than U.S. exports to Mexico, this type of calculation typically leads to a finding that U.S. jobs were lost as a result of NAFTA and results in claims brandished by NAFTA opponents that millions of U.S. jobs were lost as a result. (It is usually not mentioned that this implies millions of job gains in Mexico.) Burfisher et al. (2001, pp. 130–132) provide examples and analysis.

Unfortunately, this calculation has no basis in any real economic logic. A thorough discussion of trade deficits is deferred until Chapter 16, but the point can be made here that there is no necessary connection between a country's trade deficit and that country's domestic demand for labor. What a trade deficit indicates is that investment spending in the country exceeds saving by that country's citizens.[11] A surge in a country's trade deficit could mean that its citizens have decided to reduce their savings or that global investors have suddenly become enthusiastic about investing in that country, and so a surge of investment funds is charging into the country. The former is probably a good interpretation of recent trends in the U.S. trade deficit (but why savings rates have fallen is a matter of debate; see Chapter 16); the latter is a good description of South Korea's surging trade deficit in the 1960s,

---

[11] Briefly, recall the basic national accounts identity from macroeconomics, $Y = C + I + G + X - M$. This can be rewritten as $I - (Y - C) = I - S = M - X$, where Y is national income, $S = Y - C$ is national savings, I is investment, and $M - X$ is the trade deficit. Again, see Chapter 16 for details.

for example. Neither interpretation suggests that a trade agreement is likely to be the cause of the deficit or that the deficit will be a job-killer. (Obviously the second interpretation implies a *boom* in hiring, as occurred in South Korea.)

Moreover, a *bilateral* trade deficit could simply be an indication of comparative advantage. For a simple example, think of a three-good economy, with bluejeans, software, and wine as the three goods. Suppose the United States imports bluejeans from Mexico but exports nothing to Mexico, and Europe imports software from the United States but sells nothing to the United States, while Mexico imports wine from Europe while exporting nothing to Europe. Then the United States has a trade deficit with Mexico and a trade surplus with Europe. The bilateral trade deficit with any one country is not necessarily an indication that anything is wrong—just an indication that a country's foreign suppliers and foreign customers need not all be in the same country.

Readers of this text henceforth have an obligation to speak up when trade-deficit-based arguments about the effects of trade agreements on jobs are floated in public discourse.[12]

15.6.2 National Bargaining-Power Issues

Some objections to PTAs arise from distributional issues *across* partner countries. A pattern pointed out by some observers such as Perroni and Whalley (2000) is that PTAs between a large-country partner and a small one tend to feature trade liberalization paired with small-country concessions to the large on issues such as intellectual property rights. The CAFTA-DR, for example, requires the Latin American signatories to tighten up their copyright law in ways that will help U.S. firms receive royalties on DVDs and music, and provide additional patent protections to help U.S. pharmaceutical firms. The U.S. free-trade agreement with Peru required legislation to help open up natural resources in the interior of the country to U.S. firms, as discussed in Section 14.3.2. This sort of measure is not what would spring to mind for most people at the mention of free trade.

Such an outcome was predicted by Mayer (1981), whose argument can be summarized as follows. Consider bargaining over trade policy by the governments of two countries that are very different in size; say, for the sake of argument, that they are the two economies in the Ricardian model of Chapter 2, but that America is much larger than Nigeria (as in Section 2.6). Given this consideration, the world relative price will always be equal to the American autarky price, and so the Nigerian government will not be able to affect its terms of trade, no matter what it does. This implies that Nigeria will have no terms-of-trade benefit from a tariff, only production and consumption distortions, and so—as with small countries in general—its optimal tariff will be equal to zero (recall Section 7.4.2). As a result, the kind of international tariff bargaining described in Chapter 8, in which each country offers to reduce or eliminate its tariff in return for the other country doing the same, cannot occur; Nigeria's tariff is zero even without bargaining. The only way the small

---

[12] Even our best economists sometimes fall prey to this "trade-deficit-equals-jobs-lost" fallacy. A particularly egregious example, in which a pillar of the field, Paul Krugman, analyzes the U.S. trade deficit with China in exactly these terms, can be found at http://krugman.blogs.nytimes.com/2009/12/31/macroeconomic-effects-of-chinese-mercantilism/. (We humans can only hope we will not be judged on our lowest moments.)

country can persuade the large one to lower its tariff is, then, to offer something else—such as intellectual property rights, a crackdown on pirated DVDs,
restrictions on generic pharmaceuticals, enhanced rights for multinationals,
and so on.

These bargaining-power issues emerge most starkly when the dynamic
adjustment of an economy to trade is taken into account. If an economy
becomes very specialized toward one trade partner over time, and if it is costly
to reorient the economy once that has happened (because of retraining costs,
the cost of retooling capital or redesigning products to appeal to a different
market), then a small economy can have very weak bargaining power relative to a large one once a bilateral trade relationship has been established.
A striking example of this situation is the nineteenth-century relationship
between the independent kingdom of Hawaii and the United States. The U.S.
government wanted to build a naval station at Pearl Harbor, but the Hawaiian
king refused and declared it a nonnegotiable request because the location was
a sacred site for the Hawaiian people. However, after several years of a free-
trade agreement that exempted Hawaii from the high U.S. sugar tariffs, the
Hawaiian economy was completely specialized in sugar, with the United
States as essentially its only market. When the U.S. government threatened to
abrogate the free-trade treaty unless the Kingdom relented on Pearl Harbor, the
King reluctantly agreed, and the naval station was built (see McLaren, 1997,
for details and sources). Large countries can indeed have an enormous bargaining power advantage in trade negotiations with small ones and so can
extract significant nontrade concessions in exchange for a trade deal.

15.6.3 Preferential Agreements and
the Multilateral Process

So far, we have discussed what Jagdish Bhagwati (1993) has called the static
impact effects of NAFTA and similar agreements—namely, what the agreement does to trade flows, prices, and incomes. However, many observers care
at least as much about what he calls the dynamic time-path effect, meaning
the effect that such agreements will have on the process of multilateral trade
liberalization over the long run. Put differently, will "these arrangements more
readily serve as building blocks of, rather than stumbling blocks to, GATT-
wide free trade" (Bhagwati, 1991, p. 77)?

In principle, a case can be made either way. Here are some of the more
prominent theories that have been proposed regarding the effect of PTAs on
the multilateral process. (Recall that a WTO member's *MFN tariff* is the tariff
it charges to other WTO members, other than those with whom it has a preferential agreement—see Chapter 8.) First, consider an optimistic interpretation:

(i) *A building-block theory: Trade diversion as a spur to liberalization.*
Richardson (1994) and Orñelas (2005) both show in very different
models[13] that providing a tariff preference to one country can provide a
strong incentive to reduce tariffs to all other countries, because doing
so reduces the inefficiencies created by trade diversion. For example,

---

[13] Richardson uses a perfectly competitive model with comparative advantage, much like the model of
Chapter 7, while Orñelas uses an oligopolistic model, much like the Cournot model of Chapter 10.

suppose that the U.S. government had set its optimal tariff on sugar, as discussed in Chapter 7, taking into account terms-of-trade effects, production, and consumption distortions, as well as the government's political bias in favor of sugar producers compared with consumers. Now, suppose that as part of NAFTA the U.S. government offers a reduction in sugar tariffs that Mexican exporters need to pay to sell in the United States.[14] To the extent that this causes some substitution of imports from Mexico in place of some cheaper sources of sugar outside of North America, such trade diversion raises the cost of the MFN tariff on sugar at the margin and lowers the optimal MFN tariff from the point of view of the U.S. government. Therefore, *signing a preferential trade agreement can induce a country to lower its MFN tariffs, facilitating multilateral liberalization.*

This is contrasted with a much more cynical and pessimistic interpretation:

(ii) *Stumbling-block theory I: Protecting preferential rents.* Limão (2006) has suggested a reason that preferential agreements can put the brakes on multilateral liberalization. Reducing a tariff against one country's products but not any other country's products creates an income-generating opportunity for the country that receives the tariff reduction. This benefit can be thought of as a preferential rent, similar in character to the quota rent created by a voluntary export restraint (see Chapter 7). The value of this rent is reduced if multilateral tariffs come down. Limão points out that if the preferential rent is part of an implicit bargain between the two countries, with the preference-receiving country providing some noneconomic favor to the preference-granting country in return, then the preference-granting country may now have an incentive to keep its MFN tariffs high in order to keep the tit-for-tat going. For example, under NAFTA, Canadian manufacturers such as the furniture manufacturers discussed in Chapter 3 enjoy duty-free access to the U.S. market. This access is more valuable if that market is protected from, for example, labor-abundant exporters of the Third World, allowing Canadian manufacturers to sell in the United States at high prices. Under the Limão theory, the U.S. government could use this as a bargaining chip, threatening to cancel or renegotiate NAFTA if the Canadian government does not support U.S. foreign policy positions, help enforce U.S. intellectual-property claims, and so forth. This is a more effective threat if the preferences in NAFTA are very valuable—and they are *especially* valuable if the United States is a protected market. Under this story, then, *signing a preferential trade agreement can induce a country to cling to high MFN tariffs to protect preferential rents, grinding multilateral liberalization to a halt.*

Evidence on these two theories is mixed. Estevadeordal et al. (2008) looked at tariffs of Latin American countries from 1991 to 2000 and found a strong pattern. A country that offers a preferential tariff reduction to one country for a given industry tends to lower its MFN tariff for the same

---

[14] The actual effect of NAFTA on Mexican access to the U.S. sugar market is complex and falls far short of full free trade; see Hufbauer and Schott (2005, pp. 315–317).

industry in subsequent years. This is exactly the pattern that would be predicted by the Richardson and Orñelas theories discussed above: Once a preference is in place, it tends to create trade diversion, which makes it attractive to start lowering the MFN tariff to limit the trade diversion. This supports the idea of preferential agreements as building blocks to multilateral trade. On the other hand, Limão (2006) studied U.S. tariffs from the late 1970s to the conclusion of the Uruguay Round of the GATT in 1993−1994 and found evidence for the stumbling-block theory. Specifically, he found that although U.S. MFN tariffs were generally falling over this period, for products that the United States imported from a country with whom the United States had signed a preferential trade agreement in the intervening years, the reduction in tariffs was significantly smaller than average. In particular, the United States cut its MFN tariffs the least on products that it imports from its NAFTA partner countries. This fits nicely with Limão's theory about the incentive to maintain preferential rents. On balance, the jury is still out on the question of whether PTAs do more to hurt or help the multilateral process.

A third theory is more difficult to test, but it could be the most pessimistic of all.

(iii) *Stumbling-block theory II: The self-enforcing prophecy.* One feature of preferential trade liberalization that is clear from watching its history is its self-reinforcing character: When two countries mutually reduce trade barriers, businesses in both countries adapt their products to the other country's markets, becoming more oriented toward each other's markets, thus making trade with the rest of the world relatively less important than it otherwise would be. McLaren (2002) shows that this can result in preferential trade blocks as a self-fulfilling prophecy, to the detriment of world welfare. To see the idea in a simple, stark form, think of a three-country economy in which each country has a comparative advantage in a different good. Suppose that each worker must first choose an industry in which to specialize, which can be thought of as acquiring the training that is needed for that industry, and then after workers have made their decisions on that, governments meet to negotiate whether to pursue preferential trade liberalization, multilateral liberalization, or no liberalization. If everyone expected multilateral free trade, then each worker in each country would choose his or her own country's comparative-advantage industry; all countries would be perfectly specialized; and there would be no resistance to multilateral free trade. On the other hand, if Countries 1 and 2 are expected to form a PTA that excludes Country 3, then some workers in Country 1 will enter Country 1's comparative-advantage industry and some will enter Country 3's industry because Country 3's comparative-advantage good will be expensive in Country 1 under a PTA that excludes Country 3. Similarly, some workers in Country 2 will enter Country 2's comparative-advantage industry, and some will enter Country 3's.

As a result, the expectation of a PTA can *increase* specialization and the potential gains from trade between the countries that are members of the PTA, while *reducing* specialization and the potential gains from trade between the PTA bloc and the rest of the world. But this then is likely to imply an enhanced political demand for the governments to negotiate the PTA and a reduced political demand for governments to negotiate multilateral liberalization. If negotiating trade agreements is difficult and costly, this may mean that the pattern of international specialization induced by the expectation of a PTA creates the conditions that lead to a PTA as the political outcome: It is a self-fulfilling prophecy.

This could help explain both the rise of major trade blocs that divide world trade into big, distinct pieces (such as NAFTA, the EU, MER-COSUR, and ASEAN) and the loss of momentum in the multilateral process, with the Doha Round of the GATT sputtering along limply after several years of attempts. Under this interpretation, even though a given PTA can be advantageous given the economic conditions under which it is negotiated, the existence of the possibility of PTAs puts the world on the wrong path, bypassing multilateral trade and lowering world welfare.

15.7 Conclusion

We can summarize the bottom line on NAFTA roughly as follows. *(i) Regarding aggregate welfare*: Despite early optimism, the most convincing empirical work suggests that the agreement was probably at least as trade-diverting as trade creating, suggesting small and quite possibly negative welfare gains. *(ii) Regarding distributional effects*: It is difficult to find any indication that the agreement harmed U.S. blue-collar workers overall, but it probably raised income inequality and hurt blue-collar workers in a number of industries quite badly. Some evidence suggests that it may have been helpful in reducing poverty rates in Mexico.

Thus, the agreement seems to have fallen far short of the expectations of its supporters, who hoped it would raise welfare in the member countries, and also to have been much more positive in its effects than its critics feared, given its apparent effects on the Mexican poor.

MAIN IDEAS

1. Preferential trade agreements (PTAs) are an important exemption from the most-favored-nation principle of the GATT, sanctioned by Article XXIV of the GATT text.

2. There are two main types of PTA: free-trade agreements, which merely specify free trade between members of the agreement, and customs unions, which take the added step of creating a common external tariff. Rules of origin are important in free-trade agreements, but not in customs unions.

3. PTAs lower trade barriers, but they also introduce a discriminatory element to trade policy, which creates its own distortion. This can lead to losses from trade diversion, as higher-cost sources of supply within the PTA substitute for lower-cost

sources of supply outside of the PTA. These losses from trade diversion must be weighed against the gains from trade creation in evaluating the welfare effects of a PTA.

4. Some observers have theorized that the proliferation of PTAs can help encourage multilateral liberalization because trade diversion acts as an incentive to reduce most-favored-nation (MFN) tariffs.

5. Others argue that PTAs can *inhibit* multilateral liberalization because it can give preference-granting countries an incentive to preserve preferential rents, or because an expectation of PTAs can become a self-fulfilling prophecy, inducing private investments that reinforce regional

patterns of trade. Evidence on these theories is mixed.

6. Dispute-settlement mechanisms matter a great deal in weighing the effect of PTAs. In the case of NAFTA, these mechanisms were set up in a way that appears to have endangered the ability of signatory governments to pass environmental regulation, at least initially.

QUESTIONS AND PROBLEMS

1. Suppose that there are two goods, clothes and mobile phones, and two factors of production, skilled and unskilled labor. There are three countries: Sweden, with a high ratio of skilled to unskilled workers; Mexico, with a medium ratio; and Bangladesh, with a low ratio. In each country, both goods are produced from the two kinds of labor using constant-returns-to-scale technology, and the two production functions are the same for all three countries. In each country, mobile phone production is skilled-labor-intensive relative to clothes production. Suppose that, initially, each country has a high MFN tariff, high enough that trade is reduced essentially to zero. Initially, there are no PTAs.

    (a) Suppose that Sweden and Mexico form a free-trade agreement, and once it is in effect each country's MFN tariff is unchanged and both countries still produce both goods. For both countries in the agreement, what will be the effect on (i) real incomes for both kinds of labor in both countries in the agreement; (ii) real income for the country as a whole; and (iii) income inequality? (Obviously numbers are not possible, but you should be able to identify the direction of change in each case.)

    (b) Now, answer the same question, but instead of a free-trade agreement between Sweden and Mexico, suppose that it is between Mexico and Bangladesh.

    (c) If your predicted outcome for Mexico is different in (a) and (b), briefly explain why.

2. The demand curve for spark plugs in the United States is given by $Q = 100 - P$, where Q indicates the number of spark plugs purchased and P is the price. Suppose that there are no spark plugs produced in the United States, but they can be imported either from Mexico or from the rest of the world. The price of spark plugs in Mexico is $20, and the price from the lowest-cost supplier in the rest of the world is $10. In each case, spark plugs are produced with a horizontal supply curve, so these prices are fixed and will not change with changes in U.S. policy. The U.S. MFN tariff on spark plugs is a specific tariff in the amount of $15 per unit imported.

    (a) If there is no PTA, so that every country must pay the same tariff, from where will U.S. consumers import their spark plugs, Mexico or the rest of the world? Compute the equilibrium price of spark plugs in the United States, the quantity imported and consumed, and U.S. consumer surplus, tariff revenue, and social welfare.

    (b) Now, suppose that the United States and Mexico sign a free-trade agreement that eliminates the tariff on spark plugs from Mexico, but leaves the tariff on spark plugs from the rest of the world unchanged. How will the equilibrium change? Answer the same questions as in (a) under the new policy regime.

    (c) Identify the welfare change due to trade creation and the welfare change due to trade diversion, and draw them on a carefully marked graph with the equilibrium prices and quantities before and after the free-trade agreement marked. Does this trade agreement raise or lower U.S. welfare?

    (d) Now, how would your answer in (c) change if the MFN tariff had been $50? Explain clearly; a diagram might help, but there is no need for additional calculation.

    (e) Now, how would your answer change if the MFN tariff had been $5? Again, no calculation is needed.

3. Consider a model such as in Krishna (2003). Suppose that utility functions are such that a 1-percentage-point reduction in Country 1's tariff on Country 2's good will always increase Country 1's imports of Country 2's good by 5 units and reduce Country 1's imports of Country 3's good by 4 units. (In other words, in the notation of equation 15.1, $\Delta m^{21} = 5$ and $\Delta m^{31} = -4$, regardless of the value of the initial tariff level.)

    (a) Suppose that initially there are no trade preferences. Country 1's tariffs against both of the other countries' goods are set at a value of 10%. Would a preferential reduction in Country 1's tariff on Country 2's goods to 9%, holding the tariff on Country 3's goods constant, raise or lower Country 1's welfare?

(b) Now, suppose that initially Country 1's tariff on Country 2's good is 1%, while its tariff on Country 3's good is still 10%. If Country 1 eliminated its tariff on Country 2's good, holding its tariff on Country 3's good constant, would Country 1's welfare go up or down?

(c) Explain the difference between the result in parts (a) and (b), making reference to trade creation and trade diversion.

4. (More challenging, and based on Krishna,1998.) Suppose that lithium-ion batteries are produced by three firms, one each in Countries A, B, and C. The firms are called Firm A, Firm, B, and Firm C, respectively. Each firm produces with a marginal cost of $10 per battery, and the batteries they produce are identical. The firms compete as Cournot competitors. In each country, the demand for lithium-ion batteries is given by $Q = 100 - P$, where Q indicates the number of batteries purchased and P is the price. Initially, each country charges an MFN tariff of $10 per

battery imported from any source. Assume that no- one can move a shipment of batteries from one country to another except for the three firms that make them, so we can analyze the three markets separately.

(a) Compute the initial MFN equilibrium. *Note*: With three Cournot competitors, in each country we have three quantities being chosen simultaneously, and hence three unknowns, but we also have three equations, namely, the best-response equations for the three firms. However, under MFN, for each country the two foreign firms face an identical situation and will choose identical quantities. This allows one to write the problem as two equations (one domestic and one foreign) with two unknowns (the domestic quantity and the quantity sold by each foreign firm).

(b) Now, suppose that countries A and B sign a free-trade agreement, setting their mutual tariffs equal to zero, while all of the MFN tariffs are unchanged. How does this affect the equilibrium? Do firms A and B gain or lose from this free-trade agreement? How about firm C? Explain.

REFERENCES

Austen, Ian (2008). "Trade Pact Controversy in Democratic Race Reaches into Canadian Parliament." *The New York Times*, March 7, p. A14.

Bhagwati, Jagdish N. (1991). *The World Trading System at Risk*. Princeton, NJ: Princeton University Press.

———— (1993). "Regionalism and Multilateralism: An Overview," in Jaime De Melo and Arvind Panagariya (eds.), *New Dimensions in Regional Integration*. Cambridge, UK: Cambridge University Press, 1993.

Brown, Sherrod (2004). *Myths of Free Trade: Why American Trade Policy Has Failed*. New York: The New Press.

Burfisher, Mary E., Sherman Robinson, and Karen Thierfelder (2001). "The Impact of NAFTA on the United States." *Journal of Economic Perspectives* 15:1 (Winter), pp. 125–144.

DePalma, Anthony (2001). "Nafta's Powerful Little Secret; Obscure Tribunals Settle Disputes, but Go Too Far, Critics Say." *The New York Times*, March 11, Section 3, p.1.

Duggan, Paul (1999). "NAFTA a Mixed Blessing for Laredo." *The Washington Post*, Sunday, April 18, p. A17.

Estevadeordal, Antoni, Caroline Freund, and Emanuel Orñelas (2008). "Does Regionalism Affect Trade Liberalization

Toward Nonmembers?" *The Quarterly Journal of Economics* 123 (November), pp. 1531–1575.

Feenstra, Robert C. and Gordon H. Hanson (1996). "Foreign Investment, Outsourcing and Relative Wages," in R. C. Feenstra, G. M. Grossman, and D. A. Irwin (eds.), *The Political Economy of Trade Policy: Papers in Honor of Jagdish Bhagwati*. Cambridge, MA: The MIT Press, pp. 89–127.

Freund, Caroline, and Emanuel Orñelas (2010). "Regional Trade Agreements." *Annual Reviews of Economics* 2, pp. 139–166.

Fukao, Kyoji, Toshihiro Okubo, and Robert Stern (2003). "An Econometric Analysis of Trade Diversion under NAFTA." *North American Journal of Economics and Finance* 14:1 (March), pp. 3–24.

Gould, D. (1998). "Has NAFTA Changed North American Trade?" Federal Reserve Bank of Dallas *Economic Review*, First Quarter, pp. 12–23.

Grossman, Gene M., and Esteban Rossi-Hansberg (2008). "Trading Tasks: A Simple Theory of Offshoring." *American Economic Review*, 98:5, pp. 1978–1997.

Hakobyan, Shushanik, and John McLaren (2010). "Looking for Local Labor-Market Effects of NAFTA." NBER Working Paper #16535 (November).

Hanson, Gordon H. (2007). "Globalization, Labor Income, and Poverty in Mexico," in Ann Harrison (ed.), *Globalization and Poverty*. Chicago: University of Chicago Press.

Hufbauer, Gary Clyde, and Jeffrey J. Schott (2005). *NAFTA Revisited: Achievements and Challenges*. Washington, DC: Institute for International Economics.

Kass, Stephen L., and Jean McCarroll (2008). "NAFTA'S Chapter 11 and U.S. Trade Agreements." *New York Law Journal*, June 27.

Krishna, Pravin (1998). "Regionalism and Multilateralism: A Political Economy Approach." *Quarterly Journal of Economics* 113, pp. 227–250.

_____ (2003). "Are Regional Trading Partners 'Natural'?" *The Journal of Political Economy* 111:1 (February), pp. 202–226.

Kumar, Anil (2006). "Did NAFTA Spur Texas Exports?" *Southwest Economy* (Federal Reserve Bank of Dallas), March/April, pp. 3–7.

Leonhardt, David (2008). "The Politics of Trade in Ohio." *The New York Times*, February 27, p. C1.

Limão, Nuno (2006). "Preferential Trade Agreements as Stumbling Blocks for Multilateral Trade Liberalization: Evidence for the United States." *American Economic Review* 96:3 (June), pp. 897–914.

Mayer, Wolfgang (1981). "Theoretical Considerations on Negotiated Tariff Adjustments." *Oxford Economic Papers* 33:1 (March), pp. 135–153.

McLaren, J. (1997). "Size, Sunk Costs, and Judge Bowker's Objection to Free Trade," *American Economic Review* 87:3 (June), pp. 400–420.

_____ (2002). "A Theory of Insidious Regionalism." *Quarterly Journal of Economics* 117 (May), pp. 571–608.

McMillan, Margaret, Alix Peterson Zwane, and Nava Ashraf (2007). "My Policies or Yours: Does OECD Support for Agriculture Increase Poverty in Developing Countries?" In Ann Harrison (ed.), *Globalization and Poverty*, pp. 183–237. Chicago: University of Chicago Press.

Orñelas, Emanuel (2005). "Rent Destruction and the Political Viability of Free Trade Agreements." *Quarterly Journal of Economics* 120, pp. 1475–1506.

Oxfam (2003). "Dumping without Borders: How U.S. Agricultural Policies Are Destroying the Livelihoods of Mexican Corn Farmers." Oxfam Briefing Paper 50.

Perroni, Carlo, and John Whalley (2000). "The New Regionalism: Trade Liberalization or Insurance?," *Canadian Journal of Economics* 33:1 (February), pp. 1–24.

Prina, Silvia (2009a). "Who Benefited More from NAFTA: Small or Large Farmers? Evidence from Mexico." Working Paper, Department of Economics, Case Western Reserve University.

_____ (2009b). "Effects of NAFTA on Agricultural Wages and Employment in Mexico." Case Western Reserve University.

Richardson, Martin (1994). "Why a Free Trade Area? The Tariff Also Rises." *Economics and Politics* 6, pp. 79–96.

Romalis, John (2007). "NAFTA's and CUSFTA's Impact on International Trade." *The Review of Economics and Statistics* 89:3 (August), pp. 416–435.

Sethupathy, Guru (2009). "Offshoring, Wages, and Employment: Theory and Evidence." Working Paper, Columbia University.

Viner, Jacob (1950). *The Customs Union Issue*. New York: Carnegie Endowment for International Peace.

16 Is the Trade Deficit a Time Bomb?

"But we're not just talking about buying a car—we're talking about confronting this country's trade deficit with Japan."

Mort Gerberg/Cartoon Bank

16.1 Not a Subtle Change

One of the most striking facts that jumps out from even a casual inspection of U.S. trade data is the explosive growth of the trade deficit. This can be seen in Figure 16.1, which shows the *trade balance*, or the value of exports minus the value of imports, for the United States as a fraction of GDP since 1960. Positive values in the time-plot indicate a *trade surplus*, meaning that the value of exports exceeds the value of imports, and negative values indicate a *trade deficit*, meaning that imports exceed exports. When the trade balance is equal to zero, exports and imports are equal and trade is said to be *balanced*.

Before the mid-1980s, the U.S. trade balance was usually in surplus, as shown by the positive values shown in the time-plot. Trade deficits began to be common at that point, but before 2000, the U.S. trade deficit was never as high as 3% of GDP, and usually was much lower than that. Since 2000, the trade deficit has always been well above 3% of GDP, and in fact is more often closer to 5%. In one generation, the trade deficit has gone from nonexistent to enormous, and it does not appear to be going away.

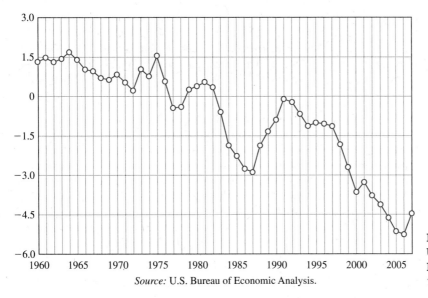

FIGURE 16.1
U.S. Trade Balance as Percentage of GDP, 1960–2007.

Source: U.S. Bureau of Economic Analysis.

It has become commonplace to list the trade deficit as one of the country's problems. In 2000, Senator Chuck Schumer (D-NY) called it "one of the few black marks on our economy."[1] In 2005, Senator Byron Dorgan (D-ND) declared on the Senate floor: "This trade deficit is growing. It is dangerous. It is harmful to the long-term economic interests of this country. We have to do something about it."[2] In 2008, Senator Sherrod Brown (D-OH) implied that the trade deficit was responsible for destroying 10 million American jobs.[3] Further, Senator Dorgan introduced legislation (S.355, February 10, 2005) to require U.S. trade officials to create an emergency action plan whenever the trade deficit reaches 5% of GDP, and the famed investor Warren Buffett has proposed a policy that would essentially enforce a zero trade deficit by administrative fiat.[4] (Neither proposal went anywhere.)

We will look here at whether or not this concern over the deficit makes sense. Can the trade deficit be a problem? Can it be a *symptom* of a problem? Can it be "cured?" Or is it a benign by-product of a well-functioning economy? We will analyze these questions, but first we need to look at some basics.

16.2 What Is a Trade Deficit?

16.2.1 Definitions, and Why It Hasn't Shown Up Before

The topic of trade deficits and surpluses has not come up so far in this text because in our explorations of trade because we have been studying static

[1] Testimony to the Trade Deficit Review Commission, March 13, 2000.
[2] Remarks introducing S.355: Foreign Debt Ceiling Act of 2005, February 10, 2005. *Congressional Record.*
[3] On the floor of the Senate, Senator Brown suggested—citing President George H.W. Bush as a source!—that each $1 billion of trade deficit destroys on average 13,000 jobs. U.S. Senate, April 16, 2008. *Congressional Record.*
[4] Buffett's proposed law would require importers to purchase an "Import Certificate" for each dollar of imports they bought, which would be purchased from exporters. The exporters would be issued an Import Certificate for each dollar of exports they sold (Buffett, 2003).

models—models with no time dimension. In a static model, trade must be balanced in equilibrium. To see this, recall the model from Chapter 6, in which the United States exports pharmaceuticals and imports apparel. Consider U.S. consumer i, with income y^i, who must choose how much apparel c^{Ai} and pharmaceuticals c^{Pi} to consume given the prices P^A and P^P of these two goods. The budget constraint is:

$$P^A c^{Ai} + P^P c^{Pi} \le y^i,$$

which will be satisfied with equality since in a static model consumer i has no incentive to save. Now add this up for all American consumers, to obtain:

$$P^A \Sigma_{i=1}^n c^{Ai} + P^P \Sigma_{i=1}^n c^{Pi} = \Sigma_{i=1}^n y^i,$$

where n is the number of U.S. consumers. Now, the right-hand side of this is total U.S. income, which is of course equal to the value of U.S. output. Thus, we have

$$P^A \Sigma_{i=1}^n c^{Ai} + P^P \Sigma_{i=1}^n c^{Pi} = P^A Q^A + P^P Q^P,$$

where Q^A and Q^P are U.S. production of the two goods, respectively. Rearranging, we have:

$$P^A \left(\Sigma_{i=1}^n c^{Ai} - Q^A \right) = P^P \left(Q^P - \Sigma_{i=1}^n c^{Pi} \right).$$

The left-hand side is the value of U.S. imports of apparel, and the right-hand side is the value of U.S. exports of pharmaceuticals. In other words, this is just a statement of balanced trade. The point is that in a static model *balanced trade follows logically from the consumer's budget constraint.* (An important exception is the case of international transfers, as, for example, if the U.S. government needs to tax its citizens to pay some foreign debt or gives a donation of foreign aid to another country. In that case, the value of U.S. consumption will lie below U.S. GDP, and a trade surplus will result.)

In a dynamic model, consumers face an *intertemporal* budget constraint: The present discounted value of consumption must be equal to the present discounted value of income. In an infinite-horizon model, this yields:

$$\Sigma_{t=1}^\infty \frac{P_t^A \left(\Sigma_{i=1}^n c_t^{Ai} - Q_t^A \right)}{(1+r)^t} = \Sigma_{t=1}^\infty \frac{P_t^P \left(Q_t^P - \Sigma_{i=1}^n c_t^{Pi} \right)}{(1+r)^t},$$

where a t subscript denotes consumption or production at date t and r denotes the interest rate. In other words, the country's trade must be balanced in present discounted value: The present discounted value of a country's imports must be equal to the present discounted value of its exports. Along the way, it can run trade deficits and surpluses that balance each other out in the long run.

16.2.2 The National Income Identity

A very useful way of thinking about trade deficits comes from national income accounting. Recall the basic equation from macroeconomics:

$$Y = C + I + G + X - M,$$

where Y stands for GDP, C for aggregate domestic private consumption expenditure, I for domestic investment expenditure, G for domestic government consumption expenditure, X for exports, and M for imports. If we subtract taxes T and add government transfers R (social security payments, unemployment insurance, and the like), the left-hand side becomes personal disposable income:

$$Y - T + R = C + I + G - T + R + X - M.$$

This can be rearranged as:

$$[Y - T + R - C] + [T - G - R] + [M - X] = I. \qquad (16.1)$$

The first term in square brackets is personal savings, the excess of personal disposable income over personal consumption. The second term in square brackets is the government's budget surplus (which of course can be negative); this can be interpreted as government savings, since it is the excess of the government's income (T) over its spending ($R + G$). The third term in square brackets is, of course, the trade deficit, but it can also be interpreted as a kind of savings: Since it measures how much more the rest of the world is selling to us than buying from us, it measures the excess of foreign income over foreign consumption, and so we can call it foreign savings.

Thus, these three pieces of the national income accounts show the three different sources of finance for a country's investment. As a result, when the trade deficit shoots up, one can ask: (a) Did the country's rate of investment rise? (b) Did its personal savings rate fall? Or (c) did the government budget deficit rise (or surplus fall)? Or was it some combination of the three? Equation (16.1) shows us that at least one of these *must* have occurred in order for an increase in the trade deficit to be possible.

In the U.S. case, both (b) and (c) appear to describe the rise of the trade deficit. (There has been no dramatic rise in investment rates, so (a) is not part of the explanation.) Figure 16.2 shows the path of the personal savings rate, which is personal savings as a percentage of personal disposable income, as reported

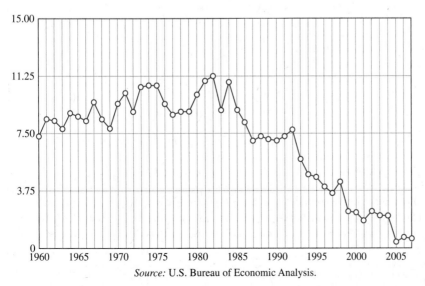

Source: U.S. Bureau of Economic Analysis.

FIGURE 16.2
U.S. Personal Savings
Rate, 1960–2007.

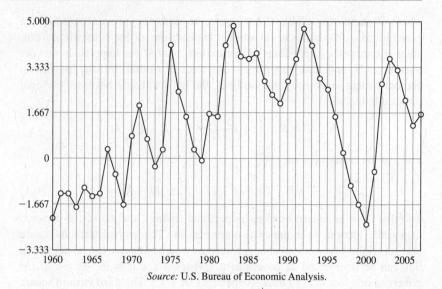

FIGURE 16.3
U.S. Federal Government Budget Deficit as a Percentage of GDP, 1960–2007.

Source: U.S. Bureau of Economic Analysis.

by the BEA. Before the mid-1980s, the personal savings rate was almost always above 8% and often well above. Since the mid-1980s it has never been as high as 8%; it has been in steady decline, and now it hovers around zero. Figure 16.3, which shows the budget deficit as a percentage of GDP, is only slightly less dramatic. Before the 1970s, the U.S. federal government was usually in surplus; since the 1980s, it has almost always been in deficit.

Now, to say that the rise in the U.S. trade deficit is "due to" the fall in U.S. domestic personal and government savings is only an accounting exercise rather than a causal explanation. We will turn to the economic interpretation of the trade deficit in the next section, to see if we can begin to understand the question of causation.

But first, we need two important clarifications.

16.2.3 The Current Account and the Financial Account

The first clarification is the relationship between the trade deficit and another concept often mentioned in the same contexts, the current account. The *current account deficit* is the trade deficit plus net payments abroad for debt service (such as interest payments Americans pay to foreigners, minus interest payments paid to Americans from abroad), plus net payments abroad for factor services (such as dividends paid to foreigners on U.S. corporate stock they own, minus dividends paid to Americans on their holdings of foreign stock, and profits repatriated to foreign multinational corporations from their U.S. affiliates, minus profits repatriated to Americans). The current account deficit is a fuller measure of the extent to which the country is borrowing from foreigners. It matches up with the *financial account surplus*, which is essentially the net acquisition of foreign claims on domestic output (foreign acquisition of domestic stocks and bonds minus domestic acquisition of foreign stocks and bonds, plus net foreign lending to domestic entities, and so on).[5] Apart from

---

[5] In older writing on this subject, the term "capital account" was used in place of "financial account."

statistical errors, the financial account surplus must be equal to the current account deficit. In most of this chapter, we will ignore international interest and factor payments for simplicity, and so we will focus on the trade deficit instead of the current account. First, however, we should make sure we understand the fuller accounting of these flows.

An example of this accounting in practice is presented in Table 16.1. This is a simplified version of the International Transactions table for the U.S. economy for 2010; the full version is available from the U.S. Bureau of Economic Analysis at www.bea.gov. Each item is listed in billions of U.S. dollars. The current account is listed in rows 1 through 6, with payments into the United States listed as positive numbers and payments outside listed as negative numbers. Rows 1 and 3 show the value of trade flows. If U.S. firms sell $1 billion worth of merchandise to foreign consumers, that is listed in Row 1 as +1, while if U.S. consumers buy $1 billion worth of merchandise from a foreign firm, that is listed in Row 3 as − 1. The U.S. trade surplus is therefore Row 1 plus Row 3, which is a negative number indicating a trade deficit. Rows 2 and 4 show income payments across borders, which include, for example, profits of U.S. multinational firms repatriated from other countries (listed as a positive number in Row 2) and profits of foreign multinational firms repatriated from the United States to those firms' home countries (listed as a negative number in Row 4), among other forms of income. Row 5 shows government

Table 16-1 International Transactions of the U.S. Economy 2010

	Current Account	
	(Positive for payments into U.S., negative for payments to other countries from U.S.).	
1	Exports of goods and services and income receipts (+)	1838
2	Income receipts by Americans from other countries (+)	663
3	Imports of goods and services (−)	−2338
4	Income payments from Americans to foreigners (−)	−498
5	Unilateral current transfers, net government grants plus pensions and other transfers (positive if into the U.S. from other governments, otherwise negative)	−55
6	Private remittances (positive if sent into U.S., negative if sent out of U.S.).	−81
	Financial Account	
	U.S.-owned assets abroad (increase/financial outflow (−))	
7	Official assets	5.7
	Private assets	
8	Direct investment	−351
9	Foreign securities plus U.S. claims reported by banks, security brokers and other concerns	−660
	Foreign-owned assets in U.S. [increase/financial inflow (+)]	
10	Official assets (mainly U.S. government securities)	350
	Private assets	
11	Direct investment	236
12	Securities, currency, and liabilities to foreigners reported by banks, security brokers, and other concerns.	660
13	Statistical discrepancy (sum of above terms with sign reversed)	230.3

transfers to other countries, including, for example, foreign aid, as negative values, and Row 6 shows private remittances, which are the payments made by private citizens living out of their home country to persons back home. For example, a Guatemalan worker picking grapes in California who sends home $100 to help his family back home will show up as a − $100 in Row 6.

Rows 7 through 12 show the financial account. Each entry in these rows shows the *change* in the U.S. net asset position, with an increase in U.S. holdings of foreign assets recorded as a negative number (in Rows 7 through 9) and an increase in foreign holdings of U.S. assets recorded as a positive number (in Rows 10 through 12). Row 7 records changes in official assets, meaning assets owned by the U.S. government; for example, if the U.S. Federal Reserve system increases its holdings of foreign currency reserves by the equivalent of $1 billion, it will show up in this row as −1. Row 8 shows changes in U.S. private holdings of direct investment abroad, and Row 9 shows changes in U.S. private financial assets abroad. In 2010, holdings of FDI abroad by U.S. firms and individuals increased by $351 billion, according to these figures. Rows 10, 11, and 12 correspond exactly to the analogous lines 7, 8, and 9, except that they pertain to foreign holdings of U.S. assets. Foreign governments increased their holdings of U.S. securities by $350 billion during 2010, for example.

Now, if all of these statistics have been collected without errors or omissions and correctly added to the table, then lines 1 through 12 will add up to zero, by definition. For example, suppose that every row of the current account (lines 1−6) was equal to zero except for the $81 billion in private remittances. If, say, Guatemalan workers in the United States send home $81 billion, and that money is just saved locally in Guatemala as U.S. currency, then it will show up in line 12 as an $81 billion increase in foreign private holdings of U.S. currency, with a positive sign. Therefore, lines 6 and 12 will sum to zero. On the other hand, if it is deposited in a Guatemalan bank, which deposits the money with the Guatemalan central bank, then it shows up as $81 in line 10, with a positive sign, and so Rows 6 and 10 will sum to zero. On the other hand, if that $81 is used to purchase U.S.-made goods and services, it will show up in Row 1, with a positive sign, and the current account will sum to zero on its own. Any story about what happens to the $81 billion must produce an $81 billion somewhere in the table, with a positive sign, so that the rows sum to zero. This thought experiment need not start with private remittances; it can be based on any line in the table, and the conclusion will always be the same: The rows must sum to zero.

Of course, in truth there are always errors and omissions in data collection, so the rows do not exactly sum to zero in practice. Row 13 shows the extent of this discrepancy, which is quite sizable at $230.3 billion.

16.2.4 Bilateral versus Multilateral Deficits

The difference between the trade balance and the current account was the first clarification we needed. The second clarification has to do with bilateral trade deficits. A country can have a trade deficit with another country without having an overall trade deficit. This is called a *bilateral trade deficit*; for example, the U.S. bilateral trade deficit with Mexico is U.S. imports from Mexico minus U.S. exports to Mexico. The overall trade deficit we have been discussing is the sum of the country's bilateral trade deficits with each country (including any negative ones, if there are any bilateral trade surpluses); we can call the overall trade deficit the *multilateral trade deficit* for contrast.

We have pointed out that the multilateral trade deficit has something to do with the balance between domestic savings and domestic investment, but that is not necessarily true of a bilateral trade deficit. A bilateral deficit may arise purely out of comparative advantage. For example, despite having a large multilateral trade deficit, the United States generally has a bilateral trade surplus with Brazil. This is driven largely by exports of capital-intensive heavy manufactures, such as aircraft engines and parts, which are useful for Brazil's quite substantial regional-jet industry.

These two deficits are sometimes muddled in public debate. For example, the U.S. bilateral deficit with China often seems to be identified as the main cause of the U.S. multilateral deficit; Bown et al. (2005) show why that is not credible[6] and why efforts to reduce the U.S.-China deficit are unlikely to have much impact on the multilateral deficit. For the remainder of this chapter, we will focus solely on the multilateral trade deficit.

16.3 Why Would a Country Run a Trade Deficit?

To analyze a trade deficit in an economic equilibrium, we need a dynamic model. The simplest dynamic model has two periods (anything fewer and it's a static model), and only one good. A model of that sort is often called a Fisher model, after the pioneering early-twentieth-century economist Irving Fisher. The main points that emerge will carry over to a more realistic many-good model.

Suppose that the Home economy can produce a single good, called corn. This is also the only consumption good. Apart from being consumed, corn can also be invested; by using a portion of the crop as seed, output of corn next period can be increased. The economy's production-possibilities frontier is shown in Figure 16.4. The horizontal axis measures Period 1 net output of corn, meaning output net of corn diverted for seed. The vertical axis measures

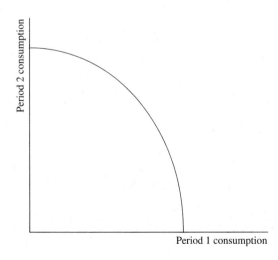

FIGURE 16.4
Production Possibilities
in the Fisher Model.

---

[6] For example, the U.S.-China deficit is too small compared to the overall deficit to be a prime driver of it.

Period 2 output of corn (since there are only two periods, there is no use of corn for seed in Period 2). The more corn is invested as seed in Period 1, the lower is the net Period 1 output, but the higher is the Period 2 output, yielding the downward-sloping curve in the figure.

Corn can be traded internationally. Since there is no other good to exchange it for, importing corn in Period 1 requires giving the supplier an IOU for corn in Period 2. (In other words, importing corn in Period 1 is really a form of borrowing. For this reason, this model is often called a model of intertemporal trade.)

The interest rate on world markets is denoted r, and Home takes that interest rate as given.

Assuming that all Home residents have the same production possibilities (think of them as farmers with identical plots of land) and the same preferences, we can represent equilibrium as in Figure 16.5, which is often called the *Fisher diagram*.

Note that utility is now a function of Period 1 corn and Period 2 corn consumed. Since any corn borrowed in Period 1 must be paid back in Period 2 with interest, each consumer's budget constraint is:

$$C_2 \leq Y_2 - (1+r)(C_1 - Y_1),$$

where C_t denotes consumption in Period t and Y_t denotes production in Period t. The term in brackets on the right-hand side, $(C_t - Y_t)$, is corn borrowed in Period 1. Subtracting interest and principal from that loan off of Period 2 output gives the maximum Period 2 consumption possible, which is the right-hand side of the budget constraint. We can rewrite this as:

$$C_1 + \frac{C_2}{(1+r)} \leq Y_1 + \frac{Y_2}{(1+r)}.$$

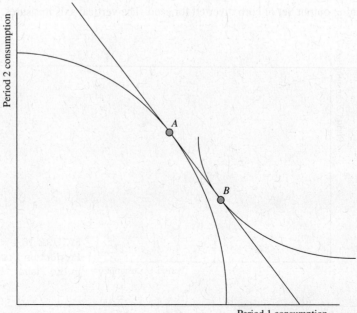

FIGURE 16.5
Equilibrium in the
Fisher Model, with a
Trade Deficit.

In other words, the present discounted value of consumption cannot be greater than the presented discounted value of production. Of course, in equilibrium this will hold with equality.

Since anything that increases the right-hand side of this budget constraint makes the consumer better off, Home households will adjust their production plan to maximize the present discounted value of production. That implies production at point A in Figure 16.5, where the marginal rate of transformation of Period 1 corn into Period 2 corn equals $(1+r)$. The straight line with slope equal to $-(1+r)$ going through that point is, then, the Home consumer's intertemporal budget line. Optimal consumption is at point B, where this budget line is tangent to an intertemporal indifference curve.

As pictured, optimal consumption is southeast of optimal production, implying that initially each Home consumer is consuming more than it produces. *This is, therefore, a picture of a Period 1 trade deficit*, followed by a Period 2 trade surplus. The opposite, a trade surplus followed by a trade deficit, would be the outcome if B was northwest of A. A zero trade deficit (usually the same thing as balanced trade, but here it really means no trade) would occur when B and A are the same point.

We can now discuss the situations in which the outcome will be a Period-1 trade deficit as shown. We will note two different situations that can give rise to a trade deficit.

Situation 1: Disaster. Suppose that initially equilibrium is at point A in Figure 16.6, so that there is no trade deficit. Now, suppose that a disaster hits this economy, destroying a portion of Period 1 output. This could be locusts that eat some of the corn, or it could be a war that destroys part of the output, but let us assume that the disaster strikes in Period 1 and will not reoccur in Period 2. This shifts the net production possibilities frontier parallel to the left as shown by the broken curve. Any given level of seed-corn investment will

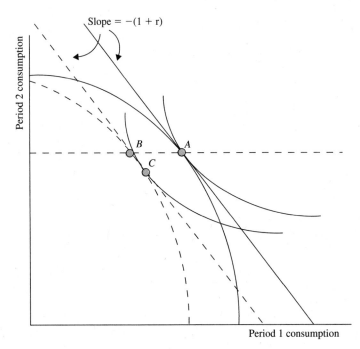

FIGURE 16.6
Disaster as a Motivation for a
Trade Deficit.

produce the same level of Period 2 output as before the disaster but will result in lower Period 1 net output. The new optimal production point is B, which is directly to the left of A because the production possibilities frontier has shifted parallel to the left (so that the slope is the same for any height as it was before the disaster). However, the new consumption point is *not* at B, since the lower Period 1 consumption at point B implies that the marginal rate of intertemporal substitution (the slope of the indifference curve) is strictly higher at B than at A.[7] Thus, the indifference curve cannot be tangent to the budget line at B; the equilibrium must lie to the right of B, at a point like C. This implies a trade deficit followed by a trade surplus. What we see in this case is *a trade deficit caused by a temporary shock, as Home consumers borrow or dissave in Period 1 in order to smooth out their consumption.*

This is actually a fairly good description of what happened in Europe following the devastation of World War II. The European economies ran huge trade deficits from the end of the war through much of the 1950s as they rebuilt their economies, while the United States and Canada, which had not suffered the same kind of destruction, ran trade surpluses. This is shown in Figure 16.7, which shows the balance of trade for selected European countries, the United States, and Canada from 1948 to 1970. Initially, all of the European countries are clearly in deficit, with the U.S. trade surplus looming over all of the other figures. Germany was the first to begin running trade surpluses. In more recent years than is shown on this time-plot, the two countries' roles have reversed, with the United States running huge trade deficits and Germany running huge surpluses.

Incidentally, a large problem during the postwar period was the inability of European economies to run deficits as large as they needed to, because of currency convertibility problems and general difficulties in borrowing (see De Grauwe,

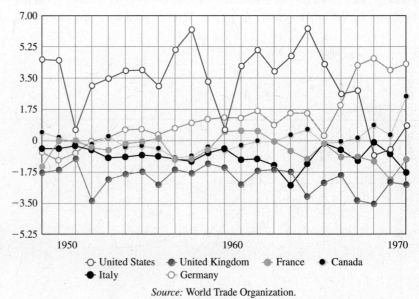

FIGURE 16.7
Balance of Trade,
Selected Countries,
1948–1970 ($ billions).

-O- United States -●- United Kingdom -●- France -●- Canada
-●- Italy -O- Germany

Source: World Trade Organization.

---

[7] Since Period 1 consumption is lower at point B but Period 2 consumption is just as high, the marginal utility of Period 1 consumption will be higher, and the marginal utility of Period 2 consumption no lower, at B than at A. Since the slope of the indifference curve is the ratio of these marginal utilities, that tells us that the indifference curve is steeper at B than at A.

1989, for an account of this period). This was a prime motivation for establishing the International Bank for Reconstruction and Development (IBRD), an intergovernmental agency that made loans to governments having trouble borrowing from the private sector for their reconstruction efforts. The IBRD grew into what we now know as the World Bank, whose primary mission is lending to the governments of middle- and low-income countries for development projects. Most people do not realize that the World Bank grew out of postwar Europe's inability to run sufficiently large trade deficits.

Situation 2: Sunny horizons. Now, return to the "pre-disaster" situation from Figure 16.6, and this time suppose that citizens of Home realize that the marginal product of each bit of corn invested as seed is higher than it used to be. This makes the production possibilities frontier steeper at each point, shifting it upward as in the broken line in Figure 16.8. Since it is steeper than the original production possibilities frontier, the new production point B is not only higher but also farther to the left compared to the original production point A. As a result, the marginal rate of intertemporal substitution is higher at B than at A, and so B cannot be the new consumption point.[8] The new consumption point is southeast of B and is marked as C. Again, this implies a trade deficit followed by a trade surplus. What we see in this case is a trade deficit caused by an improvement in the economy's future prospects, as Home consumers borrow to finance an expansion in domestic investment.

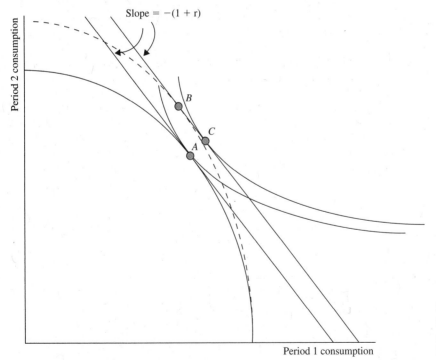

FIGURE 16.8
Sunny Horizons as a Motivation for a Trade Deficit.

---

[8] An increase in Period 2 consumption holding Period 1 consumption constant lowers the marginal utility of Period 2 consumption, raising the marginal rate of intertemporal substitution. A drop in Period 1 consumption holding Period 2 consumption constant raises the marginal utility of Period 1 consumption, also raising the marginal rate of intertemporal substitution.

Aurora Photos/Alamy

Part of what the Korean trade deficit helped finance. Shipworks near Pusan.

This is a good description of South Korea's trade deficits during its remarkable growth spurt during the 1960s to the 1980s. The government encouraged the domestic business sector to launch aggressively into a wide range of manufacturing investment through a combination of policies including targeted subsidies. See Rodrik, 1995, for a detailed analysis of that story. The result was a huge investment boom, financed partly through a large increase in foreign savings (that is, a trade deficit), as shown in Figure 16.9. Again, the figures are from the WTO, and again, they show exports minus imports, so negative values indicate a trade deficit. The trade balance did not begin to show a surplus until the late 1980s. The negative values in the graph of Figure 16.9 are a large part of how the people of South Korea have propelled themselves into prosperity within one generation.

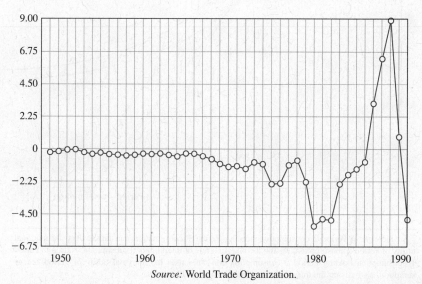

FIGURE 16.9
Balance of Trade,
South Korea,
1948–1990 ($ billions).

Source: World Trade Organization.

We see that a trade deficit can result both from a temporary adverse shock and from good news about the future of the economy—and it must be underlined that in each of these cases as analyzed here, *the trade deficit is part of the economy's optimal, efficient response to these events.*

16.4 Can the Trade Deficit Ever Be a Problem?

The previous analysis seems to have suggested that the trade deficit cannot be a problem and that tampering with it can only do harm. But is there any conceivable way that the common view of the trade deficit as a problem (or a "dangerous black mark" that is destroying millions of jobs) could have any validity?

We have assumed that people plan their futures optimally (setting their intertemporal indifference curves tangent to their intertemporal budget lines). However, many observers dispute that assumption, including many economists. They argue instead that the complexity of calculation required for retirement planning, together with the difficulty of forecasting future conditions, leads to large-scale errors, and that the remarkable drop in savings rates over the past generation is not an optimal response to changed circumstances but rather a colossal mistake.[9]

This text takes no stand on that debate. We simply point out that *if* one believes that private saving is suboptimal, *then* it is quite consistent to believe that the trade deficit is larger than optimal and that a policy to reduce it can improve welfare.

To see a stylized example, let us return to our corn-based two-period model. Suppose that in each period the Home government needs to withdraw 100 units of corn to shore up the levees that protect Home from floods. (Piled-up corn helps keep the levees standing up. It's hard to come up with more realistic examples in a one-good economy.) The government can tax these required corn supplies from Home citizens, or borrow them on the world market, which is effectively the same thing as running a budget deficit. The situation is depicted in Figure 16.10, where the dotted production possibilities frontier shows the original production possibilities frontier shifted down and to the left by 100 units to correct for the government requirement. Suppose that optimal consumption is at point A, with no trade deficit, and if the government taxes 100 units of corn in Period 1 and explains that it will do the same again in Period 2, then that is what consumers will choose.

Suppose now that the government chooses deficit financing, borrowing 100 units of corn on the world market in Period 1, understanding that it will need to pay back $(1 + r)100$ units in Period 2. If Home consumers *understand* that, the deficit financing will not change their consumption decision. They will pay no taxes now, but they will understand that they will need to pay $(2 + r)100$ units in tax next period—that is, 100 units for the levee, plus $(1 + r)100$ to enable the government to pay back the loan. Their budget line is unchanged by the deficit finance, and they will still consume at point A. Put differently, they

---

[9] The issues are reviewed in Lazear (1994). Bernheim (1994) presents a concise case that Americans do not save enough. A more recent analysis is found in Council of Economic Advisers (2006).

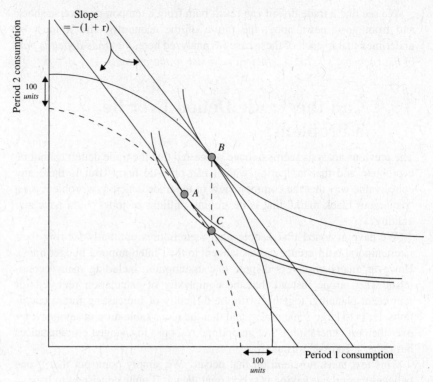

FIGURE 16.10
A Trade Defeicit as a Symptom of a Savings Problem.

will save the 100 units of corn they would otherwise have been taxed, and those savings will be used to help pay tax in Period 2. This is a property of government deficits in simple models with informed, rational consumers, called Ricardian equivalence and pointed out in a famous paper by Robert Barro (1974).

If, however, Home consumers do not read the newspaper and do not know about the levee problem and do not know that their government is borrowing on the world market, then they may *believe* that they are working with the original, solid-line net production possibilities frontier. They will, in that case, choose to consume at point B.[10] Home consumers will then be shocked to learn, when they arrive at Period 2, that they must pay not only 100 units of corn for the levees, but $(1 + r)100$ units for the foreign loan. Their actual consumption will be at point C, directly below B. Note that C is not only on a lower indifference curve than B but on a lower indifference curve than A. Their misunderstanding of the government's fiscal situation has made them worse off.

Note also that point C exhibits a Period 1 trade deficit followed by a Period 2 trade surplus. As claimed at the outset, this is a case in which inefficiently low private savings lead to an inefficiently high trade deficit, lowering Home welfare.

So in this case, the trade deficit is a symptom of a savings problem. If the government could prevent a trade deficit through trade policy—say, by

---

[10] For simplicity, point B is depicted as a point where the production possibilities frontier is tangent to an indifference curve, but this is not necessarily the case and the main point does not depend on it.

coercing exports of 100 units of corn in Period 1 and prohibiting imports, it could in principle improve matters by pushing the economy back to point *A*. However, if possible, it would be better to bypass the symptom and address the cause of the problem—either by abandoning deficit financing and raising taxes to pay the government's expenses as they are incurred, or at least by making sure the public is better informed about its savings situation. This would be better than policy to regulate the trade deficit for a number of reasons. Coercion and prohibitions breed evasion and inefficiencies of their own, for one. For another, the optimal trade deficit will not generally be zero, and the government likely will not know the optimum trade deficit to enforce since it depends on preferences and technology (such as the slopes of the indifference curves and production possibilities frontiers), which government can know only imperfectly.

An additional note is that even in cases in which the trade deficit is a symptom of a problem, it is hard to see how it can be responsible for destroying jobs. In the example here, the problem is not that the economy does not produce enough jobs, but rather that the consumers do not allocate their consumption resources optimally over their lifespan. The total output of the economy is unaffected by the deficit. Rules of thumb that suggest a given number of jobs are destroyed for each billion dollars of the trade deficit—such as the one Senator Brown says he learned from President George H.W. Bush (recall footnote 3)—appear to be the result of simple economic confusion.

In sum, if one believes (as some do and some do not) that the United States is suffering from a market failure that is leading to insufficient savings, then that implies that the current trade deficit is indeed excessively high. In this case, government action to lower the trade deficit directly, such as the Buffett proposal, may well improve welfare. But this is attacking the symptom, while the ideal solution would be to target the alleged savings problem directly.

MAIN IDEAS

1. The trade deficit is the value of a country's imports minus the value of its exports. The trade surplus is the value of a country's exports minus the value of its imports. A country's trade is balanced if the value of its exports is equal to the value of its imports.

2. In a static model of trade, trade must be balanced in equilibrium because of the budget constraint, unless there are international transfers of wealth or income.

3. In the period right after World War II, European economies ran large trade deficits while the U.S. economy ran surpluses. In the last two decades, those roles have been reversed. European trade on the whole has tended to be fairly balanced, while the U.S. economy has been running gigantic, unprecedented trade deficits.

4. If we interpret the trade deficit as "foreign savings," then national accounting identities imply that domestic savings (public and private) plus foreign savings must equal domestic investment. This helps in interpreting a given change in the trade deficit.

5. A country may run a trade deficit as an optimal response to a temporary adverse shock (such as Europe in the aftermath of World War II) or an improvement in growth prospects (such as South Korea in the 1960s to the 1980s). In these cases, efforts to "cure" the deficit would be harmful.

6. If a country's citizens are not saving as much as they optimally should, the economy will tend to run a trade deficit higher than it optimally should. In this case, policies to reduce the deficit directly might help, but it is better to address the savings problem directly if possible. This unresolved and contentious issue is at the heart of contemporary debates about the U.S. trade deficit.

QUESTIONS AND PROBLEMS

1. In Table 16.1, pick a row that is part of the current account and assume that the value in that row goes up by $100 billion. Explain four different ways that other rows in the table could change so that the rows will still add up to zero, in each case explaining what the economic meaning of the change in the row is (as was done in the discussion of private remittances in Section 16.2.3).

2. Recall from Section 16.2 that a country can have a trade surplus or a trade deficit even in a static model if there is some sort of international transfer. Think of three real-world examples of such transfers either in current events or in history, and explain how they could result in unbalanced trade.

3. In a many-country static trade model, suppose that country i receives a transfer of income from country j and there are no other intergovernmental transfers. Does this imply that i will have bilateral trade deficit with j, or that i will have a multilateral trade deficit and j will have a multilateral trade surplus? Explain.

4. From the 'trade flows data.xls' spreadsheet, identify a country with a trade deficit (other than the United States) and another with a trade surplus. Comment on what may be driving this deficit or surplus, in either case, using what you know about the country in question, and using the theory we have seen in this chapter.

5. Recall from Chapter 9 the model of learning by doing in the production of memory chips. Suppose that an economy has just entered large-scale production of these chips, and that a large fraction of the workforce is employed in the industry. Because of the learning curve, GDP grows, rapidly at first, then more slowly as the workers become experienced. Suppose that consumers in this economy plan well for the future, and that preferences are such that their consumption is constant over time (in other words, they consume their permanent income).

Draw a graph to show what the time path of GDP, consumption, and the trade deficit will look like for this country. Assuming that the economy is a net borrower on the world market rather than a net lender, draw the time path for the economy's foreign debt as well. Obviously, no numbers are needed, just an illustration of the qualitative appearance of these time paths.

6. Consider the two-period corn economy of the text. Suppose that initially the equilibrium has a zero trade deficit. Now, increase the interest rate. Show how the Fisher diagram changes. Will trade still be balanced? If not, will there be a trade deficit or a trade surplus?

7. *Do poor countries run trade deficits?* Consider again the two-period corn economy. Suppose that initially the equilibrium has a zero trade deficit, and draw the Fisher diagram. Now, on the same diagram, draw the production possibilities frontier for an economy with the same preferences but half the productive capacity. That is, for each point on the original production possibilities frontier, the new production possibilities frontier has a corresponding point with half the Period 1 net output and half the Period 2 output. Draw the new equilibrium, with the new point of tangency with an indifference curve. Is there a trade deficit in the new equilibrium? Why or why not? If the answer is ambiguous, what assumptions could you make to provide an definitive answer? Your explanation is as important as the diagram.

8. *Can protectionism cause trade deficits?* Recall the model of U.S.-China trade presented in Chapter 6, in which the United States exports plastics to China and China exports apparel to the United States. Suppose that the Chinese government simply refused to allow any U.S. plastics to be imported into the country. Would that cause a U.S. trade deficit? Why or why not?

REFERENCES

Barro, Robert (1974). "Are Government Bonds Net Wealth?" *Journal of Political Economy* 82:6 (November–December), pp. 1095–1117.

Bernheim, B. Douglas (1994). "Comment on Chapters 4 and 5," in David A. Wise (ed.), *Studies in the Economics of*

Aging, pp. 171–179. Chicago: University of Chicago Press for the NBER.

Bown, Chad P., Meredith A. Crowley, Rachel McCulloch, and Daisuke J. Nakajima (2005). "The U.S. Trade Deficit:

Made in China?" *Economic Perspectives* (Federal Reserve Bank of Chicago) (4th quarter), pp. 2–17.

Buffett, Warren E. (2003). "America's Growing Trade Deficit Is Selling the Nation Out From Under Us. Here's a Way to Fix the Problem—And We Need to Do It Now." *FORTUNE*, November 10.

Council of Economic Advisers (2006). *Economic Report of the President*. Washington, DC: United States Government Printing Office.

De Grauwe, Paul (1989). *International Money: Post-War Trends and Theories*. Oxford: Oxford University Press.

Lazear, Edward P. (1994). "Some Thoughts on Savings," in David A. Wise (ed.), *Studies in the Economics of Aging*, pp. 143–169. Chicago: University of Chicago Press for the NBER.

Rodrik, Dani (1995). "Getting Interventions Right: How South Korea and Taiwan Grew Rich." *Economic Policy: A European Forum* 20 (April), pp. 53–97.

17

Trade and Exchange Rates: Is the Renminbi the Culprit?

Dennis Galante/©Corbis

The accused.

17.1 The Ultimatum

In the fall of 2003, Senator Charles Schumer (D-NY) ran out of patience. As he saw it, China had refused time and again to do anything about its policy of currency market manipulation, which he claimed maintained an artificially low value for Chinese currency (called the *renminbi*, or "people's currency," with units called *yuan*) and thereby gave an unfair advantage to Chinese manufacturing over American manufacturing. He entered Senate bill S. 1586 to start playing tough. The text of the bill claims:

> *The undervaluation of the yuan makes exports from the People's Republic of China less expensive for foreign consumers and makes foreign products more expensive for Chinese consumers. The effective result is a significant subsidization of China's*

exports and a virtual tariff on foreign imports, leading the People's Republic of China to enjoy significant trade surpluses with its international trading partners. . . . China's undervalued currency and the United States trade deficit with the People's Republic of China is contributing to significant United States job losses and harming United States businesses. In particular the United States manufacturing sector has lost over 2,600,000 jobs since March 2001.

The action the bill prescribed was dire: Unless the president could specify within 180 days that China had ceased currency manipulation, the U.S. government would impose a 27.5% tariff on all Chinese products. One journalist observed that it was "like holding a gun to the head of U.S. consumers and saying to China, 'reform, Or I'll shoot'" (Ramzy, 2006). The bill went nowhere and was unsuccessfully reintroduced in 2005. Finally, years later, a similar bill passed the Senate 63–35 in October 2011—but went nowhere in the House (Steinhauer, 2011).

Despite the troubles the bill has encountered that have kept it from becoming law, the views expressed in the bill are quite common. Prominent economist C. Fred Bergsten (2007) has argued that the Chinese government is "exporting unemployment" through its exchange-rate policy, which is threatening a "devastating impact" on the world trading system, and is "by far the single most important issue in US-China economic relations." President Obama appears to agree.[1]

Is this right? Does the Chinese government adopt policies that make its currency artificially cheap? Does that create a bilateral U.S. trade deficit with China? Does it destroy U.S. jobs? Should the U.S. government get tough and insist that the Chinese government raise the value of the renminbi?

We will attempt to shed light on these questions, but first we need to develop a certain level of understanding of foreign-exchange markets. We will first develop some basic institutional knowledge and then construct a simple equilibrium model of exchange-rate determination that can then be used to analyze the renminbi question.[2]

17.2 Basic Facts about Foreign-Exchange Markets

Mexico has its own currency, the peso; the United States has its own, the U.S. dollar; and Japan has the yen. This is the pattern for most countries: Each country has its own currency. However, there are exceptions. A few countries use another country's currency (as Panama, for example, uses the U.S. dollar), and other countries jointly maintain a shared currency, called a *currency union* or a *monetary union*. The best-known currency union is the Economic and Monetary Union (EMU) of the European Union (EU), comprising most of the

---

[1] In the runup to the presidential election in 2008, the Obama campaign issued a Fact Sheet on China, for example, that mentioned "China's manipulation of the value of its currency, a practice that contributes to massive global imbalances and provides Chinese companies with an unfair competitive advantage." Obama restated his belief that the yuan is undervalued in a joint press conference with President Hu Jintao on January 19, 2011.

[2] This chapter will provide an introduction to these questions. See Tatom (2007) and Bown et al. (2005) for much more detailed background on U.S.-Chinese macroeconomic issues. Staiger and Sykes (2010) cover much of the terrain of this chapter in a readable nontechnical form.

countries of Europe, whose shared currency is the euro. Another important currency union is the CFA franc zone in Africa, comprising several French-speaking countries such as the Côte-d'Ivoire and Niger that share the CFA franc. Most currencies can be freely traded one for another, and the markets for exchange of one currency for another are called *foreign-exchange markets*, with the price of one currency in terms of another called an *exchange rate*. (More precisely, this is a *nominal exchange rate*; we will introduce a concept of real exchange rates later. For now the qualifier "nominal" will be implicit.) For example, the yuan–dollar exchange rate tells how many yuan need to be offered on foreign-exchange markets to purchase one U.S. dollar. If a currency's price goes up in terms of another, it is said to *appreciate*, and if its price falls, it is said to *depreciate*. Logically, the appreciation of one currency implies a depreciation of the other. For example, if the yuan/dollar rate goes from 8 to 6, the renminbi has appreciated against the dollar, and the dollar has depreciated against the renminbi.

It is crucial to keep in mind that exchange rates are prices, determined by the balance of supply and demand (including speculative demand) for the different currencies on foreign-exchange markets. This was not always the case; in the past, there have been many *inconvertible currencies*, particularly in the Third World, meaning currencies that could not be traded on foreign-exchange markets due to government restrictions. For those currencies the government would simply declare the exchange rate as a matter of policy (commonly creating a black market in the process). Now, however, inconvertible currencies are uncommon, and so exchange rates are market-determined. As a result, when we hear that a government is *pegging* its currency to a particular value in terms of another currency, what is usually meant is that the central bank of that country is engaging in *open market operations*—buying and selling the currencies in question and financial securities denominated in those currencies in order to manipulate the market exchange rate. For example, the Central Bank of China (called the People's Bank of China, or the PBC) can keep the value of the renminbi down against the dollar by issuing large quantities of new yuan and using them to buy dollars or U.S. dollar-denominated bonds.

Thus, when observers of the world economy make a distinction between *fixed* and *flexible* (or *floating*) exchange rates, they are really making a distinction between different types of monetary policy. A country has a fixed exchange rate policy if its central bank engages in open market operations to keep its exchange rate within a narrow range around a fixed target value; it has a flexible or floating rate if it abstains from open market operations and merely lets the exchange rate fluctuate. In practice, most countries maintain a practice somewhere in between these two extremes, keeping the rate within a broad band or intervening in the foreign-exchange markets only in case of sharp movements. This type of middle ground is often called a *managed float*. Occasionally a government that is trying to keep its currency within a narrow band will announce a shift in the band it is targeting. A shift in the direction of making its currency less valuable is called a *devaluation*, although once again it is best interpreted as a change in monetary policy.

Following World War II, the international community attempted to avoid the economic disasters of the 1930s and the war by creating new institutions. Along with the United Nations for resolving conflicts without war, the

IBRD/World Bank for postwar reconstruction as mentioned in Chapter 16, and the GATT discussed in Chapter 8, they also constructed a new inter-governmental bank called the International Monetary Fund (IMF) to help maintain order in the international financial system. Essentially, IMF member countries agreed to a system whereby the U.S. dollar would be permanently pegged to a fixed value in terms of gold, and the other currencies would be pegged to a fixed value in terms of the dollar. The main role of the IMF was to lend to countries that temporarily needed help in order to undertake the open market operations required to maintain the agreed-upon exchange rate. Thus, the IBRD was a bank that did long-run lending for development projects, while the IMF did short-run lending for international financial stability. This system, called the *Bretton Woods system* after the resort community in New Hampshire where it was hatched, lasted until 1971, when most countries abandoned the agreed-upon pegs and simply adopted managed floats.

When the People's Republic of China was a planned, socialist economy, the currency was inconvertible with a government-declared exchange rate, but with the market reforms of the early 1990s it was transformed into a convertible currency. The official rate had been between 2 and 3 yuan to the dollar, but the renminbi's value quickly fell to more than 8 to the dollar, as seen in Figure 17.1, which shows the yuan/dollar rate from 1990 to the present.[3] (Note that an upward movement in the figure indicates a depreciation of the renminbi and an appreciation of the dollar.) The government held the value steady at exactly 8.28 to the dollar for several years, before allowing it to appreciate gradually beginning in July 2005. The figure thus shows several of the basic

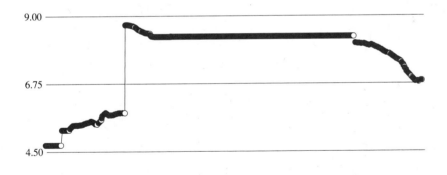

Source: Econstat.com.

FIGURE 17.1
Yuan/Dollar Exchange Rate, Monthly, 1990–2008.

---

[3] To avoid confusion, recall that the name of the *currency* is the renminbi, but its *units* are called yuan. Thus, a depreciation of the renminbi implies that it now takes more yuan to purchase one dollar.

types of exchange-rate policy at a glance: an inconvertible currency, followed by a convertible currency with a fixed exchange rate, and finally followed by a convertible currency with a managed float (the emphasis being more on the "managed" than on the "float").

The question, now, is whether or not, and how, this matters. Does the yuan/dollar rate hurt the U.S. economy by being too high (indicating that the renminbi is too cheap)? We cannot answer that question without thinking of the general equilibrium of the system. A common habit practiced by observers of international macroeconomic policy is to ask, in effect, what would happen to, say, the U.S. unemployment rate if the yuan/dollar rate was to fall without any change to any other variable in the system. But this is not a helpful way to think about it, because in order for the yuan/dollar rate to fall, something else in the system must have changed, such as Chinese monetary policy, U.S. monetary policy, supply and demand conditions for relevant traded commodities, Chinese or American productivity, or expectations about any of these items. Any of these changes would also have an effect on the U.S. unemployment rate. *The exchange rate is not an exogenous variable driving changes in the system, but rather an endogenous variable that responds to exogenous shocks along with all of the other endogenous variables.* Given that, it does not make sense to hold other variables unchanged when analyzing an appreciation of the renminbi, but rather to look at how the whole equilibrium (including, for example, prices of traded commodities in both countries) changes when an exogenous change occurs.

For example, we can ask the question: What would happen if the PBC raised the value of the renminbi? To answer this question, we need to remember that this issue entails not just a change in the yuan/dollar rate, but a change in PBC monetary policy—which in general could change all prices in the system, not just the exchange rate. To analyze this question, we need a general-equilibrium model with currency in it. We develop such a model in the next section.

17.3 A Dynamic, General-Equilibrium Model of Exchange-Rate Determination

17.3.1 The Setup

We construct a simple model of international trade with a market for foreign exchange. To smooth our path, we will take a familiar model of trade and add currency to it. For the main points of this analysis, it does not matter much which trade model we use, as long as it is a general-equilibrium model. Recall the Heckscher-Ohlin model of Chapter 6, with the United States and China using skilled and unskilled labor to produce and trade apparel (A) and plastics (P). To simplify matters, we will stick with the version of the model with fixed-coefficients (Leontieff) technology, as presented in Section 6.2, and assume free trade.

Suppose that we add currency to this model as follows. Assume that the Federal Reserve System, which is the central bank for the United States, has issued a total stock of M dollars and that the PBC has issued a total stock of M^* yuan. (Throughout, any nominal variable with no asterisk is dollar-denominated, while any nominal variable with an asterisk is yuan-denominated.) Suppose for now that all of this currency is being held by individual consumers, and that everyone knows that these stocks of currency will never change. We will ignore the distinction, crucial for many topics in monetary economics, between the different kinds of money, currency versus demand deposits, time deposits, and so on. For simplicity, we will assume that the only medium of exchange is currency (M0, in the classification scheme of monetary economics).

In order to have a determinate equilibrium exchange rate, there must be a demand for each currency. There are many ways of incorporating such a demand into the model, but perhaps the simplest is to introduce what is known as a *cash-in-advance constraint*: The assumption is that in order to buy a product made in the United States, one must first have in hand the required amount of money in U.S. dollars; and in order to buy a product made in China, one must first have in hand the required amount of money in yuan. (Cash-in-advance models of international trade were pioneered by Stockman (1980). The main points of the analysis would still carry through if, for example, this constraint applied only to some fraction of goods.)

Currency is an asset, whose market value (the exchange rate) at any date depends partly on the expectation that it will be useful in the future. To capture this element of the economics of exchange rates, we need a dynamic model. Consequently, we will define consumer preferences over the whole span of lifetime consumption (to eliminate some unnecessary complications, we will treat consumers as having infinitely long lives). Suppose that all consumers have the same utility function and that it is defined over the whole horizon of current and future consumption of both goods. Thus, we can write utility for a given consumer as:

$$ U(c_0^A, c_0^P, c_1^A, c_1^P, \ldots, c_t^A, c_t^P, \ldots), $$

where c_t^j is consumption of good j at time t, and U is an increasing and concave function. We will make a couple of assumptions on this function. First, at any date, utility maximization implies a relative demand curve that is the same as at any other date, so that:

$$ \frac{c_t^A}{c_t^P} = RD\left(\frac{P_t^A}{P_t^P}\right), $$

where P_t^j denotes the price of good j at time t, and RD is a decreasing function that does not vary over time. This works exactly as it did in the static model of Chapter 6. In fact, we will work out an example in which the relative demand curve is the same as the relative demand curve of the static model of Chapter 6, as laid out in Section 6.3. One can think of the consumer as first deciding how to allocate her spending across time and then, for each period, choosing that period's c_t^A and c_t^P to maximize that period's utility, taking as given the amount of spending money the consumer has allocated to that period.

Second, recall the concept of the marginal rate of intertemporal substitution, which is the slope of the indifference curve in diagrams such as Figure 16.5. In this model, we have two goods, so in principle we could have two different marginal rates of intertemporal substitution; for either good, it is the marginal utility of date-t consumption of the good, divided by the marginal utility of date $t + 1$ consumption of the same good. We assume here that if consumption is equal at two consecutive dates, $c_t^j = c_{t+1}^j$ for both goods, $j = A$ and P, then for either good, the intertemporal marginal rate of substitution is equal to $(1 + \gamma)$, where γ is a positive constant called the *rate of time preference*. In other words, consumers are impatient; there is a bias toward consuming now rather than later, so that, starting from a steady state, a consumer would need more than one unit of consumption next period to compensate for the loss of one unit of consumption this period.[4] We can call this the impatience assumption.

To understand the implications of the impatience assumption, a note on optimal consumption over time is in order. Recall from the two-period intertemporal optimization problem summarized by the Fisher diagram in Figure 16.5 that optimal consumption over time requires that the marginal rate of intertemporal substitution equals the slope of the intertemporal budget line, which we can call the marginal rate of intertemporal transformation. The same point works in a many-period problem such as we have here. For U.S. consumers the marginal rate of intertemporal transformation is equal to:

$$(1 + i_t)\frac{P_t^j}{P_{t+1}^j}$$

for good j, where i_t is the (nominal) interest rate at date t, since one unit of good j not consumed today saves P_t^j dollars that can be lent, yielding $(1 + i_t)P_t^j$ dollars next period, each of which can then be used to buy $\frac{1}{P_{t+1}^j}$ units of j. This marginal rate of intertemporal transformation is usually approximated by 1 plus the *real interest rate*, which is defined as $i_t - \pi_t^j$, where $\pi_t^j \equiv \frac{P_{t+1}^j - P_t^j}{P_t^j}$ is the rate of inflation for good j.[5] The approximation works very well as long as the inflation rate is not very large. From here on in, we will drop the "marginal rate of intertemporal transformation" language and just refer to the real interest rate for short.

So to a very good approximation we can state that optimal consumption requires that at each date the marginal rate of intertemporal substitution will be equal to 1 plus the real interest rate. The impatience assumption then implies that in order for consumers to be willing to budget for the future to consume as much tomorrow as today, the real interest rate must be equal to γ. If the real interest rate is greater than this value, consumers will budget even more for future consumption, implying greater consumption next period than in the current period. If the real interest rate is less than this value, consumers will budget less, and next period's consumption will be less than today's.

---

[4] It is easy to construct examples in which these two assumptions are satisfied. For example, if

$$U(c_0^A, c_0^P, c_1^A, c_1^P, \ldots, c_t^A, c_t^P, \ldots) = \sum_{t=0}^{\infty} \frac{1}{(1+\gamma)^t} v\left(\left(c_t^A c_t^P\right)^{1/2}\right),$$

where v is an increasing, concave function, it is easy to check that they are satisfied. In that case, the relative demand curve is just:

$$\frac{c_t^A}{c_t^P} = \frac{P_t^P}{P_t^A}.$$

This is just one example. We use a different relative demand curve in the example we work out in the text in order to keep the example in conformity with the model of Chapter 6.

[5] The marginal rate of intertemporal transformation can be written as $1 + (1 + i_t)\frac{P_t^j}{P_{t+1}^j} - 1$, which reduces to $1 + \frac{(1+i_t)}{(1+\pi_t^j)} - 1 = 1 + \frac{(i_t - \pi_t^j)}{(1+\pi_t^j)}$.

This is very well approximated by 1 plus the real interest rate, unless π_t^j is very large.

Importantly, we will assume that all economic agents in this model understand the model and are able to anticipate correctly what the future will be in any equilibrium. This is usually called a rational-expectations assumption.

Here is how a typical day works in this model. At the beginning of each period t, each consumer in each country can take his or her currency stored from last period and exchange part or all of it at the foreign-exchange market for the other currency. They may also borrow or lend currency in the process. In these transactions, they face the market-clearing exchange rate, which we will denote e_t, the price of a dollar in terms of yuan in period t; the market-clearing interest rate, i_t, for borrowing and lending dollars; and the market-clearing interest rate, i_t^*, for yuan. Then, each consumer takes this currency to the goods market and places orders for the goods he or she wishes to consume that period; payment is made at the time the orders are placed, at dollar prices P_t^A and P_t^P for goods made in the United States and at yuan prices P_t^{A*} and P_t^{P*} for goods made in China. Next, the firms that have accepted payment use the currency to hire skilled and unskilled workers to produce the output to fill the orders. (These workers are, of course, also consumers, who then will store this currency they receive as wages for consumption in the next period.) Finally, production occurs, the goods are sent to consumers, and consumption occurs. The period ends, and a new one begins with exactly the same sequence, which repeats from one period to the next over and over again.

17.3.2 Equilibrium

We will be able to make the main points by focusing on the simplest case: an equilibrium starting from an initial state in which consumers in both countries initially hold only their own country's currency and both countries initially have a zero net foreign asset position. This simply means that initially people in neither country owe the other money. We will see that under these conditions, with the model as specified, there is a simple *steady-state* equilibrium, meaning a time-path along which the endogenous variables are not changing. The conditions for equilibrium in this situation can be described as follows (of course, they are somewhat more complicated than in the models without money, but they are easily managed).

First, we must have market clearing in the markets for skilled and unskilled labor in both countries. This is exactly as laid out in Section 6.3. It takes 2 units of unskilled labor and 1 unit of skilled labor to produce 1 unit of apparel, and 3 units of both kinds of labor to produce 1 unit of plastics. Given that the United States has 72 million units of unskilled labor and 60 million units of skilled labor, labor-market clearing implies that the U.S. economy produces 12 million units of apparel and 16 million units of plastics. Given that China has 540 million unskilled workers and 300 million skilled workers, labor-market clearing implies that the Chinese economy produces 240 million units of apparel and 20 million units of plastics.

Second, we must have the same prices for each product in each country, regardless of where the product was produced. A Chinese consumer can buy a unit of plastics from a Chinese firm, paying P^{P*} yuan, or from a U.S. firm, paying P^P dollars, which requires eP^P yuan. Since in equilibrium Chinese consumers will buy some portion of their plastics from suppliers in both countries, these must be equal. Similar logic applies to U.S. consumers' purchase of apparel, which costs them P^A dollars from American suppliers and P^{A*}/e dollars from Chinese suppliers. As a result:

$$P^{P*} = eP^P$$
$$P^{A*} = eP^A \qquad (17.1)$$

This is called the *law of one price*; that is, each commodity will sell at the same price anywhere it is sold, after correcting for exchange rates. (Of course, it is not really a law; it follows from the assumptions of this model and a lot of other models, but whether or not it holds in the real world is an empirical question, to be discussed later.) A related concept is *purchasing power parity*. Define the *real exchange rate* as the yuan-denominated consumer price index for Chinese consumers, divided by e times the dollar-denominated consumer price index for U.S. consumers. Given that in this model consumers in both countries have the same preferences, and given the law of one price, the real exchange rate in this model will always be equal to 1. The *purchasing power parity hypothesis* is the hypothesis that the real exchange rate between any two countries will be a constant. Clearly, that will be true in this model. All of these propositions, however—the law of one price, the real exchange rate taking a value of 1, purchasing power parity—hold in some models but not in others, and none of them holds exactly in real-world data.

Third, the world goods market must clear, which implies that the relative price of apparel must be such that the relative demand for apparel by each consumer is equal to the world relative supply. Once again, this follows the analysis of Chapter 6 and implies, using the assumed relative demand curve used there, that:

$$\frac{P^A}{P^P} = \frac{P^{A*}}{P^{P*}} = 0.42.$$

(See Section 6.3.) Fourth, we must have zero profits in both industries in both countries, which we can ensure by deriving wages for skilled and unskilled workers in both countries once we have found product prices, as in Section 6.4. Now that we know that the relative price of apparel is 0.42, we can compute $(w^U/P^A) = 0.0867$, $(w^S/P^A) = 0.247$, $(w^U/P^P) = 0.206$, and $(w^S/P^P) = 0.587$.

Fifth, world lending markets must be in equilibrium. Forgetting for the moment that we are discussing a steady state, suppose that the U.S. and Chinese interest rates at time t are equal to i_t and i_t^*, respectively, and the exchange rate is equal to e_t and e_{t+1} at time t and $t+1$, respectively. People in financial markets are always looking for a new way to make money, and one method they may try is a scheme called *triangular interest arbitrage*. Under this scheme, an investor can borrow \$1 at time t, convert it into e_t yuan, lend the yuan, receive $(1 + i_t^*)e_t$ yuan back from the loan next period, and then convert it back into dollars to receive $\frac{(1+i_t^*)e_t}{e_{t+1}}$ dollars. Paying back the original dollar loan (don't forget the original dollar loan!) with interest, the profit on the transaction is equal to $\frac{(1+i_t^*)e_t}{e_{t+1}} - (1 + i_t)$, which is positive if $\frac{(1+i_t^*)}{(1+i_t)} > \frac{e_{t+1}}{e_t}$. In other words, triangular interest arbitrage starting from a dollar loan makes a profit if the rate of depreciation of the renminbi (the right-hand side of this inequality) is less than the Chinese interest-rate premium (the left-hand side of this inequality). If this occurs, then we will not have equilibrium in financial markets, because everyone will be trying to borrow dollars for this purpose, and no one will be willing to lend. A similar situation emerges on the other side of the market if the inequality has the opposite sign, with everyone wanting to borrow yuan for arbitrage. The implication is that in order to have equilibrium in the financial markets, we must have:

$$\frac{(1+i_t^*)}{(1+i_t)} = \frac{e_{t+1}}{e_t}, \tag{17.2}$$

This condition is called *uncovered interest parity*.[6] It ensures that if there is any anticipated appreciation of a currency, then the interest rate for the other country will be higher by just enough that investors will be willing to hold either currency. Of course, given that we are focusing on a steady state, (17.2) is easy to satisfy: In a steady state, the exchange rate will be constant, the right-hand side of (17.2) will be equal to 1, and uncovered interest parity simply requires that the two countries' interest rates are equal. Later, we will explore situations in which an anticipated depreciation leads the interest rates to differ.[7]

Note, by the way, that the law of one price (17.1) combined with uncovered interest parity (17.2) together imply that the marginal rate of intertemporal transformation $(1+i_t)\frac{P_t^j}{P_{t+1}^j}$ for U.S. consumers is equal to the corresponding rate $(1+i_t^*)\frac{P_t^{j*}}{P_{t+1}^{j*}}$ for Chinese consumers. In other words, interest-rate parity plus the law of one price together ensure that real interest rates in the two countries are always equal.

Sixth, interest rates must adjust so that at each date total world consumption demand is equal to total world production. In this steady-state situation, that means that interest rates must adjust so that consumers are willing to consume constant amounts of both commodities over time. Recall from the discussion following the impatience assumption in Section 17.3.1 that this implies that the real interest rate in each country must be equal to the rate of time preference, γ. Note that in the steady state of this model, there will be no inflation, so there will be no difference between real and nominal interest rates. This implies that in a steady-state equilibrium $i = i^* = \gamma$: Both currencies' interest rates are simply equal to the rate of time preference. (From this point, we will drop the time subscripts on all variables, since they are superfluous in a steady state.)

Seventh, the price level in each country must adjust so that the demand for that country's currency is equal to its supply. We know that $P^A/P^P = 0.42$, so we can write U.S. nominal GDP, in millions of dollars, as:

$$\begin{aligned} GDP^{US} &= P^A Q^A + P^P Q^P \\ &= P^P(0.42 Q^A + Q^P) \\ &= P^P(0.42 \cdot 16 + 12) \\ &= P^P 18.72. \end{aligned} \tag{17.3}$$

---

[6] The condition is most often expressed in the form $i_t^* - i_t = \hat{e}_t$, where $\hat{e}_t \equiv \frac{e_{t+1}}{e_t} - 1$ is the expected rate of depreciation. This is a fairly good approximation for (17.2) when the interest rates and the depreciation rate are not too large.

[7] In the steady state of this model, there is no borrowing or lending, since there is no capital to invest in and there are no differences in the situations of different people in the same country that might lead one to lend to another. Thus, the interest rate in each country is merely the rate at which each consumer optimally chooses zero borrowing. It is still instructive to see how the interest rate changes with various shocks to the system. Later, we will look at a productivity shock that hits China alone and that will cause borrowing to occur in equilibrium.

This is the income of U.S. consumers. Given that we are studying a steady state, consumers have no reason to save, so they spend their income in each period; however, this means that (17.3) is also per-period U.S. consumer spending in this model. Now, note that U.S. consumers spend their currency holdings each year, with the U.S. dollars all spent on U.S. goods. (Some of these dollars are spent by Chinese consumers, who purchase the dollars at the start of the period in order to import something from the United States, but one way or another each dollar held at the beginning of the period will be spent on a U.S. product.) As a result, nominal U.S. consumer spending is represented equally well by (17.3) and by M. Equating these gives:

$$P^P = M/18.72. \tag{17.4}$$

In other words, the U.S. price level is proportional to the U.S. money supply. A parallel calculation for China provides the parallel result. Representing China's nominal GDP by GDP^{CH^*}, we find:

$$GDP^{CH^*} = P^{P^*}120.8, \tag{17.5}$$

which leads to:

$$P^{P^*} = M^*/120.8. \tag{17.6}$$

Finally, the exchange rate must adjust so that the foreign-exchange market is in equilibrium. Due to the law of one price (17.1), the equilibrium value of the exchange rate can be found as the yuan-denominated price of plastics in China divided by the dollar-denominated price of plastics in the United States (or the same calculation for apparel). This can be found by dividing (17.6) by (17.4). This yields:

$$e = \frac{M^*}{M} \frac{18.72}{120.8}. \tag{17.7}$$

This is the key finding. The exchange rate is the product of two terms. The first term is the ratio of the money supplies in the two countries. Other things being equal, doubling the number of yuan in circulation, or cutting the number of dollars in half, will double the yuan/dollar rate, cutting the value of each yuan in half. The second term is the ratio of the sizes of the two economies. Note from the calculation of (17.3) and (17.5) that 18.72 is U.S. GDP divided by the U.S. price of plastics (or, equivalently, U.S. GDP evaluated with the price of plastics set equal to 1 and the price of apparel set equal to 0.42). Similarly, 120.8 is Chinese GDP divided by the price of plastics. Thus, the second ratio in (17.7) is the relative size of the two economies. Other things being equal, an increase in the size of the Chinese economy relative to the U.S. economy will raise the demand for yuan and cause the renminbi to appreciate.

17.4 Equilibrium Responses

Now that we understand how equilibrium works in this model, we can ask how it would respond to a wide variety of events—including, most importantly, how it would respond if the PBC capitulated to the Schumer ultimatum.

17.4.1 What Happens If the Value of the Renminbi Is Raised?

We can now pose the question of what happens in this model if the People's Bank of China grants the wishes of Senator Schumer, and so many other commentators, and raises the value of the renminbi. Once again, as emphasized in Section 17.2, this does *not* mean *lowering* the value of e, keeping all other variables as given. What it does mean is a change in Chinese monetary policy, specifically, choosing a lower value of M^*, the supply of yuan, with all of the attendant changes in the equilibrium that that implies. For concreteness, suppose that M^* is decreased by 27.5%, the figure proposed by the senator himself.

Going through the seven points of equilibrium analysis, we see that the quantities of both goods produced by both countries are unchanged, and as a result so are the relative prices of the two goods. Both countries' interest rates remain equal to the rate of time preference, as required in any steady state. The price level in the United States is unchanged, as shown by (17.4). It is not until we reach nominal GDP in China (17.5), and the nominal price level for China (17.6), that we see a change: The yuan prices for both goods fall by exactly 27.5% as a result of the policy change, lowering nominal GDP in China also by exactly 27.5%. Of course, from (17.7), the yuan appreciates by 27.5%.

The budget line for every Chinese consumer is unchanged because all incomes fall in nominal terms by exactly the same fraction as all consumer prices. Therefore, the utility attained by each Chinese consumer is unchanged. Trade is also unchanged, since each country's production and consumption of each good are unchanged. The change in exchange-rate policy has certainly not had any effect on the trade balance, which was and remains zero.

As a result, the revaluation of the renminbi in this example has had no meaningful effect on anything. In particular, it has not made U.S. manufacturers more competitive. The revenue earned by an American plastics exporter on a unit sold in China is P^{P*}/e, after converting into dollars. The denominator has fallen, which is the effect most commentators who recommend a crackdown on the renminbi point out, but the numerator has fallen by the same amount, leaving the dollar price unchanged.

Within the framework of this model, bickering over the value of the renminbi is not helpful or harmful; the issue is simply irrelevant.

Advocates of a renminbi crackdown are either making the mistake of partial equilibrium thinking on a general-equilibrium question—forgetting that changing the exchange rate will require policy changes that will in turn change other prices in the system—or they are relying on a different model. Shortly we will discuss important additions to this model that can change some of the conclusions. First, we will examine a few other illuminating experiments we can perform with the basic model.

17.4.2 Anticipated Devaluation

It is useful to analyze the effects of a change in currency policy that is announced one period in advance. Because currency is in a way a financial asset (one that pays no interest or dividends but that can provide capital gains or losses), a pre-announced policy change could have a significant effect before the policy actually goes into effect. For a concrete example, suppose that the PBC announces at date $t = 0$ that it will print extra yuan equal to 10% of the existing stock and will distribute them equally to all Chinese citizens as of the beginning of date $t = 1$. Because such a change will inevitably reduce the value of the yuan at least at date $t = 1$, we can call this a case of anticipated devaluation.

The analysis of the model from date $t = 1$ forward is just as we have seen, with steady-state values for the exchange rate and for yuan-denominated goods prices that are 10% higher than they would otherwise be, but no change in anything else. Date $t = 0$ is slightly trickier. At date $t = 0$, production and relative supply of both goods are unchanged, so the relative supply of apparel is unchanged and as a result so is its relative price. There is nothing new in the calculation of nominal U.S. GDP or the U.S. price level, so (17.3) and (17.4) hold without any change. Once we know the yuan-denominated price of plastics, the calculation of nominal Chinese GDP is the same as it was without the devaluation, so equation (17.5) still holds. Further, during period 0 the supply of yuan, M^*, is unchanged (it increases by 10% only at the beginning of period 1). As long as all of those yuan are actually spent at date $t = 0$, then they have to be spent on Chinese-produced goods, so M^* is still equal to nominal Chinese GDP, and (17.6) still holds as well. We can conclude that the date $t = 0$ price level in China is unchanged by the announcement, and so, by (17.7), so is the date $t = 0$ exchange rate.[8]

So far, we know that production, consumption, prices, and the exchange rate at date $t = 0$ are unchanged by the devaluation announcement. By process of elimination, then, the only thing that can change at date $t = 0$ is the interest rate. The U.S. interest rate cannot change because dollar prices are the same in both periods, so there is no U.S. inflation; thus, there is no difference between the real interest rate and the nominal rate; and the real rate is equal to γ. Recalling now the uncovered interest parity condition (17.2):

$$\frac{(1 + i_0^*)}{(1 + i_0)} = \frac{e_1}{e_0}, \tag{17.8}$$

this reduces to:

$$\frac{(1 + i_0^*)}{(1 + \gamma)} = 1.1. \tag{17.9}$$

The right-hand side is the expected rate of yuan devaluation, which takes a value of 1.1 because the exchange rate rises by 10% between date $t = 0$ and date $t = 1$. Condition (17.9) says that the equilibrium yuan interest rate at date $t = 0$ is equal to $i_0^* = 1.1(1 + \gamma) - 1 = 0.1 + \gamma + (0.1)\gamma$, which is pretty well approximated by the rate of time preference plus 10%.

In sum, the announcement of the devaluation does create an anticipated effect: It raises the yuan nominal interest rate immediately, by just enough to compensate for the expected loss in the yuan's value, so that the yuan is just as attractive an investment as the dollar (or, put differently, there is no way to profit from

---

[8] The finding that the date $t = 0$ exchange rate is unchanged by the announcement of the date $t = 1$ devaluation is forced by the structure of the model, which requires that the velocity of money, or the ratio of GDP to the money stock, is always equal to 1. A richer model would allow for an announced devaluation to cause an immediate depreciation.

triangular interest arbitrage). However, the *real* interest rate facing all consumers, in both countries is unchanged; it is still equal to the rate of time preference.

This simple example makes a more general point about exchange rates: Anticipated *future* changes in exchange-rate policy can have large *current* effects on economic outcomes. Here, an anticipated future devaluation of the yuan leads to a current increase in Chinese interest rates. This is an example of what international economists sometimes call a *Peso problem*, a situation in which speculators anticipate a devaluation and act accordingly. For a long time in the early 1980s, when Mexico maintained a fixed exchange rate, investors thought a devaluation was likely, despite government denials; this expectation raised Mexican interest rates and put pressure on the central bank.

17.4.3 Productivity Effects

Exchange rates will respond not only to monetary policy, but also to any change in supply or demand conditions. Here is a simple example. Suppose that the productivity of each worker in China rises by 10%, so that in China, it takes only $2/1.1 = 1.8$ units of unskilled labor and $1/1.1 = 0.9$ units of skilled labor to produce a unit of apparel, and only $3/1.1 = 2.7$ units of either kind of labor to produce one unit of plastics. The productivity of workers in the United States is unchanged. The situation is, for our purposes, identical to the situation we would have if China's skilled and unskilled labor forces increased in size by 10% (but it is not identical from the point of view of Chinese workers, because a productivity improvement allows their *per capita* incomes to rise).

The first thing to note about the new equilibrium is that the output of both industries in China would rise by 10%, so China would produce 264 million units of apparel instead of 240 and 22 million units of plastics instead of 20. The second thing to note is that, although neither country's relative supply curve in Figure 6.6 would change, the increased size of the Chinese economy would imply that the world relative supply curve is closer to the Chinese one than it was before the productivity change. Thus, as a result of the rise in Chinese productivity, RS^W shifts to the right and the world relative price of apparel falls below its original value of 0.42. For concreteness, suppose that the new value of the relative price is 0.4. Then the new value of nominal GDP in China is:

$$
\begin{aligned}
GDP^{CH*} &= P^{A*}Q^A + P^{P*}Q^P \\
&= P^{P*}(0.4Q^A + Q^P) \\
&= P^{P*}(0.4 \cdot 264 + 22) \\
&= P^{P*}127.6.
\end{aligned}
\tag{17.10}
$$

U.S. nominal GDP is changed only slightly, due to the change in the relative apparel price:

$$
\begin{aligned}
GDP^{US} &= P^P(0.4 \cdot 16 + 12) \\
&= P^P 18.4.
\end{aligned}
\tag{17.11}
$$

Tracing through the same logic as before in equations (17.3) to (17.7), we find the new value of the exchange rate:

$$
e = \frac{M^*}{M} \frac{18.4}{127.6} < \frac{M^*}{M} \frac{18.72}{120.8}.
\tag{17.12}
$$

The expression on the right-hand side of the inequality in (17.12) is the exchange rate before the productivity change from (17.7). Clearly, the productivity improvement increases the value of the renminbi against the dollar. The point is that, with a larger Chinese economy and more Chinese-produced goods to purchase, the demand for yuan has gone up relative to the demand for dollars.

17.4.4 Anticipated Productivity Changes

Now, consider again the permanent productivity change just discussed, but suppose that it occurs at date $t = 1$, while productivity at date $t = 0$ is as in the original model. Suppose that everyone knows that this productivity change will occur. For date $t = 0$, the nominal prices of both goods in the two currencies, as well as the exchange rate, can be found to be exactly as they were in the original model in Section 17.3.2. For date $t = 1$, these prices can be seen to be as they were in the steady state with the productivity change just discussed above. Therefore, we have an expected appreciation of the renminbi between date $t = 0$ and date $t = 1$, and uncovered interest parity (17.2) requires that the nominal dollar interest rate be higher than the nominal yuan interest rate.

Something a bit more interesting happens in this example, however. Notice that at date $t = 1$ and thereafter, world output of both goods is higher than at date $t = 0$. Therefore, world consumption must also be higher. Now, uncovered interest parity together with the law of one price guarantees that real interest rates will be equal in both countries (recall the discussion following (17.2)). Therefore, either (i) the real interest rate is equal to γ, and everyone in the world has the same consumption level at date $t = 0$ and at date $t = 1$; or (ii) the real interest rate exceeds γ, and everyone in the world has higher consumption at date $t = 1$ compared with date $t = 0$; or (iii) the real interest rate is less than γ, and everyone in the world has lower consumption at date $t = 1$ compared with date $t = 0$. In light of the fact that worldwide consumption must be higher at date $t = 1$ compared with date $t = 0$, only (ii) is possible.

We conclude that the anticipated future improvement in Chinese productivity leads to a current rise in world real interest rates. One way of interpreting this fact is that Chinese consumers expect an increase in their future income and wish to borrow in order to begin enjoying the benefits of their increased wealth right away. The increased demand for loans pushes real interest rates up, encouraging American consumers to lend part of their income. What this implies is that the United States runs a trade surplus at date $t = 0$, consuming less than its GDP as it lends to China, followed by a trade deficit at all dates after that, consuming *more* than its GDP as it receives interest payments on its date $t = 0$ loans. This is really a richer example of the case of a trade deficit because of optimism as developed in Section 16.3 (here, China plays the role that Korea played in that example).

17.4.5 A Fiscal Interpretation

There is a case to be made that the story of U.S.-Chinese economic relations is largely a matter of managing U.S. budget deficits. Consider the following very stylized representation of that story within this model.

Suppose that instead of 72 million unskilled workers, the U.S. economy has 80 million, and instead of 60 million skilled workers, it has 66.67 million.

Suppose that for unavoidable public works projects such as national defense, the government needs to hire 8 million unskilled workers and 6.67 million skilled workers every period. That is 10% of the total for both types of worker, and it leaves 72 million unskilled and 60 million skilled for the private sector—just as in the basic model. Assume that the workers hired by the government are paid the same as workers are paid in the private sector.

Now, suppose that instead of paying for this expense with taxes, the government prints money. Because its expense will be 10% of GDP, it can meet the need by printing money equal to 10% of the existing money supply. This is a simple form of deficit financing, called seigniorage; in practice, the U.S. government does not finance deficits in this way, but rather by issuing Treasury bonds, but the distinction does not make much difference to this particular discussion. Think of the government as hiring the labor at the beginning of the period, just before the foreign-exchange market, so that workers hired by the government can take their newly received (and newly printed) dollars and exchange some of them for yuan. Suppose that the PBC decides to help the U.S. government out by buying up a fraction x of those newly issued dollars, paying in newly printed yuan, and putting the dollars it buys into its vault permanently. In effect, the PBC is financing a fraction x of the U.S. budget deficit.

Each period, then, the U.S. money stock increases by $0.1(1 - x)M_t$, which is the new dollars printed, $0.1M_t$, minus the amount purchased by the PBC, $0.1(x)M_t$ (recalling that in equilibrium U.S. nominal GDP always equals M_t). The rate of change of the U.S. money supply is, then, this increase divided by the current total supply, or $0.1(1 - x)$.

The number of yuan spent by the PBC to buy the specified quantity of dollars on the foreign-exchange market is $e_t(0.1)(x)M_t$, so the rate of growth of the stock of yuan is:

$$e_t(0.1)(x)\frac{M_t}{M_t^*}.$$

The dollar supply grows faster than the yuan supply if

$$0.1(1 - x) > e_t(0.1)(x)\frac{M_t}{M_t^*},$$

which, following from the fact that each country's nominal GDP is equal to its money supply in this model, can be rearranged to:

$$x < \frac{GDP^*/e_t}{GDP^*/e_t + GDP}.$$

In other words, the U.S. money supply grows faster than the Chinese money supply if the PBC finances a fraction of U.S. deficit spending that is less than China's share of the world economy. If China finances less than this, it will allow the dollar to depreciate without end. If China finances more than this, it will be gobbling up dollars and making the dollar appreciate without end. If the fraction of the U.S. budget deficit that it finances is equal to China's share in the world economy, then the exchange rate will be fixed. This will produce a history of the exchange rate that looks a lot lot like Figure 17.1 from 1995 to 2006, with a very constant level of the exchange rate, and in the background huge, continuous purchases of U.S. government securities by the PBC.[9]

The point may be driven home by considering the situation of a typical unskilled U.S. plastics worker. The real wage of an unskilled plastics worker is determined by the logic of the Heckscher-Ohlin model and is consequently the same regardless of monetary policy (and is the same as the real wage of an unskilled apparel worker), so it does not depend on x. Of course, the *nominal* wage *does* depend on monetary policy. Suppose that given the current monetary state, the unskilled wage last period amounted to $100. Given the wages relative to output prices as described in Section 17.3.2, this implies that the price of a unit of apparel, P^A, last period was equal to $1,153,[10] and the price of a unit of plastics, P^P, was equal to $485. Suppose first that $x = 0$. Now, that $100 wage has been saved at the end of last period to be used for consumption this period, but by the time the goods market opens this period there is 10% more U.S. currency on the market, causing the prices of both products to rise by 10% (hence, $1,268 for apparel and $534 for plastics). As a result, the $100 wage saved from last period will buy 10% less than it would have with no inflation. Now, suppose that $x = 1$. In this case, there is no dollar price inflation, so when the worker spends today the $100 she earned last period, she can do so at the same prices, $P^A = \$1153$ and $P^P = \$485$, that prevailed yesterday. In this case, the cost of U.S. national defense is paid for by Chinese workers, who shoulder the burden of the inflation themselves.

Thus, the history of U.S.-China macroeconomic relations is something like a model with x equal to China's share in the world economy, producing a steady yuan/dollar exchange rate. Is this a problem? In particular, should the United States try to insist that China choose a smaller value for x? Within this model, the short answer is No. The public works project is not free; the printing of money causes the money to lose value constantly by causing product prices to increase constantly. Americans save money at the end of one period and then find that it does not buy as much at the beginning of the next period. This capital loss on money reduces consumption, as is needed to free up resources for the public works project. If $x = 0$, all of that burden falls on Americans, with no price inflation to bother Chinese consumers. If $x = 1$, all of the inflation tax falls on Chinese consumers, with no inflation in the United States. The more of the U.S. budget deficit the PBC finances, the lower is U.S. inflation, and the better off the American consumers are.

By this interpretation, Senator Schumer is asking the PBC to lower the value of x, in effect imploring the Chinese government to stop sending such a generous gift to the American people.

---

[9] In practice, the U.S. government does not finance its deficits by printing money, but by issuing Treasury bonds, and these are what the PBC buys. However, the effects are, for the purposes of this discussion, similar. In the real world, the money supply is not simply currency (M0); demand deposits are a larger component, and these are generated through the banking system with fractional-reserve banking. The more Treasury bonds there are, the more reserves there are for the banking system, and the more money the banking system will create.

[10] This follows from the information that $(w^U/P^A) = 0.0867$, together with the assumption that $w^U = \$100$.

17.5 Adding Nominal Rigidity

To sum up, this model has suggested that the value of the renminbi in and of itself is irrelevant to the U.S. trade deficit and U.S. welfare. However, we need to consider whether or not this conclusion is driven by the particular assumptions of the model—perhaps the model omits effects that are important in the real world, and that would give us a different answer if we included them. The single most important assumption we made is that all prices adjust quickly to market-clearing levels no matter what happens. For that reason, this type of model is called a *flexible-price* model. However, many economists argue that the dynamics of international adjustment cannot be understood without allowing for the possibility that at least some fraction of product prices is fixed in terms of one of the currencies for at least a short while. This is called a *nominal rigidity*. It can have a big impact on the relationship between monetary policy, exchange rates, and welfare.

The questions of whether or not nominal rigidities matter in the world economy, and exactly how, are the subjects of a vast amount of research and debate. Recall (from Section 17.3.2) that the flexible-price model studied in the previous sections features the law of one price and purchasing power parity. Many economists have pointed out that there are substantial deviations from both of these principles in the data, and a substantial literature has emerged to estimate how persistent deviations from purchasing power parity are. Crucini, Telmer, and Zachariadis (2005) and Crucini and Shintania (2008) summarize much of that research. However, it is not necessary therefore to conclude that nominal rigidities are important in practice. The law of one price could fail to hold, for example, because of transport costs, because some goods are not tradable, or because consumers in different countries consume different qualities of the same good. Indeed, Crucini et al. present evidence that when one looks at product-level prices (rather than aggregate price indices, which are what are used in real exchange-rate research), the patterns of deviations from the law of one price do not appear to be the sort of patterns that would be created by nominal rigidities.

We make no attempt to settle the debate over nominal rigidities here, but we *will* comment on how nominal rigidities would affect the analysis of the policy questions. Adding nominal rigidity to a model such as this in a thorough way is a large project beyond the scope of this volume. However, we can point out some of the more important effects that have been developed by economists who have done so.

By far the most influential approach to nominal rigidities in an international monetary model is that of Obstfeld and Rogoff (1995). The model that they construct is similar to the one studied here in many respects, but it exhibits three particularly important differences: (i) The model features monopolistic competition (recall Chapter 3). (ii) Workers have an upward-sloping labor-supply schedule (unlike the model here, in which labor is inelastically supplied). (iii) Prices exhibit nominal rigidity, in a particular form, called *producer-currency pricing*: In each country, at each date, each firm chooses the price it will charge to *all* of its customers for the following date *in its own currency*. Thus, at date t, each American firm sets its prices for date $t + 1$ in dollars, taking into account what it expects market conditions to be like at that time. Consequently, if, say, the renminbi unexpectedly appreciates by 10% between dates t and $t + 1$, that will not affect the U.S. firms' price for

U.S. consumers at that date, but it *will* affect the U.S. firms' price for *Chinese* consumers because the price will have dropped by 10% in yuan. Notice that the law of one price automatically holds with producer-currency pricing; consequently, if the two countries consume the same basket of goods purchasing-power parity will also hold.

Obstfeld and Rogoff show that in a model of that sort, an unexpected devaluation can have significant real effects. Suppose that the supply of dollars has been constant and is expected to remain constant until date $t = T$, at which time the U.S. government suddenly increases the supply of dollars by 10% by printing up new money and delivering it evenly to American consumers. Then, at that date, the dollar will depreciate, but the prices charged by each firm in its own currency will be, for the moment, unchanged—having been set by each firm at date $t = T - 1$. As a result, for each U.S. consumer, the dollar price of each Chinese good will be suddenly higher, so Chinese goods will be (for the moment) relatively expensive compared to U.S.-produced goods; and for each Chinese consumer, the yuan price of each U.S.-produced good will be suddenly lower, so U.S.-made goods will be (for the moment) relatively cheap compared to Chinese-produced goods. The result is that consumers the world over will increase their spending on U.S.-made goods and reduce their spending on Chinese-produced goods. This expenditure-switching effect will raise U.S. GDP relative to Chinese GDP, boosting U.S. incomes.[11]

This expenditure-switching effect is temporary, however. As of date $t = T + 1$, firms in both countries will have set their new prices to take the new monetary landscape into account, and the economy enters its new permanent steady state. Since as of date $t = T$, U.S. consumers understand that the boost in their relative incomes is temporary, they save most of it, running a current-account surplus at date $t = T$, followed by a permanent current-account deficit afterward. In effect, Americans receive a temporary windfall and use it to increase their permanent consumption by lending out most of the windfall to the Chinese. As a result, at date $t = T$, Americans consume less than their income, and at every date after that they consume more than their income.

An alternative approach to nominal rigidities in an international equilibrium is called *pricing to market* (PTM). Under this assumption, a firm sets its price in terms of the consumer's currency. Thus, under PTM a U.S. firm will set a price in dollars for the U.S. market and a price in yuan for the Chinese market. Notice that the law of one price will not generally hold in this type of model, since a sudden movement in the exchange rate will change the dollar price of the good sold in the Chinese market but not the dollar price of the good sold in the U.S. market. Because the law of one price will not hold, purchasing-power parity will not either.

Devereux (2000) shows how a devaluation will affect the current account differently in a model with PTM compared to a model with producer-currency pricing. In a model just like the Obstfeld-Rogoff model except that it features PTM, Devereux shows that a sudden increase in the U.S. money stock launches two effects. First, it temporarily raises U.S. income relative to the rest of the world's income not because of expenditure-switching effects (these are absent, because the devaluation does not change any consumer's prices, and so

---

[11] The details matter: The fact that the expenditure-switching effect increases U.S. GDP is a consequence of the monopolistic competition and upward-sloping labor supply.

cannot make U.S. goods cheaper relative to Chinese-produced goods), but because each U.S. firm now receives more dollars for each sale it makes in China at its fixed yuan price, while each Chinese firm now receives fewer yuan for each sale it makes in the United States at its fixed dollar price. This temporary boost to U.S. income provides an incentive for U.S. consumers to increase their savings at date $t = T$, creating a temporary current-account surplus, as in the Obstfeld-Rogoff model.

Second, it temporarily lowers the U.S. real interest rate, because as of date $t = T$, prices have not changed yet, but everyone knows that prices in the United States will adjust upward at date $t = T + 1$. Put differently, everyone knows that the U.S. economy will go through significant inflation between $t = T$ and $t = T + 1$. As a result, consumption for U.S. consumers is temporarily cheap at date $t = T$, and this provides an incentive for U.S. consumers to *lower* their savings at date $t = T$, creating a temporary current-account *deficit*. For these reasons, either a U.S. trade surplus or trade deficit could occur at date $t = T$, depending on which of these two effects dominates.

This line of research is rich and complex, and has identified many ways in which monetary shocks can affect exchange rates, trade, savings, investment, the current account, and welfare in an open-economy general equilibrium setting. However, it should be underlined that one thing it does *not* do is to make a case that a particular value of the yuan-dollar rate, or any other nominal exchange rate, is preferable to any other. In all of these models, multiplying the quantity of U.S. currency by 10% at each date will reduce the value of the dollar and increase the dollar-denominated prices by 10% at each date, with no effect on any real variable such as production, consumption, or any consumer's utility. The effects that the literature focuses on have to do with *unanticipated changes* in exchange-rate policy; *the absolute value of the nominal exchange rate, in and of itself, remains irrelevant.*

MAIN IDEAS

1. An exchange rate is the price of one currency in terms of another. Inconvertible currencies tend to have a price set by government and are now uncommon. Exchange rates for convertible currencies are set by supply and demand forces on foreign-exchange markets.

2. Central banks can influence exchange rates for convertible currencies through open market operations on foreign-exchange markets. They can choose a strategy of fixed or floating rates, or the intermediate strategy of a managed float.

3. An exchange rate is a *price*, determined in general equilibrium by every facet of the economy, including productivity, demand, monetary policy, and possibly expectations of all of these for the future. As a consequence, it does not make sense to ask what would happen if, say, a particular currency was devalued, all else equal. We need to ask what would happen if, say, monetary policy was changed in such a

way as to devalue the currency, and then trace through the general-equilibrium ramifications of that change in policy.

4. Generally, a larger supply of a currency, *ceteris paribus*, lowers its value on foreign- exchange markets, while an increase in the productivity or size of the national economy that issues it raises its value.

5. An important equilibrium condition in foreign-exchange markets is uncovered interest parity, which requires nominal interest rates across countries to differ by the expected rate of depreciation of the exchange rate.

6. In dynamic general equilibrium open-economy models, in general, if the supply of a currency is increased by a fixed percentage at each date, the exchange rate will be proportionally reduced at each date, and production, trade, consumption, and utility will be unchanged. In this sense, the

absolute level of the exchange rate is irrelevant. This is true of flexible-price and nominal-rigidity models.

7. The law of one price and purchasing power parity are both properties of equilibrium in the simplest flexible-price models. They are both rejected by the data. Whether or not this implies that nominal-price models are better than flexible-price models for analyzing policy is a matter of debate.

8. In models with nominal rigidities, an unanticipated change in monetary policy can cause an unanticipated swing in exchange rates and real effects on production, consumption, and utility.

9. In a model with nominal rigidities in the form of producer-currency pricing, a sudden devaluation of a currency leads to a temporary expenditure-

switching effect that increases GDP in the devaluating country relative to the rest of the world, giving that country a temporary current-account surplus and long-run current-account deficits.

10. In a model with nominal rigidities in the form of pricing to market (PTM), a sudden devaluation could lead to a current-account surplus or deficit depending on parameters.

11. The idea that the Chinese government is hurting the United States economy with a sustained "undervaluation" of the renminbi is hard to support with a coherent general equilibrium analysis. A more plausible interpretation is that the Chinese government is helping the U.S. economy by financing U.S. fiscal deficits that would otherwise be paid for by Americans.

QUESTIONS AND PROBLEMS

1. Pick a pair of countries and download data on their exchange rate, from a site such as oecd.org or econstat.com. Plot the exchange rate over time, and describe briefly the main features of the history. Can you come up with a good economic explanation of the major movements (or lack of movement) in this exchange rate, consistent with the sort of logic we have seen in the model of Sections 17.3 and 17.4 and what you know about those two countries?

2. Suppose that a newspaper commentator calls for a quick devaluation of the U.S. dollar as a temporary boost to the U.S. economy in order to get it out of a slump. Could you endorse such a suggestion? Under what circumstances? Using the theory in this chapter, describe how such a move would be implemented and what its effects would be. Make it clear which model of the economy you are using in your analysis.

3. In the flexible-price model of Section 17.3, suppose that the nominal interest rate in China is 15% and the nominal interest rate in the United States is 10%.

   (a) Which currency is expected to depreciate, and at what rate?

   (b) Describe an event that can create a situation like that within this model.

   (c) Can we conclude anything about differences in *real* interest rates across the two countries? Why or why not?

4. Consider two countries, East and West, that produce and trade two goods, Food and Clothing, using skilled and unskilled labor. Each unit of Food requires 1 unit of unskilled labor and 2 units of skilled labor to produce. Each unit of Clothing requires 2 units of unskilled labor and 1 unit of skilled labor to produce. East has 900,000 unskilled workers and 600,000 skilled workers. West has 600,000 unskilled workers and 900,000 skilled workers. The rate of time preference is $\gamma = 0.1$ and the relative demand curve is:

$$\frac{c_t^F}{c_t^C} = \frac{P_t^C}{P_t^F},$$

where c_t^i is the price of good i and P_t^i is the consumption of good i. The money supply in East is permanently kept at 1 million East dollars (denoted E$), and the money supply in West is permanently kept at 1 million West dollars (W$). Calculate:

   (a) The supply of both goods in each country, the world relative supply, and the relative price.

   (b) The nominal price of each good in each currency, and the equilibrium exchange rate.

   (c) Real and nominal interest rates in each currency.

   (d) Finally, describe briefly how the calculations in (a) through (c) would change if the money supply in East was doubled. Would welfare in either country change?

5. In the East and West economy described in the previous question, with both money supplies equal to 1 million units of currency, suppose that 300,000 unskilled workers move from East to West. Repeat the calculations (but not part (d)). Does the immigration have an effect on exchange rates? Why or why not? Does it have an effect on the utility attained by workers who do not move? Does it have an effect on the utility attained by workers who do move?

6. Again, consider the East and West economy, in its first version of Question 4 with equal money supplies in the two countries. Suppose that at date 0 a technological breakthrough is announced that will allow West permanently to produce 50,000 more units of Food and 50,000 more units of Clothing with the same number of workers as before, thus keeping world relative supply unchanged. However, the increased output will begin only at date $t = 1$. How does this announcement change the equilibrium? Discuss consumption, production, nominal prices and

exchange rates, both at date $t = 0$ and at date $t = 1$.

7. For the fiscal example of Section 17.4.5, what would the outcome be if the U.S. government simply taxed each U.S. household to pay for the public works project? Specifically, suppose that at the beginning of each period, the government taxes from each worker an amount of cash equal to 10% of that worker's expected wage that period, and then the government uses that money to hire workers for the public works. What would be the equilibrium outcome, prices, quantities, and exchange rate? How would it be different from the outcome discussed in the text, with money printing to pay for the public works and $x = 0$ (so that the Chinese government is not helping)?

8. *(Hard.)* Again for the fiscal example of Section 17.4.5, calculate each U.S. worker's consumption of the two goods with $x = 0$ and with $x = 1$. How would you describe the effect of the PBC's currency intervention on U.S. consumption?

REFERENCES

Bergsten, C. Fred (2007). "The Dollar and the Renminbi." Statement before the Hearing on U.S. Economic Relations with China: Strategies and Options on Exchange Rates and Market Access, Subcommittee on Security and International Trade and Finance, Committee on Banking, Housing and Urban Affairs, United States Senate, May 23, 2007.

Bolt, Kristen Millares (2007). "Baucus Looks Beyond Tariffs in Trade Dispute." *Seattle Post-Intelligencer*, April 2.

Bown, Chad P., Meredith A. Crowley, Rachel McCulloch, and Daisuke J. Nakajima (2005). "The U.S. Trade Deficit: Made in China?" *Economic Perspectives* (Federal Reserve Bank of Chicago) (4th quarter), pp. 2–17.

Crucini, Mario J., Chris I. Telmer, and Marios Zachariadis (2005). "Understanding European Real Exchange Rates." *American Economic Review* 95:3 (June), pp. 724–738.

Crucini, Mario J., and Mototsugu Shintania (2008) "Persistence in Law of One Price Deviations: Evidence from Micro-data." *Journal of Monetary Economics* 55:3 (April), pp. 629–644.

Devereux, Michael B. (2000). "How Does a Devaluation Affect the Current Account?" *Journal of International Money and Finance* 19, pp. 833–851.

Obstfeld, Maurice, and Kenneth Rogoff (1995). "Exchange Rate Dynamics Redux." *The Journal of Political Economy* 103:3 (June), pp. 624–660.

Ramzy, Austin (2006). "10 Questions for Charles Schumer." *TIME* Magazine, Sunday, March 26.

Staiger, Robert W., and Alan O. Sykes (2010). "Currency 'Manipulation' and World Trade: A Caution," In Simon Evenett (ed.), *The US-Sino Currency Dispute: New Insights from Economics, Politics and Law*, Chapter 13, pp. 109–113. London: Center for Economic Policy Research.

Steinhauer, Jennifer (2011). "Senate Jabs China Over Its Currency." *The New York Times* (October 11), p. B1.

Stockman, Alan C. (1980). "A Theory of Exchange Rate Determination," *The Journal of Political Economy* 88:4 (August), pp. 673–698.

Tatom, John A. (2007). "The US-China Currency Dispute: Is a Rise in the Yuan Necessary, Inevitable or Desirable?," *Global Economy Journal* 7:3, pp. 1–13.

INDEX